Beginning Groovy, Grails and Griffon

Vishal Layka
Christopher M. Judd
Joseph Faisal Nusairat
Jim Shingler

Apress®

Beginning Groovy, Grails and Griffon

ISBN-13 (pbk): 978-1-4302-4806-4

ISBN-13 (electronic): 978-1-4302-4807-1

President and Publisher: Paul Manning
Lead Editor: Steve Anglin
Developmental Editor: Richar Carey
Technical Reviewer: Rohan Walia

Coordinating Editor: Katie Sullivan
Copy Editor: Carla Spoon
Compositor: SPi Global
Indexer: SPi Global
Artist: SPi Global
Cover Designer: Anna Ishchenko

Distributed to the book trade worldwide by Springer Science+Business Media New York, 233 Spring Street, 6th Floor, New York, NY 10013. Phone 1-800-SPRINGER, fax (201) 348-4505, e-mail orders-ny@springer-sbm.com, or visit www.springeronline.com. Apress Media, LLC is a California LLC and the sole member (owner) is Springer Science + Business Media Finance Inc (SSBM Finance Inc). SSBM Finance Inc is a Delaware corporation.

For information on translations, please e-mail rights@apress.com, or visit www.apress.com.

Apress and friends of ED books may be purchased in bulk for academic, corporate, or promotional use. eBook versions and licenses are also available for most titles. For more information, reference our Special Bulk Sales–eBook Licensing web page at www.apress.com/bulk-sales.

Any source code or other supplementary materials referenced by the author in this text is available to readers at www.apress.com. For detailed information about how to locate your book's source code, go to www.apress.com/source-code/.

Contents at a Glance

Contents

About the Authors

Vishal Layka has over a decade of experience in Java/JEE. His thesis on building compilers for dynamic languages propelled his career in dynamic languages. Other than Groovy, his work and research interests involve Clojure, Erlang, Haskell, and Scala.

Christopher Judd is president and primary consultant for Judd Solutions, LLC. He is an international speaker, open source evangelist, leader of the Central Ohio Java Users Group, and co-author of *Enterprise Java Development on a Budget* (Apress, 2003). He has spent 12 years architecting and developing software for Fortune 500 companies in various industries, including insurance, retail, government, manufacturing, and transportation. His focus is consulting, mentoring, and training with Java, Java EE, Java Platform, Micro Edition (Java ME), mobile technologies, and related technologies.

Joseph Faisal Nusairat, author of *Beginning JBoss Seam* (Apress, 2007) and co-author of *Beginning Groovy & Grails* (Apress, 2008), is a software developer who has been developing web-based applications in the Columbus and Phoenix area since 1997, primarily focused on Java/Groovy development. His career has taken him into a variety of Fortune 500 industries including military applications, data centers, banking, Internet security, pharmaceuticals, and insurance. Joseph is a graduate of Ohio University with dual degrees in Computer Science and Microbiology, with a minor in Chemistry. Currently, Joseph works as the Groovy Sage at Integrallis Software (`www.integrallis.com`). In his off-hours he enjoys watching bodybuilding and Broadway musicals, but not at the same time.

Jim Shingler is VP of Application Development for J.P. Morgan Chase. The focus of his career is on using cutting-edge technology to develop IT solutions for the banking, insurance, financial services, and manufacturing industries. He has 16 years of large-scale Java experience and significant experience in distributed and relational technologies.

About the Technical Reviewer

Rohan Walia is a software consultant with extensive experience in client-server, web-based enterprise application development. He is responsible for designing and developing end-to-end Java/J2EE applications consisting of various cutting-edge frameworks and utilities. His areas of expertise are Spring, Hibernate, Groovy, and ADF. When not working, Rohan loves to play tennis, travel, and study photography.

Acknowledgments

I would like to personally thank my wife Wendy and son Tyler for their support and patience through the writing of the book and in our journey together through life. I would like to thank the many people that have contributed to my personal and professional growth: Wendy Shingler, James L. Shingler Sr., Linda Shingler, George Ramsayer, Tom Posival, Chris Judd, Andres Almiray, Soren Neal Ford, Greg Wilmer, Tim Heller, Dustin Potts, Chris Nicholas, Seth Flory, Henry Wang, Mukund Chandrasekar, Chris Schmitz, John Keyes, Awnish Bhatt, Frank Neugebauer, Tim Resch, Kevin Smith, David Duhl, Nate Beyene, Teresa Whitt, Rick Burchfield, Gerry Wright, and the many others who have touched my life.

—James Shingler

CHAPTER 1

Introduction to Groovy

Modern Java programmers live in the dissonance of two conflicting schools of thought. On one hand, dynamic languages such as Groovy, JRuby, and Jython offer advances in expressive power. On the other, many Java purists reject these languages as too impractical. Groovy with its new version addresses this conflict, establishing itself as an expedient language.

Anachronistically, as programming languages evolve in a benign continuum, one or the other contender language is impeached upon on its performance merits. However, with progressive enhancements of compilers, runtime systems, or even processing power, it became apparent that the performance penalties were not so big as envisaged. The contender language not only survived, but also had rather favorable consequences on the programming sphere. It is now apparent that Groovy is not a fad that will fade away next year or the year after.

Beautifully-engineered Groovy seamlessly integrates with the existing Java libraries and aims at dynamicity to Java without introducing a steep learning curve for Java developers. Groovy, however, is not alone in the new feature-rich JVM landscape—other languages such as JRuby, Jython, Jaskell, Clojure, Scala are its contemporaries. All these languages are designed to, when not leveraging Java, assuage some of Java's problems. But there are a few factors that ascertain Groovy's position as first among equals. Groovy was designed from scratch to run on Java virtual machines, as were Clojure and Scala, which gives Groovy, Clojure, and Scala few notches. Jython and JRuby were ported on JVM. Jaskell is a JVM counterpart of pure functional language Haskell. Other than execution environment, all these languages except Groovy lack Java's immense libraries. Groovy is designed to be both source-compatible and binary-compatible with Java. This means that a Groovy class could extend a Java class or implement a Java interface, and that a Java class could extend a Groovy class or implement a Groovy interface. Grails, the leading next-generation Groovy-based framework, is built on widely-held Spring and Hibernate frameworks. Griffon, another Groovy-based MVC framework, brings a revolution in the world of desktop applications. Groovy's source and binary compatibility with Java, combined with two Groovy-powered next-generation frameworks supported by the starfleet of SpringSource, strongly indicates that Groovy's future is assured. It is only logical.

In this chapter, we will introduce the Groovy language, describe how to install it, and give you an idea of the benefits of Groovy over Java by working through an example. Then we will give you a general overview of key features of the Groovy language.

Installation

Groovy comes bundled as a .zip file or platform-specific installer for Windows, Ubuntu, and Debian (as well as openSUSE until recent versions). This section explains how to install the zipped version, since it covers the most platforms.

To install Groovy:

1. Download the most recent stable Groovy binary release .zip file from `http://groovy.codehaus.org/Download`.

2. Uncompress `groovy-binary-X.X.X.zip` to your chosen location.

3. Set a GROOVY_HOME environment variable to the directory in which you uncompressed the .zip file.
4. Add the %GROOVY_HOME%\bin directory to your system path.

To validate your installation, open a console and type the following:

```
>groovy -v
```

You should see something like this:

```
Groovy Version: 2.0.0 JVM: 1.6.0_31 Vendor: Sun Microsystems Inc. OS: Windows 7
```

Groovy by Example

The best way to grasp the power and elegance of Groovy is to compare it to Java using an example. In the remainder of this chapter, we will show you how to convert the simple Java class in Listing 1-1 into Groovy. Then we will demonstrate how to adapt the code to use common Groovy idioms.

Listing 1-1. Simple Java Class

```
1.    package com.apress.bgg;
2.
3.    import java.util.List;
4.    import java.util.ArrayList;
5.
6.
7.    public class Todo {
8.            private String name;
9.            private String note;
10.
11.           public Todo() {}
12.
13.           public Todo(String name, String note) {
14.                   this.name = name;
15.                   this.note = note;
16.           }
17.
18.           public String getName() {
19.                   return name;
20.           }
21.
22.           public void setName(String name) {
23.                   this.name = name;
24.           }
25.
26.           public String getNote() {
27.                   return note;
28.           }
29.
```

```
30.         public void setNote(String note) {
31.                 this.note = note;
32.         }
33.
34.         public static void main(String[] args) {
35.                 List<Todo> todos = new ArrayList<Todo>();
36.                 todos.add(new Todo("1", "one"));
37.                  todos.add(new Todo("2", "two"));
38.                 todos.add(new Todo("3","three"));
39.
40.                 for(Todo todo : todos) {
41.                         System.out.println(todo.getName() + " " + todo.getNote());
42.                 }
43.         }
44. }
```

If you have any Java experience, you will recognize Listing 1-1 as a basic Todo JavaBean. It has getters and setters for name and note attributes, as well as a convenience constructor that takes a name and note for initializing new instances. As you would expect, this class can be found in a file named `Todo.java` in the `com.apress.bgg` package. The class includes a `main()` method, which is required for Java classes to be executable and is the entry point into the application. On line 35, the `main()` method begins by creating an instance of a `java.util.ArrayList` to hold a collection of `Todo`s. On lines 36-38, three `Todo` instances are created and added to the todos list. Finally, on lines 40–43, a `for` statement iterates over the collection and prints the `Todo`'s name and note to `System.out`.

Converting Java to Groovy

To convert the Java Todo class in Listing 1-1 to Groovy, just rename the file to `Todo.groovy`. That's right, Groovy derives its syntax from Java. This is often referred to as copy/paste compatibility. So congratulations, you are a Groovy developer (even if you didn't know it)! This level of compatibility, along with a familiar API, helps to reduce the Groovy learning curve for Java developers. It also makes it easier to incorporate Java examples found on the Internet into a Groovy application and then refactor them to make them more Groovylike, which is what we will do with Listing 1-1.

To run this Groovy application, from the command line, type the following:

```
> groovy com\apress\bgg\Todo.groovy
```

If you are coming from a Java background, you may be a little surprised that you did not need to first compile the code. Here's the Java equivalent:

```
> javac com\apress\bgg\Todo.java
> java com.apress.bgg.Todo
```

Running the Java application is a two-step process: Compile the class using `javac`, and then use `java` to run the executable class in the JVM. But Groovy will compile to byte code at runtime, saving a step in the development process and thereby increasing Groovy's productivity. Groovy provides a lot of syntactic sugar and is able to imply more than Java. You'll see this in action as we make our Groovy application more Groovy by applying some of the Groovy idioms.

Converting a JavaBean to a GroovyBean

Let's begin by simplifying the JavaBean, which could also be referred to as a Plain Old Java Object (POJO). Groovy has the GroovyBean, which is a JavaBean with a simpler Groovy syntax, sometimes referred to as a Plain Old Groovy Object (POGO). GroovyBeans are publicly scoped by default. Listing 1-2 shows our example using a GroovyBean.

Listing 1-2. Simple Example Using a GroovyBean

```
1.   package com.apress.bgg;
2.
3.    import java.util.List;
4.    import java.util.ArrayList;
5.
6.
7.    public class Todo {
8.
9.           String name;
10.          String note;
11.
12.           public static void main(String[] args) {
13.                  List <Todo> todos = new ArrayList<Todo>();
14.                 todos.add(new Todo(name:"1", note:"one"));
15.                 todos.add(new Todo(name:"2", note:"two"));
16.                 todos.add(new Todo(name:"3", note:"three"));
17.
18.                 for(Todo todo : todos) {
19.
20.                 System.out.println(todo.name + " " + todo.note);
21.                 }
22.          }
23.  }
```

Listing 1-2 is significantly shorter than Listing 1-1, primarily because Groovy has a concept of native properties, which means getters and setters do not need to be declared. By default, all class attributes—such as the `name` and `note` attributes on lines 9 and 10—are public properties and automatically generate corresponding getters and setters in the byte code. So if the class is used from Java code, or reflection is used to interrogate the class, you will see the getters and setters. These properties also have a more intuitive usage model. They can be assigned or used directly, as on line 20, where the name and note properties, rather than the getters, are used to generate the output. Also, rather than needing to explicitly create a convenience constructor for initializing a GroovyBean, you can pass named parameters in the constructor to initialize any properties you want, as in lines 14–16.

GroovyBeans have a very useful initialization feature called Named parameters. We can pass a Map to the constructor of a bean that contains the names of the properties, along with an associated initialization value. Every GroovyBean has this built-in Map constructor, which works by iterating the map object and calling the corresponding property setter for each entry in the map.

Suppose we have a GroovyBean Book, which has the properties id and title. We can initialize such bean with a map:

```
map = [id: 1, title: "Beginning Groovy, Grails and Griffon"]
Book = new Book( map)
We can pass the map directly to the bean:
Book = new Book ( id: 1, title: "Beginning Groovy, Grails and Griffon")
```

Simplifying the Code

Some of the syntax sugar included in the Groovy language is making semicolons, parentheses, and data typing optional. Other interesting features to simplify code include implicit imports like the `java.util.*` package, common methods like `println()` applying to all objects including Java objects, and more flexible strings. Listing 1-3 applies these features to our example.

Listing 1-3. Simple Example Applying Syntactic Sugar, Implicit Imports, Common Methods,and String Features

```
1.   package com.apress.bgg;
2.
3.   public class Todo {
4.
5.            String name
6.            String note
7.
8.            public static void main(String[] args) {
9.                    def todos = new ArrayList()
10.                   todos.add(new Todo(name:"1", note:"one"))
11.                   todos.add(new Todo(name:"2", note:"two"))
12.                   todos.add(new Todo(name:"3", note:"three"))
13.
14.                   for(Todo todo : todos) {
15.
16.                             println "${todo.name} ${todo.note}"
17.                   }
18.           }
19.  }
```

In Listing 1-3, under the package declaration we no longer need to import `java.util.List`, `java.util.ArrayList`, and `java.util.Iterator`. These are implicitly imported since they are in the `java.util.*` package. Other implicitly included packages are `java.lang.*`, `java.net.*`, `java.io.*`, `groovy.lang.*`, and `groovy.util.*`. Also notice that, other than in the `for` statement (which we will clean up in the next round of refactoring), all the semicolons were removed. On line 16, we used optional parentheses with the implicit `println()` method. But that is not the only change to line 16. The println() method was modified to use Groovy's GString format, which is similar to the Apache Ant property format, rather than concatenating two strings. We'll cover Groovy strings in Chapter 2. At this point, just notice how much simpler this is to read. Line 9 has been changed to use optional typing. The variable `todos` is no longer typed to List. Groovy uses "duck typing," which means if it sounds like a duck and walks like a duck, it must be a duck. Do you really care what the type of an object is, as long as you can pass it a message and it will handle the request if it can? If the object cannot handle the request, you will receive a `groovy.lang.MissingMethodException` or `groovy.lang.MissingPropertyException`. Of course, where you think typing is necessary, you always have the option of explicitly typing variables.

Using Groovy Collection Notation and Closure

The next step in refactoring the example is to take advantage of Groovy's collection and map notation, as well as replace the ugly `for` statement with a more elegant closure. Listing 1-4 shows this version.

Listing 1-4. Example with the Groovy Collection Notation and Closure

```
1.    package com.apress.bgg;
2.
3.    public class Todo {
4.
5.            String name
6.            String note
7.
8.            public static void main(String[] args) {

9.                    def todos = [
10.                           new Todo(name:"1", note:"one"),
11.                           new Todo(name:"2", note:"two"),
12.                           new Todo(name:"3", note:"three")
13.                   ]
14.
15.                   todos.each {
16.                           println "${it.name} ${it.note}"
17.                   }
18.           }
19.   }
```

Notice how the ArrayList was replaced with [ ]. Again, this is just syntactic sugar; Groovy really is instantiating an ArrayList. Similarly, we can create maps with the [:] syntax. To make the code more clean, we can initialize the list without needing to call the add() method for each entry. Then to simplify the iteration, we call the each() method, passing a closure that prints out the string. Notice that, by default, the iteration variable is it. Chapter 2 will provide more explanations and examples of Groovy lists, maps, and closures.

Getting Rid of main()

One bit of Java ugliness left in our example is the main() method. After all these improvements, the main() method now stands out. Fortunately, Groovy has a concept of scripts as well as classes, and we can turn this into a script, removing the need for the main() method. To begin, the file must be renamed to something like Todos.groovy. This is because a script will also be compiled to a class, and if we didn't change the name, there would be a name clash between the Todo class and the Todo script. Then we simply move the code that currently exists in the main() method outside the Todo class. Note that, in Groovy, any code that is not inside a class is called a script. When the script is run, it will behave the same as before. Listing 1-5 shows the script version.

Listing 1-5. Example as a Script

```
1.    package com.apress.bgg;
2.    public class Todo {
3.    String name
4.    String note
5.    }
6.    def todos = [
7.    new Todo(name:"1", note:"one"),
8.    new Todo(name:"2", note:"two"),
9.    new Todo(name:"3", note:"three")
10.   ]
```

```
11.  todos.each {
12.  println "${it.name} ${it.note}"
13.  }
```

Finally, we have elegant, easy-to-read code at a fraction of what we started with in Java. It should be obvious that if we had started with the Groovy idioms to begin with, the Groovy approach would have been much more productive.

Groovy Language Key Features

This section gives a general overview of the language features that make Groovy a commendable extension to the Java platform. A detailed treatment of all these features is given in subsequent chapters.

Assertion

An assertion is used to validate that an expected condition is true. Assertions in Groovy are more powerful than in Java because assertion in Java works only on Boolean, whereas assertion in Groovy can accept any type. Assertions in Java can be disabled, whereas assertions in Groovy are always executed and are recommended to be used in the production code.

Listing 1-6. Assertion Example

```
def list = [1, 2, 'x'] // list of 3 elements
assert list.size() == 3
```

Annotations for AST Transformation

When the Groovy compiler compiles Groovy scripts and classes, the Groovy parser (the front end of the compiler) creates an Abstract Syntax Tree (AST) before generating the final byte code for the class. The AST is the in-memory representation of the source code, comprising class, method, property, statement, and variables. AST transformation is the capability to add new code (methods, checks) into source code before the final byte code is generated. The objective of the AST transformation is to let developers structure their code while focusing more on the business code rather than on boilerplate code or cross-cutting concerns. Groovy provides annotations you can use to annotate code structures for AST transformation. Here is one example of AST transformation using `@Singleton` annotation provided by Groovy:

Listing 1-7. Using Annotations for AST Transformation

```
@Singleton
class SomeSingleton
{
//..
}
```

The `@Singleton` annotation creates a private constructor and a static method, which gives us an instance of the Singleton through AST transformations.

Builder

Generating the simplest XML document in Java is enormously difficult and time consuming. Groovy simplifies generating XML by providing built-in builder classes that make it possible to build a tree-like structure from within the code itself. That is, the structure of the code itself resembles the tree-like structure we are trying to build, thus making the task of generating tree-like structure painless.

Listing 1-8. Tree-like Structure in XML

```
<employee>
<name>John Doe</name>
<gender>male</gender>
</ employee >
```

Listing 1-9. Groovy Code to Generate Preceding Tree-like Structure

```
def builder = new groovy.xml.MarkupBuilder()
builder.employee {
name    'John Doe'
gender  'male'
}
```

Closure

A Groovy closure is a block of reusable code within curly braces {}, which can be assigned to a property or variable, or passed as a parameter to a method. The code within the curly braces is executed when the closure is invoked.

Listing 1-10. Using Closure

```
def name = "Chris"
def printClosure = { println "Hello, ${name}" }
printClosure()
name = "Joseph"
printClosure()
```

Here is the output:

```
Hello, Chris
Hello, Joseph
```

GDK

Groovy as a whole comprises Groovy language, libraries specific to Groovy-specific libraries, and GDK. The GDK is Groovy's extension to some of the existing classes in the JDK. You can access the full API specification at `http://groovy.codehaus.org/groovy-jdk`.

Metaprogramming

Metaprogramming means writing a program that creates, queries, and manipulates other programs or (more often) itself. Metaprogramming can occur at either compile-time or runtime.

The covenant of compile-time metaprogramming is byte-code generation. In Groovy, compile-time metaprogramming lets you modify the AST before generating final byte code. We illustrated an example of compile-time metaprogramming in the "Annotations for AST Transformation" section. Runtime metaprogramming is centered on enabling dynamic method-invocation and synthesis of methods and classes. In Groovy, runtime metaprogramming is realized using meta-object protocol. The MOP, in Groovy, comprises categories, expandos, and metaclasses.

Listing 1-11. Runtime Metaprogramming

```
String.metaClass.firstUpper = {->

    return delegate[0].toUpperCase() + delegate[1..delegate.length() - 1]
}

println "iiii".firstUpper()
```

Listing 1-11 shows how you can add an additional method to a class on the fly. We added an additional method to `String` class, which is immutable.

Here is the output:

```
Iiii
```

Native JSON Support

JSON (JavaScript Object Notation) is a lightweight data interchange format, used as an alternative to XML for serializing and transmitting structured data over a network.

As a simple example, data about an employee can be written in JSON as follows:

Listing 1-12. Example of JSON

```
var person= {
          "name" : "John Doe",
          "age" : "40"
};
```

This creates an object that can be accessed using the employee variable. Groovy 1.8 introduced native JSON support through `JsonSlurper` for reading JSON and `JsonBuilder` for writing JSON.

Listing 1-13. Reading JSON

```
import groovy.json.JsonSlurper
 def slurper = new JsonSlurper()
 def result = slurper.parseText('{"person":{"name":"John Doe","age":40,"cars":["bmw","ford"]}}')

 println result.person.name
 println result.person.age
 println result.person.cars.size()
 println result.person.cars[0]
 println result.person.cars[1]
```

Here is the output:

```
John Doe
40
2
bmw
ford
```

Native Support for Lists and Maps

Java has no language-level support for collections that it has for arrays. Groovy enhanced the Java collection classes by adding and improving the declaration syntax and additional methods.

Groovy contains first-class constructs for `List` and `Map`. It also adds the new collection type—`Range`—at the language level, which provides special-purpose syntax for managing ranges of values.

Listing 1-14. Support for Lists as a Language Feature

```
authors = [ 'Vishal', 'Chris', 'Joseph', 'Jim' ]
println authors
println authors[0]
```

Here is the output:

```
["Vishal", "Chris", "Joseph", "Jim"]
Vishal
```

Native Support for Regular Expression

Groovy builds regular expression handling right into the language via the =~ operator and matcher objects.

Object Orientation: Everything is an Object in Groovy

Unlike Java, everything in Groovy is an object; there are no primitive types. As a result, in Groovy, no auto boxing is needed because everything is an object.

For example, Groovy executes `2 + 2` as `2.plus(2)`. The plus operator is implemented via the `plus()` method. In Groovy, all operators are method calls. This makes it possible to apply object-orientation to operators; for example, it is possible to overload/override any operator to give a new implementation.

String interpolation

String interpolation is the ability to substitute an expression or variable within a string. Java doesn't support string interpolation. You must manually concatenate the values. Here is an example of the type of code you need to write in Java:

Listing 1-15. String Concatenation in Java

```
String lastName= "Layka";
String fullname= "Vishal " + lastName;
System.out.println(fullname);
```

Listing 1-16. String Interpolation in Groovy

```
def lastName = "Layka"
def fullname = "Vishal ${lastName} " // string interpolation (also called Gstring)
println fullname
```

Static and Dynamic Typing

Groovy supports both static and dynamic typing when declaring variables. Dynamic typing can be achieved by using the def keyword.

Listing 1-17. Dynamic and Optional Typing in Groovy

```
def var = 10
var = "It's a String"
```

The def keyword is optional in scripts.

Listing 1-18. Static and Optional Typing in Groovy

```
String  s1 = " A String " // static
s2 = "Another String " // optional typing :type is left to be determined at the time of assignment.
```

Static Type Checking

Groovy 2.0 introduces a @TypeChecked annotation, which annotates a method or a class that needs to be static type checked. This type-checked mode, enabled through annotation, indicates the errors at compile time.

The static type checker is built using Groovy's existing powerful AST transformation mechanisms. Being an optional feature, you are not forced to use it if you don't need it. To trigger static type checking, just use the @TypeChecked annotation on a method or on a class to turn on checking.

Listing 1-19. Using TypeChecked Annotation

```
import groovy.transform.TypeChecked

void doIt() {}

@TypeChecked
void test() {

    dott ()//compilation error:cannot find matching method dott()

}
```

Figure 1-1 illustrates the @Typechecked annotation in action in Eclipse.

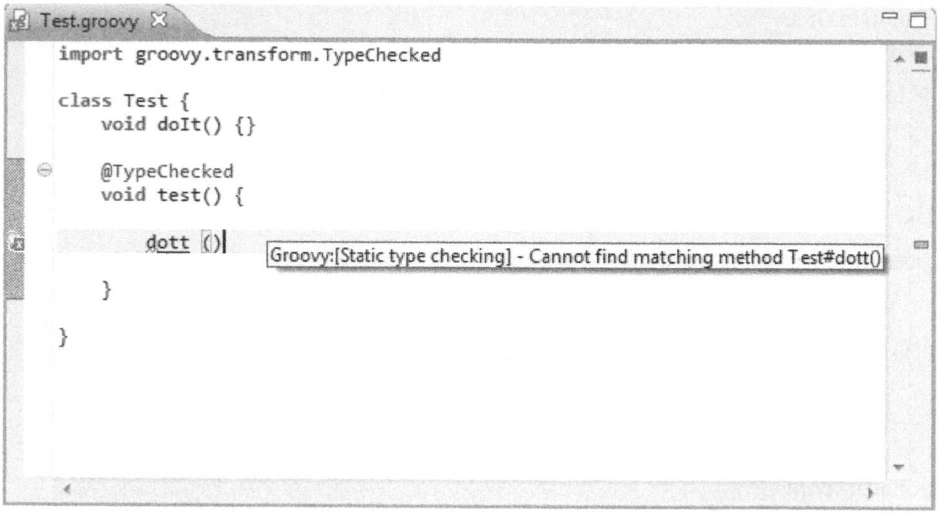

Figure 1-1. *Using the @TypeChecked annotation*

Static Compilation

Groovy 2.0 also makes it possible to enable static compilation via `@CompileStatic`. This mode eliminates the runtime overhead of dynamic dispatch.

Listing 1-20. Using CompileStatic Annotation

```
import groovy.transform.CompileStatic

@CompileStatic
int doubleIt(int num) {
    2* num
}

assert doubleIt(2) == 4
```

Using `@CompileStatic` will statically compile the code, and the generated byte code will run just as fast as java's byte code. Like the `@TypeChecked` annotation, `@CompileStatic` can annotate classes and methods, and `@CompileStatic(SKIP)` can bypass static compilation for a specific method when its class is marked with `@CompileStatic`.

Optional Syntax

Now let's look at the optional syntax.

Access Modifiers

In Groovy, classes without an access modifier are considered public. Attributes without an access modifier are considered private. Methods without an access modifier are public. This is in contrast with Java, where methods and fields default to package access. The reason Groovy chose to make the public access modifier the default is that it is the most frequently used modifier, whereas package access is used far less frequently.

Checked Exceptions

In Groovy, checked exceptions need not be declared or caught, as Groovy automatically wraps exceptions as a `RuntimeException`.

Getters and Setters

Similar to JavaBeans, Groovy introduces GroovyBeans, which support the notion of properties. Properties in GroovyBeans look just like public fields, with no need to define explicit getters and setters.

Listing 1-21. Properties in Groovy

```
class Employee{
String name
}
Employee emp = new Employee()
emp.setName("John Doe" )

println emp.name
```

Import Statements

By default, Groovy always imports the following packages:

```
groovy.lang.*
groovy.util.*
java.lang.*
java.util.*
java.util.regex.*
java.net.*
java.io.*
java.math.BigDecimal, java.math.BigInteger
```

Parentheses and Semicolons

Parentheses and semicolons are optional in Groovy. The following statements are valid in Groovy:

Listing 1-22. Optional Semicolons and Parentheses

```
println ("hello");
println "hello"
```

Return Type and the return Keyword

In Groovy, the return type for a method and the `return` keyword as the last statement in the method are optional. The result value of the last statement is always returned from a method call.

Listing 1-23. Optional return Keyword

```
String greeting() {
result = "Hello world"
result
}
println greeting()
```

Listing 1-23 shows that `return` keyword is optional.

If the `def` keyword is used as a return type, Groovy dynamically figures out the return type during runtime depending on the value returned.

Listing 1-24. Optional Return Type

```
def greeting() {
result = "Hello world"
result
}
println greeting()
```

Listing 1-24 shows that Return type is dynamic.

In both Listing 1-23 and Listing 1-24, the output is:

```
Hello world
```

■ **Note** It appears that removing constructs like parentheses and semicolons is unessential and rather mundane, but as you will see in domain-specific languages, one of the key areas of Groovy, removing these constructs brings code close to the natural language.

Summary

The purpose of this chapter was to provide a preview of some key features of Groovy. We demonstrated how you can dramatically reduce the code it takes to write the equivalent Java class in Groovy, while increasing the readability and expressiveness. In the next chapter, we will continue exploring Groovy by looking at its basic language features.

CHAPTER 2

Groovy Basics

Chapter 1 introduced you to Groovy, its relationship to Java, and where the two languages differ. This chapter will delve into the Groovy language. First, you will learn about Groovy scripts, including compiling and running Groovy scripts using the command Line, Groovy Shell, and Groovy Console. Then we will focus on specific aspects of the Groovy language: assertions, strings, regular expressions, collections, ranges, control structures, methods, closures, and operators.

Scripts

You will be using the Groovy language to build domain objects, controllers, and services. But that isn't the only way to use Groovy. In addition to building classes, you can use Groovy as a scripting language. You will see detailed examples of scripts in subsequent chapters. But here we'll start with a simple script.

Listing 2-1 is an example of a very simple Groovy "Hello" script that takes an argument and uses it to print a message.

Listing 2-1. A Simple Groovy Script: Hello.groovy

```
println "Hello ${args[0]}, may Groovy be with you."
```

Execute the script by typing the following on the command Line:

```
>groovy Hello "Luke Skywalker"
```

The script will output the results:

```
Hello Luke Skywalker, may Groovy be with you.
```

On execution of the script, Groovy generates a class with the same name as the script source file, including a main method that contains the script source. The equivalent Java application would look like Listing 2-2.

Listing 2-2. The Java Version: HelloJava.java

```
package com.apress.beginninggrails.cli.scripts;
public class HelloJava {
    public static void main(String[] args) {
        System.out.println( "Hello "+ args[0]+", may Java be with you." );
    }
}
```

Notice how much more verbose the Java version is compared to the Groovy version. With Java, you need to define a class and a main method. You also must fully qualify the println method, add parentheses, and terminate it with a semicolon. Then you need all of the closing curly braces. Even if you are a Java fan, you have to admit that the Groovy example is a good bit shorter and easier to read! Furthermore, you don't need to go through a separate step of compiling Groovy before it is executed.

Using Script Functions

Like with most scripting languages, you can organize Groovy scripts into blocks of reusable code. In scripts, these blocks are called functions. Listing 2-3 is an example of creating and using a function. It creates a simple function to print a name and calls the function with two different names.

Listing 2-3. A Script Function:PrintFullName.groovy

```
def printFullName(firstName, lastName) {
println "${firstName} ${lastName}"
}
printFullName('Luke', 'SkyWalker')
printFullName('Darth', 'Vader')
```

This example defines the `printFullName` function, which takes two parameters. Next, the function is invoked twice: once to print Luke Skywalker and again to print Darth Vader.

Compiling Groovy

In the previous examples, we let Groovy compile the script on the fly. Like with Java, you can compile Groovy to Java byte code. Listing 2-4 illustrates compiling the Groovy script from Listing 2-1.

Listing 2-4. Compiling Groovy with groovyc

```
groovyc Hello.groovy
```

As you might expect, compiling Hello. Groovy results in `Hello.class`. Because Groovy compiles to Java bytecode, you can use the Java command line to execute it.

Listing 2-5. Running the Groovy Program Using Java

```
java -cp %GROOVY_HOME%/embeddable/groovy-all-2.0.0.jar;. Hello "Luke Skywalker"
```

Here is the output:

```
Hello Luke Skywalker
```

Being able to run the Groovy program using Java proves it—Groovy is Java. If you look at Listing 2-5, you'll see that the only thing special required to run the Groovy compilers to include `groovy-all-<version>.jar` on the classpath.

The Groovy compiler is a joint compiler. It can compile Groovy and Java code at the same time. The joint compiler first became available in Groovy 1.5 through a generous donation by JetBrains, the makers of IntelliJ IDEA. The joint compiler allows you to compile Groovy and Java files with a single compile statement. Listings 2-6 and 2-7 are a Groovy file and a Java file, respectively, to demonstrate joint compilation.

Listing 2-6. A Sample Groovy File: Name.groovy

```
class Name
{
String firstName
String toString() { return "Hello ${firstName}, Java calling Groovy" }
}
```

Listing 2-7. A Sample Java File:SayHello.java

```
public class SayHello
{
    public static void main(String args[ ])
    {
        Name name = new Name();
        name.setFirstName( args[0] );
        System.out.println( name.toString() );
    }
}
```

The Java class, `SayHello`, instantiates the Groovy class `Name` and sets the `firstName` property to a value passed in on the command Line. Listing 2-8 illustrates compiling and executing the programs.

Listing 2-8. Joint Compile and Execute

```
groovyc *.groovy *.java
java -cp %GROOVY_HOME%/embeddable/groovy-all-2.0.0.jar;. SayHello "Luke"
```

Here is the output:

```
Hello Luke, Java calling Groovy
```

Compiling the Groovy and Java classes is accomplished by telling `groovy` to compile files matching the file pattern ending in `.groovy` and `.java`. You run the program in the same way that you run any other Java program—just include `groovy-all-<version>.jar` in the classpath.

Running Groovy

You can run Groovy scripts and classes through the command Line, Groovy Shell, or Groovy Console. Let's look at each technique.

Command Line

To run Groovy from the command line, you have several options:

- Use Groovy directly by typing `groovy MyPgm` at the command line.

  If you are running a script, Groovy will generate a class with a `main` method containing the script commands, compile the script, and execute it. If you don't want to recompile the file each time it is run, you can use the third option.

- Compile the file using groovy into a class and execute it using Java. You saw an example of this approach in the previous section.
- If you're in the Windows environment and Groovy was installed with the Windows installer with the `PATHEXT` option, you can omit the leading `groovy` and just type `MyPgm.groovy`. The `PATHEXT` option associates files ending with `.groovy` to the Groovy runtime. On Unix platforms, you can use a shebang at the top of the file to get the same result:

```
#!/usr/bin/groovy
println "Hello ${args[0]}, may Groovy be with you."
```

Groovy Shell

The Groovy Shell is an interactive command-line application (shell) that allows you to create, run, save, and load Groovy scripts and classes. To start the Groovy Shell, run groovysh. Figure 2-1 illustrates using the Groovy Shell to execute a simple script.

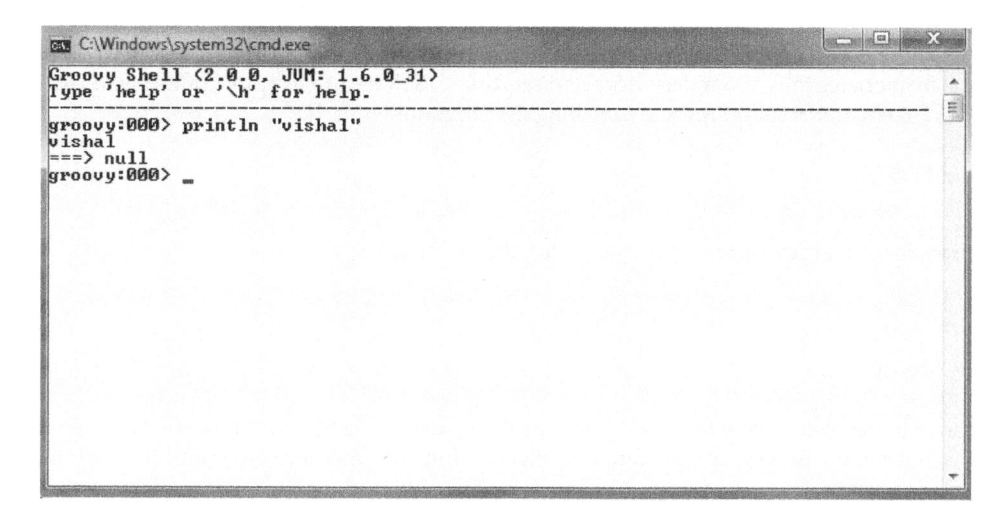

Figure 2-1. *Using the Groovy Shell*

As you can see, the script prints vishal. Then you see `===> null`. As a matter of convention, Groovy always returns the results of methods. In this case, there is no result, so null is returned.

The Groovy Shell contains a built-in help facility that you can use to learn more about the shell. To access it, type help at the prompt. Figure 2-2 shows the help listing.

```
C:\Windows\system32\cmd.exe
Groovy Shell (2.0.0, JVM: 1.6.0_31)
Type 'help' or '\h' for help.
-------------------------------------------------------------------------------
groovy:000> println "vishal"
vishal
===> null
groovy:000> help

For information about Groovy, visit:
    http://groovy.codehaus.org

Available commands:
  help      (\h ) Display this help message
  ?         (\? ) Alias to: help
  exit      (\x ) Exit the shell
  quit      (\q ) Alias to: exit
  import    (\i ) Import a class into the namespace
  display   (\d ) Display the current buffer
  clear     (\c ) Clear the buffer and reset the prompt counter.
  show      (\S ) Show variables, classes or imports
  inspect   (\n ) Inspect a variable or the last result with the GUI object brow
ser
  purge     (\p ) Purge variables, classes, imports or preferences
  edit      (\e ) Edit the current buffer
  load      (\l ) Load a file or URL into the buffer
  .         (\. ) Alias to: load
  save      (\s ) Save the current buffer to a file
  record    (\r ) Record the current session to a file
  history   (\H ) Display, manage and recall edit-line history
  alias     (\a ) Create an alias
  set       (\= ) Set (or list) preferences
  register  (\rc) Registers a new command with the shell

For help on a specific command type:
    help command

groovy:000>
```

Figure 2-2. *Groovy Shell help information*

Groovy Console

The Groovy Console, shown in Figure 2-3, is a graphical version of the Groovy Shell. It is written using SwingBuilder, a Groovy module that makes building a Swing user interface easier.

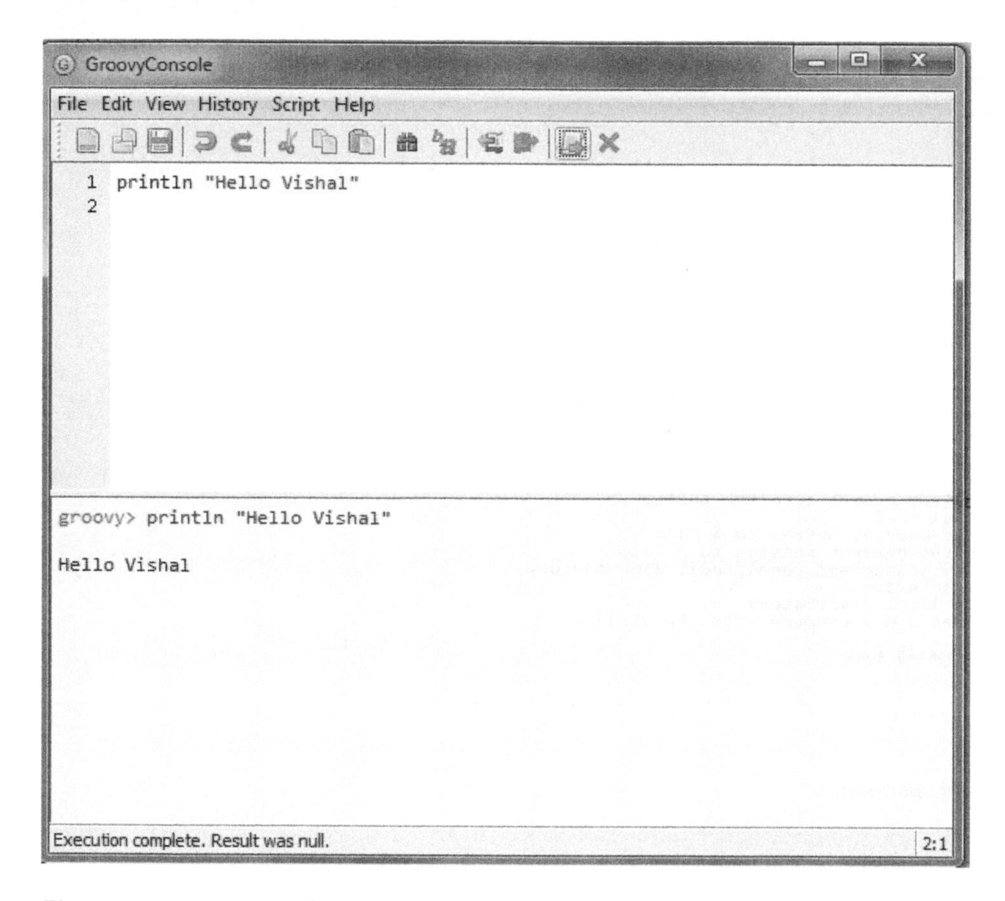

Figure 2-3. *Groovy Console*

Figure 2-4 shows the Groovy Console with the output detached. You can start the Groovy Console in a number of ways, depending on your environment and how you installed Groovy. The easiest way is to execute Groovy Console, which is located in the Groovy bin directory.

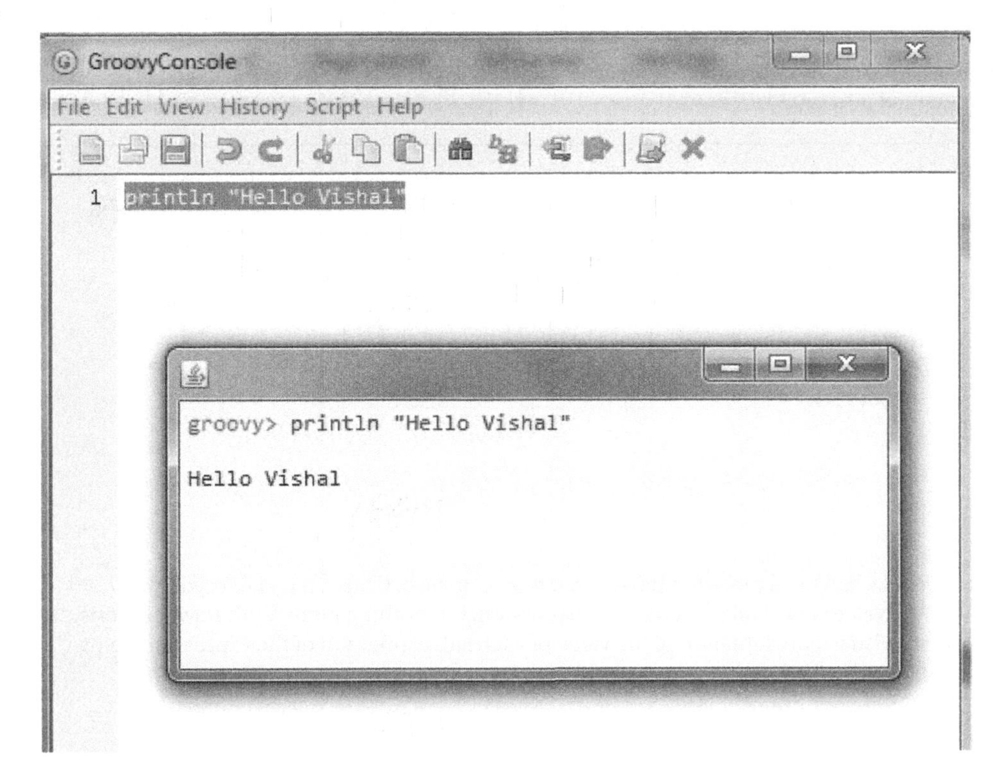

Figure 2-4. *Groovy Console with detached output*

The console provides the ability to create, save, load, and execute classes and scripts. Some of the nice features of the console are undo/redo and the ability to inspect variables. If you have to choose between using the Groovy Shell and the Groovy Console, we recommend the Groovy Console.

Assertions

As a developer, if you have used JUnit (or any of the flavors of JUnit), you already have some idea what an assertion is. An assertion is used to validate that an expected condition is true. If the expected condition is not true, a `java.lang.AssertionError` is thrown. You test that the expected condition is true by using Groovy expressions. Listing 2-9 illustrates the Java and Groovy versions of assert.

Listing 2-9. Java and Groovy Assertions

```
// Java assert
assert 1==2 : "One isn't Two";
// Groovy assert
assert 1==2 : "One isn't Two"
```

As you can see, the Groovy assert syntax is the same as Java's, except for the ending semicolon. The message is to the right of the expression and separated by a colon. As with Java, the message portion of the assert is optional.

■ **Tip** As a best practice, when you are using assertions, you should include a message. It will help the next person maintaining your code to understand its intent.

When an assertion fails, Groovy throws a `java.lang.AssertionError`. Listing 2-10 is the output of the failing Groovy assertion in Listing 2-9.

Listing 2-10. Assertion Failure

```
Caught: java.lang.AssertionError: One isn't Two. Expression: <1 == 2>
java.lang.AssertionError: One isn't Two. Expression: <1 == 2>
        at Hello.run<Hello.groovy:2>

D:\groovy\groovy-2.0.0>
```

Power Asserts

Groovy's `assert` keyword just checks that the expression passed to it is true or false. If false, it just tells you the expression was false, and gives the value of variables used in the expression, but nothing more. With Power Asserts, the output of the assert provides a visual representation of the value of each sub expression of the expression being asserted, as illustrated in Listing 2-11.

Listing 2-11. Power Assert Feature

```
assert new File('HelloWorld.txt') == new File('Hello.txt')

Caught: Assertion failed:

assert new File<'HelloWorld.txt'> == new File<'Hello.txt'>
       |                           |  |
       HelloWorld.txt              |  Hello.txt
                                  false

Assertion failed:

assert new File<'HelloWorld.txt'> == new File<'Hello.txt'>
       |                           |  |
       HelloWorld.txt              |  Hello.txt
                                  false

         at Hello.run<Hello.groovy:2>
```

Assertions are very handy and one of the cornerstones of good testing. They also do a great job of clarifying intentions. You will see assertions in many of the examples throughout this book.

Strings

Groovy supports two kinds of strings: regular Java strings and GStrings. A string in Groovy is an instance of `java.lang.String` if it is surrounded by single quotes or if it is surrounded by double or triple quotes with no unescaped dollar sign ($).

GStrings

GStrings are an instance of groovy.lang.GString and allow placeholders to be included in the text. GStrings are not a subclass of String because the String class is final and can't be extended. A GString is just like a normal string, but it allows the embedding of variables within it using ${..}. The curly braces are only required if the embedded variable is a placeholder for an expression.

Groovy supports a concept found in many other languages such as Perl and Ruby called string interpolation. String interpolation is the ability to substitute an expression or variable within a string. If you have experience with Unix shell scripts, Ruby, or Perl, this should look familiar. Java doesn't support string interpolation. You must manually concatenate the values.

Listing 2-12 is an example of the type of code you need to write in Java.

Listing 2-12. Building Strings with Java

```
String name = "Jim";
String helloName = "Hello " + name;
System.out.println(helloName);
```

Listing 2-13. String Interpolation in Groovy/GString

```
1. str1= "Jim"
2. str2 = "Hello "
3. println "$str2$str1"
```

In Line 3, curly braces are not used because curly braces are only required if the embedded variable is a placeholder for an expression.

When Groovy sees a string defined with double quotes or slashes and an embedded expression, Groovy constructs an org.codehaus.groovy.runtime.GStringImpl instead of a java.lang.String. When the GString is accessed, the expression is evaluated. Notice that you can include any valid Groovy expression inside the ${} notation; this includes method calls or variable names.

Single Line Strings

Single line strings can be single quoted or double quoted. A string enclosed in single quotes is taken literally. Strings defined with single quotes do not interpret the embedded expressions, as illustrated in Listing 2-14.

Listing 2-14. Single Quote String does not Interpret Embedded Expressions

```
name = "vishal"
s1 = 'hello $name'
println s1
```

Here is the output:

```
hello $name
```

Listing 2-15. Nested Double Quote in Single Quote

```
s1 = 'hello "vishal"'
println s1
```

Here is the output:

```
hello "vishal"
```

Strings defined using double quotes will interpret embedded expressions within the string, as illustrated in Listing 2-16.

Listing 2-16. Double Quote Strings Interpret Embedded Expressions

```
def name = "vishal"
s1 = "hello $name"
println s1
```

Here is the output:

```
hello vishal
```

Listing 2-17. Nested Single Quote in Double Quote

```
s1 = "hello 'vishal'"
println s1
```

Here is the output:

```
hello 'vishal'
```

Multiline Strings

Groovy supports strings that span multiple lines. A multiline string is defined by using three double quotes or three single quotes.

Multiline string support is very useful for creating templates or embedded documents (such as XML templates, SQL statements, HTML, and so on). For example, you could use a multiline string and string interpolation to build the body of an e-mail message, as shown in Listing 2-18. String interpolation with multiline strings works in the same way as it does with regular strings: Multiline strings created with double quotes evaluate expressions, and single-quoted strings don't.

Listing 2-18. Using Multiline Strings

```
def name = "Jim"
def multiLineQuote = """
Hello, ${name}
This is a multiline string with double quotes
"""
println multiLineQuote
println multiLineQuote.class.name
def multiLineSingleQuote = '''
Hello, ${name}
This is a multiline string with single quotes
'''
println multiLineSingleQuote
println multiLineSingleQuote.class.name
```

Running the code in Listing 2-18 results in the following output:

```
Hello, Jim
This is a multiline string with double quotes

org.codehaus.groovy.runtime.GStringImpl

Hello, ${name}
This is a multiline string with single quotes

Java.lang.String
```

Slashy Strings

As mentioned earlier, slashes can be used to define strings. The slashy notation has a very nice benefit: Additional backslashes are not needed to escape special characters. The only exception is escaping a backslash: \/. The slashy notation can be helpful when creating a regular expression requiring a backslash or a path. Listing 2-19 illustrates the difference between using regular quotes and slashes to define a regular expression to match a file system path.

Listing 2-19. Using Slashy Strings

```
def winpathQuoted='C:\\windows\\system32'
def winpathSlashy=/C:\windows\system32/
println winpathSlashy // C:\windows\system32
assert winpathSlashy ==~ '\\w{1}:\\\\.+\\\\.+'
assert winpathSlashy ==~ /\w{1}:\\.+\\.+/
```

Listing 2-19 defines two variables and assigns them to a directory path. The first variable definition, `winpathQuoted`, uses the single-quote notation to define a string. Using the single-quote notation requires that the embedded backslash be escaped using an additional backslash. The first assert statement, which tests the regular expression defined using single quotes, also requires the addition of an extra backslash to escape a backslash.

Notice how using the slashy notation doesn't require the additional backslashes.

Clearly, it is easier to write and read winpath Slashy, and the second regular expression is easier to write and read as well. Regular expressions and the ==~ operator will be covered in more detail in the "Regular Expressions" section later in this chapter.

Multiline Slashy Strings

Slashy strings can also span multiple lines. This is particularly useful for multiline regexs when using the regex free-spacing comment style.

Listing 2-20. Using Multiline Slashy Strings

```
1. def name = "vishal"
2. def path= "c:/groovy"
3. def multilineSlashy = /
4.     Hello $name
5.     path= $path
```

```
6.      dollar = $
7.      path = c:\/groovy
8.      /
9. println multilineSlashy
```

Here is the output:

```
Hello vishal
path= c:/groovy
dollar = $
path = c:/groovy
```

Let's take a look at Listing 2-20 in a little more detail:

- Line 1 defines a variable, `name`, and assigns the value "vishal" to it.
- Line 2 defines a variable, `path`, and assigns the value "c:/groovy" to it.
- Line 3 defines a variable, `multilineSlashy`, and assigns a multiline string to it that includes up to Line 8, between the slashes.
- Line 4 has an expression, `$name`, that is evaluated to `vishal`, as shown in the output.
- Line5 has an expression, `$path`, that is evaluated to `c:/groovy`, as shown in the output.
- Line 6 has a $ sign but it is not an expression, so it is displayed in the output.
- Line 7 has a slash, which needs to be escaped.

Dollar Slashy Strings

In multiline slashy strings, a slash still needs to be escaped. Moreover, in multiline slashy strings, an unescaped dollar sign that is not an expression results in a `MissingPropertyException`, as illustrated in Listing 2-21.

Listing 2-21. MissingPropertyException in Multiline Slashy String

```
1.  def name = "vishal"
2.  def path= "c:/groovy"
3.
4.  def multilineSlashy = /
5.      Hello $name
6.      path= $path
7.      dollar = $test
8.      path = c:\/groovy
9.      /
10. println multilineSlashy
```

```
Caught: groovy.lang.MissingPropertyException: No such property: test for class:
Hello
groovy.lang.MissingProperyException: No such property: test for class: Hello
        at Hello.run<Hello.groovy:4>
```

In Listing 2-21, there is no such property as test; $test in Line 7 is interpreted as an expression, which results in a `MissingPropertyException`.

Now, let us look at the code in the Listing 2-22, specifically Line 7.

Listing 2-22. Unescaped Dollar Sign in Multiline Slashy String

```
1.  def name = "vishal"
2.  def path= "c:/groovy"
3.
4.  def multilineSlashy = /
5.      Hello $name
6.      path= $path
7.      dollar = $ test
8.      path = c:\/groovy
9.
10.     /
11.
12. println multilineSlashy
```

This time Groovy does not interpret `$ test` in Line 7 as an expression, as there is an empty space between $ and `test`, and renders the output as follows:

```
Hello vishal
path= c:/groovy
dollar = $ test
path = c:/groovy
```

With dollar slashy string, you are no longer required to escape slash with a preceding backslash (multiline slashy strings require the slash to be escaped) and you can use $$ to escape a $ or $/ to escape a slash if needed, as illustrated in Listing 2-23.

Listing 2-23. Using Dollar Slashy String

```
1.  def name = "vishal"
2.  def path= "c:/groovy"
3.
4.  def dollarSlashy = $/
5.      Hello $name
6.      path= $path
7.      dollar = $$test // escaping $test with a $
8.      path = c:/groovy
9.      /$
10. println dollarSlashy
```

```
Hello vishal
path= c:/groovy
dollar = $test
path = c:/groovy
```

Let's take a look at Listing 2-23 in more detail:

- Line 4 defines a dollarSlashy string that includes up to Line 9.
- Line 7 has a $test, which had caused a MissingPropertyException in the case of the multiline slashy string in Listing 2-21, which we now escape using a $.

Regular Expressions

Regular expressions, sometimes referred to regex, are a technique for identifying and manipulating text using a pattern notation. They have been popular in scripting languages such as Unix shell scripting and Perl for a long time, and were added to Java in version 1.4.

Note Regular expressions are extremely robust and powerful. This section discusses Groovy's support of regular expressions. For a full exploration of regular expressions, refer to a book devoted to that subject. You can also find many useful tutorials on the Internet.

A regular expression is a sequence of characters to create a pattern that is applied to a string. The pattern is defined by a pattern language. Table 2-1 shows some of the more common patterns in the Java regular expression language.

Table 2-1. Summary of Regular-Expression Constructs

Construct	Matches
Characters	
x	The character x
\\	The backslash character
\t	The tab character (\u0009)
\n	The newline (line feed) character (\u000A)
\r	The carriage-return character (\u000D)
\f	The form-feed character (\u000C)
\e	The escape character (\u001B)
Character Classes	
[abc]	a, b, or c (simple class)
[^abc]	Any character except a, b, or c (negation)
[a-zA-Z]	a through z or A through Z, inclusive (range)
[a-d[m-p]]	a through d, or m through p: [a-dm-p] (union)
[a-z&&[def]]	d, e, or f (intersection)
[a-z&&[^bc]]	a through z, except for b and c: [ad-z] (subtraction)
[a-z&&[^m-p]]	a through z, and not m through p: [a-lq-z] (subtraction)

(*continued*)

Table 2-1. (*continued*)

Construct	Matches
Predefined Character Classes	
`.`	Any character (may or may not match line terminators)
`\d`	A digit: [0-9]
`\D`	A nondigit: [^0-9]
`\s`	A whitespace character: `[ \t\n\x0B\f\r]`
`\S`	A non-whitespace character: `[^\s]`
`\w`	A word character: [a-zA-Z_0-9]
`\W`	A nonword character: `[^\W]`
Boundary Matchers	
`^`	The beginning of a line
`$`	The end of a line
`\b`	A word boundary
`\B`	A nonword boundary
`\A`	The beginning of the input
`\G`	The end of the previous match
`\Z`	The end of the input but for the final terminator, if any
`\z`	The end of the input
Greedy Quantifiers	
X?	*X*, once or not at all
*X**	*X*, zero or more times
X+	*X*, one or more times
X{*n*}	*X*, exactly *n* times
X{*n*,}	*X*, at least *n* times
X{*n*,*m*}	*X*, at least *n* but not more than `m` times
Reluctant Quantifiers	
X??	*X*, once or not at all
*X**?	*X*, zero or more times
X+?	*X*, one or more times
X{*n*}?	*X*, exactly *n* times
X{*n*,}?	*X*, at least *n* times
X{*n*,*m*}?	*X*, at least *n* but not more than *m* times

(*continued*)

Table 2-1. *(continued)*

Construct	Matches
Possessive Quantifiers	
X?+	*X*, once or not at all
*X**+	*X*, zero or more times
X++	*X*, one or more times
X{*n*}+	*X*, exactly *n* times
X{*n*,}+	*X*, at least *n* times
X{*n*,*m*}+	*X*, at least *n* but not more than *m* times
Logical Operators	
XY	*X* followed by *Y*
X|*Y*	Either *X* or *Y*
(*X*)	*X*, as a capturing group

Groovy Regular Expression Operators

Groovy leverages Java's regular expression support and makes it easier through Groovy's String support. Groovy also adds three convenience operators:

- The match operator (`==~`)
- The find operator (`=~`)
- The pattern operator (`~string`)

Match Operator

The match operator (`==~`) returns true if the regular expression exactly matches the subject.

Listing 2-24 shows some examples of using the match operator.

Listing 2-24. Using the Match Operator

```
1. assert "abc" ==~ 'abc'
2. assert "abc" ==~ /abc/
3. assert "abcabc" ==~ /abc/ // Fails - not an exact match
4. assert "abc" ==~ /^a.c/ // Starts with a, 1 char, ends with c
5. assert "abc" ==~ /^a../ // Starts with a, 2 chars
6. assert "abc" ==~ /.*c$/ // One or more chars end with c
7. assert "abc" ==~ ".*c\$" // Slashy string is better
```

Line 3 shows that unless it is an exact match, the match will fail (return false). Lines 4–6 illustrate a couple of ways of defining a regular expression that matches the subject. Line 7 is another example of defining the regular expression on Line6, except it uses double quotes instead of slashes. The important thing to note is that using the double quotes requires the $ to be escaped using a (==~)backslash.

Find Operator

The find operator (=~) returns a `java.util.regex.Matcher`. A matcher is a component that applies a regular expression to a string. The result is a two-dimensional array of matches.

The first dimension contains the match, and the second dimension contains the groups within the match. A group is defined within the regular expression using parentheses. In the example in Listing 2-25, the regular expression defines four groups. When the expression is applied to a string, the groups are individually accessible. This is useful for identifying and accessing portions of a string.

Listing 2-25. Using the Find Operator

```
1. def winpath=/C:\windows\system32\somedir/
2. def matcher = winpath =~ /(\w{1}):\\(\w+)\\(\w+)\\(\w+)/
3. println matcher
4. println matcher[0] // ["C:\windows\system32\somedir", "C", "windows",
5. // "system32", "somedir"]
6. println matcher[0][1] // C
7. def newPath = matcher.replaceFirst('/etc/bin/')
8. println newPath // /etc/bin
```

Here is the output:

```
java.util.regex.Matcher[pattern=(\w{1}):\\(\w+)\\(\w+)\\(\w+) region=0,27
lastmatch=]
["C:\windows\system32\somedir", "C", "windows", "system32", "somedir"]
C
/etc/bin/
```

Line 1 defines `winpath` as a directory path string. Line 2 applies a regular expression to the `winpath` variable using the find operator and returns a `java.util.regex.Matcher`. The regular expression is set up as a series of group-capturing expressions. Referring to Table 2-1, you can see that \w is a word character and the + means one or more. When the regular expression matches the variable, the individual group values are available from the matcher. When Line 3 is invoked, you can see that matcher is in fact a `java.util.regex.Matcher` and the pattern matches. Lines 4 and 5 illustrate printing the contents of the first match using an index notation. In this example, there will be only one match. If `winpath` had been a multiline string with multiple directory paths, then matcher would have had multiple matches. Line 6 shows accessing the first group within the match using a second index. Now that you have a match, you can start applying `java.util.regex.Matcher` methods. Line 7 is an example of replacing the first match with a new value. When you replace a match, it returns a new string.

Pattern Operator

The pattern operator (`~string`) transforms a string into a pattern (`java.util.regex.Pattern`), which is a compiled regular expression. When you plan to use a regular expression over and over, consider creating a pattern. Reusing a pattern will give the application a performance boost.

Listing 2-26. Creating and Using a Pattern

```
1. def saying = """Now is the time for all good men (and women) to come to the aid
2. of their country"""
3. def pattern = ~/(\w+en)/
4. def matcher = pattern.matcher(saying)
```

```
5. def count = matcher.getCount()
6. println "Matches = ${count}"
7. for(i in 0..<count) {
8. println matcher[i]
9. }
```

Here is the output:

```
Matches = 2
["men", "men"]
["women", "women"]
```

Lines 1 and 2 assign a famous quote to the saying variable. Line 3 defines a regular expression pattern that should find the words that end in en, such as men and women.

■ **Caution** Notice the space between the = and ~ for the pattern operator in Listing 2-26. Without the space, it would be the find operator.

Line 4 applies the pattern to the saying and returns a matcher that contains the results.

Lines 5 and 6 print the number of matches. Lines 7–9 loop through and print the matches.

Common Uses of Regular Expressions

By now, you are starting to get an idea of how regular expressions work. Now let's see how they can be applied in real-world scenarios. It is common for web applications to allow the user to enter personal information such as a telephone number. Two common tasks are to check that the phone number is a valid format and to parse the phone number into the individual parts. Listing 2-27 is an example of using the match operator to validate a phone number.

Listing 2-27. Validating a Phone Number

```
def phoneValidation = /^[01]?\s*[\(\.-]?(\d{3})[\)\.-]?\s*(\d{3})[\.-](\d{4})$/
assert '(800)555-1212' ==~ phoneValidation
assert '1(800) 555-1212' ==~ phoneValidation
assert '1-800-555-1212' ==~ phoneValidation
assert '1.800.555.1212' ==~ phoneValidation
```

In this example, you see the same phone number in four different valid formats. The regular expression to validate the phone number format is assigned to the variable phoneValidation. The match operator is used to validate the phone numbers by applying the regular expression to the phone number. If the phone number is valid, the match operator returns true.

Another common task is parsing a phone number so that the values can be put into a domain class. Listing 2-28 illustrates parsing the phone number into the individual parts and loading it in the domain class.

Listing 2-28. Parsing the Phone Number

```
class Phone {
String areaCode
String exchange
String local
}
```

```
def phoneStr = '(800)555-1212'
def phoneRegex = ~/^[01]?\s*[\(\.-]?(\d{3})[\)\.-]?\s*(\d{3})[\.-](\d{4})$/
def matcher = phonePattern.matcher(phoneStr)
def phone = new Phone(
areaCode: matcher[0][1],
exchange: matcher[0][2],
local: matcher[0][3])
println "Original Phone Number: ${phoneStr}"
println """Parsed Phone Number\
\n\tArea Code = ${phone.areaCode}\
\n\tExchange = ${phone.exchange}\
\n\tLocal = ${phone.local}"""
```

In this example, the Phone object, the phone number to parse (phone1), and the phone regular expression pattern (phoneRegex) are defined. Next, the phone pattern is applied to the phone number to be parsed. The pattern is defined with groups, which allows the regular expression to be used to parse the phone number into the individual parts. The construction of the Phone object illustrates accessing the individual parts using the second index. Lastly, we print out the phone number to prove that the parsing worked.

Collective Datatypes

Groovy supports a number of different collections, including arrays, lists, maps, ranges, and sets. Let's look at how to create and use each of the collection types.

Arrays

A Groovy array is a sequence of objects, just like a Java array. Groovy makes working with arrays a little easier, but you have the same limitations as with Java arrays.

Listing 2-29. Creating and Using Arrays

```
1.  def stringArray = new String[3]
2.  println stringArray.size()
3.  stringArray[0] = "Chris"
4.  println stringArray // {"Chris", null, null}
5.  stringArray[1] = "Joseph"
6.  stringArray[2] = "Jim"
7.  println stringArray // {"Chris", "Joseph", "Jim"}
8.  println stringArray[1] // Joseph
9.  stringArray.each { println it} // Chris, Joseph, Jim
10. println stringArray[-1..-3] // ["Jim", "Joseph", "Chris"]
```

Line 1 creates a string array of size 3. Lines 3–8 use an index to access the array. Line9 illustrates using the each() method to iterate through the array. That deserves a second look. Yes, the each() method is available on the array, which is very convenient. The each() method is used to iterate through and apply the closure on every element. A closure always has at least one argument, which will be available within the body of the closure via the implicit parameter it if no explicit parameters are defined. Both the each() method and the it variable are discussed in detail in the Closures section of this chapter. Line 10 also shows something interesting—it uses a range, which will be discussed shortly, to access the array. In this case, the example goes one step further and shows accessing the array from left to right.

Lists

A Groovy list is an ordered collection of objects, just as in Java. It is an implementation of the `java.util.List` interface. In the course of building Grails applications, it is common to see lists returned from the controllers and services. Listing 2-30 illustrates creating a list and common usages.

Listing 2-30. Creating and Using Lists

```
1.  def emptyList = []
2.  println emptyList.class.name // java.util.ArrayList
3.  println emptyList.size // 0
4.
5.  def list = ["Chris"] // List with one item in it
6.  // Add items to the list
7.  list.add "Joseph" // Notice the optional () missing
8.  list << "Jim" // Notice the overloaded left-shift operator
9.  println list.size // 3
10.
11. // Iterate over the list
12. list.each { println it } // Chris Joseph Jim
13.
14. // Access items in the list
15. println list[1] // Joseph // Indexed access
16. list[0] = "Christopher"
17. println list.get(0) // Christopher
18.
19. list.set(0, "Chris") // Set the 0 item to Chris
20. println list.get(0) // Chris
21.
22. list.remove 2
23. list-= "Joseph" // Overloaded - operator
24. list.each { println it } // Chris
25.
26. list.add "Joseph"
27. list+="Jim" // Overloaded + operator
28. list.each { println it } // Chris Joseph Jim
29. println list[-1] // Jim
```

On Line 1 of Listing 2-30, an empty list is created by assigning a property the value of [ ] . Line 2 prints out the list's class name so that you can see that it is a `java.util.ArrayList`. Line 3 prints the list's size, which is 0. Lines 5–9 create a list with an item already in it and show two ways to add items to the list.

Line 12 iterates over the list, invoking the closure to print out the contents. The `each()` method provides the ability to iterate over all elements in the list, invoking the closure on each element. This is an example of using a closure as a parameter to a method. Lines 15–17 illustrate using an index to access a list. Lists are zero-based. Line 15 shows accessing the second item in the list. Line 16 shows using an index to assign `position()` the value "Christopher". Line 17 accesses the list using the `get()` method. Lines19–20 use the `set()` method to assign the first position in the list and then print it out. Lines 22–24 remove items from the list using the `remove()` method and the minus operator. Lines 26–28 add items to the list using the `add()` method and the plus operator. Line 29 is interesting—it uses the index value -1. Using a negative index value causes the list to be accessed in the opposite order, or from last to first.

Maps

A Groovy map is an unordered collection of key/value pairs, where the key is unique, just as in Java. It is an implementation of `java.util.Map`. By default, unless you specify otherwise, a Groovy map is a `java.util.LinkedHashMap`. If you are familiar with `LinkedHashMap` maps, you know that they are ordered by insert. If you need a map other than a `LinkedHashMap`, you can create any type of map by instantiating it; for example, `def aTreeMap = new TreeMap()`. In general, we encourage you to think of it as a regular map.

Listing 2-31 illustrates creating maps and common usages.

Listing 2-31. Creating and Using Maps

```
1.  def emptyMap = [:]
2.  // map.class returns null, use getClass()
3.  println emptyMap.getClass().name //java.util.LinkedHashMap
4.  println emptyMap.size() // 0
5.
6.  def todos = ['a':'Write the map section', 'b':'Write the set section']
7.  println todos.size() // 2
8.  println todos["a"] // Write the map section
9.  println todos."a" // Write the map section
10. println todos.a // Write the map section
11. println todos.getAt("b") // Write the set section
12. println todos.get("b") // Write the set section
13. println todos.get("c", "unknown") // unknown, Notice "c" wasn't defined
14. // and now it is
15. println todos // ["a":"Write the map section", "b":"Write the set section",
16. // "c":"unknown"]
17.
18. todos.d = "Write the ranges section"
19. println todos.d // Write the ranges section
20. todos.put('e', 'Write the strings section')
21. println todos.e // Write the strings section
22. todos.putAt 'f', 'Write the closure section' // Notice () are optional
23. println todos.f // Write the closure section
24. todos[null] = 'Nothing Set' // Using null as a key
25. println todos[null] // Nothing set
26.
27. // Print each key/value pair on a separate Line
28. // Note: it is an implicit iterator
29. todos.each { println "Key: ${it.key}, Value: ${it.value}" }
30. // Print each key/value pair on a separate Line with index
31. todos.eachWithIndex { it, i -> println "${i} Key: ${it.key},Value: ${it.value}" }
33. // Print the value set
34. todos.values().each { println it }
```

In Line 1, an empty map is created by assigning a property the value `[:]`. Compare the creation of an empty list to the creation of an empty map. An empty list is created using the value `[]`; an empty map is created using the value `[:]`. You can see from Line 2 that the map is implemented as a `java.util.LinkedHashMap`.

Line 6 illustrates defining a map with multiple entries. When using the square bracket notation, the colon separates the key from the value. Line 6 is `[key1: value1,key2 : value2]`.

Lines 8–16 show several different techniques for accessing the map. The most interesting is Line 10. It shows using the key as a property to the map. You can use this technique to read an item from the map and put an item into the map.

Lines 18–25 show several different techniques for putting items into the map. You can see that they mirror the techniques used on lines 8–16.

Lines 29, 31, 32, and 34 illustrate iterating. Line 29 iterates over the map to print the key and value. Lines 31 and 32 iterate with an index. Line 34 iterates over the map values.

Ranges

A range is a list of sequential values. Logically, you can think of it as 1 through 10 or a through z. As a matter of fact, the declaration of a range is exactly that: 1..10, or 'a'.'z'. A range is a list of any objects that implements `java.lang.Comparable`. The objects have `next()` and `previous()` methods to facilitate navigating through the range. This means that with a bit of work, it is possible to use your own Groovy objects within a range. Listing 2-32 illustrates some of things you can do with ranges.

Listing 2-32. Creating and Using Ranges

```
1.  def numRange = 0..9
2.  println numRange.size() // 10
3.  numRange.each {print it} // 0123456789
4.  println ""
5.  println numRange.contains(5) // true
6.
7.  def alphaRange = 'a'..'z'
8.  println alphaRange.size() // 26
9.  println alphaRange[1] // b
10.
11. def exclusiveRange = 1..<10
12. println exclusiveRange.size() // 9
13. exclusiveRange.each {print it} // 123456789
14. println ""
15. println exclusiveRange.contains(10) // false
16.
17. def reverseRange = 9..0
18. reverseRange.each {print it} // 9876543210
```

Lines 1, 7, 11, and 17 illustrate defining ranges. Line 1 defines an inclusive range of numbers. Line 7 defines an inclusive range of lowercase letters. Line 11 defines an exclusive list of numbers. The range results in a range of numbers 1–9, excluding 10. Line 17creates a range in reverse order, 9 through 0.Frequently, ranges are used for iterating. In Listing 2-32, `each()` was used to iterate over the range. Listing 2-33 shows three ways you could use a range to iterate: one Java and two Groovy.

Listing 2-33. Iterating with Ranges

```
1.  println "Java style for loop"
2.  for(int i=0;i<=9;i++) {
3.  println i
4.  }
5.
```

```
6.  println "Groovy style for loop"
7.  for (i in 0..9) {
8.  println i
9.  }
10.
11. println "Groovy range loop"
12. (0..9).each { i->
13. println i
14. }
```

Listing 2-33 starts off by showing a classic Java style for loop. Lines 7-9 are an example of the same loop using the Groovy style `for` loop. The `for` loop syntax is discussed in detail in the next section. Lines 12-14 illustrate yet another technique for looping, by using a range and the `each()` method. The `each()` method is used to iterate through and apply the closure on every element. A closure always has at least one argument, which will be available within the body of the closure via the implicit parameter `it` if no explicit parameters are defined. Both the `each()` method and `it` variable are discussed in detail in Closures section of this chapter.

Sets

A Groovy set is an unordered collection of objects, with no duplicates, just as in Java. It is an implementation of `java.util.Set`. By default, unless you specify otherwise, a Groovyset is a `java.util.HashSet`. If you need a set other than a `HashSet`, you can create any type of set by instantiating it; for example, `def aTreeSet = new TreeSet()`. In general, we encourage you to think of it as a regular set. Listing 2-34 illustrates creating sets and common usages.

Listing 2-34. Creating and Using Sets

```
1.  def emptySet = [] as Set
2.  println emptySet.class.name // java.util.HashSet
3.  println emptySet.size() // 0
4.
5.  def list = ["Chris", "Chris" ]
6.  def set = ["Chris", "Chris" ] as Set
7.  println "List Size: ${list.size()} Set Size: ${set.size()}" // List Size: 2 Set
    Size: 1
8.  set.add "Joseph"
9.  set << "Jim"
10. println set.size() // 3
11. println set // ["Chris", "Jim", "Joseph"]
12.
13. // Iterate over the set
14. set.each { println it }
15.
16. set.remove 2
17. set-= "Joseph" // Overloaded - operator
18. set.each { println it } // Chris
19. set+= "Joseph"
20. set+= "Jim"
21. set.each { println it } // Chris Joseph Jim
22.
23. // Convert a set to a list
```

```
24. list = set as List
25. println list.class.name // java.util.ArrayList
26. println set.asList().class.name // java.util.ArrayList
27. println set.toList().class.name // java.util.ArrayList
```

Creating an empty set is similar to creating an empty list. The difference is the addition of the as Set clause. Lines 5–7 illustrate that a list allows duplicates and a set doesn't. Lines 8–21 shouldn't be any surprise. One of the important differences between a list and a set is that a list provides indexed-based access and a set doesn't. Lines 24 and 26 show two different techniques to convert a set into a list.

Control Structure

Groovy provides the same control structures as in Java and makes them simpler. The control structures evaluate the expression and determine if the result of the expression is true or false, and on the basis of that alters the flow of control.

Groovy Truth

In Groovy, any expression can be evaluated, unlike in Java where only boolean variables and expressions can evaluate to true or false. In Groovy truth, null Object references evaluate to false. Non-empty collections, arrays, and maps, strings with non-zero length, and non-zero numbers will all evaluate to true. This is very helpful, especially with strings and collections, as illustrated in Listing 2-35.

Listing 2-35. Null Check for Collections and Strings in Java

```
if (collection != null && !collection.isEmpty()) { ... } // collection
if (str != null && str.length() > 0) { ... }// string
```

Listing 2-36. Null Check for Collections and Strings in Groovy

```
if (collection) { ... } // collection
if (str) { ... }// string
```

In Groovy, it is possible to provide a method for coercion to boolean in your own classes. Listing 2-37 illustrates how Groovy offers the ability to coerce SomeClass instances to true or false, using the implementation of the boolean asBoolean() method.

Listing 2-37. Using asBoolean() Method

```
class SomeClass{
boolean value
boolean asBoolean() { value }
}
assert new Test(value: true)
assert !new Test(value: false)
```

Logical Branching

Groovy has three conditionals: the `if` statement, the ternary operator, and the `switch` statement. The `if` statement and ternary operator are the same as in Java, though Groovy enhances the ternary operator with the Elvis operator. The Elvis operator is discussed in Chapter 3. The `switch` statement is more powerful in Groovy than in Java, in that the `switch` accepts any kind of object (unlike Java), as illustrated in Listing 2-38.

Listing 2-38. Using switch

```
def x = 3.14
def result = ""

switch ( x ) {
    case "foo": result = "String"

    case [4, 5, 6 ]:
        result = "List"
        break

    case 12..30:
        result = "Range"
        break

    case Integer:
        result = "Integer"
        break

    case Number:
        result = "Number"
        break

    default:
        result = "Default"
}

assert result == "Number"
```

Looping

In addition to supporting Java `for` loops, Groovy also provides a much simpler `for` loop that works with any kind of array collection, as illustrated in Listing 2-39.

Listing 2-39. Using the for Loop

```
for (i in 'Hello')Iterate over a string
    println i

for (i in 0..10)   //Iterate over a range
    println i
```

```
for (i in [1,2,3,4]) //Iterate over a list
    println i

authors = [1:'Vishal', 2:'Jim', 3: 'Chris', 4:'Joseph']

for (entry in map) //Iterate over a map
  println entry.key + ' ' + entry.value
```

Listing 2-39 shows the for loop for iterating over string, range, list, and map using the in operator as a shortcut for the contains method in a collection.

Exception Handling

Exception handling in Groovy is the same as in Java. Just as in Java, you can specify a try-catch-finally sequence of blocks, or just try-catch, or just try-finally. In addition to that, in Groovy, declarations of exceptions in the method signature are optional, even for checked exceptions, and a type declaration is optional in the catch expression.

In Groovy it is possible for try/catch/finally blocks to return a value when they are the last expression in a method or a closure. There is no need to explicitly use the return keyword inside these constructs, as long as they are the latest expression in the block of code. If an exception is thrown in the try block, the last expression in the catch block is returned instead. finally, blocks don't return any value, as illustrated in Listing 2-40.

Listing 2-40. Returning Value from try/catch/finally

```
def method(bool) {
    try {
        if (bool) throw new Exception("foo")
        1
    } catch(e) {
        2
    } finally {
        3
    }
}

assert method(false) == 1
assert method(true) == 2
```

In Groovy, it is also possible to define several exceptions to be catch and treated by the same catch block with the multi-catch block, as illustrated in Listing 2-41.

Listing 2-41. Multi-catch Block

```
try {
    /* ... */
} catch(IOException | NullPointerException e) {
    /* one block to handle 2 exceptions */
}
```

Methods

Listing 2-42 illustrates defining a method in Groovy the Java way.

Listing 2-42. Defining aMethod the Java Way

```
public String hello(String name) {
return "Hello, " + name;
}
```

Listing 2-43 illustrates defining the method using the Groovy idiom.

Listing 2-43. Defining aMethod Using the Groovy Idiom

```
def hello(name) {
"Hello, ${name}"
}
```

The Groovy way of defining a method is a bit more compact. It takes advantage of a couple of Groovy's optional features:

- The return type and the return statement are not included in the body of the method. Groovy always returns the results of the last expression—in this case, the `GString` "Hello, . . .".
- The access modifier public is not defined. By default, unless you specify otherwise, Groovy defaults all classes, properties, and methods to public access.

■ **Note** Strictly speaking, the Groovy version of the `hello` method (Listing 2-43) is not exactly like the Java version (Listing 2-42). The corresponding Java signature of the method would be: `public Object hello (Object name)`. But, functionally, they are almost the same.

Closures

In *Old Times on the Mississippi,* Mark Twain wrote: "When I was a boy of 14, my father was so ignorant I could hardly stand to have the old man around. But when I got to be 21, I was astonished at how much the old man had learned in seven years."

Functional programming is the old man who comes to the rescue when learning to write robust concurrent software. Functional programming gives you the right foundation to think about concurrency. The three keystones of this foundation are referential transparency, higher-order functions, and immutable values. Understanding these key elements is crucial to understanding closures (and other functional features recently introduced in Groovy) and to that end we will give a brief introduction to functional programming. This introduction is by no means comprehensive, but sufficient enough to see Groovy in the functional light.

Groovy is not a pure functional language like Haskell, but we can still apply functional principles with it. Functional programming is built on the premise of pure functions. In mathematics, functions are pure in that they lack side effects. Consider the classic function sin(x): y = sin(x). No matter how many times sin(x) is called, no global or contextual state is modified internally by sin(x). Such a function is pure, free of side effects and oblivious to the context. This obliviousness to the surrounding context is known as referential transparency. If no global state is modified, concurrent invocation of the function is steadfast.

In functional programming, functions are first-class citizens, meaning functions can be assigned to variables, functions can be passed to other functions, and functions can be returned as values from other functions. And such functions, which take functions as arguments or return a function, are called higher-order functions.

Referential transparency, higher-order functions, and immutable values together make functional programming a better way to write concurrent software. Though functional languages are all about eliminating side effects, a language that never allowed for side effects would be useless. As a matter of fact, introducing side effects is crucial to any language. All functional languages have to provide mechanisms for introducing side effects in a controlled manner because even though functional languages are about pure programming, a language that does not sanction side effects would be useless, as input and output is essentially the ramification of side effects. One of the techniques to introduce side effects in a controlled manner is closure. A closure definition in Groovy follows the syntax:

```
{ [closure parameters ->] closure body}
```

Where `[closure parameters->]` is an optional comma-delimited list of arguments, and closure body can be an expression as well as 0 or more Groovy statements. The arguments look similar to a method's parameter list, and these arguments may be typed or untyped.

A Groovy closure is a block of reusable code within curly braces `{}`, which can be assigned to a property or a variable, or passed as a parameter to a method. A closure is executed only when it is called—not when it is defined. Listing 2-44 illustrates this.

Listing 2-44. Calling a Closure

```
1. def closureVar = {println 'Hello world'}
2.     println "closure is not called yet"
3.     println " "
4.   closureVar.call()
```

- Line 1 has the closure with no parameters and consists of a single `println` statement. As there are no parameters, the parameter `List` and the `->` separator are omitted. The closure is referenced by the identifier `closureVar`.
- Line 4 uses the explicit mechanism using the `call()` method to invoke the Closure. You may also use the implicit nameless invocation `approach:closureVar()`.

As can be seen from the output, closure prints "Hello world" when it is called in Line 4, not when it is defined in Line 1. Here is the output:

```
closure is not called yet

Hello world
```

Listing 2-45 illustrates the same closure as in Listing 2-44, but with the parameter.

Listing 2-45. Closure with Parameter

```
1. def closureVar = {param -> println "Hello ${param}"}
2. closureVar.call('world')
3. closureVar ('implicit world')
```

- Line 2 is an explicit call with the actual argument 'world.'
- Line 3 is an implicit call with the actual argument 'implicit world.'

Here is the output:

```
Hello world
Hello implicit world
```

As Listing 2-46 illustrates, the formal parameters to a closure may be assigned default values.

Listing 2-46. Parameters with Default Values

```
1. def sayHello= {str1, str2= " default world" -> println "${str1} ${str2}" }
2. sayHello("Hello", "world")
3. sayHello("Hello")
```

- In Line 1, the `sayHello` closure takes two parameters, of which one parameter, `str2`, has a default value.
- In Line 3, only one actual parameter is provided to the closure and the default value of the second parameter is used.

Here is the output:

```
Hello world
Hello default world
```

Closures always have a return value. The value may be specified via one or more explicit return statement in the closure body, as illustrated in Listing 2-47, or as the value of the last executed statement if return is not explicitly specified, as illustrated in Listing 2-48.

Listing 2-47. Using Return Keyword

```
1. def sum = {list -> return list.sum()}
2. assert sum([2,2]) == 4
```

Listing 2-48. Return Keyword Optional

```
1. def sum = {list -> list.sum()}
2. assert sum([2,2]) == 4
```

There are several ways to declare a closure. But before that, let's look deeper into the mechanics of closure. To understand closure, you have to understand the concept of free variables. A closure is formed when the body of a function refers to one or more free variables. Free variables are variables that are not local to the function and are not passed as arguments to the function, but are defined in the enclosing scope where the function is defined. Thus, closures refer to variables not listed in their parameter list (free variables). They are "bound" to variables within the scope where they are defined. Listing 2-49 illustrates this.

Listing 2-49. Free Variables

```
1. def myConst = 5
2. def incByConst = { num -> num + myConst }
3. println incByConst(10) // => 15
```

The runtime "closes over" the free variable (myConst in Listing 2-49) so that it is available when the function is executed. That is, the compiler creates a closure that envelops the external context of free variables and binds them.

Implicit Variables

Within a Groovy closure, several variables are defined that have special meaning:

it

If only one argument is passed to the closure, the arguments list and the -> symbol can be omitted and the closure will have access to `it` that represents that one argument, illustrated in the Listing 2-50.

Listing 2-50. Using it

```
def clos = {println "Hello ${it}"}
clos.call('world')
```

Here is the output:

```
Hello world
```

A closure always has at least one argument, which will be available within the body of the closure via the implicit parameter `it` if no explicit parameters are defined. The developer never has to declare the `it` variable—like the `this` parameter within objects, `it` is implicitly available. If a closure is invoked with zero arguments, then `it` will be `null`.

this, owner, and delegate

The `this` refers to the instance of the enclosing class where a closure is defined. If the closure is defined within the scope of a script, the enclosing class is the script class. The owner is the enclosing object of the closure. The owner is similar to `this` except in the case of nested closures where the enclosing object is the outer closure. The delegate is by default the same as owner, but changeable; for example, in a builder or `ExpandoMetaClass`. Listing 2-51 illustrates these three implicit variables.

Listing 2-51. Using this, owner, and delegate

```
1.  class Class1{
2.    def closure = {
3.      println "---in closure---"
4.      println this.class.name
5.      println owner.class.name
6.      println delegate.class.name
7.      def nestedClosure = {
8.      println "---in nestedClosure---"
9.         println this.class.name
10.        println owner.class.name
11.        println delegate.class.name
12.     }
13.     nestedClosure()
14.   }
15. }
16.
17. def clos = new Class1().closure
18. clos()
19. println ""
20. println "===changing the delegate==="
21. clos.delegate = this
```

```
22. clos()
23. println ""
24.
25. def closure2 = {
26.  println "--- closure outside the class(in the script)---"
27.  println this.class.name
28.     println delegate.class.name
29.     println owner.class.name
30.
31. }
32.
33. closure2()
```

- In Listing 2-51, the implicit variables `this`, `owner`, and `delegate` occur inside the outer closure from Line 4 to Line 6, inside the nested closure from Line 9 to Line 11, outside the class (closure2) from Line 27 to Line 29.
- The `this`, `owner`, and `delegate` inside the outer closure from Line 4 to Line 6 refer to the class name; for example, `Class1`.
- The `this` inside the nested closure from Line 9 to Line 11 refers to the class name (for example, `Class1`), and the `owner` and `delegate` refer to the closure class of the outer closure; for example, `Class1$_closure1`.
- The `this`, `owner`, and `delegate` outside the class from Line 27 to Line 29 refer to the name of the script; for example, `Hello`.
- In Line 21 we change the `delegate` of the closure (the outer closure in `Class1`) to the `this`, as we mentioned that the `delegate` is changeable.

Here is the output:

```
---in closure---
Class1
Class1
Class1
---in nestedClosure---
Class1
Class1$_closure1
Class1$_closure1

===changing the delegate===
---in closure---
Class1
Class1
Hello
---in nestedClosure---
Class1
Class1$_closure1
Class1$_closure1

--- closure outside the class<in the script>---
Hello
Hello
Hello
```

Explicit Declaration of Closure

All closures defined in Groovy are essentially derived from the type `Closure`. Because `groovy.lang` is automatically imported, we can refer to `Closure` as a type within our code. This is explicit declaration of closure. The advantage of declaring closure explicitly is that a non-closure cannot be inadvertently assigned to such variable.

Listing 2-52. Explicit Declaration of Closure

```
Closure clos = { println it }
```

Reusing the Method as a Closure

Groovy provides the method closure operator (`.&`) for reusing the method as a closure. The method closure operator allows the method to be accessed and passed around like a closure. Listing 2-53 illustrates this.

Listing 2-53. Reusing the Method as a Closure

```
1. def list = ["Vishal","Chris","Joseph","Jim"]
2. list.each { println it }
3. String printName(String name) {
4. println name
5. }
6. list.each(this.&printName)
```

Listing 2-53 creates a list of names and iterates through the list to print out the names. In Line 6, the method closure operator (`.&`) causes the method `printName` to be accessed as a closure.

Here is the output:

```
Vishal
Chris
Joseph
Jim
Vishal
Chris
Joseph
Jim
```

A closure is an object. You can pass closures around just like any other objects. A common example is iterating over a collection using a closure.

Listing 2-54. Passing a Closure As a Parameter

```
def list = ["Chris", "Joseph", "Jim"]
def sayHello = { println it }
list.each(sayHello)
```

Notice that `sayHello` is a property whose value is a closure. It is passed to the `each()` method so that as `each()` iterates over the list, the `sayHello` closure is invoked.

Closures and Collection

Lists, Maps, and Ranges include a number of methods (GDK methods) that have a closure parameter, which makes it effortless to iterate over the elements of the collection or range. We will discuss any, collect, each, every, and find methods.

any

The any method iterates through each element of a collection, checking whether a condition is valid for at least one element. The condition is provided by a closure. The signature of the any method is:

```
boolean any(Closure closure)
```

Listing 2-55. Using the any Method

```
def anyElement= [1, 2, 3, 4].any {element -> element > 2}
assert anyElement == true
```

The any method in Listing 2-55 iterates through the list and returns true if any element is greater than 2.

collect

The collect method iterates through a collection, converts each element into a new value as specified in the closure and returns a new List. It has the signature:

```
List collect(Closure closure)
```

Listing 2-56. Using the collect Method

```
def doubled = [1, 2, 3, 4].collect {element -> return 2*element}
assert doubled == [2,4,6,8]
```

each

The each method is used to iterate through a collection and apply the closure on every element. The signature of the each method is:

```
void each(Closure closure)
```

Listing 2-57. Using the each Method

```
[1, 2, 3].each {println it}
```

Listing 2-50 prints the values 1, 2, 3 on separate lines.

Here is the output:

```
1
2
3
```

every

The every method is used to iterate through a collection to check if all the elements in the collection matches the condition specified in the closure. The signature of the every method is:

```
boolean every(Closure closure)
```

Listing 2-58. Using the every Method

```
def allElements1 = [1, 2, 3, 4].every {element -> element > 1}
assert allElements1 == false

def allElements2 = [2, 3, 4, 5].every {element -> element > 1}
assert allElements2 == true
```

find

The `find` method finds the first value in a collection that matches some condition as specified in the closure. The signature of the `find` method is:

```
Object find(Closure closure)
```

Listing 2-59 illustrates using the `find` method to find the first element that is greater than 2.

Listing 2-59. Using the find Method

```
def foundElement = [1, 2, 3, 4].find {element -> element > 2}
assert foundElement == 3
```

Closures as Map Keys and Values

It's possible to put closures in a map, both as keys and values. You can use a closure as a key and as a value and call that closure as if it were a method on the map. However, when putting it into the map, you must escape it by enclosing it in parentheses. When accessing the value of the closure in the map, you must use `get(key)` or `map[key]`, as map. Key will treat key as a string.

Listing 2-60. Using Closure as Key and Value

```
1. key1 = { println "closure as key" }
2. map1 = [ (key1): 100 ]
3.
4. println  map1.get(key1)
5. println  map1[key1]
6.
7. map1 = [ key1: { println "closure as value" } ]
8. map1.key1()
```

The output is:

```
100
100
closure as value
```

- In Line 1, a closure is used as a key: key1.
- In Line 2, key1 is stored in the map and the value is 100.
- Line 4 prints the value stored in the map.
- Line 5 is another technique to retrieve the value.
- In Line 7, a closure is used as a value.
- Line 8 calls the closure stored as the value and prints "closure as value".

Currying Closure

Currying is the technique of transforming a function that takes multiple arguments in such a way that it can be called as a chain of functions, each with a single argument. In Groovy, you can use the curry() method to form curried closures.

Listing 2-61. Using Closure

```
1. def add= { x, y -> return x + y }
2. assert add(1,2) == 3
```

- Line 1 defines an add closure that takes two parameters and adds them.
- Line 2 replaces the formal parameter x with the value 1, replaces y with the value 2, and asserts that the sum is 3.

Now consider that instead of providing actual values to both formal parameters (x and y), we only provide a value to one of the parameters. The definition of the new closure with one actual value looks like this:

```
newAdd= { 1, y -> return 1 + y }
```

We just defined a new closure (newAdd) by providing actual value 1 to a formal parameter (x) of the closure add. This is what curry() method does for us; for example, we can define the closure newAdd by calling curry() on closure add, and provide the actual value 1 to one of the formal parameters, like so:

```
newAdd = add.curry(1)
```

The definition of this closure newAdd is still the same; for example, newAdd= {1,y -> 1+y}. We can fix the value of y in the same way by calling curry() on the closure newAdd; for example, newAdd.curry().

Listing 2-62. Currying Closure

```
1. def add= { x, y -> return x + y }
2. def newAdd = closure.curry(1)
3. assert "${ newAdd(2)}" == 3
```

Closure Trampoline

As we discussed earlier, in functional programming, because of the immutability of variables, it is not possible to have loop counters that change through a loop on each pass. The pure functional way of implementing such loop counter is through recursion.

Recursion, in a large measure, plays a crucial role in functional programming. That said there are two latent problems associated with recursion: the performance penalty of repetitive function calls and the probability of stack overflow. Performance penalty associated with repetitive function calls can be addressed with memorization, as discussed next. Stack overflow can be avoided by converting the recursive calls into a loop called trampoline.

Listing 2-63. Stack Overflow Error in Recursion

```
1. def factorial
2. factorial={n,BigInteger acc=1->
3.                 n == 1 ? acc:
4. factorial(n-1, n*acc)
5. }
6. factorial(1000)
```

A trampoline is a loop that works through a list of functions, calling each one in turn. In Groovy, a trampoline is formed by adding `.trampoline()` to a closure declaration, as illustrated in Listing 2-64.

Listing 2-64. Using Trampoline

```
1. def factorial
2.
3. factorial={n, BigInteger acc=1->
4.
5.         n == 1 ? acc:
6. factorial.trampoline(n-1, n*acc)
7. }.trampoline()
8.
9. factorial(1000)
```

Closure Memoization

Performance penalty associated with repetitive function calls in recursion can be addressed with memoization.

Memoization is a technique used to perform internal optimizations by caching previously computed values. Caching introduces side effects, in otherwise side effect free, pure functional programming, as the state of the cache is modified.

Listing 2-65. Using Memoization

```
1. closure = {param1, param2 ->  sleep(100); param1 + param2 }
2.
3. memoizedClosure = closure.memoize()
4.
5. def testTime(param1, param2) {  begin = System.currentTimeMillis()
6.                                 memoizedClosure(param1, param2)
7.                                 timeElapsed = System.currentTimeMillis()
8.                                 println "param1 = $param1, param2 =
   $param2   time :${timeElapsed - begin } ms."
```

```
9. }
10.
11. testTime(1, 2)
12. testTime(3, 4)
13. testTime(1, 2)
```

The output is:

```
param1 = 1,  param2 = 2    time :153 ms.
param1 = 3,  param2 = 4    time :100 ms.
Param1 = 1,  param2 = 2    time :0 ms.
```

Listing 2-65 illustrates memoization in action. In Line 3, closure is memoized. That is why the testTime closure call in Line 13 with the same parameters as in Line 11 takes 0 ms.

Operators

You use operators every day. They probably have become so familiar to you that you don't even think of them anymore. Common operators include = for assignment, + to add two numbers, * to multiply two numbers, and ++ to increment a number. Of course, there are many more, but you get the idea.

Operator Overloading

Operator overloading has been around for some time, but absent from Java. Operator overloading was omitted from Java because of the bad experiences it brought with its usage in C++. Groovy embraces operator overloading and makes it easy to define and use. An overloaded operator executes a method on object. Groovy has predefined the relationship between the overloaded operator and the object method. Table 2-2 lists the Groovy operators and their corresponding methods. When an overloaded operator is encountered, the corresponding method is invoked.

Table 2-2. *Operator Overloading*

Operator	Method
`a + b`	`a.plus(b)`
`a - b`	`a.minus(b)`
`a * b`	`a.multiply(b)`
`a ** b`	`a.power(b)`
`a / b`	`a.div(b)`
`a % b`	`a.mod(b)`
`a | b`	`a.or(b)`
`a & b`	`a.and(b)`
`a ^ b`	`a.xor(b)`
`a++ or ++a`	`a.next()`
`a-- or --a`	`a.previous()`

(*continued*)

Table 2-2. (continued)

Operator	Method
`a[b]`	`a.getAt(b)`
`a[b] = c`	`a.putAt(b, c)`
`a << b`	`a.leftShift(b)`
`a >> b`	`a.rightShift(b)`
`switch(a){case(b):}`	`b.isCase(a)`
`~a`	`a.bitwiseNegate()`
`-a`	`a.negative()`
`+a`	`a.positive()`

At first glance, you may not see the benefits of operator overloading. Groovy uses operator overloading to create shortcuts that make Java friendlier. For example, adding an object to a list in Java looks like this: `myList.add(someObject)`. The corresponding Groovy way of adding an object to a list is `myList << someObject`. Operator overloading isn't limited to the predefined instances that Groovy supplies; you can add operator overloading to your Groovy classes by implementing the corresponding method.

Specialized Operators

Groovy includes many of the standard operators found in other programming languages, as well as operators that are specific to Groovy that enable it to be so powerful.

Spread Operator

The spread operator (`*.`) is a shorthand technique for invoking a method or closure on a collection of objects. Listing 2-66 illustrates the usage of the spread operator for iterating over a list.

Listing 2-66. Using the Spread Operator

```
1. def map = [1:"Vishal", 2:"Chris", 3:"Joseph", 4:"Jim"]
2. def keys = [1, 2, 3, 4]
3. def values = ["Vishal", "Chris", "Joseph", "Jim"]
4. assert map*.key == keys
5. assert map*.value == values
```

Line 4 and Line 5 use the spread operator to access keys and values of the map.

Elvis Operator

The Elvis operator (`?:`) is a shorthand version of the Java ternary operator. An example of using the Java-style ternary operator is `a == 1 ? "One" : "Not One"`. If a is equal to 1, then "One" is returned; otherwise "Not One" is returned. It is literally a shorthand "`if-then else`."

As with most Java constructs, you can use the Java ternary operator in Groovy. In addition to the Java ternary operator, you can use an even shorter notation in Java: the Elvis operator. This can be very useful in defaulting values if they are not already set, meaning that they evaluate to null or false; that is, `b= a ?: 1` could be interpreted as:

```
if(a != 0)
        b = a
else
    b = 1
```

Listing 2-67 illustrates using the Java ternary and Elvis operators in Groovy.

Listing 2-67. Using the Elvis Operator

```
def firstName = user.firstName == null ? "unknown" : user.firstName // Java ternary
def firstName2 = user.firstName ?: "unknown" // Groovy Elvis
```

In both cases, if the `user.firstName` is `null`, then the `firstName` is set to “unknown”. The `user.firstName` portion of the Elvis operator example is known as the expression. If the expression evaluates to false or `null`, then the value after the `:` is returned. The two lines in the example are logically equivalent.

Safe Navigation/Dereference Operator

The safe navigation/dereference operator (`?.`) is used to avoid `NullPointerExceptions`, so it is incredibly handy. Consider the situation where you have a `User` object and you want a print the `firstName`. If the `User` object is null when you access the `firstName` property, you will get a `NullPointerException`.

Listing 2-68. Using the Safe Navigation/Dereference Operator

```
class User {
    String firstName
    String lastName
    def printFullName = {
        println "${firstName} ${lastName}"
    }
}
User user
println user.firstName
```

The code in Listing 2-68 throws a `NullPointerException`. In Java, we add a `null` check this way:

```
if (user != null) {
    println "Java FirstName = ${user.firstName}"
}
```

Listing 2-69 illustrates adding the `null`-check using the safe-navigation/dereference operator in Groovy.

Listing 2-69. Using the Safe Navigation/Dereference Operator

```
class User {
    String firstName
    String lastName
    def printFullName = {
        println "${firstName} ${lastName}"
    }
}
User user
println "Groovy FirstName = ${user?.firstName}"
```

Field Operator

In Chapter 1, you learned about properties on a class and how Groovy automatically supplies a getter. You also learned that in the event that special logic is required, you can provide your own getter. While not recommended because it is a major violation of encapsulation, Groovy provides a way to bypass the getter and access the underlying field directly.

Listing 2-70 shows an example of using the field operator (`.@`).

Listing 2-70. Using the Field Operator

```
class Todo {
    String name
    def getName() {
        println "Getting Name"
        name
    }
}
def todo = new Todo(name: "Jim")
println todo.name
println todo.@name
```

Here is the output:

```
Getting Name
Jim
Jim
```

In this example, the first `println` uses the getter to access name, and the second `println` bypasses the getter to access name directly.

Method Closure Operator

Earlier in the chapter, you learned about closures and how some of the Groovy functions accept a closure as input. But what if you would like to pass a method around in the same way that you can pass a closure? Groovy provides the method closure operator (`.&`) for just this scenario. The method closure operator allows the method to be accessed and passed around like a closure.

Listing 2-71. Using the Method Closure Operator

```
def list = ["Chris","Joseph","Jim"]
// each takes a closure
list.each { println it }
String printName(String name) {
    println name
}
// & causes the method to be accessed as a closure
list.each(this.&printName)
```

Here is the output:

```
Chris
Joseph
Jim
Chris
Joseph
Jim
```

This example creates a list of names and iterates through the list to print out the names. You have seen this before. A `printName()` method is created that prints the name parameter. Lastly and the main point of this example, the list is iterated, executing the `printName()` method as a closure.

Now because this is a really simple example, you may be thinking, "Big deal." Well actually it is, especially if you are building a domain-specific language (DSL), which you will learn more about in Chapter 3.The method really invokes `System.out.println`. How did the Groovy team get println to do that? The answer is that they used the method closure operator to assign `System.out.println` to a global property, as in `def println = System.out.&println()`. That is extremely powerful. Using the method closure operator, you are able to expose Java methods as closures.

Diamond Operator

In order to avoid the repetition of parameterized types, Groovy introduced the diamond operator. The parameterized types can be omitted and replaced with pointy brackets, which look like a diamond. Listing 2-72 shows a usual verbose way of defining a list.

Listing 2-72. A Simple Groovy Script: Hello.groovy

```
List<List<String>> list1 = new ArrayList<List<String>>()
```

Groovy allows us to use the diamond operator instead of a parameterized type to avoid repetition, as illustrated in Listing 2-73.

Listing 2-73. Using the Diamond Operator

```
List<List<String>> list1 = new ArrayList<>()
```

This means you can avoid specifying the `<List<String>>` on either side of the definition.

Summary

The focus of this chapter was Groovy language basics. The goal was to teach you enough Groovy to get you started with Grails. In this chapter, you created a simple program (script) and compared it to doing the same thing in Java. Then you learned how-to turn the script into a Groovy class, compile it, and run it using Java. Once you learned about Groovy scripts and classes, we took a quick look at the Groovy Shell and Groovy Console. The shell and console are handy for writing and testing simple programs. With some basic Groovy tooling under your belt, it was time to start taking a look at the Groovy language. Your journey into the Groovy language started with learning about Groovy's support of strings, closures, and methods, and collections (lists, maps, sets, arrays, and ranges). Next, you had a high-level overview of Groovy's regular expression support.

We covered the find (`=~`), match (`==~`), and pattern (`~string`) operators. Lastly, you learned about operator overloading and specialized operators. They are a major source of Groovy's power. This chapter is by no means a comprehensive study of Groovy. Groovy is a broad and deep topic. The goal here was to give you enough Groovy knowledge to start building an application and know where to look for more information. The next chapter will introduce you to more advanced Groovy topics.

CHAPTER 3

■ ■ ■

More Advanced Groovy

Chapters 1 and 2 offered a glimpse into the power and capabilities of Groovy by providing a basic explanation of its language features and tools. But there is far more to know about Groovy. For example, Groovy provides an ideal framework for creating unit tests. It makes working with XML simple and straightforward, and it includes a great framework for templating text. Finally, Groovy has a metaprogramming model that you can use to do amazing things, such as enabling the creation of domain-specific languages and adding methods and functionality to the Java API classes, including classes that are marked as final.

This chapter covers a variety of unrelated or loosely related advanced Groovy topics. It starts off by introducing the object-orientation in Groovy, shows you how to use Groovy to write and execute unit tests, compares how to process XML documents with both Java and Groovy, and explains how you can use Groovy's templating to generate e-mails. The chapter concludes with metaprogramming topics: implementing expando classes, extending classes with metaobject protocol (MOP), AST transformations, and creating domain-specific languages (DSLs).

Object Orientation in Groovy

Few Java purists like to engage in reductio ad absurdum in this manner: "Because you can write scripts in Groovy and scripting is not real programming, Groovy is *just* a scripting language." (Note the emphasis on "just.")This is absolutely not the case. Groovy supports all object-oriented (OO) programming concepts that are well-known to Java developers: classes, objects, interfaces, inheritance, polymorphism, and others. In fact, unlike Java, Groovy is a pure OO language in which everything is an object. You can fully organize your code into classes and packages and still use scripts with classes. The Groovy compiler will convert such scripts into Java classes; that is to say, you can mix scripts with classes.

Classes and Scripts

As Larry Wall says:

> *"Suppose you went back to Ada Lovelace and asked her the difference between a script and a program. She'd probably look at you funny, and then say something like: 'Well, a script is what you give the actors, but a program is what you give the audience.' "*

A lot of entities in Groovy are classes. Lists, sets, maps, strings, patterns, scripts, closures, functions, and expandos are all implemented under the hood as classes. Classes are the building blocks of Groovy. In Groovy, any code that is not inside a class is called a script. You cannot have any Java code outside of a class. In Java, you can have only one public class in a single file, and the name of that class must match the name of the file. In Groovy, in addition to classes, you can have scripts and the same file can include one or more classes in addition to scripting code. Unlike Java, Groovy also allows you to have more than one public class in the same file, and none of the public classes in the same file need to match the name of the containing file.

Listing 3-1 illustrates a file named Hello.groovy with a script but no classes. The compiler will generate a class for the scripting code based on the filename. Compiling this file via groovyc will generate one class: Hello.class.

Listing 3-1. Hello.groovyFile with Script but no Classes

```
println "hello"
```

Listing 3-2 illustrates a file named Hello.groovy with a script and one class. Compiling this file via groovyc will generate one class: Hello.class (for scripting code based on the filename) and HelloWorld.class.

Listing 3-2. Hello.groovy File with Script and One Class

```
class HelloWorld{
 def hello(){
  println "hello world"
 }
}
println "hello world"
```

Listing 3-3 illustrates a file named Hello.groovy with a script and one class with the name same as the file name. This file will not get compiled. By default the compiler generates a class for the scripting code based on the filename, and because we already defined a class with that name, the compiler will throw an exception.

Listing 3-3. Hello.groovy File with Script and One Classwith the Same Name as the File Name

```
class Hello{
 def hello(){
  println "hello world"
 }
}
println "hello world"
```

Listing 3-4 illustrates a file named Hello.groovy with a script and two classes. Compiling this file will generate three classes: Hello.class, HelloWorld1.class, and HelloWorld2.class.

Listing 3-4. Hello.groovy File with Script and TwoClasses

```
class HelloWorld1{
 def hello(){
  println "hello world"
 }
}
class HelloWorld2{
 def hello(){
  println "hello world"
 }
}
println "hello world"
```

Listing 3-5 illustrates a file named Hello.groovy with no script and one class. Compiling this file will generate one class: HelloWorld.class, as there is no script in the file.

Listing 3-5. Hello.groovy File with no Script and One Class

```
class HelloWorld{
 def hello(){
  println "hello world"
 }
}
```

Listing 3-6 illustrates a file named `Hello.groovy` with no script and two classes. Compiling this file will generate two classes: `HelloWorld1.class` and `HelloWorld2.class`.

Listing 3-6. Hello.groovy File with no Script and TwoClasses

```
class HelloWorld1{
 def hello(){
  println "hello world"
 }
}
class HelloWorld2{
 def hello(){
  println "hello world"
 }
}
```

Listing 3-7 illustrates a file named `Hello.groovy` with no script and one class with the same name as the file. Compiling this file will generate one class: `Hello.class`. Hazard a guess as to why the compiler does not throw an exception this time. It is because there is no script in the file.

Listing 3-7. Hello.groovy File with no Script and One Classwith the Same Name as File Name

```
class Hello{
 def hello(){
  println "hello world"
 }
}
```

Groovy Constructors

In Groovy, a constructor can be called in several ways. Listing 3-8 illustrates calling the constructor Java style. The preferred way is to use named parameters, as illustrated in Listing 3-9.

Listing 3-8. Calling the Constructor Java Style

```
class Test{
  def i
  def j
  Test(i, j){
    this.i = i
    this.j = j
  }

}
```

```
def test = new Test(1, 2)
assert test.i == 1
assert test.j == 2
```

Listing 3-9 illustrates calling the constructor using named parameters. As discussed earlier in Chapter 1, Groovy uses the map object to initialize each property. The map is iterated and the corresponding setter is invoked for each map element.

Listing 3-9. Using Named Parameters

```
1. class Test{
2.  def i = 0
3.  def j = 0
4. }
5. def test1 = new Test(i:1, j:2)
6. assert test1.i == 1
7. assert test1.j == 2
```

As can be seen in Line 5 of Listing 3-9, when we pass a map object to a constructor, the parentheses [], which is the part of the map syntax, can be skipped.

We can also list the property values in any order, like so:

```
def test2= new Test( j:2, i:1)
assert test2.i == 1
assert test2.j == 2
```

If a property is excluded, the corresponding setter will not be called and the default value is preserved, like so:

```
def test3 = new Test(i:1)
assert test3.i == 1
assert test3.j == 0
```

A class can have more than one constructor, as illustrated in Listing 3-10.

Listing 3-10. Class with More than One Constructor

```
1.  class A{
2.   def list= []
3.   A(){
4.    list<< "A constructed"
5.   }
6.   A(int i){
7.    this()
8.    list<< "A constructed with $i"
9.   }
10.  A(String s){
11.   this(5)
12.   list<< "A constructed with '$s'"
13.  }
14. }
15. def a1= new A()
16. assert a1.list == [ "A constructed" ]
```

```
17. def a2= new A(7)
18. assert a2.list.collect{it} == [
19. "A constructed",
20. "A constructed with 7",
21. ]
22. def a3= new A('test')
23. assert a3.list.collect{it} == [
24. "A constructed",
25. "A constructed with 5",
26. "A constructed with 'test'",
27. ]
```

In Listing 3-10, class A has three constructors:

- In Line 7, constructor `A(int i)` calls default parameterless constructor `A()` in its first statement.
- In Line 11, `A(String s)` calls `A(int i)` in its first statement, which in turn calls constructor `A()` in its first statement.
- In Line 18, when the constructor `A(7)` is invoked, the list will have two elements, one from `A(int i)` and one from `A()`. Note the `collect` method of `list` in Line 19. The `collect` method accepts a list and a closure argument.

Inheritance

As shown in Listing 3-11, Groovy enables one class to extend another, just as interfaces can, though classes extend at most one class.

Listing 3-11. Extending class

```
1. class A{}
2. class B extends A{}
3. def b = new B()
4. assert b in B && b in A
```

In Line 4, we test for extended classes with the in operator.

The in operator is a shortcut for the `contains()` method in a collection. The snippet below illustrates the usage of the in operator.

```
assert 1 in [1, 2, 3]
```

Public instance fields, properties, and methods defined on an extended class are also available on the extending class, as shown in Listing 3-12:

Listing 3-12. Inherited Methods and Properties

```
1.  class A{
2.   int x
3.   int y
4.   String methodA(int n){ "value ${x= y= n}" }
5.  }
6.  class B extends A{
7.   String methodB(int n){ "value $n" }
8.  }
```

```
9.  def b= new B()
10. assert b.methodB(10) == 'value 10'
11. assert b.methodA(20) == 'value 20'
12. assert b.x == 20
13. assert b.y == 20
14. b.y= 5
15. assert b.y == 5
16. assert b.getY() == 5
```

- In Line 11, we call method `A()` on extending class `B`.
- In Lines 12–16 we assert `x` and `y` on extending class `B`.

We can define an abstract class, a class with only some methods defined, the others being only declarations just like in interfaces. As shown in Listing 3-13, an abstract class and each method declaration in it must be modified with the `abstract` keyword:

Listing 3-13. Using Abstract Class

```
1.  interface X{
2.   def x()
3.  }
4.  interface Y{
5.   def y()
6.  }
7.  abstract class A{
8.   def a(){ println 1 }
9.   abstract b()
10. }
11. class B extends A implements X, Y{
12.  def x(){ println 2 }
13.  def y(){ println 3 }
14.  def b(){ println 4 }
15. }
```

- In Line 8, a method `a()` is defined.
- In Line 9, a method `b()` is declared.
- Line 14 provides the definition to method `b()`.

Interface and abstract methods cannot be declared static. Whether a method is static is part of its definition, as shown in Listing 3-14, but not its declaration.

Listing 3-14. Interface and Abstract Methods

```
1.  interface X{
2.   def x()
3.   //static x1()
4.  }
5.  interface Y{
6.   def y()
7.  }
8.  abstract class A{
9.   static a(){ println 1 }
10.  abstract b()
```

```
11.  abstract c()
12.  //abstract static c1()
13. }
14. class B extends A implements X, Y{
15.  static x(){ println 2 }
16.  def y(){ println 3 }
17.  static b(){ println 4 }
18.  def c(){ println 5 }
19. }
```

- Line 3 is commented, as interface methods cannot be declared static.
- Line 12 is commented, as abstract methods cannot be static.

A final class cannot be extended; a final method cannot be overridden:

Listing 3-15. Using Final Class

```
1. class A{
2.  final a(){ 11 }
3.  def b(){ 12 }
4. }
5. final class B extends A{
6.  //def a(){ 15 }
7.  def b(){ 16 }
8. }
9. //class C extends B{}
```

- Line 6 is commented, as method `a()` in class `A` is final and cannot be overridden.
- Line 9 is commented, as class `B` is final and cannot be extended.

Just as a class's constructor can call another constructor as we discussed in Listing 3-10, so also it can call a constructor on the superclass, as shown in Listing 3-16:

Listing 3-16. Calling Constructor of the Superclass

```
1.  class A{
2.   def list= []
3.   A(){
4.    list<< "A constructed"
5.   }
6.   A(int i){
7.    this()
8.    list<< "A constructed with $i"
9.   }
10. }
11. class B extends A{
12.  B(){
13.   list<< "B constructed"
14.  }
15.  B(String s){
16.   super(5)
17.   list<< "B constructed with '$s'"
18.  }
19. }
```

```
20. def b1= new B('test')
21. assert b1.list.collect{it} == [
22.  "A constructed",
23.  "A constructed with 5",
24.  "B constructed with 'test'",
25. ]
26. def b2= new B()
27. assert b2.list == [
28.  "A constructed",
29.  "B constructed",
30. ]
```

- In Line 16, a constructor can call its 'superclass's constructor if it's the first statement.
- In Line 27, default parameterless constructor is called, as `super()` is not called.

Polymorphism

Groovy does not really need interfaces because of dynamic typing but still includes support for them. In Groovy, polymorphism is simply a matter of matching method names. Two objects belonging to two unrelated classes can be sent in the same message, provided that the method is defined by each class, as illustrated in Listing 3-17.

Listing 3-17. A Polymorphism Example

```
1.  class Square{
2.   def display() {
3.    assert  "length:${length} width:${width}" == "length:10 width:10"
4.   }
5.   def length
6.   def width
7.  }
8.  class Rectangle{
9.   def display() {
10.   assert  "length:${length} width:${width}" == "length:10 width:12"
11.  }
12.  def length
13.  def width
14. }
15. def shapes= [new Square(length : 10, width : 10),
16.  new Rectangle(length : 10, width : 12)
17. ]
18. shapes.each { item -> item.display() }
```

- The two classes `Square` and `Rectangle` in Line 1 and Line 8 do not share a common superclass or implement the same interface (in our example).
- Line 18 iterates over the shapes collection and on each object in the collection, the `display()` method specific to that object is called.

Groovy Unit Testing

One of Groovy's best value propositions is unit testing. Using Groovy to unit-test Groovy or Java code can make the code easier to read and maintain. Unit testing is a common way to introduce Groovy to an organization, because it doesn't affect the production runtime. Once developers and managers get comfortable with Groovy in a testing capacity, they eventually begin using it in production.

Unit testing is so fundamental to Groovy that it's built right in. You don't need to download a separate framework. Groovy already includes and extends JUnit, which is a popular Java unittesting framework. The primary extension is `groovy.util.GroovyTestCase`, which inherits from `junit.framework.TestCase` and adds the additional assert methods found in Table 3-1.

Table 3-1. *GroovyTestCase Assert Methods*

Assert Method	Description
`assertArrayEquals`	Asserts two arrays are equal and contain the same values
`assertContains`	Asserts an array of characters contains the given characters or an array of `ints` contains a given `int`
`assertEquals`	Asserts two `Objects` or two `Strings` are equal
`assertInspect`	Asserts the value of the `inspect()` method
`assertLength`	Asserts the length of `char`, `int`, or `Object` arrays
`assertScript`	Asserts script runs without any exceptions being thrown
`assertToString`	Asserts the value of `toString()`

JUnit (and therefore Groovy unit testing) works by creating a class that inherits from `TestCase` or one of its descendants. `GroovyTestCase` is the appropriate class to extend for unit testing in Groovy. Notice that `GroovyTestCase` is found in the `groovy.util` package, so it is implicitly available and doesn't even require any imports. Tests can then be added by creating methods that have a name that begins with test and is followed by something descriptive about the test. For example, you could use `testAlphaRanges` for a test that validates the Groovy language feature of ranges. These test methods should take no parameters and return void. Unlike with JUnit tests written in Java, these methods don't have to declare exceptions that could be thrown, because Groovy naturally converts all checked exceptions into unchecked exceptions. This makes tests more readable than the equivalent Java implications.

Unit tests often require objects to be put into a known state. In addition, tests should be good test-harness citizens and clean up after themselves. Like JUnit tests, all Groovy tests can override the `setUp()` and `tearDown()` methods.

Unit tests are also a great way to learn new frameworks, libraries, and languages such as Groovy. You can use unit tests to validate your understanding of how they work. Listing 3-18 is a unit test used to validate some assumptions about Groovy ranges, including whether a range from `'a'..'z'` contains uppercase letters and whether ranges can be concatenated.

Listing 3-18 shows a unit test that extends from `GroovyTestCase` and contains two variables that include a range of lowercase letters on Line 3 and a range of uppercase letters on Line 4. The test case also contains three tests.

Listing 3-18. Example Unit Test That Validates Assumptions About Groovy Ranges

```
1.  class RangeTest extends GroovyTestCase {
2.
3.    def lowerCaseRange = 'a'..'z'
4.    def upperCaseRange = 'A'..'Z'
5.
6.    void testLowerCaseRange() {
7.      assert 26 == lowerCaseRange.size()
8.      assertTrue(lowerCaseRange.contains('b'))
```

```
9.      assertFalse(lowerCaseRange.contains('B'))
10.  }
11.
12.   void testUpperCaseRange() {
13.     assert 26 == upperCaseRange.size()
14.     assertTrue(upperCaseRange.contains('B'))
15.     assertFalse(upperCaseRange.contains('b'))
16.   }
17.
18.   void testAlphaRange() {
19.     def alphaRange = lowerCaseRange + upperCaseRange
20.     assert 52 == alphaRange.size()
21.     assert alphaRange.contains('b')
22.     assert alphaRange.contains('B')
23.   }
24. }
```

The first test in Listing 3-18, shown on Lines 6–10, asserts that the range has a size of 26, representing each of the letters in lowercase. It also asserts that a lowercase `'b'` is in the range but that an uppercase `'B'` is not. The second test, shown on Lines 12–16, is basically the same test but uses the uppercase range. The third test, on the other hand, validates that the two ranges can be concatenated to produce a new range that includes both. Therefore, the new range is twice the size and includes both the lowercase `'b'` and the uppercase `'B'`.

Running a Groovy unit test is just like running a script. To run this test, execute the following:

```
> groovy RangeTest
```

Because a JUnit test runner is built into Groovy, the results of the tests are printed to standard out. The results identify how many tests ran, how many failed, and how many errors occurred. Failures indicate how many tests did not pass the assertions, and errors indicate unexpected occurrences such as exceptions. In addition, because `GroovyTestCase` extends JUnit, you can easily integrate the Groovy tests into automated test harnesses such as Apache Ant and Apache Maven builds so they can be run continually.

Working with XML

Extensible Markup Language (XML) is a general-purpose markup language commonly used in enterprise applications to persist or share data. Historically, creating and consuming XML documents has been easier than working with other types of formats, because XML is text-based, follows a standard, is in an easily parseable format, and features many existing frameworks and libraries to support reading and writing documents for many different programming languages and platforms.

Most of these frameworks, however, are based on the World Wide Web Consortium's (W3C) Document Object Model (DOM), which can cause the code that manipulates XML documents to become difficult to write and read. Due to the popularity and complexity of working with XML, Groovy includes a framework that uses XML in a natural way. The next section demonstrates how complicated it is to write simple XML with standard Java code, then shows you how to process XML in the simple and elegant Groovy way.

Writing XML with Java

Generating a simple XML document like the one found in Listing 3-19 in Java is difficult, time consuming, and a challenge to read and maintain.

Listing 3-19. Simple XML Output for Todos

```
<todos>
 <todo id="1">
  <name>Buy Beginning Groovy Grails and Griffon</name>
  <note>Purchase book from Amazon.com for all co-workers.</note>
 </todo>
</todos>
```

Listing 3-20 shows the minimum Java code necessary to generate the XML shown in Listing 3-19.

Listing 3-20. Java Code to Generate the Simple Todo XML Found in Listing 3-19

```
import org.w3c.dom.Document;
import org.w3c.dom.Element;
import javax.xml.parsers.DocumentBuilder;
import javax.xml.parsers.DocumentBuilderFactory;
import javax.xml.parsers.ParserConfigurationException;
import javax.xml.transform.stream.StreamResult;
import javax.xml.transform.Transformer;
import javax.xml.transform.TransformerFactory;
import javax.xml.transform.OutputKeys;
import javax.xml.transform.Source;
import javax.xml.transform.Result;
import javax.xml.transform.TransformerException;
import javax.xml.transform.dom.DOMSource;

/**
 * Example of generating simple XML in Java.
 */
public class GenerateXML {
  public static void main (String[] args)
      throws ParserConfigurationException, TransformerException {
    DocumentBuilder builder =
      DocumentBuilderFactory.newInstance().newDocumentBuilder();
    Document doc = builder.newDocument();
    Element todos = doc.createElement("todos");
    doc.appendChild(todos);

    Element task = doc.createElement("todo");
    task.setAttribute("id", "1");
    todos.appendChild(task);

    Element name = doc.createElement("name");
    name.setTextContent("Buy Beginning Groovy Grails and Griffon");
    task.appendChild(name);
    Element note = doc.createElement("note");
    note.setTextContent("Purchase book from Amazon.com for all coworkers.");
    task.appendChild(note);
    // generate pretty printed XML document
    TransformerFactory tranFactory = TransformerFactory.newInstance();
    Transformer transformer = tranFactory.newTransformer();
```

```
    transformer.setOutputProperty(OutputKeys.INDENT, "yes");
    transformer.setOutputProperty(
        "{http://xml.apache.org/xslt}indent-amount", "2");
    Source src = new DOMSource(doc);
Result dest = new StreamResult(System.out);
    transformer.transform(src, dest);
  }
}
```

Notice how difficult it is to read Listing 3-20. It begins by using `DocumentBuilderFactory` to create a new `DocumentBuilder`. With `DocumentBuilder`, the `newDocument()` factory method is called to create a new `Document`. Elements are created using `DocumentBuilder's` factory methods, configured by adding attributes or text content, and then finally appended to their parent element. Notice how difficult it is to follow the natural tree structure of the XML document by looking at the Java code. This is partly because most elements require three lines of code to create, configure, and append the element to its parent.

Finally, outputting the XML into a humanreadable nested format isn't straightforward. Much like creating the document itself, it begins by getting a `TransformerFactory` instance and then using the `newTransformer()` factory method to create a Transformer. Then the transformer output properties are configured to indent, and the indent amount is configured. Notice that the indent amount isn't even standard. It uses an Apache Xalan-specific configuration, which may not be completely portable. Ultimately, a source and result are passed to the transformer to transform the source DOM into XML output.

Groovy Builders

Groovy simplifies generating XML by using the concept of builders, based on the builder design pattern from the Gang of Four. Groovy builders implement a concept of Groovy-Markup, which is a combination of Groovy language features such as MOP (discussed later in the chapter), closures, and the simplified map syntax to create nested tree-like structures. Groovy includes five major builder implementations, as defined in Table 3-2. They all use the same format and idioms, so knowing one builder pretty much means you'll be able to use them all.

Table 3-2. *Groovy Builders*

Name	Description
`AntBuilder`	Enables the script and execution of Apache Ant tasks
`DOMBuilder`	Generates W3C DOMs
`MarkupBuilder`	Generates XML and HTML
`NodeBuilder`	Creates nested trees of objects for handling arbitrary data
`SwingBuilder`	Creates Java Swing UIs (discussed in detail in Chapter 13)

In general, you start using a builder by creating an instance of the builder. Then you call a named closure to create the root node, which could represent a root XML element, a Swing component, or a specific builder-appropriate node. You add nodes by nesting more named closures. This format makes it easy to read the hierarchical structures.

You add attributes by using Groovy's map syntax to pass name-value pairs into the named closures. Under the covers, MOP interprets the message passed to the object, usually to determine which method to invoke. When it realizes there is no method by that name, it creates the associated node or attribute.

Writing XML with Groovy MarkupBuilder

As noted in Table 3-2, you use MarkupBuilder to create XML and HTML. Listing 3-21 shows the Groovy code in action for creating the XML shown in Listing 3-19.

Listing 3-21. Groovy Code to Generate the Simple Todo XML Found in Listing 3-19

```
1.  def writer = new StringWriter()
2.  def builder = new groovy.xml.MarkupBuilder(writer)
3.  builder.setDoubleQuotes(true)
4.  builder.todos {
5.      todo (id:"1") {
6.          name "Buy Beginning Groovy Grails and Griffon"
7.          note "Purchase book from Amazon.com for all co-workers."
8.      }
9.  }
10.
11. println writer.toString()
```

Looking at Listing 3-21, you can see how much easier it is to read than the Java equivalent shown in Listing 3-20. The example begins by creating StringWriter, so the final XML can be printed to system out on Line 11. Then MarkupBuilder is created using StringWriter. By default, MarkupBuilder uses single quotes for attribute values, so Line 3 changes the quotes to double quotes to comply with the XML specification. Lines 4–9 actually build the XML document using named closures and map syntax. You can easily see that todos contains a todo with an id attribute of 1 and nested name and note elements.

Reading XML with XmlSlurper

Groovy makes reading XML documents equally as easy as writing XML documents. Groovy includes the XmlSlurper class, which you can use to parse an XML document or string and provide access to a GPathResult. With the GPathResult reference, you can use XPath-like syntax to access different elements in the document.

Listing 3-22 shows how to use XmlSlurper and GPath to interrogate a todos XML document.

Listing 3-22. Reading XML in Groovy

```
1. def todos = new XmlSlurper().parse('c:/todos.xml')
2. assert 3 == todos.todo.size()
3. assert "Buy Beginning Groovy Grails and Griffon" == todos.todo[0].name.text()
4. assert "1" == todos.todo[0].@id.text()
```

Listing 3-22 begins by using XmlSlurper to parse a todos.xml file containing three todo items. Line 2 asserts there are three todos in the document. Line 3 shows how to access the value of an element, while Line 4 shows how to access the value of an attribute using @.

Native JSON support

As JSON becomes a natural choice for data- interchange format, Groovy added native support for JSON.

Reading JSON

A JsonSlurper class allows you to parse JSON payloads, and access the nested Map and List data structures representing that content. We illustrated JsonSlurper for reading JSON in Chapter 1.

JsonBuilder

Groovy introduces JsonBuilder to produce JSON content, as illustrated in Listing 3-23.

Listing 3-23. Reading XML in Groovy

```
1.  import groovy.json.*
2.  def builder = new groovy.json.JsonBuilder()
3.  def root = builder.Book{
4.   Groovy{
5.    title 'Beginning Groovy, Grails and Griffon'
6.    Authors(
                  1: 'Vishal',
                  2: 'Chris',
                  3: 'Joseph',
                                  4: 'James',
7.    )
8.   }
9.  }
10. println builder.toString()
```

The output is:

```
{"book":{"groovy":{"title":"Beginning Groovy, Grails and Griffon", "authors":{"1"
:"Vishal","2":"Chris","3":"Joseph","4":"James"}}}}
```

Prettyprinting JSON Content

As you can see, the output of Listing 3-23 is difficult to read. When given a JSON data structure, you may wish to prettyprint it, so that you can more easily inspect it, with a friendlier layout. So for instance, if you want to prettyprint the result of the previous example, there are two ways to fix it. We can use either the JsonBuilder or JsonOutput.

In the case of JsonBuilder, we can just replace Line 16 in Listing 3-23 with:

```
println builder.toPrettyString()
```

In the case of JsonOutput, replace Line 16 in Listing 3-23 with this line:

```
println JsonOutput.prettyPrint(builder.toString())
```

Either of these ways gives the same output:

```
{
    "book": {
        "groovy": {
            "title": "Beginning Groovy, Grails and Griffon",
            "authors": {
                "1": "Vishal",
                "2": "Chris",
                "3": "Joseph",
                "4": "James"
            }
        }
    }
}
```

Generating Text with Templates

Many web applications generate text for e-mails, reports, XML, and even HTML. Embedding this text in code can make it difficult for a designer or business person to maintain or manage. A better method is to store the static portion externally as a template file and process the template when the dynamic portions of the template are known.

Table 3-3. *Groovy Template Engines*

Name	Description
`SimpleTemplateEngine`	Basic templating that uses Groovy expressions as well as JavaServer Pages (JSP) `<% %>` script and `<%= %>` expression syntax
`GStringTemplateEngine`	Basically the same as `SimpleTemplateEngine`, except the template is stored internally as a writable closure
`XmlTemplateEngine`	Optimized for generating XML by using an internal DOM

As shown in Table 3-3, Groovy includes three template engines to make generating text easier.

The `SimpleTemplateEngine` usually is appropriate for most templating situations. Listing 3-24 shows an HTML e-mail template that we'll use in Chapter 11 for sending e-mail during a nightly batch process.

Listing 3-24. HTML E-mail Template Found in nightlyReportsEmail.gtpl

```
<!DOCTYPE HTML PUBLIC "-//W3C//DTD HTML 4.01 Transitional//EN">
<html>
<head>
<title>
    Collab-Todo Nightly Report for
    ${String.format('%tA %<tB %<te %<tY', date)}
</title>
</head>

<body bgcolor="#FFFFFF" style="margin:0;padding:0;">
<div style="padding: 22px 20px 40px 20px;background-color:#FFFFFF;">
<table width="568" border="0" cellspacing="0" cellpadding="1"
        bgcolor="#FFFFFF" align="center">
<tr>
<td>
```

```
          Dear ${user?.firstName} ${user?.lastName},
<p />
          Please find your attached nightly report for
          ${String.format('%tA %<tB %<te %<tY', date)}.
</td>
</tr>
</table>
<!-- static HTML left out for brevity -->
</div>
</body>
</html>
```

The template in Listing 3-24 is mostly HTML with a couple of Groovy expressions thrown in for the dynamic portions of the e-mail, such as formatting the date and user's name. The e-mail produces the image shown in Figure 3-1.

Dear Christopher Judd,

Please find your attached nightly report for Saturday July 28 2012.

Figure 3-1. *HTML e-mail*

To process the template, you create an instance of a template engine and use the overloaded `createTemplate()` method, passing it a `File`, `Reader`, `URL`, or `String` containing the template text to create a template. Now with the template loaded and parsed, you call the `make()` method, passing it a map that binds with the variables in the template that are based on the names in the map. Listing 3-25 shows what the code that generates the e-mail in Figure 3-1 looks like.

Listing 3-25. E-mail Template-Processing Code

```
1.  import groovy.text.SimpleTemplateEngine
2.
3.  /**
4.  * Simple User Groovy Bean.
5.  */
6.  class User {
7.   String firstName;
8.   String lastName;
9.  }
10.
11. def emailTemplate = this.class.getResource("nightlyReportsEmail.gtpl")
12. def binding = [
13.    "user": new User(firstName: "Christopher", lastName: "Judd"),
14.    "date": new Date()
15. ]
16. def engine = new SimpleTemplateEngine()
17. def email = engine.createTemplate(emailTemplate).make(binding)
18. def body = email.toString()
19.
20. println body
```

Listing 3-25 begins by importing the `SimpleTemplateEngine` on Line 1 so you have access to it on Line 16. Lines 6–9 declare a simple `User` GroovyBean. The template is loaded from the `nightlyReportsEmail.gtpl` file found on the classpath on Line 11. It contains the template text found in Listing 3-24. Lines 12–15 create the map containing the passed user and date data, which will be bound to the template when the template is processed. `SimpleTemplateEngine`, created on Line 16, is used on Line 17 to create and process the template.

Runtime Metaprogramming

With metaprogramming you can inspect, intercept, and alter the behavior of a program at runtime. In general, statically typed languages discard their type information during compilation, and thus are incapable of reflection. Some static languages (such as Java) exhibit ability to change the runtime behavior of a program; however, this ability is only limited or restrictive in order to prevent subverting or destabilizing the type system. The key features that contribute to runtime dynamicity are introspection (the ability of a program to examine itself) and intercession (the ability of a program to alter its structure).Dynamic languages such as Groovy provide these capabilities through the metaobject protocol (MOP).

Metaobject Protocol

The metaobject protocol was originally defined as an interface to a programming language to give the user of the language the ability to modify the language's behavior and even its implementation. Before long, programming languages were more or less abstractions with constructs you could build on top of them. The metaobject protocol approach draws a distinction by opening up languages to the user to regulate, so you can fine-tune the language's behavior and implementation. MOP, formally, is the collection of rules of how a request for a method call will be handled by the Groovy runtime system. Every method call that you write in Groovy is redirected to MOP. Even if the call-target (the target of the method call) was compiled with Groovy or Java, the method call is still redirected to MOP; for example, the Groovy compiler generates byte code for the method call that calls into the MOP. The key responsibility of MOP is finding and selecting the target and handling the case when the target cannot be found. In order to discover the call-target for the method call, MOP needs information, which is stored in metaclasses.

Metaclass

A metaclass provides the means of reflection and dynamic invocation. Groovy never calls methods directly in the byte code but always through the object's metaclass. In Groovy, all classes, including all Java classes, have a property of `metaClass` of type `groovy.lang.MetaClass`. When dispatching a message to an object, the metaclass not only helps to determine which behavior should be invoked, but also prescribes behavior if the class does not implement the requested behavior. As shown in Listing 3-26, the metaclass of any class can be found by accessing its `.metaClass` property.

Listing 3-26. Accessing Metaclass

```
1. class Book {
2. String title
3. }
4. def groovyMetaclass = Book.metaClass
```

Line 4 illustrates how to access the metaclass of class `Book`.

All Groovy objects implement the `groovy.lang.GroovyObject` interface, which exposes a `getMetaClass()` method for each object. Each Groovy object has an associated `MetaClass` that can be returned via a call to `getMetaClass()` in the `GroovyObject` interface, as shown in Listing 3-27.

Listing 3-27. GroovyObject Interface

```
public interface GroovyObject {
 Object invokeMethod(String name, Object args);
 Object getProperty(String propertyName);
 void setProperty(String propertyName, Object newValue);
 MetaClass getMetaClass();
 void setMetaClass(MetaClass metaClass);
}
```

`invokeMethod()`, `getProperty()`, and `setProperty()` make Groovy objects dynamic. You can use them to work with methods and properties created on the fly.

Using invokeMethod() and get/setProperty()

Groovy supports the ability to intercept method and property access via `invokeMethod()` and `get/setProperty()`.

Overriding invokeMethod

In any Groovy class you can override `invokeMethod()`, which will essentially intercept method calls. When you a call a method on a Groovy object, the method invocation is dispatched to the `invokeMethod()` of the object, as illustrated in Listing 3-28.

Listing 3-28. Overriding invokeMethod

```
1.  class Item{
2.   int itemNumber
3.   String itemName
4.   int qty
5.   Object invokeMethod(String name, Object args) {
6.    if (name == "test"){
7.     this.properties.each {
8.      println " " + it.key + ": " + it.value
9.     }
10.   }
11.  }
12. }
13. def item1 = new Item(itemNumber: 1, itemName:"Item 1", qty:100)
14. def item2= new Item(itemNumber:2, itemName:"Item 2", qty:200)
15. def itemList = [ item1, item2]
16. itemList.each { it.test()}
```

- In Line 16, the `test()` method is invoked, which does not exist.
- In Line 5, the `invokeMethod()` added to the `Item` class allows for intercept method invocations and responds to calls to `test()`, even though this method does not exist.

Here is the output from Listing 3-28:

```
class: class Item
itemName: Item 1
qty: 100
itemNumber: 1
class: class Item
itemName: Item 2
qty: 200
itemNumber: 2
```

Overriding getProperty and setProperty

You can also override property access using the `getProperty` and `setProperty` of the `GroovyObject` interface illustrated in Listing 3-29.

Listing 3-29. Overriding getProperty/setProperty

```
1. class Expandable {
2.   def storage = [:]
3.   def getProperty(String name) { storage[name] }
4.   void setProperty(String name, value) { storage[name] = value }
5. }
6. def e = new Expandable()
7. e.foo = "bar"
8. println e.foo
```

Using methodMissing()

`methodMissing()` is only invoked in the case of a failed method dispatch. Listing 3-30 illustrates the usage of `methodMissing()`.

Listing 3-30. Using methodMissing

```
1. class Missing{
2.   def methodMissing(String name, args) {
3.     "$name method does not exist"
4.   }
5. }
6. Missing m = new Missing()
7. assert m.test() == "test method does not exist"
```

When you call a method on a POGO(plain old Groovy Object):

1. Groovy looks for the method in the metaclass of the POGO.
2. If the method is not found in the metaclass, then Groovy looks for the method in the POGO itself.
3. If the method is not found in POGO as well, then Groovy looks to see if the POGO has `methodMissing()`; if it is there, it is called.

4. If methodMissing() is not there, Groovy looks to see if the POGO has implemented invokeMethod(). If the POGO has implemented invokeMethod(), it is called.

5. If the POGO has not implemented invokeMethod(), then the default implementation of invokeMethod() is called, which throws a MissingMethodException.

Expandos

The Expando class is found in the groovy.util package and is a dynamically expandable bean, meaning you can add properties or closures to it at runtime. In some situations we need an object to hold interim behaviors. In such situations, instead of creating a class merely for such behaviors, expandos come in handy so we can create objects dynamically at runtime, as illustrated in Listing 3-31.

Listing 3-31. Using Expando

```
1. def multiplier = new Expando()
2. multiplier.value = 5
3. multiplier.doubleIt = { ->  multiplier.value = multiplier.value* 2}
4. multiplier.doubleIt()
5. assert multiplier.value == 10
```

- Line1: We create an expando.
- Line 2: A state '5' is assigned to not-yet-existing property value.
- Line 3: New behavior is assigned to the not-yet-existing property doubleIt as a closure. After the assignment, it can be called as if it was a method.
- Line 7: Asserts that a new state '10' is assigned to not-yet-existing property value.

Expandos, when combined with Groovy's duck typing, are also a great way to implement mock objects during unit testing.

■ **Note** Duck typing refers to the concept that if it walks like a duck and talks like a duck, it must be a duck. In Groovy speak, if an object has properties and methods similar to another object, the two objects must be of the same type.

The reason for explaining the Expando class here is that there is an expando metaclass in Groovy that is a metaclass that works like an expando. You can add new state (properties) and new behavior (methods) in the metaclass by simply assigning a closure to a property of the metaclass.

ExpandoMetaClass

Groovy has a special metaclass called an ExpandoMetaClass that allows you to add methods, constructors, and properties at runtime by assigning a closure to a property of the metaclass. Every java.lang.Class is supplied with a special metaClass property that, when used, gives you a reference to an ExpandoMetaClass instance.

Borrowing Methods from Other Classes

With ExpandoMetaClass you can also use Groovy's method pointer syntax to borrow methods, as shown in Listing 3-32, from other classes.

Listing 3-32. Borrowing Methods from Other Classes

```
1.  class Author{
2.   String name
3.  }
4.  class Greet{
5.   def sayHello() {
6.    "hello vishal"
7.   }
8.  }
9.  def hello = new Greet()
10. Author.metaClass.greet = hello.&sayHello
11. def author = new Author()
12. assert author.greet() == "hello vishal"
```

- In Line 1, class `Author` does not have any method and class `Greet` has a method `sayHello()`.
- Line 10 uses the method closure operator that we introduced in Chapter 2 to assign the `sayHello()` method to `Author` using `ExpandoMetaclass`.
- On Line 12 we call the method `Greet()` on `Author` class. This `Greet()` method does not exist in `Author` class and has been borrowed from the `Greet` class, dynamically creating method names.

Since Groovy allows you to use strings as property names, this in turns allows you to dynamically create method and property names at runtime.

To create a method with a dynamic name, simply use Groovy's feature of reference property names as strings, as shown in Listing 3-33.

Listing 3-33. Dynamically Creating Method Names

```
1.  class Test{
2.   String name = "foo"
3.  }
4.  def newName = "bar"
5.  Test.metaClass."changeNameTo${newName}" = {-> delegate.name = "bar" }
6.  def m = new Test()
7.  assert  m.name == "foo"
8.  m.changeNameTobar()
9.  assert m.name == "bar"
```

- In Line 5, we use string interpolation to generate the name of the method, which, when called, will change the name in the test class from "foo" to "bar".
- Note that within the scope of the closure, the delegate variable is equivalent to `this` in a standard method.
- In Line 8, we use the method `changeNameTobar()`, which will be generated at run-time.
- In Line 9, we assert the new value of name, implying the dynamically generated method changed the name as expected.

Adding Constructors

Adding constructors is a little different than adding a method with `ExpandoMetaClass`. Essentially you use a special `constructor` property and either use the `<<` or = operator to assign a closure, as shown in Line 4 in Listing 3-34.

Listing 3-34. Adding Constructors

```
1.  class Book {
2.  String title
3.  }
4.  Book.metaClass.constructor << { String title -> new Book(title:title) }
5.  def b = new Book("Beginning Groovy, Grails and Griffon")
6.  assert "Beginning Groovy, Grails and Griffon" == b.title
```

Adding Properties

In Listing 3-35, class Book has only one property: title. We will add the author property to the Book class dynamically.

Listing 3-35. Addiing Properties

```
1.  class Book {
2.   String title
3.  }
4.  Book.metaClass.constructor << { String title -> new Book(title:title) }
5.  Book.metaClass.getAuthor << {-> "Vishal Layka" }
6.  def b = new Book("Beginning Groovy, Grails and Griffon")
7.  assert "Beginning Groovy, Grails and Griffon"== b.title
8.  assert "Vishal Layka" == b.author
```

- Line 4adds a constructor that will initialize the property `title` in Book class
- Line 5adds the property `author` and assigns it the value "Vishal Layka".
- Line 7asserts the existing property `title` as "Beginning Groovy, Grails and Griffon".
- Line 8asserts the non-existing property `author` as "Vishal Layka".

Adding Methods on Interfaces

It is possible to add methods onto interfaces with `ExpandoMetaClass`. However, you must enable this ability globally using the `ExpandoMetaClass.enableGlobally()` method before application startup.

Listing 3-36 illustrates adding a new method to all implementers of `java.util.List`:

Listing 3-36. Adding Methods on Interfaces

```
1.  List.metaClass.sizeDoubled = {-> delegate.size() * 2 }
2.  def list = []
3.  list << 1
4.  list << 2
5.  assert 4 == list.sizeDoubled()
```

- In Line 1, we add a new method `sizeDoubled()`, which we replace using = operator to the `size()`method of the list multiplied by 2.
- In Lines 3-4, we append two elements to the list so the size of the list is 2.
- In Line 5, we assert `sizeDoubled()` returns 4.

Adding or Overriding Instance Methods

With ExpandoMetaClass adding or overriding instance methods is effortless, as illustrated in Listing 3-37.

Listing 3-37. Adding Instance Methods

```
1.  class Book {
2.   String title
3.  }
4.  Book.metaClass.titleInUpperCase << {-> title.toUpperCase() }
5.  def b = new Book(title:"Beginning Groovy, Grails and Griffon")
6.  assert "BEGINNING GROOVY, GRAILS AND GRIFFON" == b.titleInUpperCase()
```

- In Line 4, the left shift << operator is used to "append" the new method. If the method already exists, an exception is thrown. If you want to replace an instance method, you can use the = operator:

  ```
  Book.metaClass.toString = {-> title.toUpperCase() }
  ```

- In Line 6, we assert by invoking the newly added `titleInUpperCase()`, which operates on the `String` title, the `toUpperCase()` assigned to it in Line 4.

Adding or Overriding Static Methods

As shown in Listing 3-38, you can also add static methods using the same technique as instance methods with the addition of the `static` qualifier before the method name:

Listing 3-38. Adding a Static Method

```
1.  class Book {
2.   String title
3.  }
4.  Book.metaClass.static.create << { String title -> new Book(title:title) }
5.  def b = Book.create("Beginning Groovy, Grails and Griffon")
6.  assert "Beginning Groovy, Grails and Griffon" == b.title
```

- In Line 5, we add a static qualifier before the `create` method. This method creates a new book object with the title "Beginning Groovy, Grails and Griffon".

Categories

Categories are used to add methods to an existing class on the fly. A category can be added to any class at runtime, by using the `use` keyword. To create a category for class, we define a class containing static methods that take as their first parameter an instance of the class that we want to extend. The category can be applied to any closure by using the `use` keyword denoting a `use` method, which Groovy adds to `java.lang.Object`. This `use` method takes two parameters: a category class and a closure. Listing 3-39 shows how you can add a method to the string class.

Listing 3-39. Using Categories

```
1.  class StringExtended {
2.   static String firstUpper(String self) {
3.    return self[0].toUpperCase() + self[1..self.length() - 1]
4.   }
5.  }
```

```
6.  use (StringExtended){
7.   assert "aaaa".firstUpper() == "Aaaa"
8.  }
```

- In Listing 3-39, the category method is the static `firstUpper()` in Line 2, which takes an instance of the class that we want to extend as its parameter. Conventionally this parameter is named as `self`. So in this case we are extending the class `String` (which is final, but we are metaprogrammers!).
- In Line 6, we pass the category class and a closure to the `use()` method.
- In Line 7, we invoke the category method on the string.

Runtime Mixins

In Java as well as Groovy:

- A class can inherit only one other class even though it can implement many interfaces.
- A class cannot inherit from a final class.

Mixin can solve both these problems. Mixins are designed for sharing features while not modifying any existing behavior of the receiver. Features can build on top of each other and merge and blend with the receiver. This can be best illustrated by example in Listing 3-40.

Listing 3-40. Using a Run-time Mixin

```
1.  class A{
2.   String genericfeatureNeededByClassB(){}
3.  }
4.  class B extends A{
5.   String getName() { "class B which already extends class A" }
6.  }
7.  final class C{
8.   static test(A self) { "I'm the final class C  and reused by ${self.name} !" }
9.  }
10. B.mixin C
11. println new B().test()
```

Note the following:

- Lines 1–3: Shows class `A`, which has the method `genericfeatureNeededByClassB()`.
- Lines 5–7: Shows class `B`, which needs to extend class `A`, so now it cannot extend any other class.
- Lines 9–11: Shows a final class `C`. So now inheriting from this class is out of question. This class has a `test()` method.
- Line 10: Shows mixin syntax for merging classes.
- Line 11: Shows that `test()` of final class `C` is available in class `B`.

With this we complete the journey through the runtime programming in Groovy. Now that you have grasped the concepts of dynamic programming, let us go back in time—not too far, just to a previous section so we can apply our recently acquired knowledge. We will revisit the code from Listing 3-25 and make it dynamic. For quick reference, Listing 3-25 is repeated here.

Listing 3-25. E-mail Template-Processing Code

```
1.  import groovy.text.SimpleTemplateEngine
2.
3.  /**
4.  * Simple User Groovy Bean.
5.  */
6.  class User {
7.   String firstName;
8.   String lastName;
9.  }
10.
11. def emailTemplate = this.class.getResource("nightlyReportsEmail.gtpl")
12. def binding = [
13.    "user": new User(firstName: "Christopher", lastName: "Judd"),
14.    "date": new Date()
15. ]
16. def engine = new SimpleTemplateEngine()
17. def email = engine.createTemplate(emailTemplate).make(binding)
18. def body = email.toString()
19.
20. println body
```

The code that we will make dynamic is in bold. The simple user GroovyBean, from Lines 6–9 is used simply to pass data to the template engine; it provides no other value, so it's a great candidate for an expando object.

Listing 3-41 shows code that creates the user GroovyBean from Listing 3-25 using expandos rather than a concrete class.

Listing 3-41. Alternative to the User GroovyBean

```
1.  def user = new Expando()
2.
3.  user.firstName = 'Christopher'
4.  user.lastName = 'Judd'
5.
6.  user.greeting = { greeting ->
7.    "${greeting} ${firstName} ${lastName}"
8.  }
9.
10. assert user.greeting("Hello") == 'Hello Christopher Judd'
```

Listing 3-41 uses an expando as a replacement for a concrete GroovyBean class. On Line 1, a new instance of the expando is created. On Lines 3 and 4, the `firstName` and `lastName` properties are added to the object dynamically and assigned values. Properties are not the only things that you can add. You can also add behaviors using closures. Lines 6–8 create and assign a closure to the greeting that concatenates the greeting parameter with the properties for the first and last names. Finally, line 10 executes greeting.

You can also initialize expandos with properties using the overloaded constructor that takes a map. Listing 3-42 uses this technique to re-implement the template example found on Line 13 in Listing 3-25.

Listing 3-42. Template Example Using Expandos Instead of User GroovyBean

```
import groovy.text.SimpleTemplateEngine
def emailTemplate = this.class.getResource("nightlyReportsEmail.gtpl")
def binding = [
  "user": new Expando([ firstName: 'Christopher', lastName:'Judd']),
        "date": new Date()
]
def engine = new SimpleTemplateEngine()
def template = engine.createTemplate(emailTemplate).make(binding)
def body = template.toString()
println body
```

Notice that Listing 3-42 reduces the amount of code and increases the readability of the earlier template example by replacing the `User` class definition with expando, which contains the `firstName` and `lastName` properties.

Now we refactor Line 11 of Listing 3-25, which seems a little more like Java than Groovy, so we will groovify it.

```
def emailTemplate = this.class.getResource("nightlyReportsEmail.gtpl")
```

Listing 3-43 shows how MOP could make this a little more Groovy by adding the `getResourceAsText()` method to `java.lang.Class`, which actually loads the file and gets the contents of the file as text rather than just the URL to the file.

Listing 3-43. Adding the getResourceAsText() Method to java.lang.Class

```
1.  import groovy.text.SimpleTemplateEngine
2.
3.  Class.metaClass.getResourceAsText = { resource ->
4.    this.class.getResourceAsStream(resource).getText()
5.  }
6.
7.  def emailTemplate = this.class.getResourceAsText('nightlyReportsEmail.gtpl')
8.  def binding = [
9.          "user": new Expando([ firstName: 'Christopher', lastName:'Judd']),
10.         "date": new Date()]
11. def engine = new SimpleTemplateEngine()
12. def template = engine.createTemplate(emailTemplate).make(binding)
13. def body = template.toString()
14.
15. println body
```

Notice how Line 7 expresses much more explicitly that it is loading the template as text and not as a URL. This is accomplished by extending the final `java.lang.Class` on Lines 3–5 by accessing the `metaClass` property and adding the `getResourceAsText()` method that takes a parameter of resource, which is the name of a file on the classpath. The implementation of this method found on Line 4 uses the `getResourceAsStream()` technique to load a file as a stream. This is generally safer than using a URL, because not everything is easily addressable with a URL. The closure then finishes by using the `getText()` method, which Groovy includes in the Groovy JDK on all `java.io.InputStreams` by means of MOP. Finally, Line 7 shows what a call to the `getResourceAsText()` method would look like on `java.lang.Class`. There are additional ways in which you might want to do the same thing and make Listing 3-25 a little more expressive. Listing 3-44 shows another implementation of doing the same thing by adding behavior to `java.lang.String`, which is also a class marked as final.

Listing 3-44. Adding the fileAsString() Method to java.lang.String

```
1. String.metaClass.fileAsString = {
2.    this.class.getResourceAsStream(delegate).getText()
3. }
4.
5. println 'nightlyReportsEmail.gtpl'.fileAsString()
```

Listing 3-44 begins by adding the `fileAsString()` method to the `metaClass` property of the `java.lang.String` class, similar to the previous example. However, it uses a delegate variable instead of a passed-in parameter. The delegate is a reference to the object instance of which the method was called, which in this case would be the string containing the file name to be loaded. Notice how nicely Line 5 reads. It is almost like reading an English sentence. It is not a mere coincidence, as we will discover in the domain-specific language section, but before that we will examine another form of metaprogramming.

Compile-time Metaprogramming

Compile-time metaprogramming provides the user of a programming language, a mechanism to interact with the compiler to allow the construction of arbitrary program fragments; for instance, to add new features to a language or apply application-specific optimizations. Many of the new Groovy features use compile-time metaprogramming to eliminate redundant or verbose code. Compile-time metaprogramming can be very useful, but is less flexible than runtime metaprogramming and should only be used if you must; that is, only if you cannot find a runtime solution for the problem at hand.

AST Transformations

AST stands for Abstract Syntax Tree: a representation of code as data. When the Groovy compiler compiles Groovy scripts and classes, the Groovy parser(the front end of the compiler) creates an AST before generating the final byte code for the class. The AST is the in-memory representation of the source code, comprising class, method, property, statement, and variables. AST transformation is the capability to add new code (methods and checks) into source code before the final byte code is generated. Groovy ships with many annotations for AST transformations that you can readily use to avoid code repetition.

The objective of an AST transformation is to let developers structure code while focusing more on the business code rather than on boilerplate code or cross-cutting concerns. Groovy offers several approaches to accomplishing AST transformations: using annotations shipped with Groovy for AST transformations, local AST transformation, and global AST transformations.

Built-in AST Transformations

To use the built-in AST transformation feature of Groovy, you just need to annotate a class or a method with the annotations provided by Groovy. You don't have to know anything about compilers or Groovy internals before using the annotations, which we describe in this section. We will cover the most popular AST transformations annotations provided by Groovy. Using all Groovy built-in AST transformations and writing your own custom transformations is a broad subject and merits a book of its own. A detailed explanation on all built-in transformations can be found on the Groovy site (`http://groovy.codehaus.org/Compile-time+Metaprogramming+-+AST+Transformations`).

Delegate Transformation

A delegate is a relationship between two classes; for example, one class will contain a reference to another class. Listing 3-45 shows a simple usage of `@Delegate` that wraps an existing class, delegating all calls to the delegate:

Listing 3-45. Using @Delegate

```
1.  class Author{
2.    String authorName
3.  }
4.  class Book {
5.    @Delegate Author author
6.    String title
7.  }
8.  def author= new Author(authorName: "vishal")
9.  def book= new Book(title: "Beginning Groovy,Grails and Griffon", author: author)
10. assert book.title == "Beginning Groovy,Grails and Griffon"
11. assert book.authorName == "vishal"
```

- Line 5: `@Delegate` annotation forms a 'has a' relationship. The class Book has a reference to class `Author`.
- Lines 8-9: `Author` is initialized and passed to book.
- Line 11: Field `authorName` is accessible from the book object because of the `@Delegate` annotation.

Immutable Transformation

Immutable objects are ones 'that don't change after initial creation. Immutability implies the following:

- The class must be final.
- Fields must be private and final.
- `equals()`, `hashCode()`, and `toString()` must be implemented in terms of the fields in order to be able to compare objects or use them as keys in maps.

Immutable transformation allows you to write classes in the shortened form, as illustrated in Listing 3-46.

Listing 3-46. Adding the getResourceAsText() Method to java.lang.Class

```
1.  @groovy.transform.Immutable class Book{
2.    String title
3.    Collection authors
4.  }
5.  def book1 = new Book(title:'Beginning Groovy, Grails and Griffon', authors:['Vishal', 'Chris',
    'James', 'Joseph'])
6.  def book2 = new Book('Beginning Groovy, Grails and Griffon', ['Vishal', 'Chris', 'James',
    'Joseph'])
7.  assert book1 == book2
```

The `@Immutable` annotation instructs the compiler to execute an AST transformation, which adds the necessary getters, constructors, `equals()`, `hashCode()`, and other helper methods that are typically written when creating immutable classes with the defined properties.

Lazy Transformation

Sometimes, you want to handle the initialization of a field of your class lazily, so that its value is computed only on first use, often because it is time-consuming or memory-expensive to create. In Groovy, you can now use the `@Lazy` annotation for that purpose:

If you run the code in Listing 3-47, you will get an exception as shown.

Listing 3-47. Using @Lazy

```
1.  class Groovy {
2.   @Lazy authors= ['Vishal', 'Christopher', 'Joseph', 'James']
3.  }
4.  def g = new Groovy()
5.  assert  g.dump().contains('Vishal')
```

```
Caught: Assertion failed:

assert g.dump<>.contains<'Vishal'>
       | |       |
       | |       false
       | <Groovy@8ee016 $authors=null>
       Groovy@8ee016

Assertion failed:

assert g.dump<>.contains<'Vishal'>
       | |       |
       | |       false
       | <Groovy@8ee016 $authors=null>
       Groovy@8ee016
```

The power assert notifies us that the authors list is `null`, even if the authors list in Line 2 is not null.

This happens because of the `@Lazy` annotation. The `@Lazy` field annotation delays field instantiation until the time when that field is first used. In Line 5, `authors` is not initialized due to the `@lazy` annotation, which is corrected in Listing 3-48.

Listing 3-48. Using @Lazy Annotation

```
1.  class Groovy {
2.   @Lazy authors= ['Vishal', 'Christopher', 'Joseph', 'James']
3.  }
4.  def g = new Groovy()
5.  assert  g.authors.size() == 4
6.  assert  g.dump().contains('Vishal')
```

Logging Transformation

For logging, Groovy includes `@Log`, `@Log4j`, `@Slf4j`, and `@Commons`. Listing 3-49 illustrates using `@Log` annotation.

Listing 3-49. Using @Log

```
1. @groovy.util.logging.Log
2. class Test {
3. def someMethod() {
4. log.fine(complexMethod())
```

```
5. }
6. }
7. new Test().someMethod ()
```

- Line 1:The @Log annotation first creates a logger based on the name of the class.
- Line 4: The log method is wrapped with a conditional check whether FINE level is enabled before trying to execute the complexMethod().

The result is equivalent to wrapping the logging call in the following condition:

```
if (logger.isEnabled(LogLevel.FINE))
```

Newify Transformation

The @Newify transformation proposes two new ways of instantiating classes.

Listing 3-50 shows a Ruby-like approach to create instances with a new() class method:

Listing 3-50. Using @Newify for Ruby-like Approach to Create Instances

```
@Newify rubyLikeNew() {
 assert Integer.new(42) == 42
}

rubyLikeNew()
```

Listing 3-51. Creating a tree

```
class Tree {
    def elements
    Tree(Object... elements) { this.elements = elements as List }
}

class Leaf {
    def value
    Leaf(value) { this.value = value }
}

def buildTree() {
    new Tree(new Tree(new Leaf(1), new Leaf(2)), new Leaf(3))
}

buildTree()
```

The creation of the tree in Listing 3-51 is not very readable because of all those new keywords spread across the line. The Ruby approach in this case would not be more readable either, since a new() method call for creating each element is needed. But by using @Newify, we can improve our tree building slightly for visual clarity, using 'Python's approach by omitting the new keyword altogether. Listing 3-52 illustrates a Python-like approach to create instances.

Listing 3-52. Using @Newify for Python-like Approach to Create Instances

```
@Newify([Tree, Leaf]) buildTree() {
    Tree(Tree(Leaf(1), Leaf(2)), Leaf(3))
}
```

Singleton Transformation

We're used to creating a private constructor, a `getInstance()` method for a `static` field, or even an initialized `public static final` field. The singleton pattern requires a private constructor, and a public `static` method to access the single instance.

So instead of writing Java code, as illustrated in Listing 3-53, you just need to annotate your type with the `@Singleton` annotation, as shown in Listing 3-54:

Listing 3-53. A Singleton Class

```
public class T {
    public static final T instance = new T();
    private T() {}
}
```

Listing 3-54. Using @Singleton

```
@Singleton class T {}
```

The singleton instance can then simply be accessed with `T.instance` (direct public field access).

You can also have the lazy loading approach, shown in Listing 3-55, with an additional annotation parameter:

Listing 3-55. Using @Singleton with Lazy Loading

```
@Singleton(lazy = true) class T {}
```

The code in Listing 3-55 becomes more or less equivalent to the Groovy class created in Listing 3-56:

Listing 3-56. Groovy Class representationof @Singleton

```
class T {
    private static volatile T instance
    private T() {}
    static T getInstance () {
        if (instance) {
            instance
        } else {
            synchronized(T) {
                if (instance) {
                    instance
                } else {
                    instance = new T ()
                }
            }
        }
    }
}
```

Domain-Specific Languages

The dichotomy of *generic* and *specific* manifests itself in the programming sphere. Domain-specific languages (DSLs) are one of the forms of the manifestations of this dichotomy. Domain-specific languages are just what they are called: domain specific.

All programming languages are domain-specific languages when they come into existence, but that changes as they evolve. Domain-specific languages are created to solve problems in a certain area (or more precisely, in a certain domain) but as they gradually evolve to solve problems in several domains, the line that distinguishes them as specific blurs. Thus, such a language transgresses from the specific to the generic.

DSLs are focused on the domain or problem and can be of external or internal types.

An external DSL defines a new language with its own custom grammar and parser. An internal DSL defines a new language as well, but within the syntactical boundaries of another language. No custom parser is necessary for internal DSLs. Instead, they are parsed just like any other code written in the language.

Ant, which uses XML, is an example of an external DSL. Gant, on the other hand, uses Groovy to solve the same problem and is an example of an internal DSL. Groovy with its metaprogramming capabilities and flexible syntax is better suited to designing and implementing internal DSLs.

As an illustration, using Groovy's optional parameters and MOP, you can turn this code that only a programmer can love:

```
println this.class.getResourceAsStream('readme.txt').getText()
into:
write 'readme.txt'.contents()
```

Notice that with the second option, even a nonprogrammer has a chance of understanding the intent of the code. Listing 3-57 shows how to implement this simple DSL for writing files.

Listing 3-57. Implementation of a Simple DSL

```
1.  String.metaClass.contents = {
2.    this.class.getResourceAsStream(delegate).getText()
3.  }
4.
5.  def write = { file ->
6.    println file
7.  }
8.
9.  write 'readme.txt'.contents()
```

Lines 1-3 use the same metaprogramming implementation from the previous section to add a contents closure to the String class. The contents closure loads a file from the classpath as text based on the value of the String. Lines 5-7 implement a closure named write that simply does a `println` on whatever is passed as a parameter. This ultimately enables Line 9 to read like a sentence when the optional parentheses for the write call are not included.

Summary

Combined with the Groovy topics from the previous chapters, the advanced Groovy topics in this chapter—such as unit testing, XML processing, templates, expandos, and metaprogramming—have prepared you for developing web-based and desktop-based applications using the Groovy-based Grails and Griffon framework that is the focus of the remainder of the book.

CHAPTER 4

Introduction to Grails

Let's face it: developing web applications is hard. This problem has been exacerbated in today's environment, where applications deemed to fall into the Web 2.0 category involve lots of technologies, such as HyperText Markup Language (HTML), Cascading Style Sheets (CSS), Asynchronous JavaScript and XML (Ajax), XML, web services, Java, and databases. Then on top of the technologies sit lots of open source framework choices like model-view-controller (MVC) frameworks and Ajax frameworks. To make matters worse, while the complexity of building applications continues to grow, expected turnaround times continue to shrink.

In recent years, the Java community has tried solving these issues by building applications using Java Platform, Enterprise Edition (Java EE) and its predecessor, Java 2 Platform, Enterprise Edition (J2EE). While these platforms have proven to be scalable and robust, they don't allow for rapid, agile development. Java EE has proven over and over again that it was not written with an application level of abstraction but rather with a much lower technical level. These shortcomings led to the development of recent application frameworks and the subsequent popularity of frameworks such as Struts, Spring, and Hibernate. Furthermore, the development cycle of coding, compiling, packaging, deploying, testing, and debugging takes entirely too long for any real productivity and requires developers to switch context too frequently.

Enter Grails. Grails is an open source web development framework that packages best practices (such as convention over configuration and unit testing) with the best-of-the-best open source application frameworks (such as Spring, Hibernate, and SiteMesh). Together with the productivity of the Groovy scripting language, everything runs on top of the robust Java and Java EE platforms.

In this chapter, you will learn about the features and open source frameworks included with Grails. Then you'll learn how to take advantage of Grails' powerful scaffolding feature to build your first Grails application.

What Is Grails?

Grails is not only an open source web framework for the Java platform, but a complete development platform as well. Like most web frameworks, Grails is an MVC framework, but it's not your average Java MVC framework. Like other Java MVC frameworks, it does have models (referred to in Grails as *domain classes*) that carry application data for display by the view. However, unlike other MVC models, Grails domain classes are automatically persistable and can even generate the underlying database schema. Like other MVC frameworks, Grails controllers handle the requests and orchestrate services or other behavior.

Unlike most MVC frameworks, though, services and other classes can be automatically injected using dependency injection based on naming conventions. In addition, Grails controllers are request-scoped, which means a new instance is created for each request. Finally, the default view for Grails is Groovy Server Pages (GSP) and it typically renders HTML. The view layer also includes a flexible layout, a templating feature, and simple tag libraries.

Other Grails advantages include minimal configuration and a more agile development cycle. Grails eliminates most of the standard MVC configuration and deployment descriptors by using initiative conventions. Also, because Grails takes advantage of Groovy's dynamic language features, it is usually able to shorten the development cycle to just coding, refreshing, testing, and debugging. This saves valuable development time and makes development much more agile than with other Java MVC frameworks or Java EE.

As a complete development platform, Grails includes a web container, database, build system, and test harness out of the box. This combination can reduce project startup time and developer setup time to minutes rather than hours or days. With Grails, you typically don't have to find and download a bunch of server software or frameworks to get started. You also don't have to spend time creating or maintaining complicated build scripts. Everything you need to get started comes bundled in one simple-to-install package.

Grails has an impressive list of features and is able to provide so much functionality by integration of proven open source projects.

Grails Features

Most modern web frameworks in the Java space are convoluted, full of twists and turns, and disregard the Don't Repeat Yourself (DRY) principles. Grails, built on the concepts brought to the fore by dynamic frameworks like Rails, Django, and TurboGears, dramatically reduces the complexity of building web applications on the Java platform, leveraging already established Java technologies like Spring and Hibernate. Grails is a full stack framework and attempts to solve as many pieces of the web development puzzle through the core technology and its associated plugins. Its features include:

- An easy-to-use Object Relational Mapping (ORM) layer built on Hibernate
- An expressive view technology called Groovy Server Pages (GSP)
- A controller layer built on Spring MVC
- A command line scripting environment built on the Groovy-powered Gant
- An embedded Tomcat container configured for on-the-fly reloading
- Dependency injection with the built-in Spring container
- Support for internationalization (i18n) built on Spring's core MessageSource concept
- A transactional service layer built on Spring's transaction abstraction

All of these are made easy to use through the power of the Groovy language and the extensive use of Domain Specific Languages (DSLs).

Grails really has too many features to mention them all. In this section, we'll highlight some of the more important ones.

Convention over Configuration

Rather than using lots of XML configuration files, Grails relies on conventions to configure itself, thus making application development easier and more productive. The conventions relate to the directory structure, meaning that the name and location of files is used instead of explicit configuration. This essentially means that instead of wiring in XML configuration files, you can create a class, following the Grails conventions, and Grails will wire it into Spring or treat it as a Hibernate entity thereof. For example, if you create a new domain class called User, Grails will automatically create a table called user in the database. This convention over configuration feature is centered on its directory structure. By using the convention-over-configuration paradigm, Grails can figure out a component's responsibilities, inspecting its name and its location in the directory structure, and thus enable you to configure a particular aspect of a component only when that configuration deviates from the standard. In this way, adhering to well-known conventions, you can create an application more quickly, because you will spend less time configuring it.

Unit Testing

Unit testing is now recognized as a critical best practice to improving the quality of software deliverables and enabling long-term maintainability of an application. Furthermore, unit testing is even more important for applications written using dynamically typed languages such as Groovy, because identifying the effects of changes without the help of the compiler and unit tests can be difficult. This is why unit testing is a major Grails convention.

Grails separates its unit tests into two categories: unit and integration. Grails unit tests are free standing unit tests with no dependencies other than possibly mock objects. Integration tests, on the other hand, have access to the entire Grails environment, including the database.

Scaffolding

As you'll see in the second half of this chapter, Grails has a scaffolding framework that generates applications with create, read, update, and delete (CRUD) functionality with very little code, allowing you to focus on defining the Groovy domain by creating classes with properties, behaviors, and constraints. At either runtime or development time, Grails can generate the controller behavior and GSP views associated with the domain classes for CRUD functionality. At the same time, it can even generate a database schema, including tables for each of the domain classes.

Object Relational Mapping

Grails includes a powerful object relational mapping framework called Grails Object Relational Mapping (GORM). Like most object-relational mapping (ORM) frameworks, GORM can map objects to relational databases and represent relationships between those objects, such as one-to-one or one-to-many. But what sets GORM apart from other ORMs is the fact that it is built for a dynamic language like Groovy. It injects the CRUD methods right into the class without having to implement them or inherit from persistent super classes. Once more, it is able to provide an ORM DSL for dynamic finder methods and search criteria. You will learn more about GORM in Chapter 6.

Plugins

Grails does not propose to have all the answers to every web development problem. Instead, it provides a plugin architecture and a community where you can find plugins for things like security, Ajax, testing, searching, reporting, and web services. This plugin architecture makes it easy to add complicated functionality to your application. We will discuss plugins in more detail in "Grails Plugins," later in this chapter.

Integrated Open Source

Grails does not suffer from the Not Invented Here (NIH) syndrome. Rather than reinvent the wheel, it integrates the best of the best industry-standard and proven open source frameworks, several of which are briefly described in this section.

Groovy

Groovy is one of the pillars of Grails. Grails 2.0 comes with Groovy 1.8. As you learned in Chapters 1-3, Groovy is a powerful and flexible open source language that stands on its own. However, its integration with Java, dynamic scripting features, and simple syntax makes it a perfect complement to Grails and provides the agile nature of the entire solution.

Spring Framework

Spring Framework is best described by its creator Rod Johnson as providing an application level of abstraction on top of the Java EE API. For example, rather than having to deal with the details of handling transactions, Spring provides a means for declaring transactions around regular Plain Old Java Objects (POJOs) so that you can focus on implementing business logic. In addition, because Spring brings Java EE features to POJOs, you're able to develop and test your application code outside a Java EE container, thereby increasing productivity. Along with Hibernate, Spring was a major influence on the new Enterprise JavaBeans (EJB) 3.0 spec, which attempts to simplify Java EE development.

Grails implicitly handles much of the Spring integration. However, in Chapter 6, you will learn how to explicitly configure and integrate with Spring if you find it necessary.

Hibernate

Hibernate is an object-relational persistence framework that provides the foundation for GORM. It's able to map complex domain classes written as POJOs or POGOs (Plain Old Groovy Objects) to relational database tables, as well as map relationships between the tables. As mentioned in the previous section, Hibernate had a big influence on the EJB 3.0 specification, specifically the Java Persistence API (JPA). Hibernate is one of the many JBoss projects. For more information about Hibernate, go to `http://www.hibernate.org`.

SiteMesh

SiteMesh is a web page layout framework that implements the decorator design pattern for rendering HTML with constant components such as the header, footers, and navigation. It is one of the components found in the OpenSymphony suite and is hosted on the OpenSymphony site. Grails hides most of the SiteMesh details from you as a developer, but in Chapter 5, you'll see how to create page layouts and other web components such as GSP. You can find detailed information about SiteMesh at `http://wiki.sitemesh.org/display/sitemesh/Home`.

Ajax Frameworks

By default, Grails includes the jQuery library, but also provides support for other frameworks such as Prototype, Dojo, Yahoo UI, and the Google Web Toolkit through the plugin system. Chapter 8 will explain how to add Ajax functionality to your application to increase usability.

Tomcat

Grails 2.0 replaces Jetty with an embedded Tomcat container that is configured for on-the-fly reloading. Chapter 12 will explain how to deploy Grails applications to other containers.

H2

Grails 2.0 now uses the H2[3] database instead of HSQLDB, and enables the H2 database console in development mode (at the URI /dbconsole) so that the in-memory database can be easily queried from the browser. By default, Grails uses the embedded in-memory configuration, so that each time the application is run, the database is rebuilt from scratch and all data is lost. Chapter 12 will explain how to configure Grails to use other databases such as MySQL. We will discuss H2 further in "H2 Console," later in this chapter. To find out more about H2, including how to download it, go to `http://www.h2database.com/html/main.html`.

Grails Architecture

Now that you know some of the features and open source frameworks included in Grails, you are more prepared to understand the Grails architecture, which is illustrated in Figure 4-1.

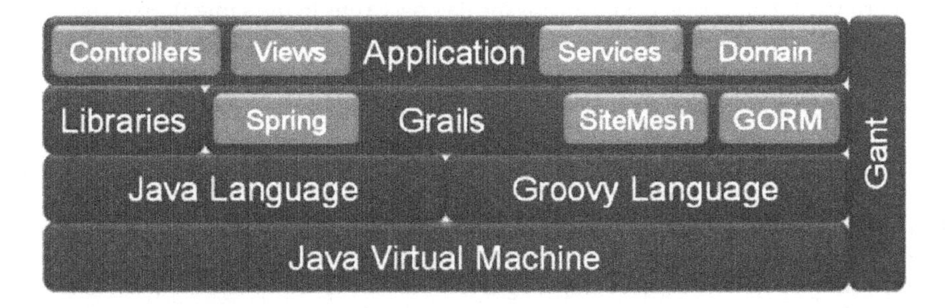

Figure 4-1. *Grails architecture*

In Figure 4-1, notice that the foundation of Grails is the Java Virtual Machine (JVM).Also, notice the separation in the architecture from the Java language and the JVM. In the past couple of years, the Java community has seen a rash of new and ported languages being run on the JVM. This is particularly important in Grails, because in the next level up from the JVM, you see that both the Java and Groovy languages are used.

The final layer of the architecture is the applications you will build with Grails. Typically, this layer follows the MVC pattern. Grails also makes it easy to organize your application to make coarse-grained services.

To simplify development, Grails includes a command-line tool for creating many Grails artifacts and managing Grails projects. The Grails command line is built on top of Gant, a build system that uses the Groovy language to script Apache Ant tasks rather than Ant's XML format. You will learn more about Gant and adding your own scripts to the Grails command line in Chapter 12.

From a runtime perspective, you can think of Grails out of the box as looking like Figure 4-2.

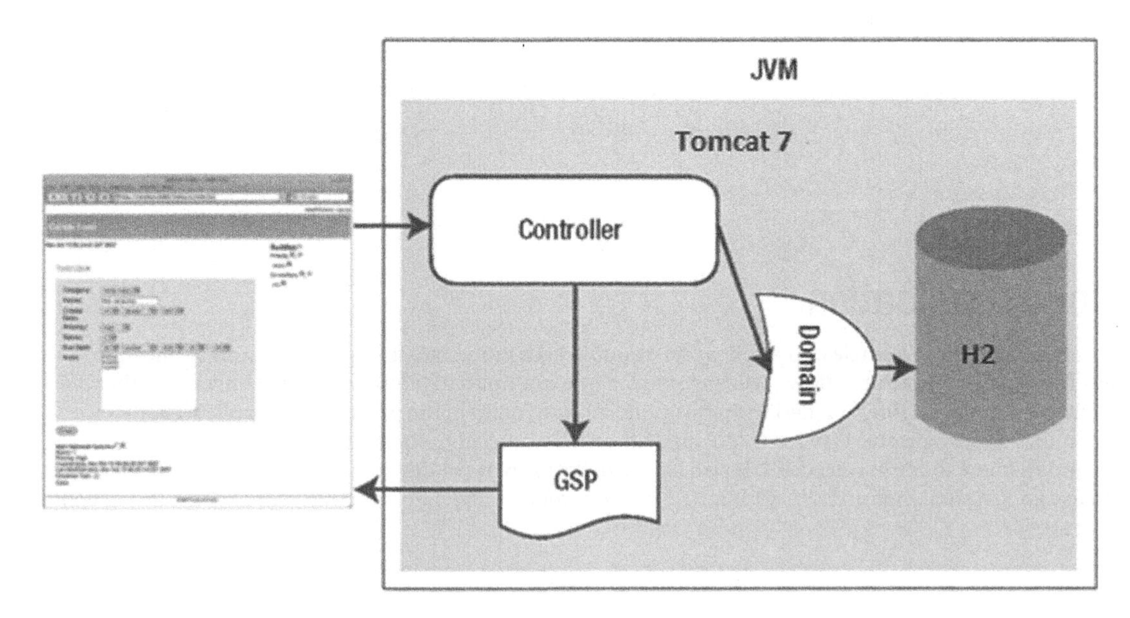

Figure 4-2. *Grails default runtime*

In Figure 4-2, you see a web browser making a request to a Tomcat web container. The container forwards the request on to a controller in a similar fashion to the standard MVC model. The controller may set or use data from a domain class (model). As mentioned earlier, all Grails domain classes are persistable through the GORM framework.

You don't need to use a Data Access Object (DAO) pattern or write SQL to persist objects. In Chapter 6, you will learn how to take full advantage of the persistable domain classes.

Out-of-the-box Grails uses an embedded H2 database, which means the database runs in the same JVM as your application and the Tomcat web container. When the controller is done, it forwards the request to a GSP, which is the view technology to render the HTML that is returned to the requesting browser.

Installing Grails

Considering the alternative to using Grails—downloading and installing a web container or application server, database, and MVC framework—installing Grails seems almost too easy. All you need to do is uncompress a file and set up some environment variables, and you're done. Most everything is self-contained. Grails does require two prerequisites, though: you must have a JDK 1.6 or above, and you must have the JAVA_HOME environment variable configured for that JDK. In this book, we will use Grails 2.1.0

Follow these steps to install Grails:

1. Download the latest Grails .zip or .tar/.gz file release from `http://grails.codehaus.org/Download`.
2. Extract the archive to your preferred location.
3. Create a GRAILS_HOME environment variable that points to the path where the Grails archive was extracted.
4. Append the GRAILS_HOME\bin directory to the PATH environment variable.

Once you complete these steps, the Grails command line will be available. You can use it to create the project, create artifacts, run the application, and package the application.

To validate your installation, open a command window and type the command grails -version:

```
> grails -version
```

If you have successfully installed Grails, the command will output the following:

```
Grails version: 2.1.0
```

Collab-Todo Application

Throughout this book, we'll use a single web application example to demonstrate how to write a web application using the Grails framework. Intermittently we will use stand-alone examples to introduce some concepts so that the learning of Grails does not get tightly coupled with the application we build in the process. The application that we will use in this book is a collaborative Web 2.0 to-do application and is called Collab-Todo. The application allows users to create and manage todos in categories. It also allows users to create buddy lists of other Collab-Todo users to make it easy to assign tasks to other users. In addition, it includes reports and batch e-mails, along with a thick client and web service access.

It is important for you to experience for yourself the power and productivity of Grails early on, so for the remainder of this chapter, you will be learning to take advantage of Grails conventions and scaffolding to create a simple but functional version of the Collab-Todo application. This initial version of the application will not be a production-suitable application from a usability and design perspective. However, the Grails scaffolding is able to render a simple but functional CRUD web application with almost no code besides your domain class code. In addition, Grails will generate a database schema and populate a database with the schema when the application is run. This scaffolding-based version of the application is suitable for testing domain objects as well as quick application prototyping.

Figure 4-3 shows an example of what the CRUD todo pages will look like by the end of the chapter.

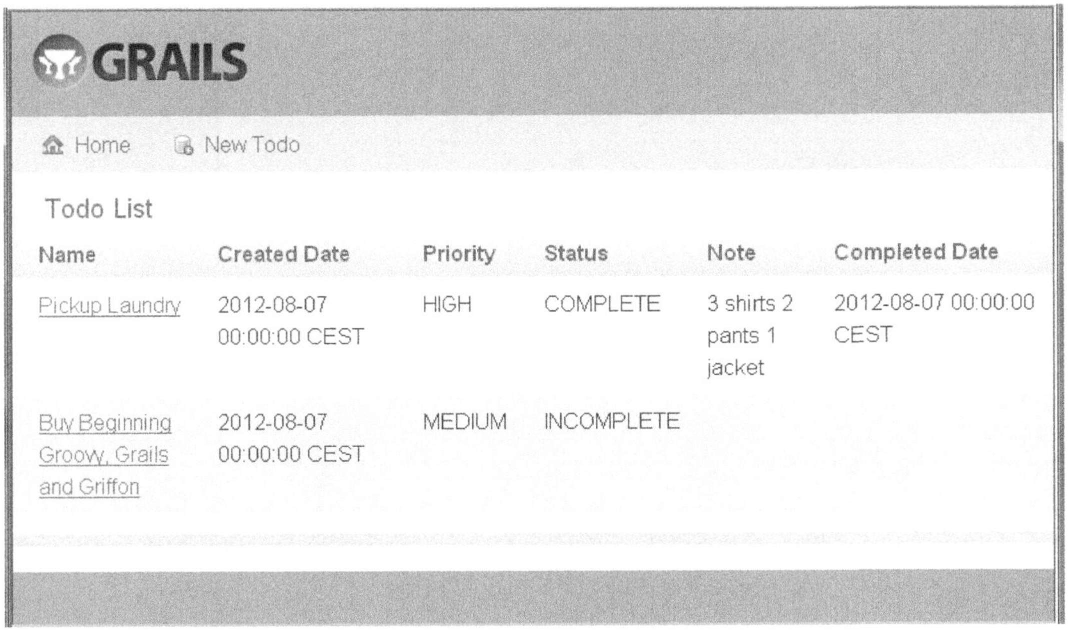

GRAILS
Home
New Todo
Todo List
Name
Created Date
Priority
Status
Note
Completed Date
Pickup Laundry
2012-08-07 00:00:00 CEST
HIGH
COMPLETE
3 shirts 2 pants 1 jacket
2012-08-07 00:00:00 CEST
Buy Beginning Groovy, Grails and Griffon
2012-08-07 00:00:00 CEST
MEDIUM
INCOMPLETE

Figure 4-3. *Todo List page*

As you can see in Figure 4-3, the Todo List page provides the ability to view all the todos in the database as well as create new todos or delete existing todos. It also provides a link to the edit page, where you can create a new todo or update an existing todo.

Figure 4-4 shows the Edit Todo page, which is basically the same page used for updating and creating todos.

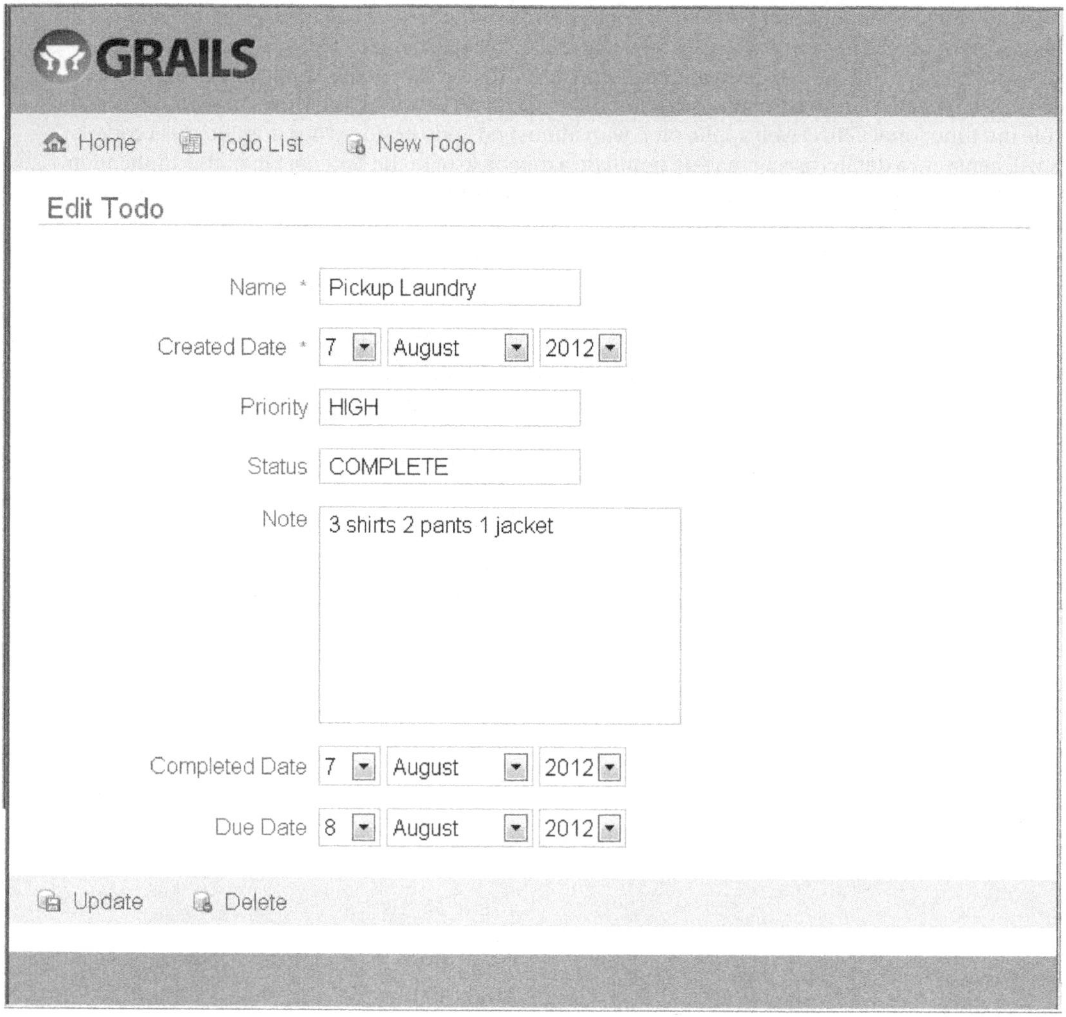

Figure 4-4. Edit Todo page

As you can tell from Figures 4-3 and 4-4, this is not the most attractive application, and you probably won't want to release this to your users. In Chapter 5, you'll learn how to make the application more usable and pleasing to your users' eyes, and in Chapter 8, you'll learn how to make it even better by adding Web 2.0 features.

Figure 4-5 is a Unified Modeling Language (UML) diagram of a subset of the Collab-Todo domain classes you'll be creating in this chapter.

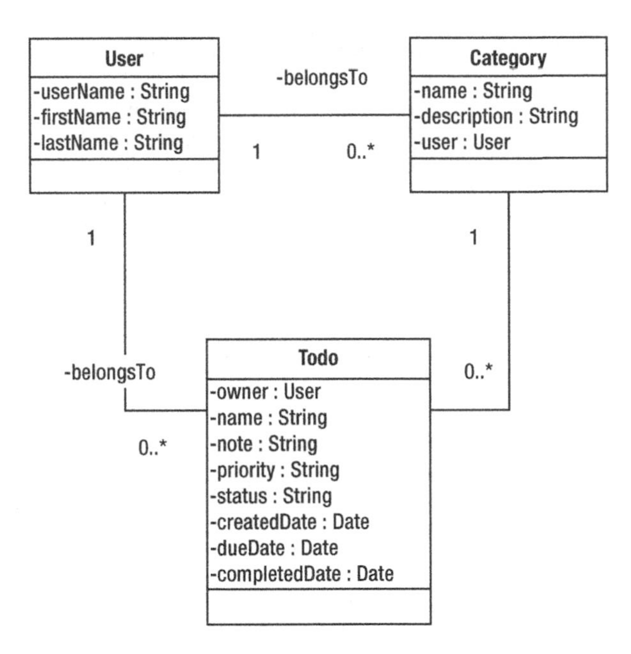

Figure 4-5. *Subset of the Collab-Todo domain classes*

Notice the domain model in Figure 4-5 is very simple and includes only three domain classes. In Chapter 6, you will extend this domain model and learn about the Grails persistence framework, GORM. Initially, the domain consists of a User class, which has a Todo (task) class, and userdefined Category classes used for organizing todos into logical groups.

Creating Collab-Todo application

To create the Collab-Todo application, you need to execute the create-app target using an optional project name on the command line, as shown here:

```
> grails create-app collab-todo
```

The entire line in the preceding command line is a command, where create-app is a target. A target is a specific task that you want Grails to execute.

If you don't supply the project name when using create-app, you will be prompted for one. On execution of this command, Grails downloads the dependencies and creates the application. The output of executing the create-app target is shown here:

```
|Downloading: D:\grails-2.1.0\lib\org.springframework.uaa\org.springframework.u
| Downloading: D:\grails-2.1.0\lib\com.google.protobuf\protobuf-java\ivy-2.4.1.x
| Downloading: D:\grails-2.1.0\lib\org.bouncycastle\bcpg-jdk15\jars\bcpg-jdk15-1
.........
 Created Grails Application at D:\devl\workspace/collab-todo
```

Instead of creating the application from command line, you can use the IDE of your choice. We recommend the Groovy/Grails Tool Suite (GGTS), which you can download from `http://www.springsource.org/downloads/sts-ggts`. This book uses the latest version: GGTS 3.0. GGTS provides the best Eclipse-powered development environment for building Groovy and Grails applications. GGTS provides support for the latest versions of Groovy and Grails, and comes on top of the latest Eclipse releases.

To create a new project in GGTS, use the menu options File ➤ New ➤ Grails Project and enter the project name as “collab-todo”.

After the create-app target has run, or after creating a new project using GGTS, you have a new directory matching the name of your project. This is the root of your new project, and you must make all subsequent Grails command-line calls from within this directory. It’s a good idea to use the cd command to get into the directory now so you don’t forget. Within the new project directory, you will find a structure matching the directory structure shown in Figure 4-6.

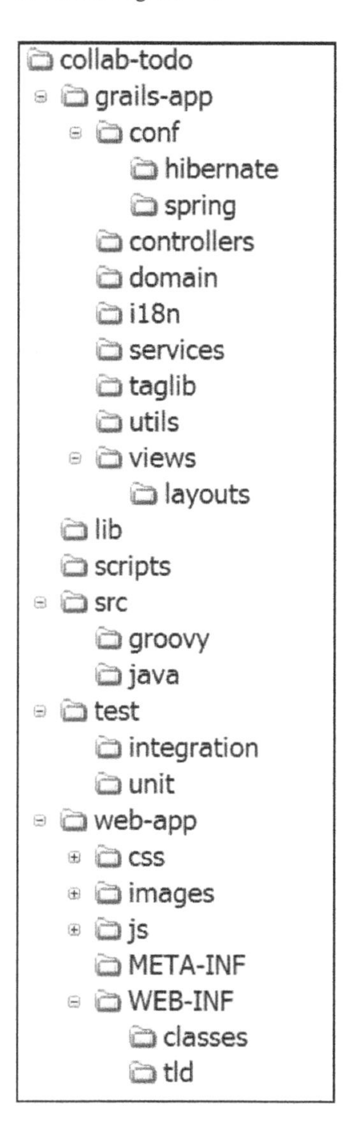

Figure 4-6. *Directory structure created by running the createapp target*

As mentioned earlier, the directory structure generated from the create-app target is a part of the Grails practice of convention over configuration. The target provides locations for placing common artifacts. Throughout the book, you will learn details about each directory. For now, Table 4-1 provides a summary of the more important directories.

Table 4-1. *Important Directories in the Grails Convention*

Directory	Description
grails-app/conf	Common configuration files such as bootstrapping, logging, data source, and URL mapping (see the "Configurations" sidebar)
grails-app/conf/hibernate	Custom Hibernate mappings, which are rarely needed (covered in Chapter 6)
grails-app/conf/spring	Custom Spring mapping files
grails-app/controllers	Application controllers that handle requests (covered in Chapter 5)
grails-app/domain	Domain model classes (covered in Chapter 6)
grails-app/i18n	Internationalized message bundles (covered in Chapter 5)
grails-app/services	Services (covered in Chapter 6)
grails-app/taglib	Custom dynamic tag libraries
grails-app/views	GSP (covered in Chapter 5)
grails-app/views/layout	Commonly shared page layouts (covered in Chapter 5)
lib	Third-party JAR files, such as database drivers
scripts	Gant script for automating tasks (covered in Chapter 12)
src/java	Additional Java source files
src/groovy	Additional Groovy files
test/integration	Integration tests
test/unit	Unit tests (introduced later in this chapter)
web-app	Web artifacts that will ultimately comprise a web application archive (WAR) (many of the artifacts are covered in Chapter 5)
web-app/css	Cascading Style Sheets (covered in Chapter 5)
web-app/images	Web graphics (covered in Chapter 5)
web-app/js	JavaScript (covered in Chapter 8)
web-app/WEB-INF	Common Servlet specification WEB-INF directory containing private artifacts such as configuration files like web.xml, the Spring application context, and the SiteMesh config

Running the Application

At this point, you have a functional application that you can run and access via a web browser. It does not do much yet, but running it now will enable you to get instant feedback as you add domain and controller classes.

To run a Grails application, execute the run-app target from your project root directory as shown here:

```
> grails run-app
```

The output of executing the run-app target is shown here:

```
Server running. Browse to http://localhost:8080/collab-todo
```

To run the application in GGTS, click on "Grails Command History" as highlighted in Figure 4-7, type "run-app" on the command window, and hit Enter.

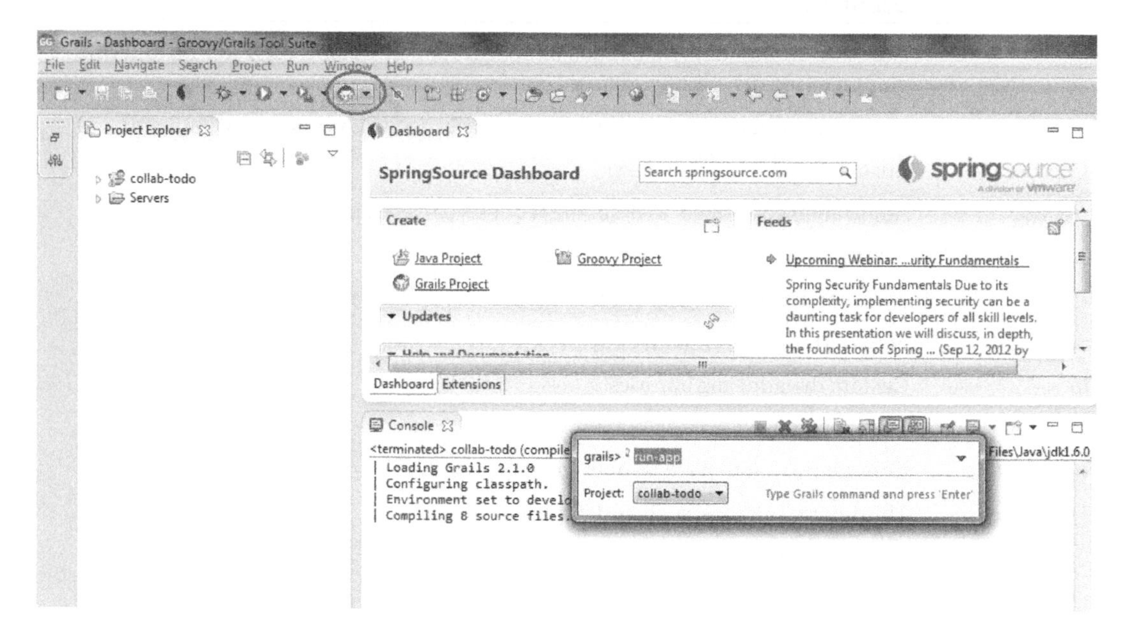

Figure 4-7. Running the application in GGTS

Running the run-app target performs some initial project setup by copying files into your web application's WEB-INF directories. Then it starts a Tomcat web container that listens on localhost port 8080. Tomcat then loads the application, causing the Grails internal classes to get initialized for filtering URL mappings and requests along with GrailsDispatchServlet. To test your app, point your web browser to that URL, as shown in Figure 4-8.

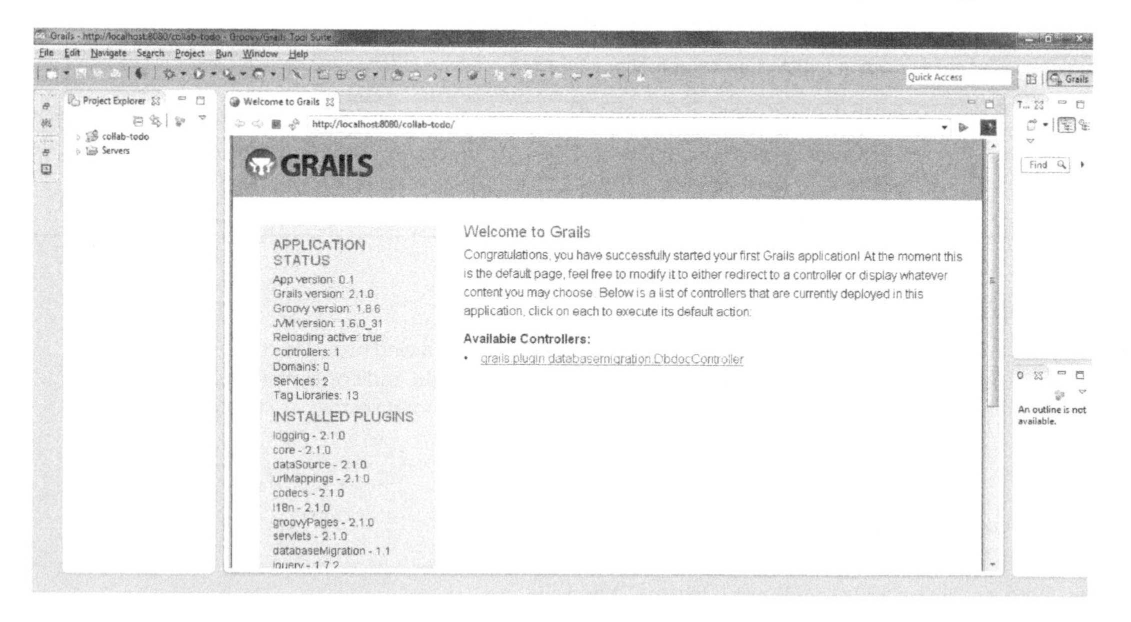

Figure 4-8. Default Grails page

Figure 4-8 shows the default Grails page. As you can see, it is not very interesting; it looks like a static page. However, as you'll see soon, there is some dynamism to this page. If you want to modify this page, it is the GSP grails-app\views\index.gsp.

Creating the Controller

A controller handles requests and creates or prepares the response. A controller can generate the response directly or delegate to a view. To create a controller class, use the Grails create-controller target. This creates a new Grails controller class in the grails-app/controllers directory, as well as the unit test for the controller class in test/unit. It also creates a grails-app/views/<controller name> directory if it doesn't exist already.

To create the TodoController class, you need to execute the create-controller target using an optional class name, as shown here:

```
> grails create-controller todo
```

If you don't supply the class name, you are prompted for one. The output of executing the create-controller target is shown here:

```
| Created file grails-app/controllers/collab/todo/TodoController.groovy
| Created file grails-app/views/todo
| Created file test/unit/collab/todo/TodoControllerTests.groovy
```

Notice that when running the create-controller with the optional class name, you can leave the class name in lowercase, and Grails will automatically uppercase it for you so that it follows the standard Groovy class naming convention.

To create the controller using GGTS, click on the controllers in the collab-todo project hierarchy, and then use New ➤ Controller as shown in Figure 4-9. Type "Todo" in the create-controller wizard as illustrated in Figure 4-10.

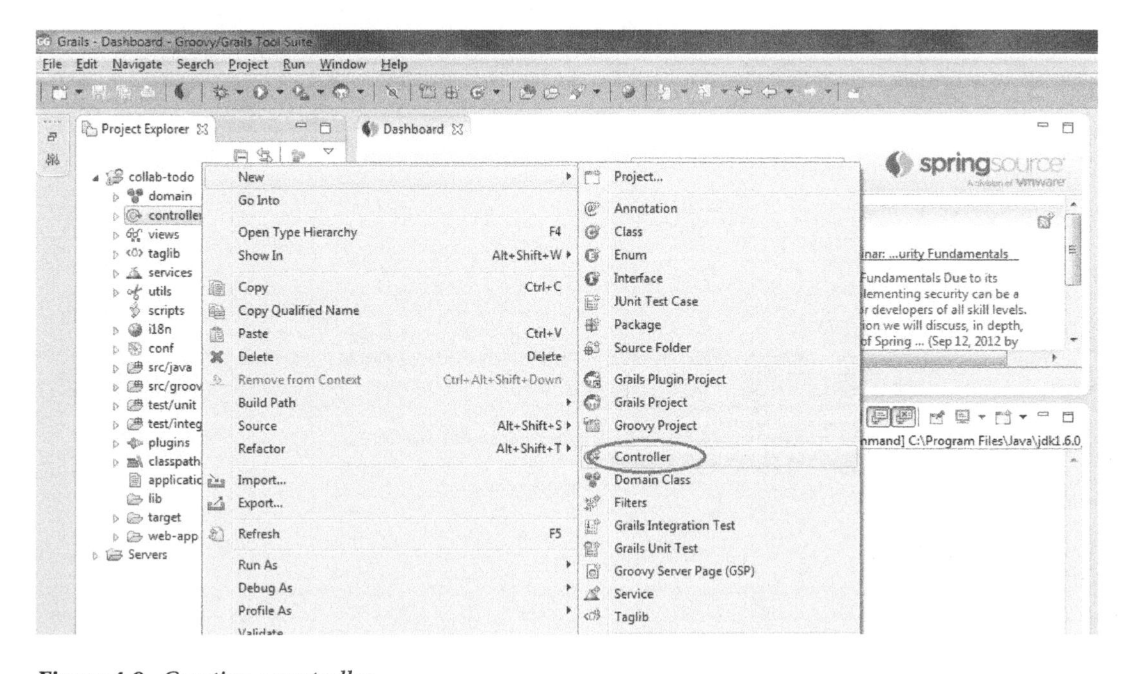

Figure 4-9. *Creating a controller*

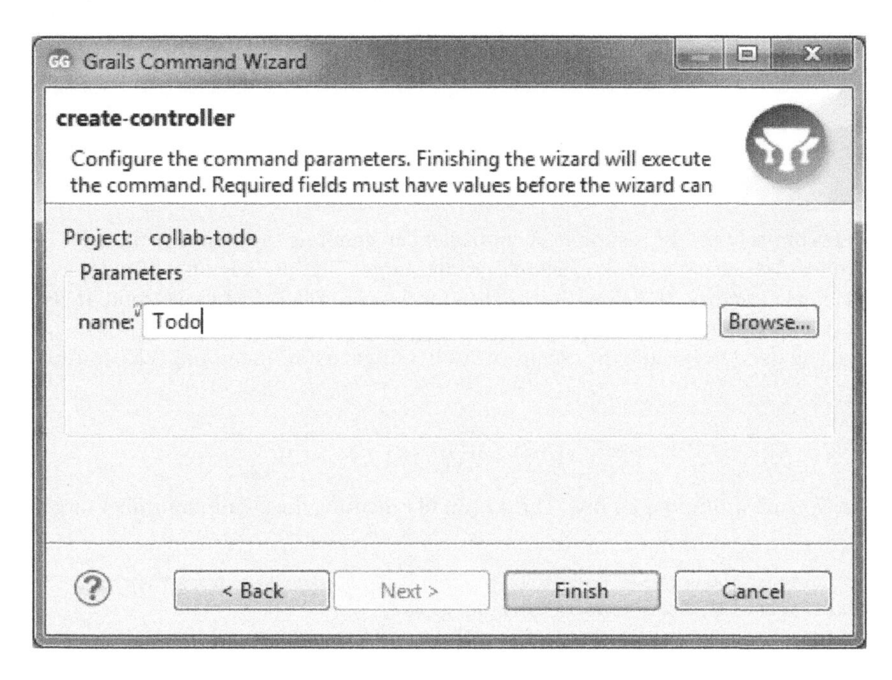

Figure 4-10. *Controller name*

This creates the controller as well as the unit test for the controller, as illustrated in Figure 4-11.

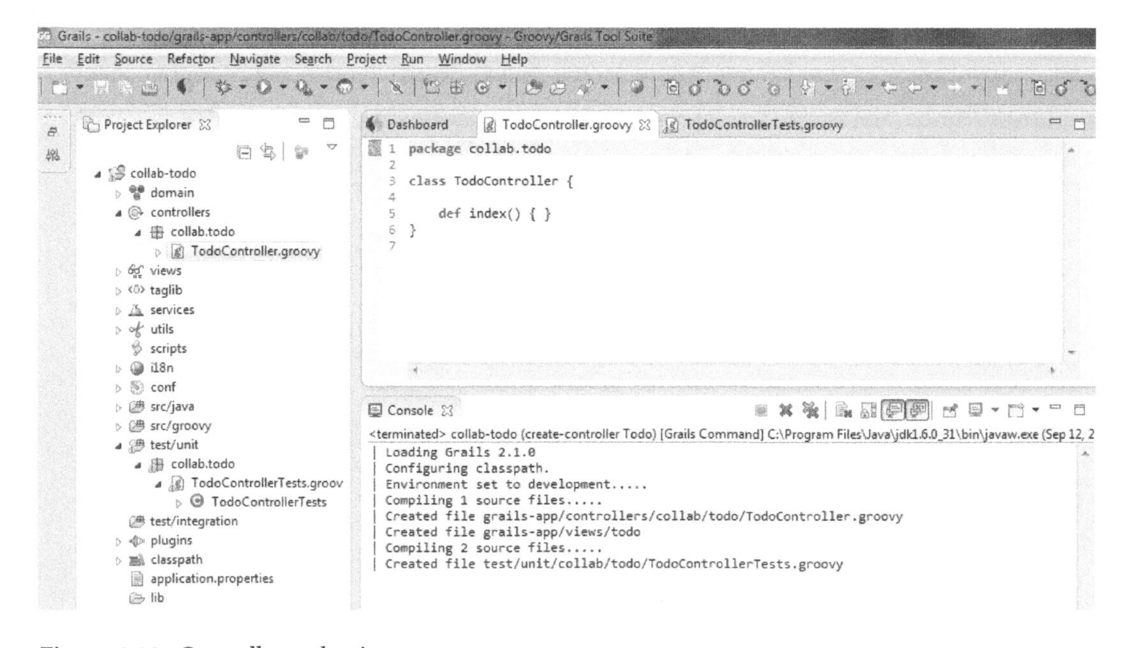

Figure 4-11. *Controller and unit test*

Listing 4-1 shows the generated TodoController class.

Listing 4-1. Grails-Generated TodoController Class

```
package collab.todo
class TodoController {

    def index() { }
}
```

The TodoController class in Listing 4-1 contains an empty index action. Chapter 5 will explain actions on the controller. We will print a simple response using one of the implicit methods, the render method, which comes with controllers in Grails, as illustrated in Listing 4-2.

Listing 4-2. Using the render Method

```
package collab.todo
class TodoController {

    def index() {
 render "create new tasks"
 }
}
```

Now run the application by typing "run-app" in the command window as explained earlier. After changing TodoController to look like it does in Listing 4-2, refresh your browser to reveal a new TodoController link on the initial page, as shown in Figure 4-12. Clicking on the controller shows the response, as illustrated in Figure 4-13.

APPLICATION STATUS

App version: 0.1
Grails version: 2.1.0
Groovy version: 1.8.6
JVM version: 1.6.0_31
Reloading active: true
Controllers: 2
Domains: 1
Services: 2
Tag Libraries: 13

INSTALLED PLUGINS

logging - 2.1.0
core - 2.1.0
i18n - 2.1.0
groovyPages - 2.1.0
dataSource - 2.1.0
codecs - 2.1.0
servlets - 2.1.0
urlMappings - 2.1.0
databaseMigration - 1.1
jquery - 1.7.2
resources - 1.1.6
tomcat - 2.1.0
webxml - 1.4.1
controllers - 2.1.0
domainClass - 2.1.0
mimeTypes - 2.1.0
converters - 2.1.0
filters - 2.1.0
scaffolding - 2.1.0
hibernate - 2.1.0
validation - 2.1.0
services - 2.1.0
cache - 1.0.0

Welcome to Grails

Congratulations, you have successfully started your first Grails application! At the moment this is the default page, feel free to modify it to either redirect to a controller or display whatever content you may choose. Below is a list of controllers that are currently deployed in this application, click on each to execute its default action:

Available Controllers:

- collab.todo.TodoController
- grails.plugin.databasemigration.DbdocController

Figure 4-12. *Initial Grails page with the TodoController link added*

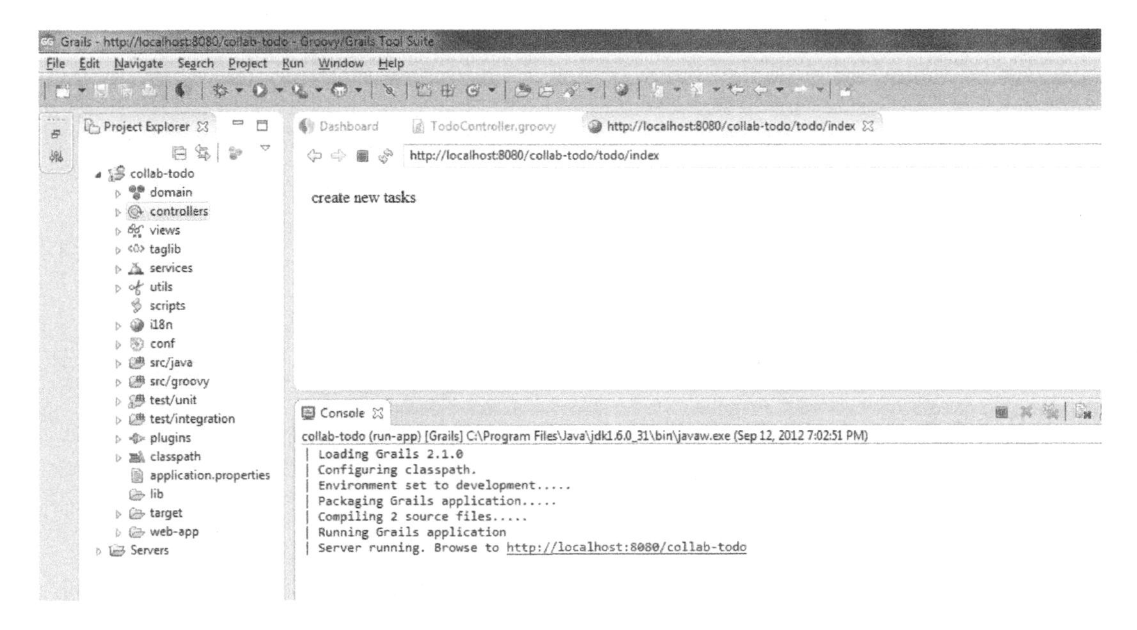

Figure 4-13. *Rendering the response*

Testing the Controller

At the time of creating the controller, Grails also creates unit tests for the controller as discussed earlier. Listing 4-3 illustrates the unit test generated by Grails, and Listing 4-4 tests the controller.

Listing 4-3. Generated Test

```
package collab.todo

import grails.test.mixin.*
import org.junit.*

/**
 * See the API for {@link grails.test.mixin.web.ControllerUnitTestMixin} for usage instructions
 */
@TestFor(TodoController)
class TodoControllerTests {

    void testSomething() {
       fail "Implement me"
    }
}
```

The TodoController class in Listing 4-2 renders a textual response. To test this controller, we assert the value of the response as illustrated in Listing 4-4.

Listing 4-4. Testing the Controller

```
package collab.todo

import grails.test.mixin.*
import org.junit.*

/**
 * See the API for {@link grails.test.mixin.web.ControllerUnitTestMixin} for usage instructions
 */
@TestFor(TodoController)
class TodoControllerTests {

    void testSomething() {
                controller.index()
       assert "create new tasks" == response.text
    }
}
```

To run the test, we use the same command window that we use to run the application. Instead of typing "run-app" in the command window, type "test-app" (you can also type this target on the command line) and browse to the URL presented in the console to view the test report as illustrated in Figure 4-14.

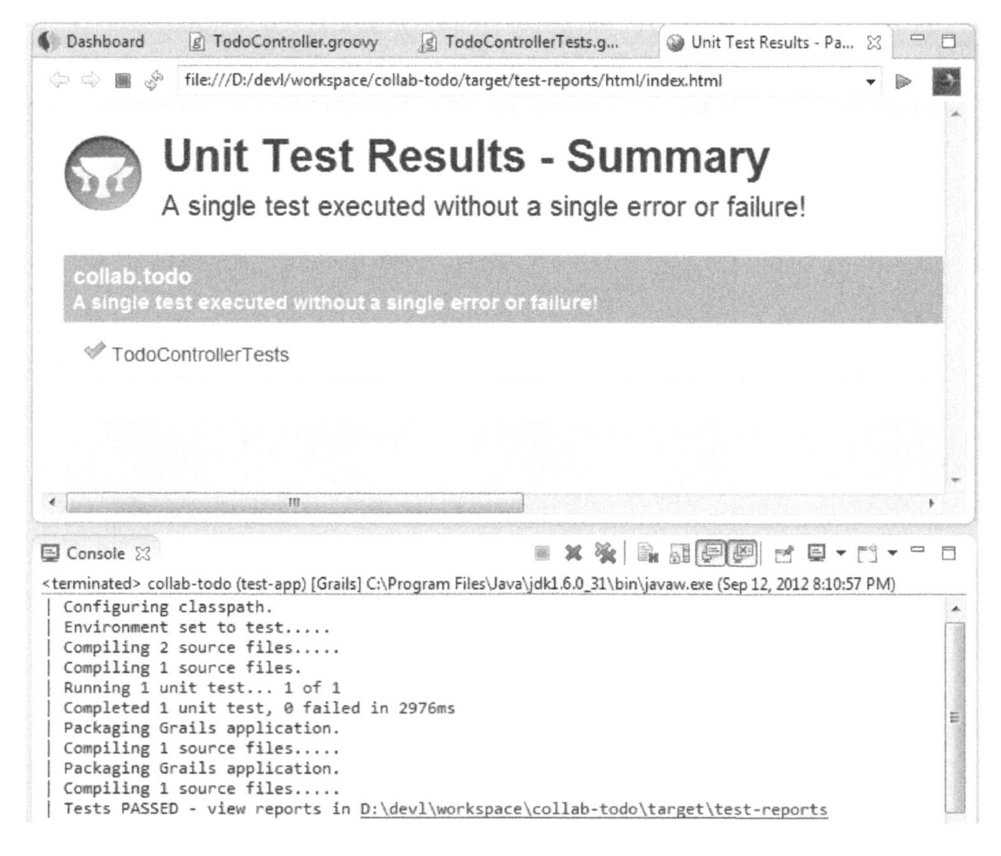

Figure 4-14. *Test report*

Scaffolding

Scaffolding lets you auto-generate a whole application for a given domain class including views and controller *actions* for CRUD operations. Scaffolding can be either static or dynamic; both types of scaffolding generate the exact same code. The main difference is that in static scaffolding, the generated code is available to the user prior to compile time and can be easily modified if necessary. In dynamic scaffolding, however, the code is generated in memory at runtime and is not visible to the user. We will explain both dynamic and static scaffolding, but before that we will create a domain class and then auto-generate a whole application for it using scaffolding.

Creating a Domain Class

At this point, the application we created doesn't really do anything; it just renders a simple textual response. We will move on by creating a domain class. To create a domain class, use the Grails create-domain-class target. This creates a new Grails domain class in the grails-app/domain directory, as well as a unit test for the domain class in test/unit.

To create the Todo domain class, you need to execute the create-domain-class target using an optional class name, as shown here:

```
> grails createdomain-class todo
```

If you don't supply the class name, you are prompted for one. The output of executing the create-domain-class target is shown here:

```
| Created file grails-app/domain/collab/todo/Todo.groovy
| Created file test/unit/collab/todo/TodoTests.groovy
```

Notice that when running the create-domain-class target with the optional class name, you can leave the class name in lowercase, and Grails will automatically uppercase it for you so that it follows the standard Groovy class naming convention.

To create the domain class using GGTS, click domain in the project hierarchy and then use New ➤ Domain Class as illustrated in Figure 4-15.

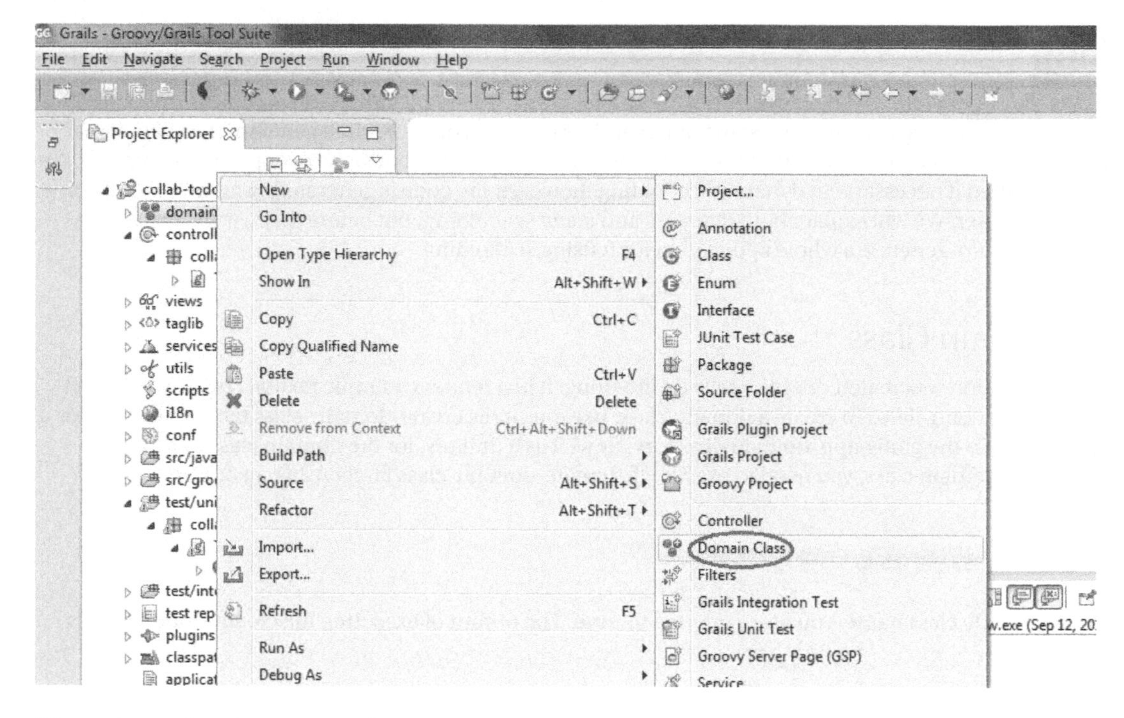

Figure 4-15. *Creating Domain class*

Listing 4-5 shows the generated Todo domain class.

Listing 4-5. Grails-Generated Todo Domain Class

```
package collab.todo
class Todo {

    static constraints = {
    }
}
```

The Todo domain class in Listing 4-5 appears to be the most basic of Groovy classes. As you will learn in the next couple of sections and in the next two chapters, there is more to Grails domain classes than meets the eye.

Listing 4-6 shows the Todo domain class after adding the fields shown in the UML diagram in Figure 4-5.

Listing 4-6. Todo Domain Class After Adding Attributes, Constraints, and the toString() Method

```
 1. class Todo {
 2.
 3.   String name
 4.   String note
 5.   Date createdDate
 6.   Date dueDate
 7.   Date completedDate
 8.   String priority
 9.   String status
10.
```

```
11.   static constraints = {
12.     name(blank:false)
13.     createdDate()
14.     priority()
15.     status()
16.     note(maxSize:1000, nullable:true)
17.     completedDate(nullable:true)
18.     dueDate(nullable:true)
19.   }
20.
21.   String toString() {
22.     name
23.   }
24. }
```

In Listing 4-6, you see that lines 3-9 are several fields of both String and Date types that you would expect to find in a Todo domain class. However, there are some additional properties you don't see that are implicit to a Grails domain class by convention. They include the id and version properties.

The id property, as you might expect, represents a unique auto-incrementing identifier and is null until the object is initially saved. The version property is a Hibernate mechanism for managing optimistic locking. Each time an object is saved, its version number gets incremented, and like the id, it is initially null. Before Hibernate saves any object, it first checks the version number in the database, and if the versions don't match the object about to be saved—meaning it was already modified since the last read—Hibernate will throw an org.hibernate.StaleObjectStateException.

Lines 11-19 demonstrate the Grails construct of constraints. These are basically rules governing the values of the properties. For example, line 12 states the name property is required and may not be empty using a blank:false constraint, while the note, completedDate, and dueDate properties on lines 16-18 are allowed to be null. Also, note that the note property on line 16 has a maximum length of 1,000 characters. In addition to constraining the properties, the constraints dictate the order of fields on the edit pages as well as the types of HTML form fields rendered by the Grails scaffolding. The order of the constraints represents the order of the fields on the page. While a String is usually represented by an HTML input field of type text, a String property with a maxSize is usually rendered as an HTML input field of a text area to support the larger amounts of input data.

Domain classes can also have behavior implemented as methods. Lines 21-23 show the toString() method being overridden. The default toString() behavior of a Grails domain class is to print the class name followed by a colon and the object ID. To make the toString() a little more helpful, line 21 prepends the name property of the Todo instance.

This section has not even scratched the surface of domain classes. You will learn more about them in Chapter 6.

Dynamic Scaffolding

As explained earlier, the dynamic scaffolding generates controller actions and views for CRUD applications at runtime. To dynamically scaffold a domain class, we need a controller. We created a controller (TodoController) in Listing 4.1. To use the dynamic scaffolding, change the index action to a scaffold property and assign it the domain class, as shown in Listing 4-7. That's all there is to it. This causes List Page, Create Page, Edit Page, and Show Page views, as well as delete functionality, to be generated for the specified domain class.

Listing 4-7. Dynamic Scaffolding-Enabled TodoController

```
package collab.todo
  class TodoController {
  static scaffold = Todo
}
```

After changing TodoController to look like it does in Listing 4-7, refresh your browser and click the TodoController link on the welcome page.

Selecting the TodoController link brings you to the Todo List page shown in Figure 4-16.

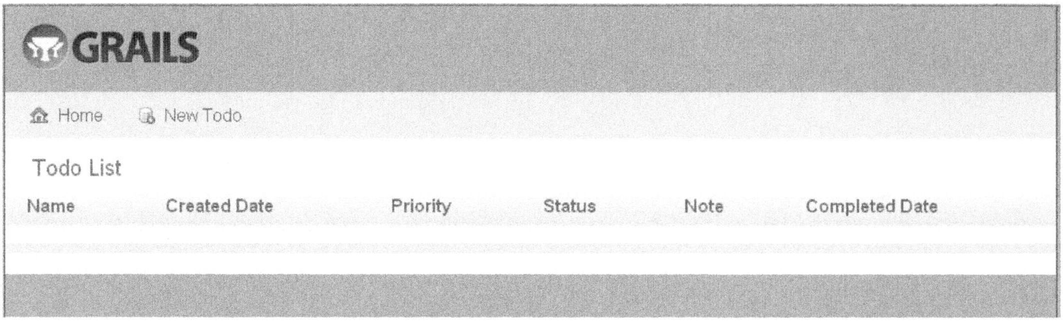

Figure 4-16. *Todo List page*

From the list page shown in Figure 4-16, you have the ability to create new domain objects (as shown in Figure 4-17) by clicking the New Todo button on the navigation bar.

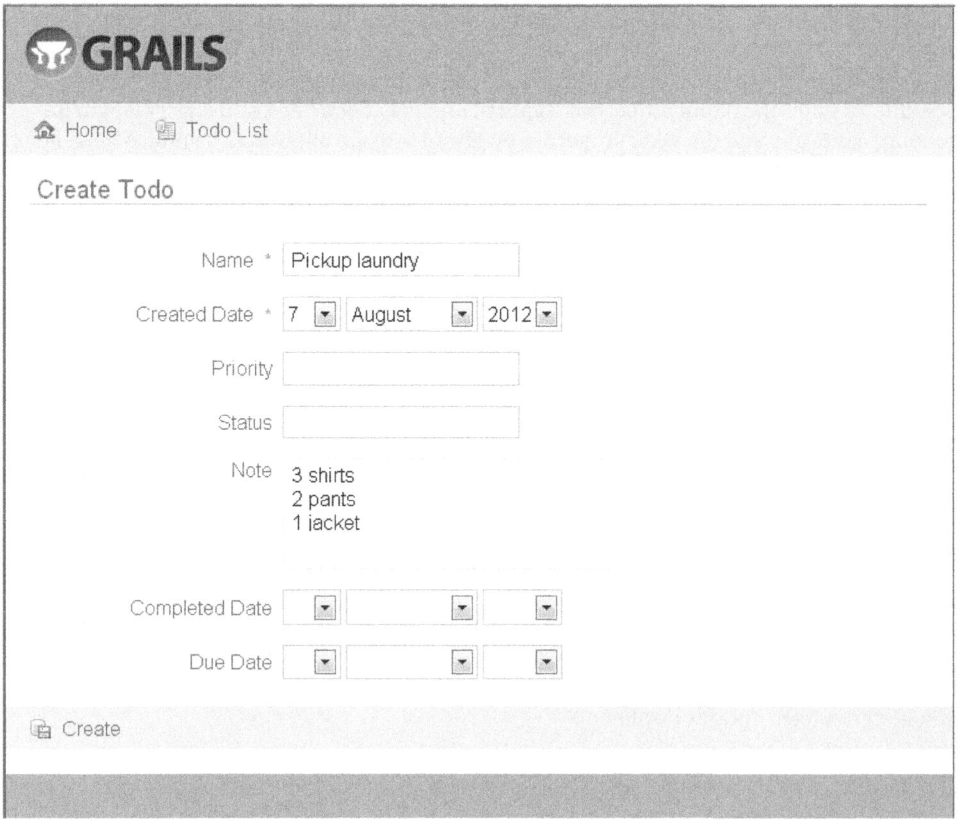

Figure 4-17. *Create Todo page*

The save page displays the list of properties in the order in which the constraints are ordered as shown in the Create Todo page in Figure 4-17. Note that the Grails scaffolding displays the edit fields in the appropriate date type format. A string is displayed as an HTML text input field, while createdDate is displayed as a series of drop-downs for the day of month, month, year, hour, and seconds. In addition, the note property is displayed as an HTML text area input due to the maxSize constraint. That's not all: the Grails scaffolding is also smart enough to use the constraints for doing form validation, as shown in Figure 4-18.

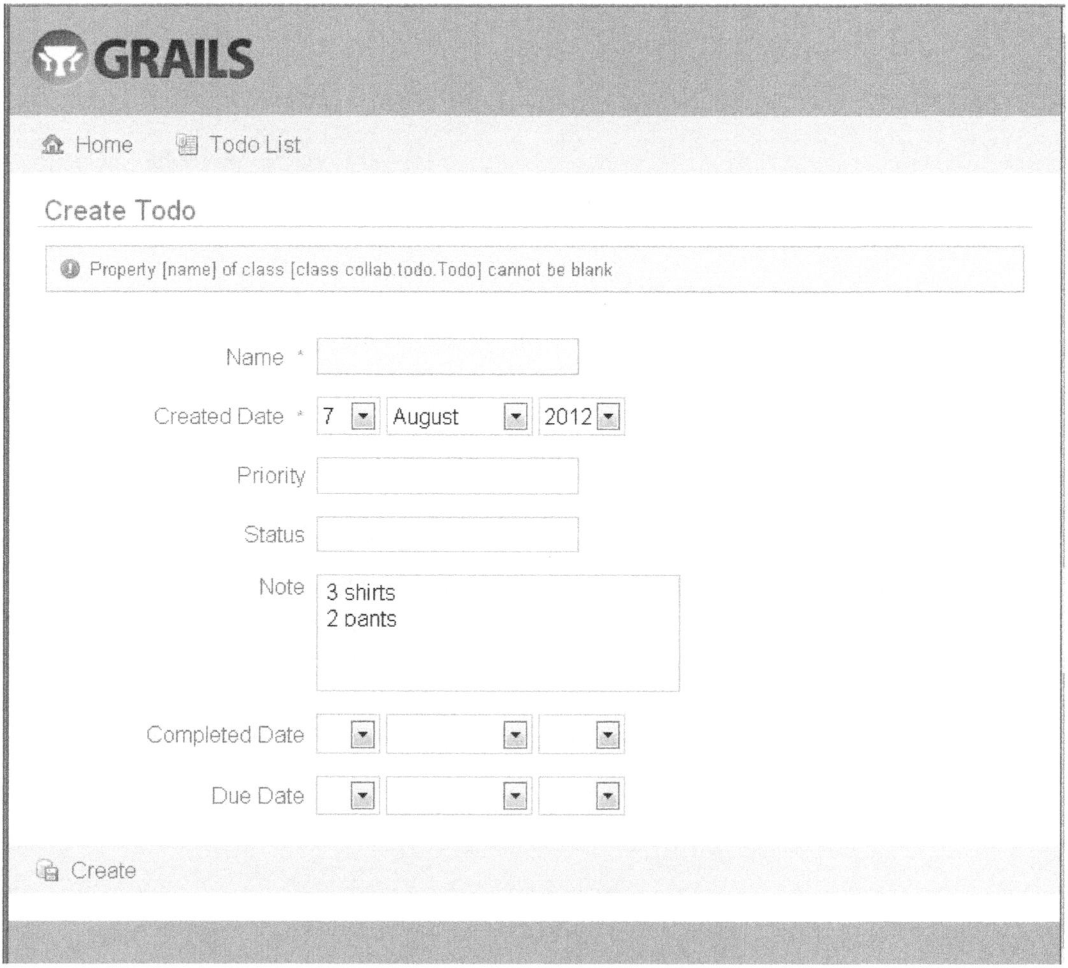

Figure 4-18. *Validation errors*

Notice in Figure 4-18 that a validation message is displayed at the top of the page if the form is submitted with an empty name. The blank:false constraint makes the name property required.

Figure 4-19 shows a read-only view.

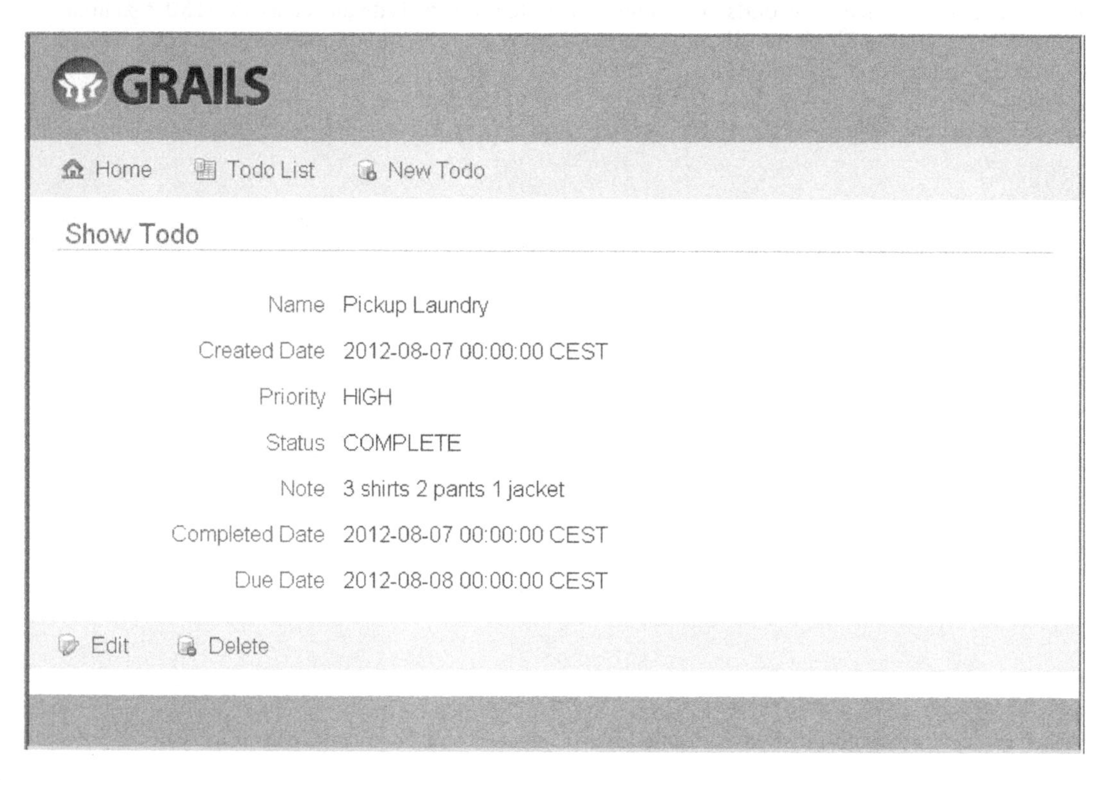

Figure 4-19. *Show Todo page*

The Show Todo page displays all the properties and values. It also provides access to the Edit Todo page, as shown in Figure 4-20, where you can delete the domain object.

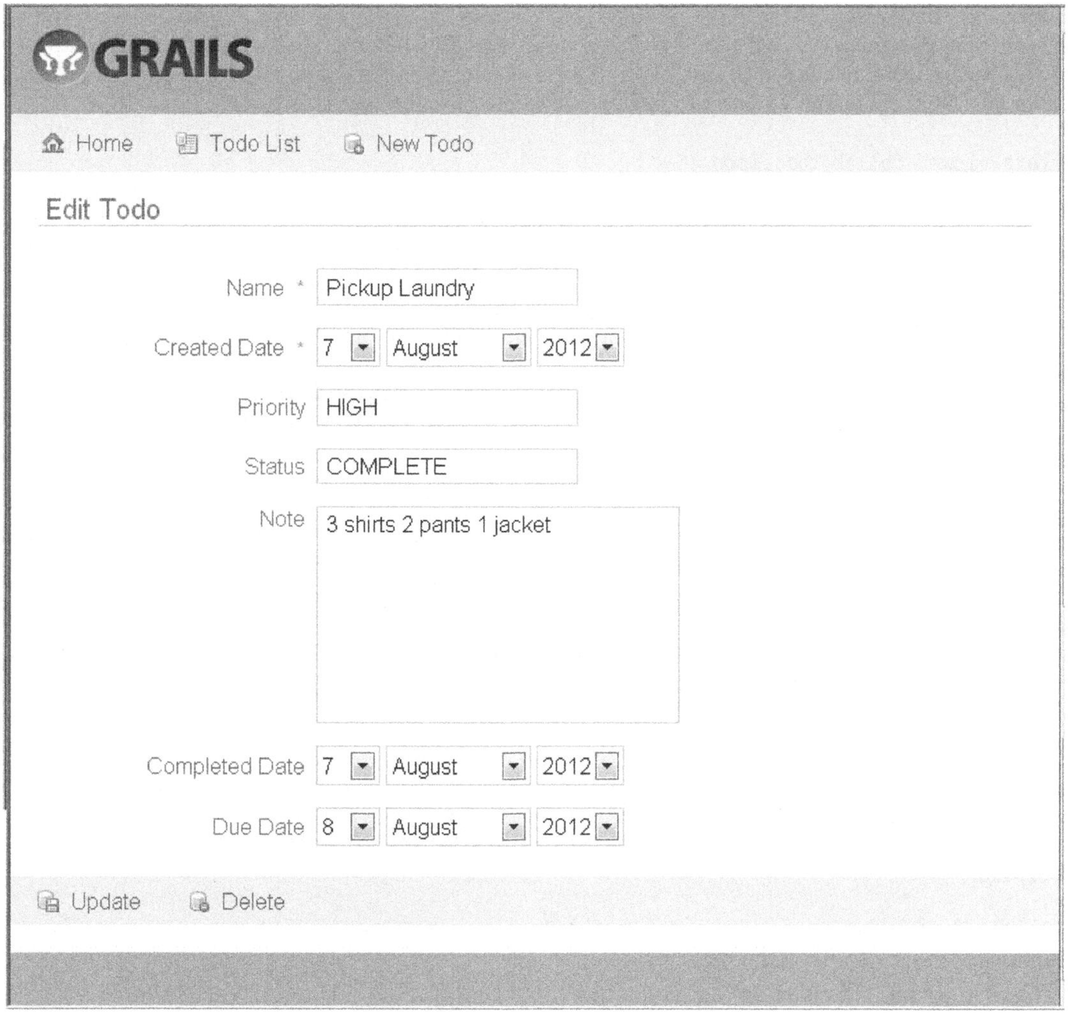

Figure 4-20. Edit Todo page

The Edit Todo page, shown in Figure 4-20, is really the same as the Create Todo page, except the data is repopulated with the domain object values, and it has Update and Delete buttons at the bottom of the page.

Static Scaffolding

Dynamic scaffolding is particularly useful in testing the domain class and developing the prototype, but you may want to customize the logic and views. You can use static scaffolding for this purpose. Static scaffolding can also serve as a great learning tool, for instance, to understand the mechanics of a CRUD application. To generate the controller for the domain class Todo using static scaffolding, use the following command:

```
> grails generate-controller  collab.todo.Todo
```

With this command, Grails generates the TodoController class inside grails-app/controllers. The generate-controller command is different from the create-controller command introduced earlier, in that the create-controller command creates an empty controller with a default action index(), while the generate-controller command creates the controller with all the code for the CRUD operation. Similarly, to generate views, use the following command:

```
> grails generate-views  collab.todo.Todo
```

With this command, Grails generates .gsp files inside grails-app/views/todo.

Grails also provides the possibility to generate both controllers and views in one command, like so:

```
> grails generate-all  collab.todo.Todo
```

One important thing to keep in mind when using static scaffolding: because all the controller code and views code are generated for the domain class, Grails will not update this code if the domain class is changed, and will relinquish this responsibility to the developer.

Finishing the Remaining Domains

Now that you've created the Todo domain and controller classes, you can repeat the steps for creating the domain classes and controller classes for the remaining domain and controllers: Category and User. Then you can add the relationships between the domain classes.

As illustrated in the UML diagram in Figure 4-5, the Category class is very simple. Listing 4-8 shows the code after generating the class using the Grails create-domain-class target and adding the properties from the UML diagram.

Listing 4-8. Category Domain Class

```
package collab.todo
class Category {
  String name
  String description

  static constraints = {
    name(blank:false)
  }

  String toString() {
    name
  }
}
```

In Listing 4-8, you see the Category class has just name and description properties and an overloaded toString() method that returns the name property. This overloaded toString() method becomes important later, because it is used to populate an HTML select field. Without it, the select field would only display the category's id, making it difficult to differentiate categories in the list. The Category class also includes a constraint, which requires the name property.

The User domain class follows the same pattern as both the Todo and Category classes. Listing 4-9 shows the code after generating the class with the Grails create-domain-class target and adding the properties from the UML diagram.

Listing 4-9. User Domain Class

```
package collab.todo
class User {
  String userName
  String firstName
  String lastName

  static constraints = {
    userName(blank:false,unique:true)
    firstName(blank:false)
    lastName(blank:false)
  }

  String  toString () {
"$lastName, $firstName"
  }
}
```

In Listing 4-9, the User class contains userName, firstName, and lastName properties. It also contains constraints that make all properties required and it forces the userName property to be unique in the database. Finally, the overridden toString()method returns the user's name in a last-name-first format.

Finishing the Remaining Controllers

The controller classes are carbon copies of TodoController. Listing 4-10 shows CategoryController after it was created with the Grails create-controller target and the scaffolding variable set.

Listing 4-10. CategoryController

```
package collab.todo
class CategoryController {

  static scaffold = Category
}
```

Listing 4-11 shows UserController.

Listing 4-11. UserController

```
package collab.todo
class UserController {

  static scaffold = User
}
```

After completing the Category and User domain and controller classes, the application start page displays all three controllers. In addition, CRUD pages for both Category and User are available when clicking on the respective controller links. Grails also provides the means to do statistics. At the command prompt, type grails stats, and you should see output similar to the following:

```
D:\devl\workspace\collab-todo>grails stats
```

```
+----------------------+-------+-------+
| Name                 | Files |  LOC  |
+----------------------+-------+-------+
| Controllers          |     3 |    12 |
| Domain Classes       |     3 |    54 |
| Unit Tests           |     6 |    60 |
+----------------------+-------+-------+
| Totals               |    12 |   126 |
+----------------------+-------+-------+
```

Creating Domain Relationships

At this point, you have three standalone domain classes—Todo, Category, and User—with no relationships between them. But remember that the UML diagram in Figure 4-5 showed that users had user-defined categories as well as todos that were organized by categories. Now it's time to represent those oneto-many relationships between the domain classes using the belongsTo and hasMany properties.

Listing 4-12 shows the new Todo class, which shows the relationships with User and Category.

Listing 4-12. Todo Domain Class with Relationships to the User and Category Domain Classes

```
class Todo {
  String name
  String note
  Date createdDate
  Date dueDate
  Date completedDate
  String priority
  String status
  User owner
  Category category

  static belongsTo = [User, Category]

  static constraints = {
    name(blank:false)
    createdDate()
    priority()
    status()
    note(maxSize:1000, nullable:true)
    completedDate(nullable:true)
    dueDate(nullable:true)
  }
```

```
  String toString() {
    name
  }

}
```

Notice in Listing 4-12 that the relationship is defined with the belongsTo property to the User and Category classes. We've also added new owner and category properties. belongsTo tells GORM to delete the todo if either the associated user or the category is deleted. Scaffolding renders these relationships as the select fields on the Create Todo and Edit Todo screens, as shown in Figure 4-21.

Figure 4-21. *Create Todo edit page with Category and Owner select fields*

Like the Todo class, the Category class has a belongsTo relationship with User, but it also has a collection of Todos, as shown in Listing 4-13.

Listing 4-13. Category Domain Class with Relationships to the User and Todo Domain Classes

```
class Category {
  String name
  String description
  User user
  static belongsTo = User
  static hasMany = [todos: Todo]

  static constraints = {
    name(blank:false)
  }

  String toString() {
    name
  }

}
```

Notice that in addition to belongsTo associated with User, Category contains a hasMany property, which is a map designating a one-to-many relationship with the Todo class. Also, the collection is available via the todos property.

Finally, the User class in Listing 4-14 has now defined its relationships with Todo and Category.

Listing 4-14. User Domain Class with Relationships to the Todo and Category Domain Classes

```
class User {
  String userName
  String firstName
  String lastName

  static hasMany = [todos: Todo, categories: Category]

  static constraints = {
    userName(blank:false,unique:true)
    firstName(blank:false)
    lastName(blank:false)
  }

  String  toString () {
    "$lastName, $firstName"
  }

}
```

As shown in Listing 4-14, the changes required to include the relationships with the Todo and Category classes only take a single line. The hasMany property identifies collections named todos and categories.

■ **Note** We'll discuss relationships in more detail in Chapter 6.

As stated earlier, when you run the application, Hibernate creates a database schema based on domain classes. Figure 4-22 shows an entity relational diagram of the domain classes so far.

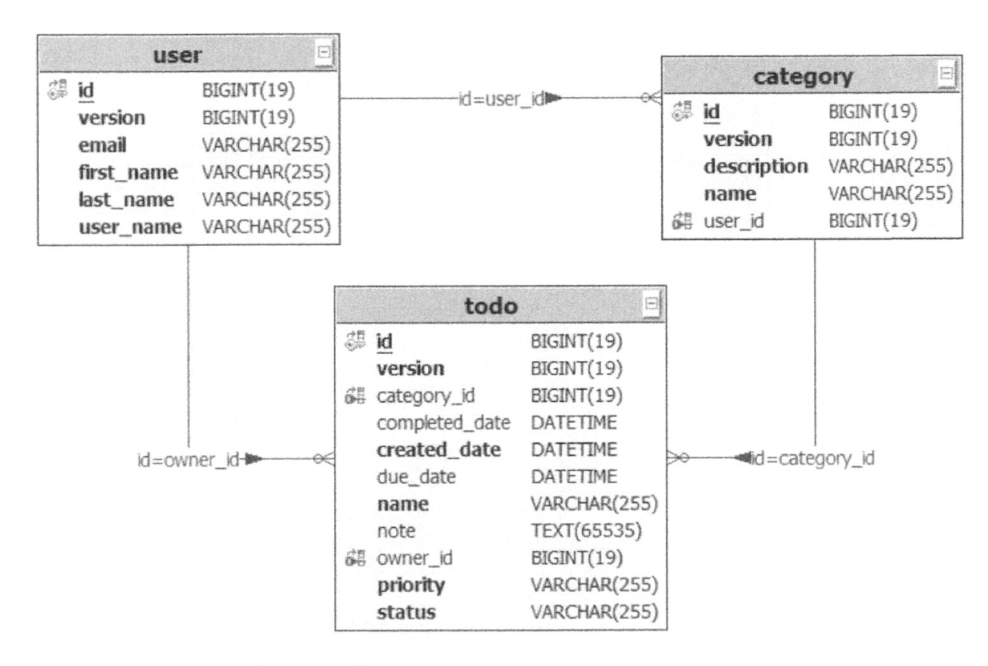

Figure 4-22. *Entity relational diagram*

Notice that the entity relational diagram looks almost identical to the UML diagram shown in Figure 4-5. Hibernate creates three tables with table names based on the class names. It also creates fields for each of the properties using underscores instead of CamelCase. Also, notice the id and version columns are the Hibernate columns for object identity and optimistic locking. Hibernate also creates foreign keys to represent the relationships between the domain classes.

During development, out-of-the-box Grail uses a Tomcat web container and an embedded H2 database. However, many operational environments use other web containers or applications servers and use server-based databases. In Chapter 12, we will look at how to package and deploy an application to an alternative operating environment.

H2 Console

As discussed earlier, Grails 2.0 enables the H2 database console in development mode (at the URI /dbconsole) so that the in-memory database can be easily queried from the browser. To see the dbconsole in action, browse to `http://localhost:8080/collab-todo/dbconsole`. The default log in parameters should match the default in grails-app/ conf/Datasource.groovy, as illustrated in Figure 4-23.

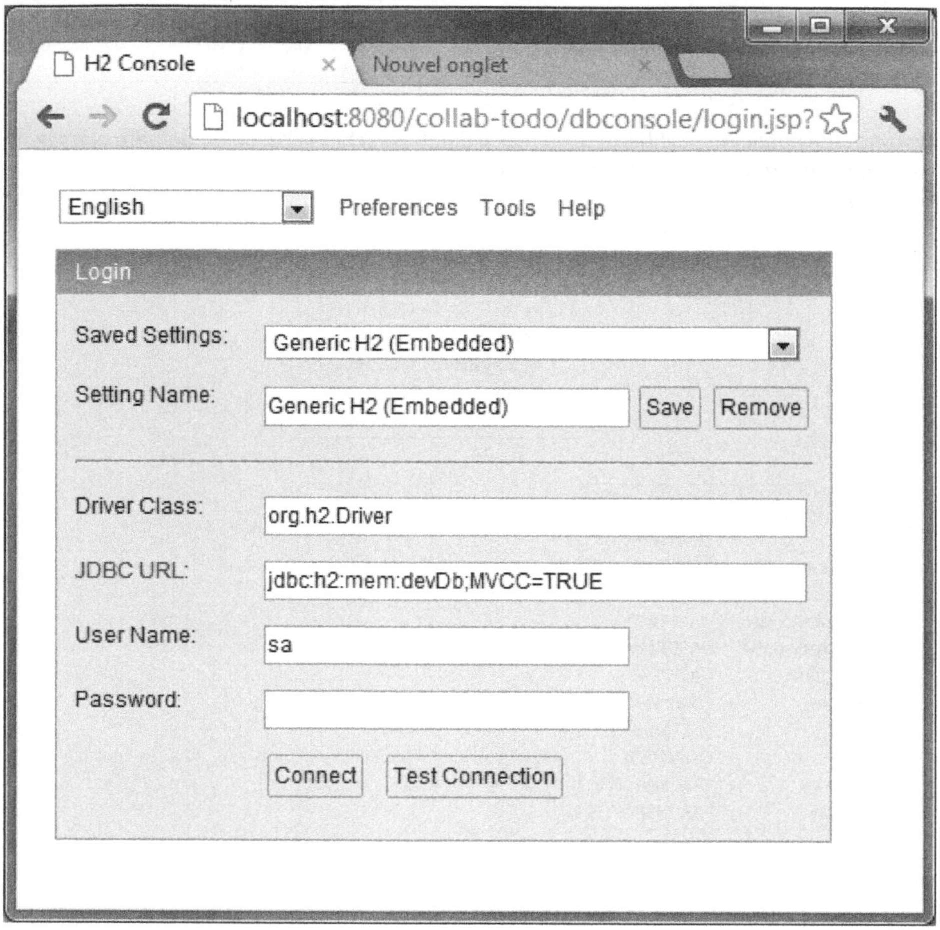

Figure 4-23. *H2 console*

Now, create a user, category, and todo task in our Collab-Todo application and then enter SELECT * from USER in the database console. The user we created in the application will show up, as illustrated in Figure 4-24.

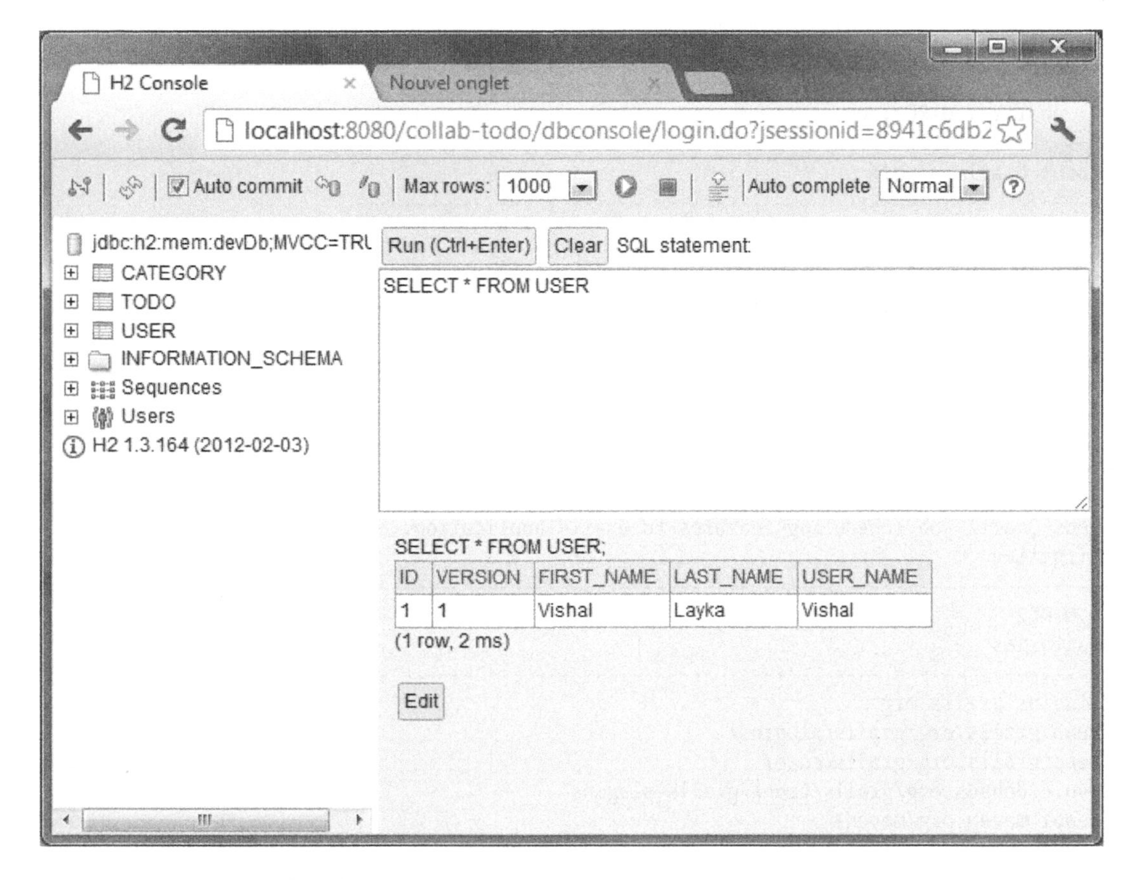

Figure 4-24. *Querying the table in H2*

Grails Plugins

In Grails, there is the likelihood that a plugin already exists that does what you need, so you may want to find out which plugins are already available. To see a list of available plugins, call the list-plugins command target:

```
> grails list-plugins
```

This command establishes a network connection to a remote server. Invoking the list-plugins target displays a table of all plugins, along with the following output:

```
.....
To find more info about plugin type 'grails plugin-info [NAME]'
To install type 'grails install-plugin [NAME] [VERSION]'
For further info visit http://grails.org/Plugins
```

You may want to know more about a particular plugin without installing it. This can be accomplished by calling the `plugin-info` command target with the plugin's name as a parameter.

```
D:\devl\workspace\collab-todo>grails plugin-info quartz
```

Invoking the command yields the output as shown:

```
| Downloading: quartz-1.0-RC2.pom
--------------------------------------------------------------------------
Information about Grails plugin
--------------------------------------------------------------------------
Name: quartz    | Latest release: 1.0-RC2
--------------------------------------------------------------------------
Quartz plugin for Grails
--------------------------------------------------------------------------
Author: Sergey Nebolsin, Graeme Rocher
--------------------------------------------------------------------------
Author's e-mail: nebolsin@gmail.com
--------------------------------------------------------------------------
Find more info here: http://grails.org/plugin/quartz
--------------------------------------------------------------------------
This plugin adds Quartz job scheduling features to Grails application.
Dependency Definition
--------------------------------------------------------------------------
    :quartz:1.0-RC2
Required Repositories
--------------------------------------------------------------------------
     http://plugins.grails.org
     http://repo.grails.org/grails/plugins/
     http://repo.grails.org/grails/core/
     http://svn.codehaus.org/grails/trunk/grails-plugins
     http://repo1.maven.org/maven2/
Transitive Dependencies
--------------------------------------------------------------------------
     org.hibernate:hibernate-core:3.6.10.Final (compile)
     org.quartz-scheduler:quartz:1.8.4 (compile)
To get info about specific release of plugin 'grails plugin-info [NAME] [VERSION]'
To get list of all plugins type 'grails list-plugins'
To install latest version of plugin type 'grails install-plugin [NAME]'
To install specific version of plugin type 'grails install-plugin [NAME] [VERSION]'
For further info visit http://grails.org/Plugins
```

Installing a plugin from the command line is just as easy. For example, to install quartz, type the following on the command line:

```
> grails install-plugin quartz
```

To remove a plugin, call the uninstall-plugin command target. To uninstall the quartz plugin:

```
> grails uninstall-plugin quartz
```

To install a plugin in GGTS, right-click on plugins under the project hierarchy and then open the Grails Plugin Manager, which is shown in Figure 4-25.

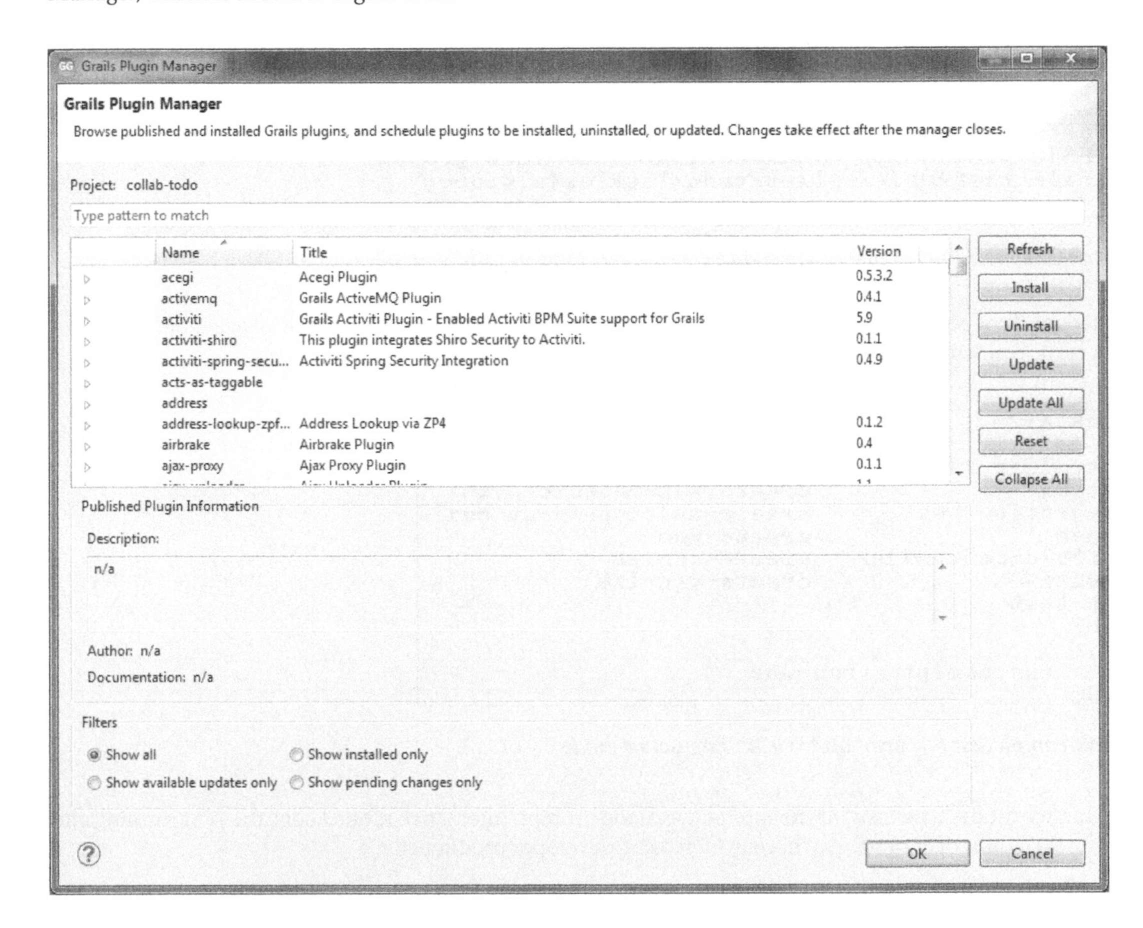

Figure 4-25. *Grails plugin manager*

Grails Interactive Mode

Until this point, all of the Grails commands that we have seen have been executed by running `grails` and passing a command name as an argument. With Grails interactive mode, there is no need to prefix every command with grails. For example, you might type something like the following on the command line:

```
grails create-domain-class collab.todo.Task
```

However, in interactive mode, you can type the shorter:

```
create-domain-class collab.todo.Task
```

To start interactive mode, enter the "`grails`" command with no arguments, as shown in Figure 4-26.

```
D:\devl\workspace\collab-todo>grails
| Enter a script name to run. Use TAB for completion:
grails>
```

Figure 4-26. *Grails interactive mode*

```
grails> create-domain-class collab.todo.Task
| Created file grails-app/domain/collab/todo/Task.groovy
| Created file test/unit/collab/todo/TaskTests.groovy
grails>
```

Figure 4-27. *Shorter commands in interactive mode*

In interactive mode, type "crea" followed by pressing Tab. Interactive mode returns a list of all available commands that start with "crea", as shown in Figure 4-28.

```
grails> create-

create-controller              create-domain-class
create-filters                 create-hibernate-cfg-xml
create-integration-test        create-multi-project-build
create-plugin                  create-pom
create-scaffold-controller     create-script
create-service                 create-tag-lib
create-unit-test
grails> run-

run-app        run-script    run-war
grails> run-
```

Figure 4-28. *Tab-completion for "crea" and "ru" in interactive mode*

To exit interactive mode, type "exit" at the interactive mode prompt. Interactive mode keeps the JVM running and allows for quicker execution of commands, thereby increasing developer productivity.

Summary

In this chapter, you learned that Grails is a new web development framework that combines the best of Java open source, conventions, the Groovy dynamic language, and the power of the Java platform.

You also saw how easy it is to develop a fully functional application using Grails scaffolding to do most of the work. In Chapter 5, you will learn how to make the application pretty and customize its look and feel, as well as how to make the controllers more functional. Then in Chapter 6, you will learn how to enhance the domain classes, including accessing more of the persistence features of GORM.

CHAPTER 5

Building the User Interface

Chapter 4 introduced the layering and components of Grails, and it showed you how to create a simple application using Grails scaffolding. In this chapter, you'll use the domain objects from Chapter 4 to start the process of creating an attractive, full-featured application using the Collab-Todo wireframe.

You will learn how to use Groovy Server Pages (GSP), Grails tags, Grails templates, and CSS to create a common look and feel across the application. You will create the login view and the controller actions to support it. Next, you will start to focus on user experience. You will look at validation, errors, and messages, and you'll learn how to customize them. To support the application, you will create a simple audit logging facility that leverages the Grails log controller property.

Starting with the End in Mind

The goal for this chapter is to create the look and feel for the Collab-Todo application's layout. Figure 5-1 shows a wireframe to give you an idea of how the application is laid out.

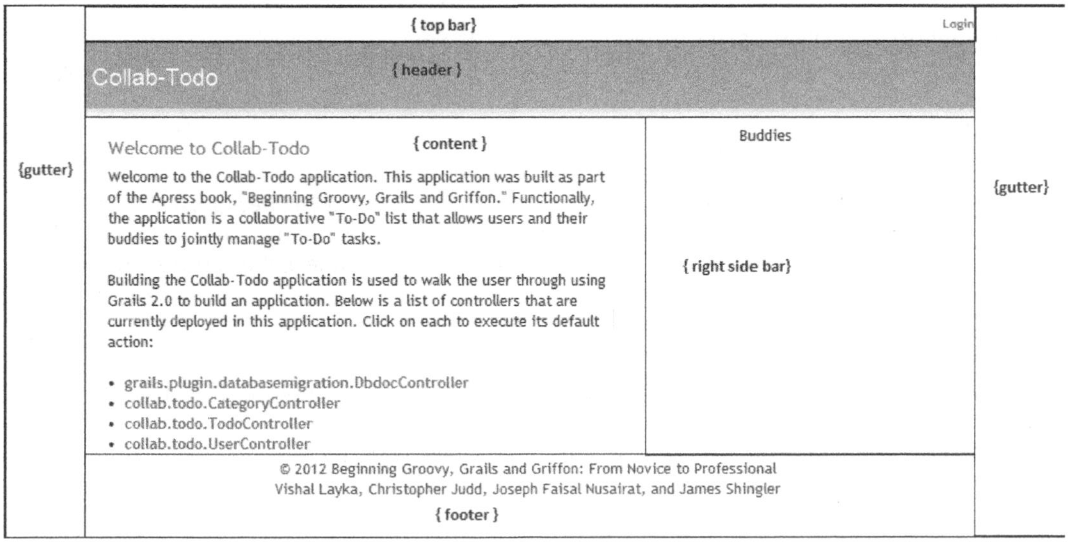

Figure 5-1. *The Collab-Todo wireframe*

The wireframe follows a common format: two columns centered on the page, gutters on both sides for spacing, and a header and footer. Table 5-1 describes each component.

Table 5-1. *Wireframe Components*

Component	Description
gutter	Provides whitespace on the edges of the browser so that the main content area is centered in the browser.
topbar	Provides the ability to log in and log out, and displays the user's first and last name when logged in.
header	Displays the application's title, "Collab-Todo."
content	This is the main content area of the application. The majority of the application data is displayed here.
right sidebar	In Chapter 8, we will use the right sidebar to display buddy list information.
footer	Displays copyright information.

Like most modern view technologies, Grails uses a layout and template-based approach to assemble the view/UI. A template is a view fragment that resides in the `grails-app/views` directory and starts with an underscore. The underscore is Grails' convention for signifying that GSP is a template. Best practices dictate that you should put templates that are associated with a specific domain, such as `User`, in the domain's view directory, such as `grails-app/views/user/_someTemplate.gsp`. You should put templates that are more generic or shared across views in a common place, such as `grails-app/views/common`.

A layout assembles the templates and positions them on the page. You create the layout using `main.gsp` (`grails-app/views/layouts/main.gsp`) and CSS (`web-app/css/main.css`). Create a couple of templates (`_topbar.gsp` and `_footer.gsp`) that will be common across all views, and then apply some CSS styling and leverage it in `main.gsp`.

Let's start with a simple footer to illustrate the point.

Creating the Footer

The goal is to display a simple copyright notice at the bottom of every page in the web site. As you might have guessed, you need to create a GSP fragment named `_footer.gsp` in the `grails-app/views/common` directory, and then add the `_footer.gsp` template to the layout using the `<g:render template="/common/footer" />`tag. You then need to style the footer by adding a `<div>` section to the main layout using a style class that you define in the `main.css`. Listing 5-1 shows what you need to do.

Listing 5-1. The Footer Template (_footer.gsp)

```
<span class="copyright">&copy; 2012 Beginning Groovy, Grails and Griffon: From Novice to
Professional<br />
Vishal Layka, Christopher Judd, Joseph Faisal Nusairat, and James Shingler
</span>
```

You need to add the copyright to the main layout (`main.gsp`) so that it's included on every page. This is where the `<g:render>` tag comes to your aid. You use the `<g:render>` tag, which has a template attribute, to insert templates into GSPs. All you have to do is add `<g:render template="/common/footer" />` to the bottom of `main.gsp`

■ **Note** By convention, the underscore and `.gsp` are omitted from the `template` attribute.

Figure 5-2 shows what happens when you reload the home page.

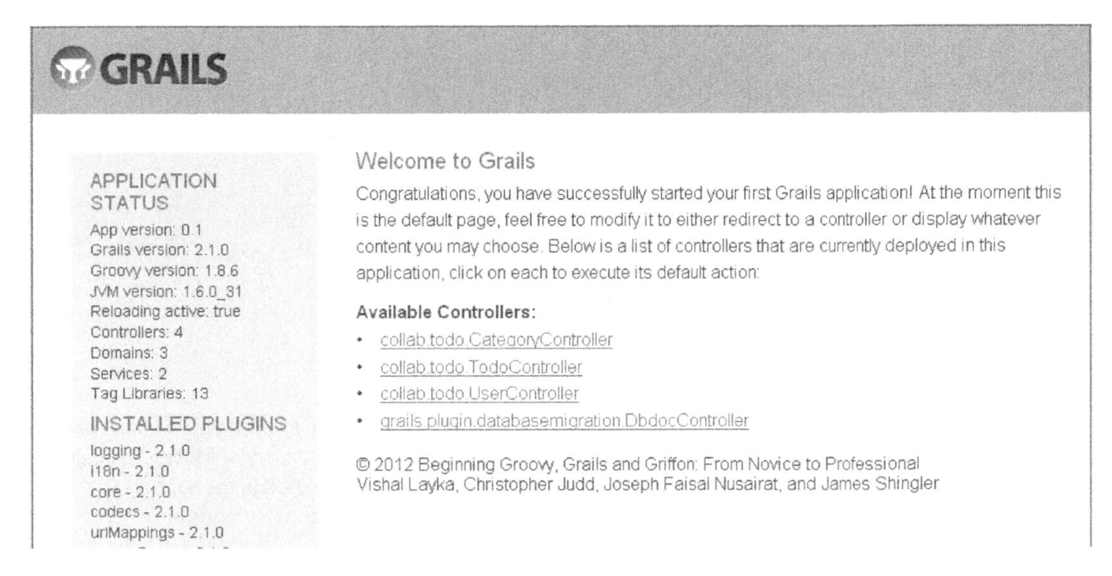

Figure 5-2. *Adding a copyright notice*

It would be nice if the copyright was centered and had a separator. You could just put the style information directly in the footer template, but a better solution, and a best practice, is to use CSS. To do so, add a `<div>` tag with the `id` attribute set to `footer` in the main layout, and define the `footer` style in `main.css`. Listing 5-2 shows the changes you need to make to `main.gsp`.

Listing 5-2. The Enhanced Main Layout (main.gsp)

```
<div id="footer">
        <g:render template="/common/footer" />
</div>
```

Listing 5-3 shows how to define the `footer` style.

Listing 5-3. The Footer Style

```
#footer {
   clear:both;
text-align: center;
   padding: 3px;
border-top: 1px solid #333;
}
```

Remove the application status block from `index.gsp`. Figure 5-3 shows the results.

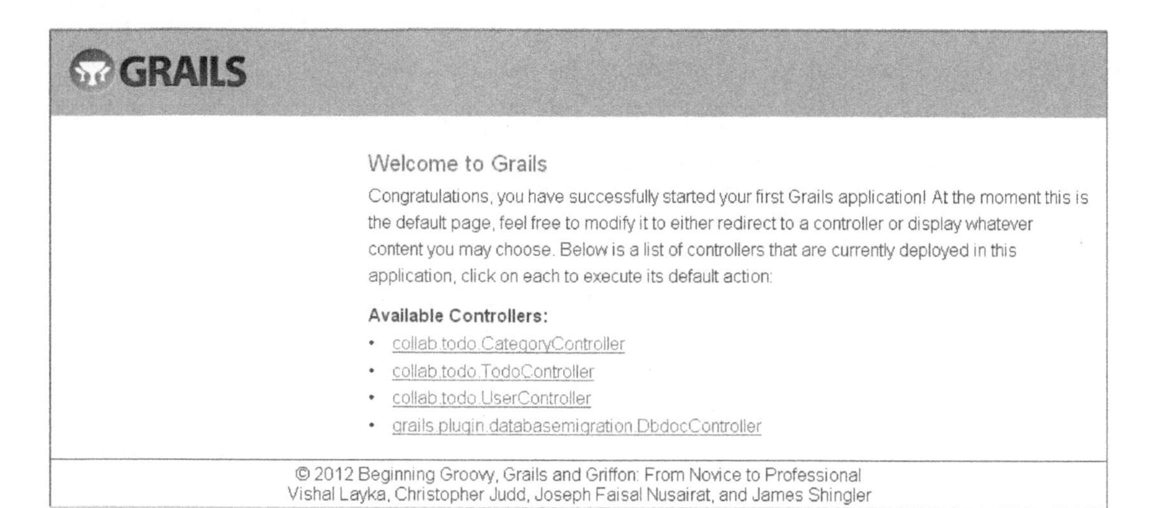
GRAILS
Welcome to Grails
Congratulations, you have successfully started your first Grails application! At the moment this is the default page, feel free to modify it to either redirect to a controller or display whatever content you may choose. Below is a list of controllers that are currently deployed in this application, click on each to execute its default action:
Available Controllers:
collab.todo.CategoryController
collab.todo.TodoController
collab.todo.UserController
grails.plugin.databasemigration.DbdocController
© 2012 Beginning Groovy, Grails and Griffon: From Novice to Professional
Vishal Layka, Christopher Judd, Joseph Faisal Nusairat, and James Shingler

Figure 5-3. *Styling the footer*

Let's review how to add the footer. First, create the `_footer.gsp` template and locate it in the `grails-app/views/common` directory. Second, add the `_footer.gsp` template to the layout using the `<g:render template="/common/footer" />` tag. Third, style the footer by adding a `<div>` section to the main layout using a style class that you defined in the `main.css`.

Now, let's take what you learned by creating the footer and start building the login/logout functionality

Creating the Topbar

You create the topbar by adding a topbar (`_topbar.gsp`) template to the main layout. The topbar template is common and should be located in the `grails-app/views/common` directory. Listing 5-4 shows the content of the topbar template.

Listing 5-4. The Topbar Template (_topbar.gsp)

```
1.  <div id="menu">
2.     <nobr>
3.       <g:if test="${session.user}">
4.         <b>${session.user?.firstName} ${session.user?.lastName}</b> |
5.          <g:link controller="user" action="logout">Logout</g:link>
6.       </g:if>
7.       <g:else>
8.         <g:link controller="user" action="login">Login</g:link>
9.       </g:else>
10.    </nobr>
11. </div>
```

Listing 5-4 uses three Grails tags: `<g:if>`,[1] `<g:else>`,[2] and `<g:link>`.[3] The `<g:if>` and `<g:else>` tags work together to create if-then-else logic. The `<g:link>` tag creates a hypertext link (for example, `http://localhost:8080/collab-todo/user/logout`). Lines 3-6 check if the session has a `User` object. If it does, the user's name followed by a | and a `Logout` link is printed. Lines 7-9 shows the `else` condition of the `if` statement, which displays the `Login` link. Listing 5-5 shows how to add the topbar to the main layout.

---

[1]http://www.grails.org/GSP+Tag+-+if
[2]http://www.grails.org/GSP+Tag+-+else
[3]http://www.grails.org/Tag+-+link

Listing 5-5. Enhancing the Main Layout for the Topbar (main.gsp)

```
<html>
   . . .
<body>
   . . .
<div id="topbar">
<g:render template="/common/topbar" />
</div>
      . . .
```

Now add the CSS fragments found in Listing 5-6 to `main.css`.

Listing 5-6. The Topbar Styles

```
#topbar {
textalign:left;
   width: 778px;
   margin: 0px auto;
   padding: 5px 0;
}
#topbar #menu {
   float: right;
   width: 240px;
   textalign: right;
   font-size: 10px;
}
```

Figure 5-4 shows the results.

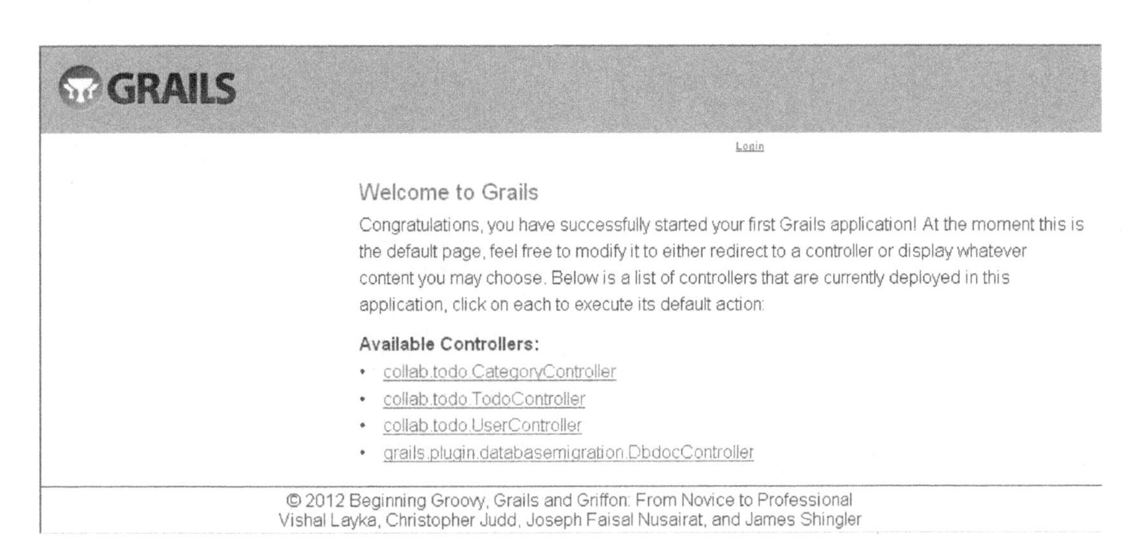
GRAILS
Login
Welcome to Grails
Congratulations, you have successfully started your first Grails application! At the moment this is the default page, feel free to modify it to either redirect to a controller or display whatever content you may choose. Below is a list of controllers that are currently deployed in this application, click on each to execute its default action:
Available Controllers:
collab.todo.CategoryController
collab.todo.TodoController
collab.todo.UserController
grails.plugin.databasemigration.DbdocController
© 2012 Beginning Groovy, Grails and Griffon: From Novice to Professional
Vishal Layka, Christopher Judd, Joseph Faisal Nusairat, and James Shingler

Figure 5-4. *Adding the topbar template*

Notice that the Login/Logout link is located in the upper-right corner of the browser.

Adding More Look and Feel

Now you need to finish the transformation so that CollabTodo has its own look and feel instead of appearing as if it came right out of the box. Do this by adding the right sidebar, replacing the Grails header, and setting the default title. Start off with some CSS styling by adding the CSS snippet in Listing 5-7 to the main style sheet (`main.css`).

Listing 5-7. CSS Styling

```
#header {
   width: 778px;
   background: #FFFFFF url(../images/header_background.gif)  repeat-x;
   height: 70px;
   margin: 0px auto;
}
#header h1 {
fontfamily:Arial,sans-serif;
   color: white;
   padding: 20px 0 0 6px;
   font-size:1.6em;
}
body {
   margin: 0px;
   padding: 0px;
text-align:center;
   fontfamily: "Trebuchet MS",Arial,Helvetica,sans-serif;
fontstyle: normal;
   fontvariant: normal;
fontweight: normal;
   fontsize: 13px;
   line-height: normal;
   fontsize-adjust: none;
   fontstretch: normal;
   color: #333333;
}
#page {
   width: 778px;
   margin: 0px auto;
   padding: 4px 0;
text-align:left;
}

#content {
   float: left;
   width: 560px;
   color: #000;
}
#sidebar {
   float: right;
   width: 200px;
```

```
    color: #000;
    padding: 3px;
}
```

■ **Note** You can find `header_background.gif` in the project source.

Now, take advantage of the CSS styling in the main layout (`main.gsp`), as shown in Listing 5-8.

Listing 5-8. Finishing the Layout (main.gsp)

```
.....
1.  <body>
2.  <div id="page">
3.  <div id="spinner" class="spinner" style="display: none;">
4.  <img src="${createLinkTo(dir:'images',   file:'spinner.gif')}"
5.                  alt="Spinner" />
6.  </div>
7.  <div id="topbar">
8.  <g:render template="/common/topbar" />
9.  </div>
10. <div id="header">
11. <h1>Collab-Todo</h1>
12. </div>
13.
14. <div id="content">
15. <g:layoutBody />
16. </div>
17.
18. <div id="sidebar">
19. <g:render template="/common/buddies" />
20. </div>
21.
22. <div id="footer">
23. <g:render template="/common/footer" />
24. </div>
25. </div>
26. </body>
```

BUDDIES TEMPLATE

Add the following snippet to the `/common/_buddies.gsp` template:

```
<div id="buddies">
<div class="title">Buddies</div>
</div>
```

Let's talk about the changes you made to the layout. Line 2 adds a `<div>` that uses the page style. Together with the body style, the page style creates a container that's 778 pixels wide and centered on the page. Lines 10-12 replace the Grails header with the Collab-Todo header. If you look carefully at the CSS `header` style, you'll see that it defines a header image (`header_background.gif`). Lines 14 and 16 wrap the view's body with the `content` style. This means that pages decorated by `main.gsp` are inserted here. The `content` style creates a container 560 pixels wide and left-aligns it within the page container. Lines 18-20 wrap the buddies template with the `sidebar` style, which creates a container 200 pixels wide and right-aligns it within the page container.

You can see the results of your work in Figure 5-5. Now you have just one more thing to do. You won't use the default index page for long, but let's change "Welcome to Grails" and the body. You can find the HTML for this in `web-app/index.gsp`. Replace the contents of `index.gsp` with the contents found in Listing 5-9.

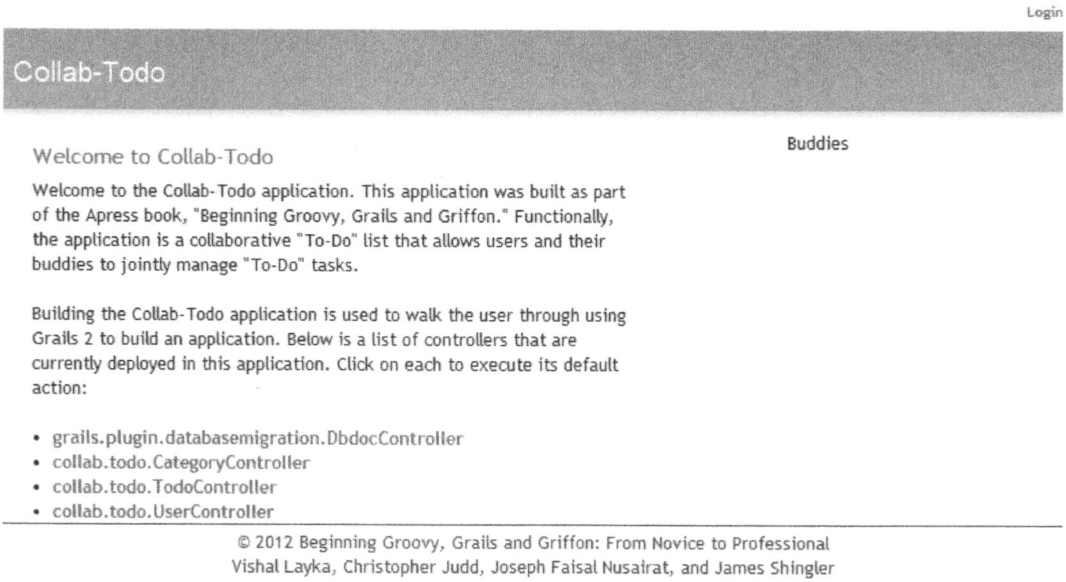

Login

Collab-Todo

Welcome to Collab-Todo

Buddies

Welcome to the Collab-Todo application. This application was built as part of the Apress book, "Beginning Groovy, Grails and Griffon." Functionally, the application is a collaborative "To-Do" list that allows users and their buddies to jointly manage "To-Do" tasks.

Building the Collab-Todo application is used to walk the user through using Grails 2 to build an application. Below is a list of controllers that are currently deployed in this application. Click on each to execute its default action:

- grails.plugin.databasemigration.DbdocController
- collab.todo.CategoryController
- collab.todo.TodoController
- collab.todo.UserController

© 2012 Beginning Groovy, Grails and Griffon: From Novice to Professional
Vishal Layka, Christopher Judd, Joseph Faisal Nusairat, and James Shingler

Figure 5-5. *The completed layout*

Listing 5-9. A New Index Page (index.gsp)

```
1.  <html>
2.      <head>
3.          <title>Welcome to Collab-Todo</title>
4.        <meta name="layout" content="main" />
5.      </head>
```

```
6.      <body>
7.          <h1 style="margin-left:20px;">Welcome to CollabTodo</h1>
8.          <p style="margin-left:20px;width:80%">
9.            Welcome to the CollabTodo application.  This application was built
10.           as part of the Apress Book, "Beginning Groovy, Grails and Griffon."
11.           Functionally, the application is a collaborative "To-Do"
12.           list that allows users and their buddies to jointly
13.           manage "To-Do" tasks.</p><br />
14.           <p style="margin-left:20px;width:80%">Building the Collab-Todo
15.           application is used to walk the user through using Grails 2 to
16.           build an application.  Below is a list of controllers that are
17.           currently deployed in this application. Click on each to execute
18.           its default action:</p>
19.           <br />
20.         <div class="dialog" style="margin-left:20px;width:60%;">
21.             <ul>
22.               <g:each var="c" in="${grailsApplication.controllerClasses}">
23.                     <li class="controller"><a href="${c.logicalPropertyName}">
24.                       ${c.fullName}</a></li>
25.               </g:each>
26.             </ul>
27.         </div>
28.     </body>
29. </html>
```

A couple of items in the file deserve explanation. Lines 22-25 illustrate the usage of `<g:each>`, an iteration tag. In this case, it is iterating over a collection of all controller classes that are a part of the application to display the name of the controller class in a list.

Line 4 is an example of using layouts by convention. In this case, the `layout` metatag causes the "main" layout (`main.gsp`) to be applied to the page. You might recall that all layouts reside within the `grails-app/views/layouts` directory.

You have created the layout, and it's looking good. You can see the results of your work in Figure 5-5.

Setting up the wireframe exposes layouts, templates, CSS, and a couple of Grails tags to you. Grails, like all modern web frameworks, supports tag libraries. The Grails tag library is similar to the JavaServer Pages Standard Tag Library (JSTL) and Struts tags. It contains tags for everything from conditional logic to rendering and layouts. The following section provides a quick overview of the Grails tags. You can find a detailed reference of Grails tags here: `http://www.grails.org/GSP+Tag+Reference`.

Grails Tags

Part of Grails' strength in the view layer is its tag library. Grails has tags to address everything from conditional logic and iterating collections to displaying errors. This section provides an overview of the Grails tags.

Logical Tags

Logical tags allow you to build conditional "if-elseif-else" logic. Listing 5-5 demonstrated the use of the `<g:if>` and `<else>` tags in `topbar.gsp`. Table 5-2 contains an overview of the logical tags.

Table 5-2. *Grails Logical Tags*

Tag Name	Tag Description
`<g:if>`	Logical switch based upon a test expression
`<g:else>`	The `else` portion of an `if` statement
`<g:elseif>`	The `elseif` portion of an `if` statement

Iteration Tags

Iteration tags are used to iterate over collections or loop until a condition is false. The `<g:each>` tag was used in `index.gsp` in Listing 5-10. Table 5-3 contains an overview of the iteration tags.

Table 5-3. *Grails Iteration Tags*

Tag Name	Tag Description
`<g:while>`	Executes a loop while a test condition is true
`<g:each>`	Iterates over a collection
`<g:collect>`	Iterates over a collection and transforms the results as defined in the `expr` parameter
`<g:findAll>`	Iterates over a collection where the elements match the GPath defined in the `expr` parameter
`<g:grep>`	Iterates over a collection where the elements match the filter defined in the `expr` parameter

Assignment Tags

You use assignment tags to create and assign a value to a variable. Table 5-4 contains an overview of assignment tags.

Table 5-4. *Grails Assignment Tags*

Tag Name	Tag Description
`<def>` (deprecated)	Defines a variable to be used within the GSP page; use `<set>` instead
`<set>`	Sets the value of a variable used within the GSP page

Linking Tags

Linking tags are used to create URLs. The `<g:link>` tag was used in `topbar.gsp` (shown in Listing 5-5), and `<g:createLinkTo>` was used as an expression in `main.gsp` (shown in Listing 5-9). Table 5-5 contains an overview of the linking tags.

***Table 5-5.** Grails Linking Tags*

Tag Name	Tag Description
`<g:link>`	Creates an HTML link using supplied parameters
`<g:createLink>`	Creates a link that you can use within other tags
`<g:createLinkTo>`	Creates a link to a directory or file

Ajax Tags

You can use Ajax tags to build an Ajax-aware application. Chapter 8 uses some of these tags to enhance the user interface. Table 5-6 contains an overview of the Ajax tags.

***Table 5-6.** Grails Ajax Tags*

Tag Name	Tag Description
`<g:remoteField>`	Creates a text field that invokes a link when changed
`<g:remoteFunction>`	Creates a remote function that is called on a DOM event
`<g:remoteLink>`	Creates a link that calls a remote function
`<g:formRemote>`	Creates a form tag that executes an Ajax call to serialize the form elements
`<g:javascript>`	Includes JavaScript libraries and scripts
`<g:submitToRemote>`	Creates a button that executes an Ajax call to serialize the form elements

Form Tags

Form tags are used to create HTML forms. Table 5-7 contains an overview of form tags.

***Table 5-7.** Grails Form Tags*

Tag Name	Tag Description
`<g:actionSubmit>`	Creates a submit button
`<g:actionSubmitImage>`	Creates a submit button using an image
`<g:checkBox>`	Creates a check box
`<g:currencySelect>`	Creates a select field containing currencies
`<g:datePicker>`	Creates a configurable date picker for the day, month, year, hour, minute, and second
`<g:form>`	Creates a form
`<g:hiddenField>`	Creates a hidden field
`<g:localeSelect>`	Creates a select field containing locales
`<g:radio>`	Creates a radio button
`<g:radioGroup>`	Creates a radio button group

(*continued*)

Table 5-7. *(continued)*

Tag Name	Tag Description
`<g:select>`	Creates a select/combo box field
`<g:textField>`	Creates a text field
`<g:textArea>`	Creates a text area field
`<g:timeZoneSelect>`	Creates a select field containing time zones

UI Tags

You use UI tags to enhance the user interface. The only official UI Grails tag is the rich text editor, but several UI tags built by the Grails community are available as plug-ins. Table 5-8 contains an overview of the UI tag.

Table 5-8. *Grails UI Tag*

Tag Name	Tag Description
`<g:richTextEditor>`	Creates a rich text editor, which defaults to fckeditor

Render and Layout Tags

Render and layout tags are used to create the layouts and render templates. As you might expect, several render and layout tags were used in `main.gsp`. Table 5-9 contains an overview of the render and layout tags.

Table 5-9. *Grails Render and Layout Tags*

Tag Name	Tag Description
`<g:applyLayout>`	Applies a layout to a body or template
`<g:encodeAs>`	Applies dynamic encoding to a block of HTML to bulk-encode the content
`<g:formatDate>`	Applies a `SimpleDateFormat` to a date
`<g:formatNumber>`	Applies a `DecimalFormat` to number
`<g:layoutHead>`	Displays a decorated page's header, which is used in layouts
`<g:layoutBody>`	Displays a decorated page's body, which is used in layouts
`<g:layoutTitle>`	Displays a decorated page's title, which is used in layouts
`<g:meta>`	Displays application metadata properties
`<g:render>`	Displays a model using a template
`<g:renderErrors>`	Displays errors
`<g:pageProperty>`	Displays a property from a decorated page
`<g:paginate>`	Displays Next/Previous buttons and breadcrumbs for large results
`<g:sortableColumn>`	Displays a sortable table column

Validation Tags

Validation tags are used to display errors and messages. Table 5-10 contains an overview of the validation tags.

Table 5-10. *Grails Validation Tags*

Tag Name	Tag Description
`<g:eachError>`	Iterates through errors
`<g:hasErrors>`	Checks if errors exist within the bean, model, or request
`<g:message>`	Displays a message
`<g:fieldValue>`	Displays the value of a field for a bean that has data binding

Static Resources

Grails 2.0 integrates with the Resources plugin to provide sophisticated static resource management. This plugin is installed by default in new Grails applications. The basic way to include a link to a static resource in your application is to use the `resource` tag. This simple approach, as shown below, creates a URI pointing to the file.

```
<g:resource dir="css" file="main.css" />
```

However, for modern applications with dependencies on multiple JavaScript and CSS libraries and frameworks (as well as dependencies on multiple Grails plugins), Grails provides `r:require` and `r:layoutResources` to enable you to easily create highly optimized web applications that run the same in development and in production. Next we illustrate the usage of `r:require` and `r:layoutResources`.

r:require

To use resources, your GSP page must indicate which resource modules it requires. For example, to use jQuery in any page on your site with the jQuery plugin, which exposes a `jquery` resource module, simply add:

```
<html>
<head>
<r:require module="jquery"/>
<r:layoutResources/>
</head>
<body>
    ...
<r:layoutResources/>
</body>
</html>
```

This will automatically include all resources needed for jQuery, including them at the correct locations in the page. However, you cannot use `r:require` in isolation: as per the examples, you must have the `<r:layoutResources/>` tag to actually perform the render.

r:layoutResources

When you have declared the resource modules that your GSP page requires, the framework needs to render the links to those resources at the correct time. To achieve this correctly, you must include the `r:layoutResources` tag twice in your page, or more commonly, in your GSP layout:

```
<html>
<head>
<g:layoutTitle/>
<r:layoutResources/>
</head>
<body>
<g:layoutBody/>
<r:layoutResources/>
</body>
</html>
```

Making the Topbar Functional

Now that you have the layout, let's make the topbar functional. You want the topbar to provide the user the ability to log in. Once the user has logged in, the topbar should display the username and provide the ability for the user to log out. When the user selects the Login link, he should be presented with a Login form.

■ **Note** The login functionality you are building initially is simply to identify who is using the system. It's not meant to provide a full, robust security system.

The Login View

Creating the login view requires you to create a GSP in the appropriate directory. The GSP contains a form that has a single selection field of usernames and a submit button. When the user submits the selection, the form invokes the `handleLogin` action on the `UserController`. Figure 5-6 illustrates the login view.

Login

Collab-Todo

Welcome to Your ToDo List. Login below

User Name:

Login

Buddies

© 2012 Beginning Groovy, Grails and Griffon: From Novice to Professional
Vishal Layka, Christopher Judd, Joseph Faisal Nusairat, and James Shingler

Figure 5-6. *The login view*

Let's take a look at the Login link, `<g:link controller="user" action="login">Login</g:link>`. When the user selects the Login link, the `login` action on the `UserController` is invoked. We'll explain the `login` action in the next section.

Based upon convention, `login.gsp` should go in the `grails-app/views/user` directory. Listing 5-10 shows the contents of `login.gsp`.

Listing 5-10. The Login View (login.gsp)

```
1.  <html>
2.     <head>
3.        <title>Login Page</title>
4.        <meta name="layout" content="main" />
5.     </head>
6.     <body>
7.        <div class="body">
8.           <g:if test="${flash.message}">
9.              <div class="message">
10.                ${flash.message}
11.             </div>
12.          </g:if>
13.          <p>
14.             Welcome to Your ToDo List. Login below
15.          </p>
16.          <g:form action="handleLogin" method="post" >
17.
18.             <span class='nameClear'><label for="login">
19.                   Sign In:
20.                </label>
21.             </span>
22.             <g:textField name="userName" value="${user?.userName}" />
23.
24.             <br />
25.             <div class="buttons">
26.                <span class="button">
27.                    <g:actionSubmit value="Login" action="handleLogin"/>
28.                </span>
29.             </div>
30.          </g:form>
31.       </div>
32.    </body>
33. </html>
```

Let's review the form. Lines 1-5 define the title and determine that the page is decorated by the `main` layout. This means that `main.gsp` acts as a container for `login.gsp`. Take a look at line 14 in Listing 5-8. In this case, the body of `login.gsp` is inserted at the `<g:layoutBody>` tag. Remember that the main layout contains a default title, `<g:layoutTitle default="CollabTodo" />`. When `login.gsp` is decorated with the `main` layout, the title in `login.gsp` is used instead of the default that was defined in the layout.

Lines 6-31 define the body of the page. Lines 9-12 display flash messages, which we'll cover shortly in the "Flash and Flash Messages" section. Lines 16-29 create the form with a selection field. Line 16 specifies that when the form is submitted, the `handleLogin` action of the `UserController` is invoked. In lines 22-23, the Grails `select` tag creates an HTML selection element. The `name` attribute sets the selection name to `userName` (which in turn is passed to the `login` action). When evaluated, the `form` attribute results in a collection that Grails uses to create the options. `optionKey` and optionValue are special attributes used to create the HTML <option> element ID and the text display in the selection field. Lines 25-28 use the Grails <g:actionSubmit> tag to create a form submission button.

If you run the application and access the view right now, you'll get a 404 error. This is because the topbar links to the login view via the UserControllerlogin action, which hasn't been created yet.

The login Action

Currently, the UserController is set up with dynamic scaffolding. You will continue to use the dynamic scaffolding and add the login action to it. Listing 5-11 shows the updated version of the UserController class.

Listing 5-11. The login Action

```
class UserController {
static scaffold = User
def login() {}
}
```

A common best practice on the Web is to use actions as a redirection mechanism. By convention, Grails uses the name of the action to look up a GSP of the same name.

If you click on the Login link now, the login view is displayed, and the User Name selection field is blank. Test the functionality of the form by creating two users. From the home page, select UserController ➤ New User. Now when you select Login, the User Name selection field is populated (see Figure 5-7).

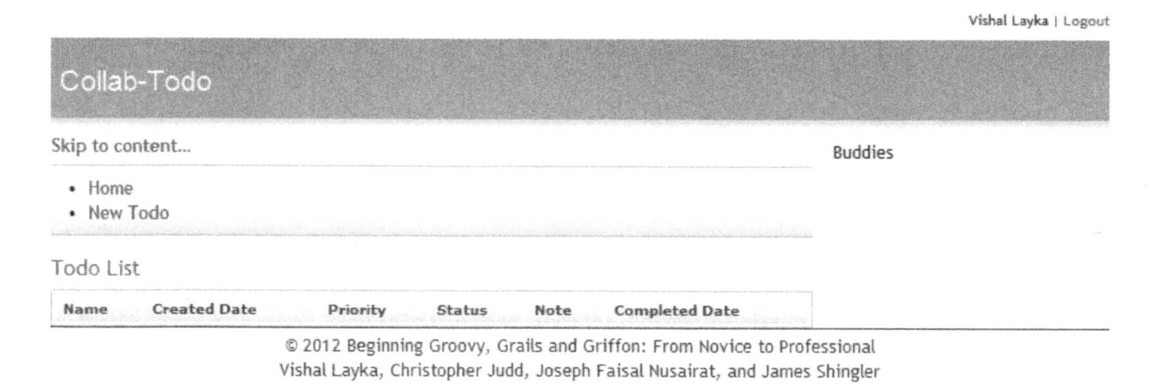

Figure 5-7. *A logged-in user*

Next, you need to implement the login logic through the UserControllerhandleLogin action.

Handling the Login and Logout Actions

You call the handleLogin action to log in a user. When you call the action, the Login form is passed the userName of the user to be signed in. Logging in is accomplished by adding the user object associated with the userName to the session. If the user cannot be found, an error message is created, and the user is redirected to the login view. In this particular example, there shouldn't be any way for the login to fail, but it is still good practice to code defensively. You use the logout action to remove the user from the session, so she can log out.

Listing 5-12 shows how you enhance the UserController.

Listing 5-12. Enhanced UserController

```
class UserController {
static  scaffold = User
   def login() {}
defhandleLogin() {
def user = User.findByUserName(params.userName)
if (!user) {
flash.message = "User not found for userName: ${params.userName}"
redirect(action:'login')
return
} else {
session.user = user
redirect(controller:'todo')
 }
}

def logout() {
if(session.user) {
session.user = null
redirect(action:'login')
 }
 }
}
```

Now, when the user logs in, she is taken to the Todo List and the topbar shows the user's first name, last name, and a Logout link.

Externalizing Strings

Like all modern Java web frameworks, Grails supports the concept of message bundles. It uses the `<g:message>` tag to look up a properties file for the text to display. For example, say you're having a difficult time deciding if the topbar should say "Login" or "Sign In." You could externalize the string and simply change the `messages.properties` file whenever you change your mind. Grails uses the message bundles to display errors. So, if you don't like the error message you're getting back, you can make it friendlier by modifying the message in the message bundle. The `messages.properties` file is located in the `grails-app/i18n` directory. Listing 5-13 shows the default contents of the `messages.properties` file.

Listing 5-13. messages.properties

```
default.doesnt.match.message=Property [{0}] of class [{1}] with value [{2}] does \
not match the required pattern [{3}]
default.invalid.url.message=Property [{0}] of class [{1}] with value [{2}] is not \
a valid URL
default.invalid.creditCard.message=Property [{0}] of class [{1}] with value [{2}] \
is not a valid credit card number
default.invalid.email.message=Property [{0}] of class [{1}] with value [{2}] is \
not a valid e-mail address
default.invalid.range.message=Property [{0}] of class [{1}] with value [{2}] \
```

```
does not fall within the valid range from [{3}] to [{4}]
default.invalid.size.message=Property [{0}] of class [{1}] with value [{2}] does \
not fall within the valid size range from [{3}] to [{4}]
default.invalid.max.message=Property [{0}] of class [{1}] with value [{2}] \
exceeds maximum value [{3}]
default.invalid.min.message=Property [{0}] of class [{1}] with value [{2}] is \
less than minimum value [{3}]
default.invalid.max.size.message=Property [{0}] of class [{1}] with value \
[{2}] exceeds the maximum size of [{3}]
default.invalid.min.size.message=Property [{0}] of class [{1}] with value \
[{2}] is less than the minimum size of [{3}]
default.invalid.validator.message=Property [{0}] of class [{1}] with value
[{2}] does not pass custom validation
default.not.inlist.message=Property [{0}] of class [{1}] with value [{2}] is \
not contained within the list [{3}]
default.blank.message=Property [{0}] of class [{1}] cannot be blank
default.not.equal.message=Property [{0}] of class [{1}] with value [{2}] \
cannot equal [{3}]
default.null.message=Property [{0}] of class [{1}] cannot be null
default.not.unique.message=Property [{0}] of class [{1}] with value [{2}] \
must be unique
default.paginate.prev=Previous
default.paginate.next=Next
```

Now we'll demonstrate how to externalize strings. Take a look at Listing 5-4to see the current topbar template. Change lines 5 and 8 to use the <g:message> tags. When completed, the topbar template should look something like what's shown in Listing 5-14.

Listing 5-14. Topbar Template with Messages

```
<div id="menu">
<nobr>
<g:if test="${session.user}">
<b>${session.user?.firstName} ${session.user?.lastName}</b> |
<g:link controller="logout"><g:message code="topbar.logout" /></g:link>
</g:if>
<g:else>
<g:link controller="login" action="auth">
<g:message code="topbar.login" /></g:link>
</g:else>
</nobr>
</div>
```

Now just add `topbar.logout` and `topbar.login` to the messages bundle:

```
topbar.login=Login
topbar.logout=Logout
```

You can easily change the text to display whatever you want without modifying the GSP. You still have to be careful, though. Depending upon how you modify the text associated with the message code, you may have to adjust the WebTest if it is looking for specific text. In a sophisticated application, you will have to make some decisions about functional testing. You need to ask yourself, "Should the functional test be run against a single locale or multiple locales?" If you decide on multiple locales, you will have to write a more robust functional test and pay particular attention to the usage of `verifyText`.

If you're an experienced web developer, you won't be surprised to find out that using the `<g:message>` tag also starts you on the path of internationalizing the application. The `<g:message>` tag is locale-aware; the `i18n` directory's name is a giveaway (and that is where the `messages.properties` file lives). By default, the tag uses the browser's locale to determine which message bundle to use.

Now that you understand message bundles, you can change the default messages that are displayed when errors occur to something more user friendly.

Errors and Validation

In this section, you'll learn the difference between errors and flash messages, and how to customize the messages.

If you try to submit a user form without entering a username, you can see error messages in action. When you violate a domain object's constraints, the red text that you see is an example of an error message. Figure 5-8 shows an example.

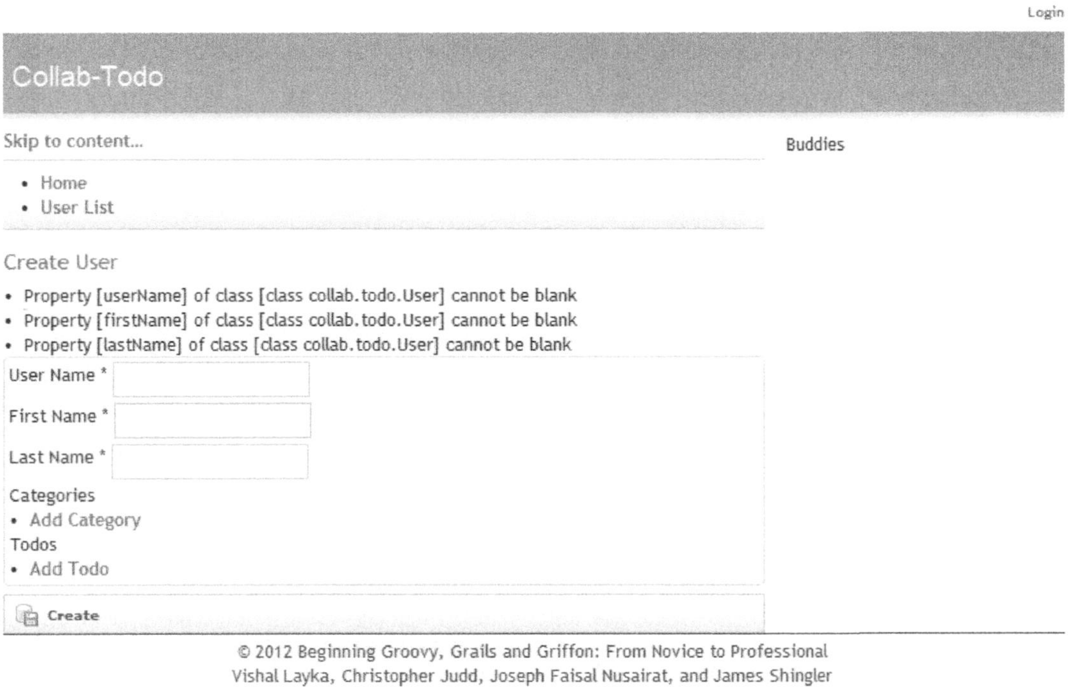

Figure 5-8. *Error message*

This screen shows the default error messages. As you saw previously in Listing 5-13, you can customize the message using the `messages.properties` file located in the `grails-app/i18n` directory. To get a better understanding of how this works, you need to switch the views and the controller from dynamic scaffolding to static scaffolding. Grails generates dynamic scaffolding on the fly when the application starts. If Grails can generate the code at runtime, it makes sense that it can generate the code at development time so you can see it. Take a precaution against losing the existing implementation of the `UserController` by making a backup copy before proceeding.

You can create the views for the `User` domain object by executing the command:

```
> grails generate-views User
```

The command uses Grails templates to generate four new GSP pages in the `grails-app/views/user` directory: `create.gsp`, `edit.gsp`, `list.gsp`, and `show.gsp`. Now you need to create static scaffolding for the controller. You can create the controller for the `User` domain object by executing the command:

```
> grails generate-controller User
```

Grails will detect that you already have an implementation of the controller and ask for permission to overwrite it. Give it permission; this is why you made a backup copy. After the `UserController` is generated, copy the `login`, `handleLogin`, and `logout` actions from the backup to the newly generated controller. Listing 5-15 contains the contents of the `save` action.

Listing 5-15. The UserController.save Action

```
1.  def save() {
2.      def user = new User()
3.      user.properties = params
4.      if(user.save()) {
5.          flash.message = "User ${user.id} created."
6.          redirect(action:show,id:user.id)
7.      }
8.      else {
9.          render(view:'create',model:[user:user])
10.     }
11. }
```

The `save` action is called when the user clicks the Create button from the New User view. When line 4 is executed, Grails validates the user constraints before attempting to persist the user in the database. If validation succeeds, the user is redirected to the Show User view with the message "User ${user.id} created." If the save fails, the Create User view is rendered so that you can correct the validation errors without losing the previous input. When validation fails, Grails inserts an error message in the `user` object's metadata, and the `user` object is passed as a model object to the view. When the Create User view is rendered, it checks to see if there are any errors and displays them if appropriate. Listing 5-16 contains a short snippet that shows how to display the errors.

Listing 5-16. Display Errors

```
<g:hasErrors bean="${user}">
<div class="errors">
<g:renderErrors bean="${user}" as="list" />
</div>
</g:hasErrors>
```

As you can see, the generated GSP uses the `<g:hasErrors>` and `<g:renderErrors>` tags to detect and display the errors. The `<g:hasErrors>` tag uses the bean attribute to detect errors in the `user` object. If errors are detected, the body of the tag is evaluated, which results in the error being displayed by the `<g:renderErrors>` tag. The `<g:renderErrors>` tag iterates through the errors in the `user` object and displays them as a list. The display process knows that it is receiving an error code and error attributes. The tag looks up the error code in the message bundle, and the attributes are substituted in the message before it is displayed.

This technique works because the page is rendered from the controller. Take another look at line 6 in Listing 5-15. In the case of a redirect, the controller instructs the browser to go to the Show User view. The browser does this by calling the `show` action on the `UserController`. The controller then executes the `show` action and renders `show.gsp`. With all of this back and forth between the controller and the browser, can you imagine what it would take to make sure that all of the message information stays intact so it can be displayed by `show.gsp`? Well, this is where flash messages come to your rescue.

Flash and Flash Messages

What is flash scope and why do you need it? The short answer is that it is a technique implemented by Grails to make passing objects across redirects much easier. In other words, it addresses the problem described at the end of the previous section. Table 5-11 illustrates various scopes associated with controllers in Grails.

Table 5-11. *Scopes Associated with Controllers*

Scope	Description
`flash`	Flash only allows the storage of objects for the current and next request.
`params`	Mutable map of incoming request query string or POST parameters.
`request`	The request object allows the storage of objects for the current request only.
`servletcontext`	This scope lets you share state across the entire web application.
`session`	The session allows associating state with a given user and typically uses cookies to associate a session with a client.

The flash object is a Map (a hash) that you can use to store key value pairs. These values are transparently stored inside the session and then cleared at the end of the next request. This pattern lets you use HTTP redirects (which is useful for redirect after post) and retain values that can be retrieved from the flash object. Figure 5-9 illustrates the problems associated with normal techniques of passing information from the controller to the view when a redirect is involved.

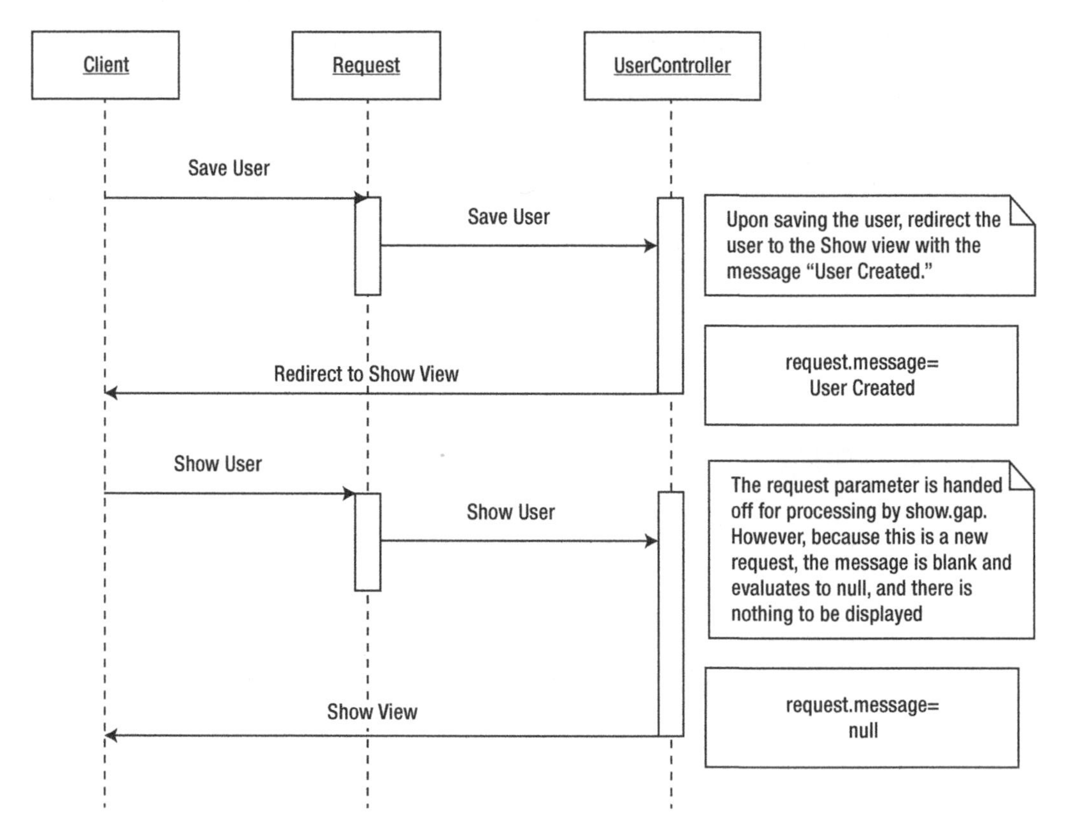

Figure 5-9. *Redirect problem*

On a redirect, if you try to use the request to carry the message to the Show view, the message gets lost when the browser receives the redirect. Another option is to stick the message in the session and have the Show view pick it up from the session. However, in the Show view, you have to remember to delete the message from the session once it has been displayed; otherwise, the same message might be displayed on multiple views. The problem with this approach is that it depends upon you doing the right thing, and it's tedious.

This is where Grails comes to the rescue: it takes the last option and implements it for you and makes it part of the Grails framework. This is the flash scope. The flash scope works just like the other scopes (application, session, request, and page) by operating off a map of key/value pairs. It stores the information in the session and then removes it on the next request. Now you don't have to remember to delete the object in the flash scope. Figure 5-10 illustrates the concept of the flash scope.

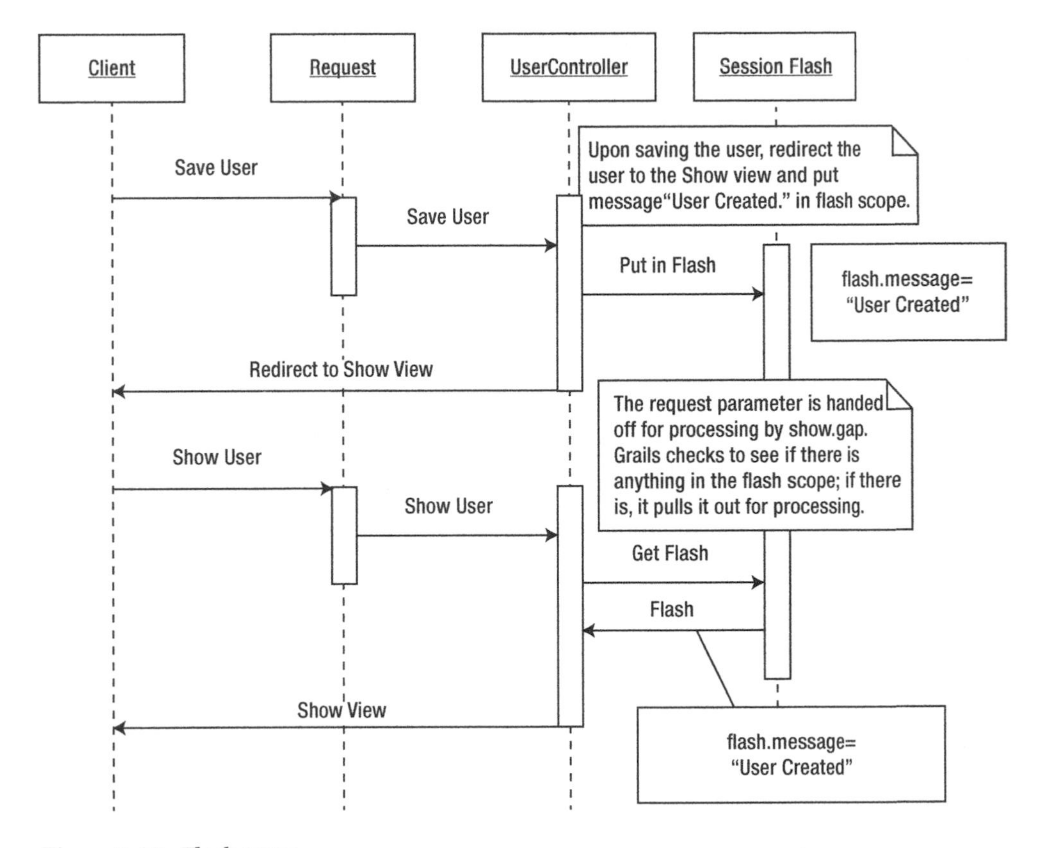

Figure 5-10. *Flash scope*

The Show view can access the flash scope objects—a message, in this case—and display them using the tags and techniques illustrated in Listing 5-17.

Listing 5-17. Access and Display a Flash Message

```
<g:if test="${flash.message}">
<div class="message">${flash.message}</div>
</g:if>
```

Grails isn't the only modern web framework that implements this technique. Ruby on Rails (RoR) developers should find this familiar.

Accessing a message from a flash scope looks pretty easy, but how do you put a message in flash? Listing 5-18 illustrates how the save action on the `UserController` puts a message into the flash scope.

Listing 5-18. Putting a Message in the Flash Scope

```
...
if(user.save()) {
    flash.message = "User ${user.id} created."
    redirect(action:show,id:user.id)
}
...
```

Grails implements a flash scope using a map. In this case, `message` is the key, and `"User ${user.id} created."` is the value.

What if you need to internationalize the code or want to change the message without editing the GSP? (Currently, the message is essentially hard-coded.) You can set it up to use message bundles just like errors do. Earlier in the chapter, you used the `<g:message>`tag to pull error messages from message bundles. You can do the same thing for flash messages using a couple of attributes. Listing 5-19 illustrates how to use the `<g:message>` tag to display flash messages.

Listing 5-19. Using the <g:message> Tag to Display a Flash Message

```
<g:message code="${flash.message}" args="${flash.args}"
    default="${flash.defaultMsg}"/>
```

Listing 5-20 illustrates the enhancements to the `save` action to set the values that the message tag will use.

Listing 5-20. Setting Values in a Flash Scope for Use by the <g:message> Tag

```
...
        if(user.save()) {
 flash.message = "user.saved.message"
 flash.args = [user.firstName, user.lastName]
 flash.defaultMsg = "User Saved"
            redirect(action:show,id:user.id)
        }
...
```

The `flash.message` property is the message code to look up in the message bundle, `flash.args` are the arguments to substitute into the message, and `flash.defaultMsg` is a default message to display in the event of a problem.

Only one thing left to do: create an entry in the message bundle with the `user.saved.message` code and whatever you would like the text to be. See Listing 5-21 for an example.

Listing 5-21. Flash Message Code Example

```
user.saved.message=User: {0} {1} was saved
```

The results should look something like what's shown in Figure 5-11.

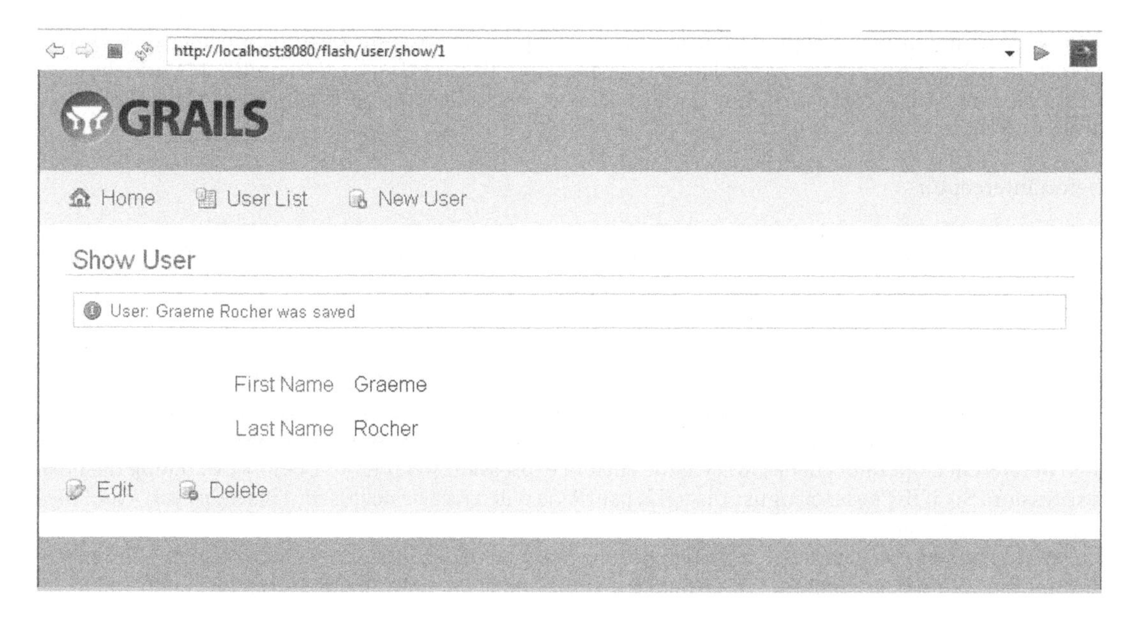

Figure 5-11. *Using Flash scope*

■ **Note** Any action can call or redirect to the Show view. At this point, you may be wondering what happens if `flash.args` and `flash.defaultMsg` aren't set. The `<g:message>` tag is pretty smart; it does the logical thing. It displays the contents of `flash.message`. To see it in action, update an existing user and take a look at the message displayed.

Now that you know about the flash scope and messages, you can create customized and internationalized application messages with a minimal investment.

You have learned quite a bit about Grails user interfaces and have established the basic look and feel. Now it's time to start implementing some logic and control.

Creating an Audit Log Using Action Interceptors

Occasionally, you'll have problems with the application. When this happens, it is useful to know the input and results of the actions being executed. This entails displaying the inputs to the action before the action is executed and the results before control is passed to the next step in the process. You could modify every action to print the inputs before executing the body of the action and then again at the end of the action. However, that's way too much work and difficult to maintain.

Grails provides a mechanism called *action interceptors* that you can use to provide the desired functionality. Experienced developers will see that this is similar to aspect-oriented programming (AOP). If you aren't familiar with AOP, you might be familiar with servlet filter interceptors for servlets, which are similar. The good news is that Grails makes it easier than either one of these.

■ **Note** Ruby on Rails developers will recognize this as a Rails filter.

Grails provides *before* and *after* interceptors. You will use both to provide the audit log functionality. You will use a before interceptor to log the userName, controller, action, and input parameters. To accomplish this, add the beforeInterceptor closure to the TodoController. Listing 5-22 is an example of the beforeInterceptor for you to add to the controller.

Listing 5-22. beforeInterceptor

```
def beforeInterceptor = {
    log.trace("${session?.user?.userName} Start action ${controllerName}
        Controller.${actionName}() : parameters $params")
}
```

If defined and unless otherwise instructed, the beforeInterceptor is called just before the action is invoked. Since it is a closure, it has full access to all of the controller properties as well as to the request parameters. It uses logging (see the "Logging" sidebar) to output the audit information. Notice that it's using the ?. safe dereference operator. The safe dereference operator checks to see if the current expression so far is null before evaluating the next portion of the expression. So, if the session or user is null, userName will never be accessed. This helps you avoid the infamous NullPointerException.

beforeInterceptor allows you to perform logic before an action is invoked, while afterInterceptor allows you to perform logic after the action has executed. Listing 5-23 is an example of the afterInterceptor for you to add to the controller.

Listing 5-23. afterInterceptor

```
def afterInterceptor = { model ->
   log.trace("${session?.user?.userName} End action
   ${controllerName}Controller.${actionName}() : returns $model")
 }
```

As you would expect, the afterInterceptor looks similar to the beforeInterceptor. The one additional piece is the passing of the model object to the interceptor; this allows you to output it to the audit log.

■ **Caution** This implementation of audit logging is a potential security hole for sensitive data. If the parameters or model contain sensitive data, take extra care to filter it out before logging any audit information.

---

beforeInterceptor and afterInterceptor are invoked for every action in the controller. Suppose you didn't want to invoke the audit log for every action. What if you didn't want to collect audit log information for the list action? You could write an if statement around the log statement. That would work, and it would work well. Grails provides an additional mechanism, called *interceptor conditions*, which allow interceptors to be applied conditionally. Listing 5-24 is an example of the before and after interceptors using conditions to exclude the list action from the audit log.

Listing 5-24. Before and After Interceptors with Conditions

```
def beforeInterceptor = [action:this.&beforeAudit,except:['list']]
def afterInterceptor = [action:{model ->this.&afterAudit(model)},
  except:['list']]
def beforeAudit = {
    log.trace("${session?.user?.userName} Start action
        ${controllerName}Controller.${actionName}() : parameters $params")
}
```

```
def afterAudit = { model ->
    log.trace("${session?.user?.userName} End action
        ${controllerName}Controller.${actionName}() : returns $model")
}
```

■ **Note** The Definitive Guide to Grails 2 from Apress shows you how to use action interceptors to build a simple security framework.

Using Filters

Filters are similar to action interceptors in that they give you the ability to execute logic before and after an action. They differ from action interceptors in that they are more flexible and can be used in situations other than actions. For example, you can define a filter that applies across multiple controllers. Filters can be applied across a whole group of controllers, a URI space, or to a specific action. Filters are far easier to plugin and maintain, and are useful for all sorts of cross-cutting concerns such as security, logging, and so on.

To create a filter, create a class that ends with the convention Filters in the grails-app/conf directory. Within this class, define a code block called filters that contains the filter definitions:

```
class SampleFilters {
   def filters = {
       // your filters here
   }
}
```

Each filter you define within the filters block has a name and a scope. The name is the method name and the scope is defined using named arguments.

Let's see how you can use filters to simplify the `UserController`. The `UserController`'s edit, delete, and update actions all contain guard logic that allows users to edit only their own user data. The actions contain logic similar to Listing 5-25.

Listing 5-25. User Modification Guard

```
. . .
     if (session.user.id != params.id) {
       flash.message = "You can only edit yourself"
       redirect(action:list)
       return
     }
. . .
```

While the logic in Listing 5-35 isn't complex, it would be repeated for each action that requires a guard. You can use filters to extract and centralize the logic to a single location. This may sound familiar to those of you who have worked with AOP. The basic idea is to extract the logic to a central location and then configure when to apply that logic.

In Grails, you extract the logic into a class ending with the name `Filters`.groovy and place it in the `grails-app/conf` directory. Each filter is contained within a method that takes parameters to define the scope of the filter, when it is applied. Listing 5-26 shows how to centralize the user modification logic.

Listing 5-26. Filter Scope

```
class UserFilters {
    def filters = {
        userModificationCheck(controller: 'user', action: '*') {

            . . .
        }
        someOtherFilter(uri: '/user/*') { }
    }
}
```

The `userModificationCheck` filter is scoped and applied to the `UserController` on all actions. Another way of scoping the filter is to use a URL. You can see an example of this option on the `someOtherFilter` filter.

Next, you need to determine if the filter should be applied `before` the action, `after` the action, and/or `afterView` rendering. In this case, the goal is to determine if the person using the system should be allowed to modify the user. This means the guard logic should be applied `before` the `edit`, `update`, and `delete` actions. Listing 5-27 illustrates how to specify the before condition.

Listing 5-27. before Filter

```
class UserFilters {
    def filters = {
        userModificationCheck(controller: 'user', action: '*') {
before = {
 . . .
 }
        }
     }
}
```

Finally, you need to limit the guard logic to the `edit`, `update`, and `delete` actions. Listing 5-28 shows the complete `userModificationFilter`.

Listing 5-28. User Modification Filter

```
1.  class UserFilters {
2.      def filters = {
3.         userModificationCheck(controller: 'user', action: '*') {
4.             before = {
5.  defcurrActionName = actionName
6.  if (currActionName == 'edit' ||
7.  currActionName == 'update' ||
8.  currActionName == 'delete') {
9.  String userId = session?.user?.id
10. String paramsUserId = params?.id
11.     if (userId != paramsUserId) {
12. flash.message = "You can only modify yourself"
13. redirect(action: 'list')
```

```
14. return false
15. }
16. }
17.                 }
18.             }
19.     }
20. }
```

Let's review the new lines. Line 5 gets the current action. Remember, you should apply the filter to the `edit`, `update`, and `delete` actions, as shown in lines 6-8.

Line 11 determines if the person attempting the modification—the logged-in user—is modifying his own user record. If not, an appropriate flash message is created, and the user is redirected to the `UserController list` action. Line 14 returns `false` to tell Grails that it shouldn't execute any other filters.

Now that you have the `userModificationCheck` filter, you can remove the redundant guard code from the `edit`, `update`, and `delete` actions.

LOGGING

While everyone uses `println` from time to time, a more mature approach is to use logging. Grails controllers are preconfigured with a log property. Each controller receives its own instance of org.apache.commons.logging.log. Apache Commons Logging component (`http://commons.apache.org/logging`) is an abstraction that allows you to plug in different logging packages. Grails comes prepackaged with log4j (`http://logging.apache.org/log4j`). The Apache Commons Logging abstraction provides the interface seen in the following code.

```
public interface log {
    void debug(java.lang.Object message)
    void debug(java.lang.Object message, java.lang.Throwable t)
    void error(java.lang.Object message)
    void error(java.lang.Object message, java.lang.Throwable t)
    void fatal(java.lang.Object message
    void fatal(java.lang.Object message, java.lang.Throwable t
    void info(java.lang.Object message)
    void info(java.lang.Object message, java.lang.Throwable t)
    void trace(java.lang.Object message)
    void trace(java.lang.Object message, java.lang.Throwable t)
    void warn(java.lang.Object message)
    void warn(java.lang.Object message, java.lang.Throwable t)
    boolean isDebugEnabled()
    boolean isErrorEnabled()
    boolean isFatalEnabled()
    boolean isInfoEnabled()
    boolean isTraceEnabled()
    boolean isWarnEnabled()
}
```

Messages have a severity level. The possible severity levels (from least severe to most severe) are:

- Trace
- Debug
- Info
- Warning
- Error
- Fatal

Grails uses its common configuration mechanism to provide the settings for the underlying log4j log system, so all you have to do is add a log4j setting to the file `grails-app/conf/Config.groovy`.

```
log4j = {
    error  'org.codehaus.groovy.grails.web.servlet',  //  controllers
           'org.codehaus.groovy.grails.web.pages' //  GSP    warn    'org.apache.catalina'
}
```

This says that for loggers whose name starts with `org.codehaus.groovy.grails.web.servlet` or `org.codehaus.groovy.grails.web.pages`, only messages logged at error level and above will be shown. Loggers with names starting with `org.apache.catalina` only show messages at the warn level and above.

For more information on logging configuration, see the online log configuration documentation at `http://www.grails.org/Logging`.

Summary

Views and controllers are broad and deep topics. We used the construction of the Collab-Todo wireframe and customization of the views and controllers to help you learn about some of the more important aspects to these topics. In the process of building the Collab-Todo application, you learned how to use layouts, templates, and CSS to build the wireframe. The wireframe was composed of topbar, header, content, sidebar, and footer components. Building the wireframe also exposed you to some of the Grails tag libraries.

Once you built the wireframe, you learned how to build a temporary login facility that allowed you to exercise the topbar login/logout functionality. Building the login facility involved creating a customized view and customized actions on the `UserController`.

You also learned about errors, validation, and flash messages. This gave you insights into how Grails renders errors and messages, and how you can control them. You also learned about the redirect message problem and how using flash-scoped messages solves the problem.

You learned how to use interceptors for things like auditing. Finally, you created a simple audit log using action interceptors and logging.

It's important to remember that even though we covered a lot, there are even more advanced things you can do with views and controllers. We'll cover more of the advanced topics in the coming chapters. The next step on your journey is to learn more about domain models and services.

CHAPTER 6

Building Domains and Services

> *King Arthur. The Lady of the Lake, her arm clad in the purest shimmering samite, held aloft Excalibur from the bosom of the water, signifying by divine providence that I, Arthur, was to carry Excalibur. THAT is why I am your king.*
>
> *Dennis, interrupting. Listen, strange women lyin' in ponds distributin' swords is no basis for a system of government. Supreme executive power derives from a mandate from the masses, not from some farcical aquatic ceremony.*

Just as King Arthur and his knights embarked on a quest to find the Holy Grail in *Monty Python and the Holy Grail*, the next step in our discovery of Grails is to search for its very heart and soul . . . or in Java terms, its *domain*.

You received your first taste of the domain in Chapter 4 when you learned how to scaffold the application. In Chapter 5, we broke out a few of those controllers to show actual calls against the domain. However, we didn't delve into the functionality of the domain. Here is where we dig deeper.

We'll show you the full power of Grails database persistence and explain all the options available to you. In addition, we'll discuss the idea of services—something that should be familiar to any enterprise developer. Unlike controllers, services don't contain any specific web knowledge like sessions and request parameters do.

GORM

We've shown you how to interact with the database, but we've left the process a bit nebulous until now. In this chapter, we'll go over the specifics behind how GORM works. Most frameworks, especially those straight out of the box, have their own mechanism for persisting to the database. Ruby on Rails uses ActiveRecord as the persistence mechanism. Java EE frameworks use the JPA (which, if you're on JBoss Application Server, is simply Hibernate underneath the covers). WebSphere uses iBATIS.

Grails uses GORM. However, GORM is not its own creation; like JBoss, it uses Hibernate for its persistence implementation. GORM simply wraps Hibernate in Groovy layers. This is a blessing, because Hibernate gives GORM all of the necessary plumbing code, allowing GORM to focus on the usability instead. In fact, if you're familiar with ActiveRecord and Hibernate, you should be about 95% good to go when it comes to writing domain objects in Grails. GORM truly is an amalgamation of the ActiveRecord and Hibernate, giving you the best of both worlds. As we move along with examples on how to use GORM, the similarities and differences will become more apparent. GORM is a broad topic and requires a book of its own; we refer you to the well written documentation (`http://grails.org/doc/latest/guide/GORM.html`), along with this chapter.

Collab-Todo's Domain

Before going into depth about how to create domains in Groovy, let's start by explaining what you'll be creating. In Chapter 4, we gave you the base of the domain structure with the `Todo`, `Category`, and `User` classes. However, this application wouldn't be that interesting if we kept just those three domain objects. We decided to wait to show you the entire domain for two major reasons:

- We didn't want to overwhelm you with the domain when you were just starting to learn the system.
- Without more background, you might not be entirely familiar with the way the domain is created.

However, now it's time introduce you to the entire domain. We'll start by going over what the Java class domain looks like. Then we'll explain the options for creating and configuring the domain components. Finally, we'll show you the database you'll create with the domain configurations.

Figure 6-1 shows a class-level diagram filled with connectors and columns. This should give you an overview of the application you'll build and explain what the individual parts mean. Also look at the source code to get an idea of how you'll transition from the diagram in Figure 6-1 to the actual code you'll use throughout the book. (You can find the code samples for this chapter in the Source Code/Download area of the Apress web site [`www.apress.com`].) Please note that this diagram contains two domains that we'll use in the next chapter as part of the security apparatus.

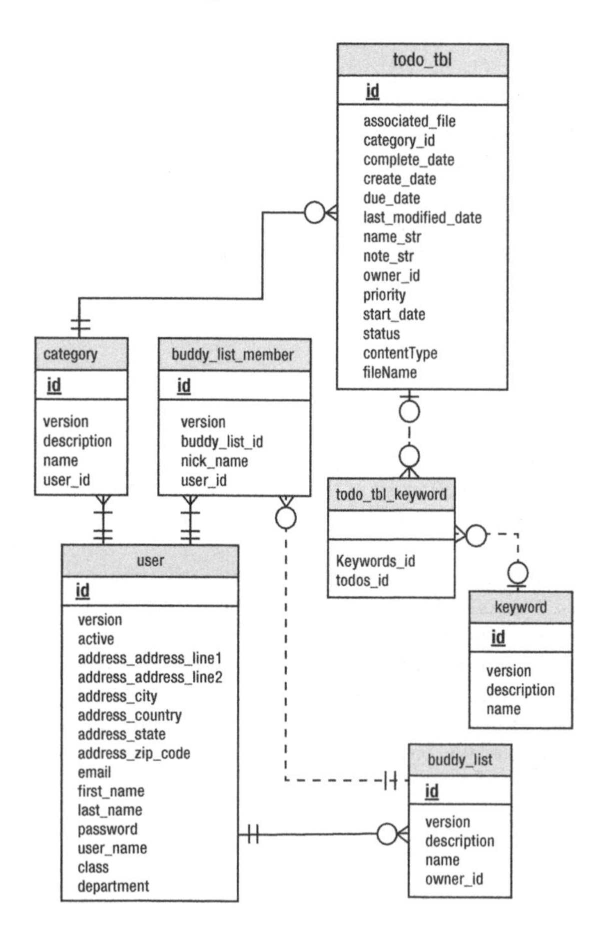

Figure 6-1. *Class-level diagram of the domain*

■ **Note** We're using the domain model to map the database; we're not using the database to map the domain model. This is becoming a fairly standard practice, although you're more than welcome to do the reverse.

A few of these tables should seem familiar to you. Table 6-1 provides a list of each domain object and a brief description of its purpose.

Table 6-1. *Domain Classes Used for the Collab-Todo Application*

Domain Name	Description
`Address`	An inner domain object to store inside the `User.groovy` file, because you'll use it as an embedded class anyway.
`Admin`	Extends the `User` class. You'll use it for administrators, where you'll track what department they are with. You will *not* use this class in permissioning, though.
`BuddyList`	Defines the buddy lists for each of the users.
`BuddyListMember`	Each person the users want in their buddy lists must be referenced in this class. The other purpose of this class is to assign nicknames.
`Category`	Creates specific names to categorize todos by.
`Keyword`	Creates keywords to differentiate the individual todos.
`Todo`	The holder for all the todos. This is the main object of the application.
`User`	Stores information about the person creating the todo.

As we move through this chapter, we will add various relations and constraints to the domain model. Let's start with how you actually create the domain object.

Creating Domain Objects

Because we're discussing how to create the domain objects that create the database, it's best to start small by examining just one table at first. In the previous two chapters, we showed you how to start the domain collection and add to it. Now we'll dive into all the options and the specifics of how domain creation works. Luckily, even if you've never worked with Hibernate or Java Data Objects (JDO), learning how to use GORM will be easy. For one, it's intuitive. For example, with normal JDOs, you have to memorize what *many-to-one*, *one-to-one*, and so on mean. With GORM, relationships are easier to define. The relationships are defined in a DSL syntax so that domain A *belongs to* domain B or domain A *has many* domain Bs associated with it. GORM was built with a DSL, so the terms you use to create the area sound like how you speak.

We'll take a few steps back before going forward. We'll start with basic domain creation, and investigate what's going on under the covers. Then we'll go into more advanced settings for the domain, including how to create complex object types and how to overwrite the storage of the domain. By the end of this section, you should be ready to create and customize almost any domain object you need.

Basic Domain Creation

Figure 6-1 showed the domain model you'll use, and in the previous chapters, you saw the implementation of a few domain objects. However, we have not detailed how you create a domain object of your own, your options in creating it, or even how it affects the underlying database. It's time to expand your knowledge. We'll detail two sets of concepts:

- Creating a fully functional domain model with constraints and relationships
- Understanding how these domain objects create and interact with the database

First, let's recreate the Todo domain object. We're not doing this to waste your time, or because we get paid by the page (we don't). We're doing this because you should see what's occurring to the database when you create the tables we defined for CollabTodo application. While it's nice that the GORM tools isolate you from having to create the database tables directly with SQL commands, you still need to have a grasp on what happens behind the scenes.

If you have ever created a domain object in EJB3 or Hibernate, this will seem familiar. Let's refresh our memory of the Todo domain and see how it interacts with the database. Listing 6-1 contains a partial listing of the domain; we're only showing the domain properties.

Listing 6-1. Revisiting the Todo Domain

```
class Todo {

    static belongsTo = [User, Category]

    User owner
    Category category
    String name
    String note
    Date createdDate
    Date dueDate
    Date completedDate
    String priority
    String status

    ...
}
```

You might be wondering, "What is GORM doing when it stores the domain in the database?" Well, that's actually pretty simple. Figure 6-2 shows a snapshot of the table from a MySQL database. Note how it is the implementation of the todo table seen in Figure 4-17 from Chapter 4.

```
mysql> describe todo;
+----------------+--------------+------+-----+---------+----------------+
| Field          | Type         | Null | Key | Default | Extra          |
+----------------+--------------+------+-----+---------+----------------+
| id             | bigint(20)   | NO   | PRI | NULL    | auto_increment |
| version        | bigint(20)   | NO   |     | NULL    |                |
| category_id    | bigint(20)   | NO   | MUL | NULL    |                |
| completed_date | datetime     | NO   |     | NULL    |                |
| created_date   | datetime     | NO   |     | NULL    |                |
| due_date       | datetime     | NO   |     | NULL    |                |
| name           | varchar(255) | NO   |     | NULL    |                |
| note           | varchar(255) | NO   |     | NULL    |                |
| owner_id       | bigint(20)   | NO   | MUL | NULL    |                |
| priority       | varchar(255) | NO   |     | NULL    |                |
| status         | varchar(255) | NO   |     | NULL    |                |
+----------------+--------------+------+-----+---------+----------------+
11 rows in set (0.01 sec)

mysql> _
```

Figure 6-2. *The todo table*

If you compare this table to the domain, you'll notice a few differences. Let's break them down into a few areas.

New Columns

Probably the first things you'll notice are the auto-generated primary key ID and the version. The ID is always used as the reference for the primary key; you can access it off the domain object at any time. The ID ties the particular detached domain object to the persisted one. Hibernate also uses a `version` field for transactional integrity and to support optimistic locking. This works much like ActiveRecord in Rails, which allows you to have the primary key and version created for you; unfortunately, the downside is that you cannot overwrite the primary key by hand.

■ **Note** It may seem like a downside that the primary key is set for you by default, but in practice, using a single unique ID primary key with Hibernate allows for the best performance when interacting with the database. We'll show you how to use mappings to change the primary key in the "Changing the Primary Key" section of the chapter.

Naming

Next, notice that the table name and column names are assigned. The names that were in CamelCase before are now switched to snake_case (lowercased and separated by an underscore).

Foreign Keys

In most databases, foreign keys or foreign key indexes are created between the `User` and `Category` tables. GORM sets up the foreign key by taking the class that has the `belongsTo` reserved word—in this case, the `Category` class has `belongsTo = User`—and saving the `user_id` column in the category table to the database. The `user_id` column is the concatenation of the `belongsTo` table name with `_id`.

Data Type

For the most part, data types are derived from the types you set in the domain itself. So `Strings` become `VARCHARs`, `Dates` become `DATETIMEs`, and so on. Of course, the exact type is dependent on the actual database you're using and the constraints applied to the property.

Setting Default Values

Many applications have a default value to store in the database if you don't select one for them. Setting a default value is easy in GORM; simply set the value as you would to a normal domain object. In general, a status usually has a starting value. In the Collab-Todo application, your value will not be "Completed" from the get-go, so start the status at Started. If the user wants to change this upon creation, he can. Listing 6-2 showcases the updated change.

Listing 6-2. The Todo with a Default Value for Status

```
class Todo {

    static belongsTo = [User, Category]

    User owner
    Category category
    String name
    String note
    Date createdDate
    Date dueDate
    Date completedDate
    String priority
    String status = "Started"

    ...
}
```

Large Object Types

Before we move on to relationships, let's discuss the treatment of large object types. Large objects are generally binary large objects (BLOBs) and character large objects (CLOBs) that get persisted to the database. Although we're storing objects to the database as an example and will be using it to highlight features in Chapter 8 on downloading and uploading files, we don't necessarily suggest using a database to store files. Files can be *very* large, and unless you need to version those files, it is unwise to waste the database as a storage place. Instead, use the file system to keep files. Remember that the point of a file system is to store files.

Of course, there are legitimate reasons to store files in the database, so if you want to store BLOBs, simply set the datatype to byte[]. Note that we've added an item to Todo called associatedFile. When you update the database in MySQL, you will notice that the object type created is TINYBLOB. In addition, setting the maxSize on the constraints produces a longtext column in the database when using MySQL.

Creating Relationships

Unless you're building a domain structure with only a few classes, you're bound to have relations to other classes. For example, the Todo object belongs to one Category and one User. Conversely, a User can have many Todos. We'll discuss the following four relationship types:

- One-to-one
- One-to-many
- Many-to-one
- Many-to-many

Writing relationships in Grails is relatively easy. In fact, the syntax and usage are virtually identical to Ruby on Rails' ActiveRecord. Knowing that GORM is based on Hibernate, you might expect the syntax and usage to be more like Hibernate or JPA, but this isn't the case. With standard JPA, you can create relations using annotations solely on one side of the bean. However, these annotations can get entirely too complex. For example, take the many-to-many relationship in JPA shown in Listing 6-3.

Listing 6-3. Example of aMany-to-Many Relationship in JPA

```
@ManyToMany
@JoinTable(name="COURSE_TO_STUDENT_TBL",
    joinColumns=@JoinColumn(name="courseId"),
    inverseJoinColumns=@JoinColumn(name="studentId"))
private Collection<Student> students;
```

Note that there are different annotations for each type of relationship. In reality, JPA configures more from the database level, whereas GORM is programmed more from the verbal level. First, we'll review the players involved, and then we'll show you how to create the relationships.

Players Involved

As you saw in Chapter 4, creating relationships is quite easy. However, we'll provide an example for those who need a refresher. You'll need to modify only two pieces of code in your classes. You'll use the following two keywords:

- `hasMany`
- `belongsTo`

The next section shows examples of these in action.

One-to-One

A oneto-one relationship exists when one record in table A references exactly one record in table B, and vice versa. For example, the `User` table contains a reference to the `Address` table. There is exactly one user at one particular address. Listing 6-4 shows an example of each table.

Listing 6-4. Example of a Oneto-One Relationship

```
class User {
    ...
    Address address
}
class Address {
    User user
}
```

■ **Note** The code for the book doesn't contain a reference to `User` in `Address`, because we're going to treat `Address` as an embedded class. This is merely one way of doing it. We actually have no pure oneto-one relationships in our code base.

One-to-Many

A oneto-many relationship exists when a record in table A can reference many records in table B, but when those records in table B can *only* reference one record in table A. Our application contains many examples of oneto-many relationships, one of which is the relationship between the user and the buddy lists. A user can have multiple buddy lists, but the buddy list can only be referenced to one user. Listing 6-5 shows an example of this in the code.

Listing 6-5. Example of a Oneto-Many Relationship

```
class User {
    ...
    static hasMany = [buddyLists: BuddyList]
}
class BuddyList {
    static belongsTo = User
}
```

hasMany, which is put on the consuming domain, tells you that this domain "has many" of this domain. The belongsTo keyword is on the other side of the object—in this case, the BuddyList. The belongsTo keyword refers to what the properties are referencing.

Let's look at another example in the BuddyList domain that has many BuddyListMembers, as shown in Listing 6-6.

Listing 6-6. Defining hasMany on BuddyListMember

```
class BuddyList {
    static hasMany = [members: BuddyListMember]
    ...
}
```

Here, members references the variable name you'll use to retrieve the BuddyListMembers from the BuddyList object. This is just one side of the relationship. The other side is actually the more important side and it ties the constraints together in the database.

Listing 6-7 shows how to define belongsTo on the BuddyList object.

Listing 6-7. Defining belongsTo on BuddyListMember

```
class BuddyListMember {
    static belongsTo = BuddyList
}
```

Putting this static reference on belongsTo tells the BuddyListMember class to put a reference to BuddyList in BuddyListMember's table upon database creation.

Managing Relationships

Adding to the relationships is quite easy and makes use of Groovy dynamic syntax. Listing 6-8 shows how to add and remove members from BuddyList.

Listing 6-8. Adding BuddyList to and Removing BuddyList from BuddyListMember

```
BuddyList myList
myList.addToMembers(someMember)
myList.removeFromMembers(someMember)
```

Many-to-One

As you've probably guessed, a manyto-one relationship is the inverse of the oneto-many relationship. Listing 6-5 shows a manyto-one relationship from the point of view of the buddy list. This is an example of what we meant when we said that GORM is more intuitive than JPA. JPA would have included an `@ManyToOne` annotation.

Many-to-Many

The manyto-many relationship further demonstrates the distinction between the way GORM and JPA implement relationships. A manyto-many relationship looks much different and is more readable than the many-to-many relationships in JPA. Readability is one benefit of using dynamic languages such as Groovy and Ruby.

In a many-to-many relationship, a record in table A can reference multiple records in table B. Conversely, a record in table B can reference multiple records in table A. To set this up, use the same keywords you used previously, so you have nothing new to learn. Both records contain `hasMany`, because they both reference many records in the other table. In addition, at least *one* class needs `belongsTo` to create the relation (it doesn't matter which one). Listing 6-9 shows an example of implementing a many-to-many relationship between the `Todo` and `Keyword` domains.

Listing 6-9. Example of aManyto-Many Relationship

```
class Todo {
    static hasMany = [keywords: Keyword]
}
class Keyword {
    static belongsTo = Todo
    static hasMany = [todos: Todo]
}
```

Here, you can add and remove the keywords the same way you did in Listing 6-8.

Overwriting Default Settings

Now that we've established the basic rules of domain creation, you should be able to do everything you need to create your domain objects. There are a few items we have not covered yet, such as constraints, but we'll wait until the "Validation" section. Here, we'll go over a few "advanced" settings for domain items. First, we'll show you how to fine-tune your tables, columns, and indexes for specific names and values. You could configure these items in a Hibernate configuration file, but we'll show you how to configure them in DSLs. In addition, we'll show you how to add properties to domains that are not persisted, and explain how to fire events when inserting, updating, and deleting a table.

Adjusting the Mappings

GORM allows you to adjust names of the tables and columns on the database itself in a DSL way without the need for extra configuration files, as Hibernate requires. To demonstrate, we'll customize the `Todo` domain. By the end, you'll see those changes reflected in the domain.

To make these adjustments, you need to add a static mapping closure to the domain object. The additional code simply adds to those static mappings. Check out the adjustment to Todo in Listing 6-10.

Listing 6-10. Todo with the Mapping Closure Defined

```
class Todo {
    ...
    static mapping = {
        // insert mappings here
    }
}
```

Now you can start adding to the static mappings, slowly growing the mapping for added functionality.

Table and Column Naming

First, change the table name and a column name; these are common changes an enterprise environment. To change the table name persisted from todo to todo_tbl, add the following line to the mapping:

```
table 'todo_tbl'
```

This simply tells GORM that the table is named todo_tbl.

That was easy enough. Now, let's update the column names. Because a table can have multiple columns, column names are grouped under one sub-block in the mapping. Change the name of the name and note to name_str and note_str. This naming convention is somewhat common for DBAs, who like to see the column type simply by glancing at the column name. To do this, add the following code to the mapping:

```
columns {
            name column:'name_str'
            note column:'note_str'
        }
```

GORM reads this as, "For columns, the name property references column name_str."

Changing the Primary Key

Earlier versions of Grails provided no easy way of changing the primary key. Even worse, you couldn't change the generation method. While this probably didn't affect smaller shops, it likely affected large companies, many of which demanded that DBAs use stored procedures or other techniques to generate a primary key. First, we'll go over how to change the generator, and then we'll discuss how to change the primary key itself.

By default, the generator uses the native implementation of the database. This could be an identity or a sequence, depending on the database. However, let's say you want to change it to use a high-low method of determining the number. You would add this entry to your mapping:

```
id generator:'hilo', params:[table:'hi_value',column:'next_value',max_lo:100]
```

This entry starts off with identifying itself by referencing to the id property, which is the default property on the domain. Next, generator defines the generator to be used, and params defines the parameters to pass into the generator. For a high-low calculation, the generator needs a table name, a column in the table, and a maximum low. Remember, this is all based on what Hibernate expects as parameters for each of the generations.

The other common approach to creating primary keys is to use a composite key, which has multiple attributes. In the example, this could be a combination of the name and the due date, the name and the user ID, and so on. Before we explain how to change the primary key to a composite key, we recommend that you don't do this unless you have to. Many would think of it as just poor design; however, the more important reason not to change it from a single ID is the fact that Hibernate performs *best* when using a primary key generated by one column.

This said, let's look at how to do it. Suppose you want the primary key to be the name plus the due date, because you cannot have the same named item due on the same date. Defining it is as simple as adding a composite ID entry in the mapping:

```
id composite:[create 'name','dueDate']
```

■ **Note** You cannot define a composite ID with a generated ID. In addition, because you can't have two different primary key techniques on one table, we've only made use of the generated ID for this chapter's source code.

Disabling Versioning

By default, GORM is configured with optimistic locking enabled and uses versioning to help maintain a version number in the database. Having versions is Hibernate's way of checking to make sure that as you're updating a record, someone doesn't update it underneath you. Whenever you update a record in the table, the version number is incremented. Before the actual save occurs, Hibernate checks the version for the record you're trying to save against the record in the database. If they're different, Hibernate doesn't allow the save to occur.

While this sounds great, there may be legitimate reasons you don't want to use versioning. In some applications, it may not matter if the record is updated by two people at the same time. To turn off versioning, simply type this command in the mapping:

```
static mapping = {
                    version false
}
```

This eliminates the column `version` from your table, and Hibernate will no longer perform any version checking.

Changing Eager Fetching and Locking

When you retrieve embedded domains from the database, GORM tells Hibernate to fetch them lazily. However, if you want to fetch them eagerly, you must disable lazy fetching for the column.

The Todo object offers no good exasmple of this, so we'll use the `User` object, which has an embedded `address` property. In Listing 6-11, you can see an example of `Todo` with the embedded `address` domain being fetched eagerly.

Listing 6-11. Todo with the Embedded Address Fetched Eagerly

```
class User {
    static mapping = {
        columns {
            address lazy:false
        }
    }
}
```

Creating Database Indexes

You can also tune the database indexes from the GORM domain level. DBAs can then create these by hand in the database, but many people (especially those without full-time database architects) find it easier to tune them via the application framework. This ensures that if you're using the automatic update feature of the database, the indexes will also get updated.

In the example, you'll define the name and createDate indexes. Name the first index Name_Idx, and name the createDate index Name_Create_Date_Idx. Listing 6-12 shows you how to define the index in the columns section.

Listing 6-12. Defining Indexes for the Todo Domain

```
class Todo {
static mapping = {
        columns {
            name index:'Name_Idx, Name_Create_Date_Idx'
            createDate index:'Name_Create_Date_Idx'
        }
    }
}
```

Class Inheritance

It's typical of a domain diagram to have class inheritance, but this concept isn't always typical in database design. Luckily, with GORM, it's literally as easy as extending a class. For the data model, the Admin class extends the User class. Listing 6-13 shows the Admin class.

Listing 6-13. The Admin Class That Extends the User Class

```
class Admin extends User {
    String department
}
```

There are two different strategies, called table-per-hierarchy or table-per-subclass, for implementing the inheritance. With table-per-hierarchy mapping, one table is shared between the parent and all child classes, while table-per-subclass uses a different table for each subclass.

By default GORM, classes use table-per-hierarchy inheritance mapping.

```
static mapping = {
    tablePerHierarchy true
}
```

This has the disadvantage that columns cannot have a NOT-NULL constraint applied to them at the database level but you're forced to have not-null constraints on all child columns because they share the same table.

The table-per-subclass might be seen as the better strategy, since each subclass is in its own table.

```
static mapping = {
    tablePerHierarchy false              // table-per-subclass
}
```

The main drawback of table-per-subclass is that the JOIN queries used to obtain the results from all the parents of a given child in a too-deep inheritance hierarchy might lead to performance issues.

Turning on the Cache

One of the big pluses with Hibernate is its ability to use second-level caching, which stores data associated with the domain class to the Hibernate cache. The advantage to this is that if you retrieve the data, it will pull it from the cache instead of making a call to the database. This is a great mechanism for retrieving data that is accessed often and is rarely changed. To configure the secondlevel cache, you have to follow a few steps. First, update the `DataSource.groovy` file, then update the domain object in question.

Configuring the cache in the data source is easy. Add the code from Listing 6-14 into your `DataSource.groovy` file.

Listing 6-14. The Entry to Initialize the Hibernate SecondLevel Cache

```
hibernate {
    cache.use_second_level_cache=true
    cache.use_query_cache=true
    cache.provider_class='org.hibernate.cache.EhCacheProvider'
}
```

This tells Hibernate that you want to use second-level caching and that the provider you'll use is `EhCacheProvider`. You can swap this line out with another provider if you like; this just happens to be the de facto Hibernate cache.

Next, initialize the cache for the individual domain objects with which you want to associate it. Initialize it for `Todo` by inserting the cache entry into the mapping constraints. Add the following line to your mapping:

```
static mapping = {
    ...
    cache true
}
```

When using `true`, it signals that the object should be stored in the cache and it will configure a "read-write" cache that includes both lazy and non-lazy properties. However, you can further adjust the cache settings to be `read-only`, `transactional`, or `non-lazy`. To do this, you use a similar entry to the previous one, but with more specifics:

```
cache usage:'read-only', include:'non-lazy'  // or cache usage: 'transactional'
```

Besides configuring the cache at the class level, you can also configure it for embedded classes at the domain level. The configuration is virtually identical to what you did previously, except you specify the column that will be cached, as shown in Listing 6-15.

Listing 6-15. Configuring the Cache for the Address on the User

```
class User {
    static mapping = {
                address cache:true
    }
```

Transient Properties

In JPA and GORM, all the properties on your domain (or entity) objects are persisted to the database by default. This can be disadvantageous when you want to have properties on your domains that either are amalgamations of other properties or simply don't need to be persisted. Luckily, in GORM, you can easily mark properties to not be persisted.

In GORM and JPA, properties that you don't want to persist are called *transient properties*. In JPA, you mark each property with the `@Transient` annotation. In GORM, you create a transient mapping of all these properties.

For the example, use the `User` table. Inside `User`, you want to have a `confirmPassword` property, so you can make sure the user typed in the correct password. Obviously, you don't need the password persisted twice, so you mark it as transient. In Listing 6-16, you can see that you add `confirmPassword` to the `transients` mapping.

Listing 6-16. User Object with the Transient confirmPassword

```
class User {
    static transients = [ "confirmPassword" ]

    String firstName
    String lastName
    String userName
    String password
    String email
    String confirmPassword
}
```

As you can see, you still add the `confirmPassword` to the normal domain, but you also add it to a list of strings called `transients`, marking it as transient.

GORM Events

Often in normal domain and DAO architectures, you could have base save/update/delete methods. However, if you ever want to add a universal concept for a particular domain, such as updating timestamps or writing to a log, you could overwrite the method, add your own custom needs, and then call the parent method. However, GORM and some of these other more modern frameworks eliminate the need for the DAO classes and allow you to access the domain class directly. However, this can pose a problem, because now the individual developers are responsible for updating fields (such as a last-modified date) that always need to be run when updating, and writing to the log file. Yuck; this could lead to disaster.

Luckily, GORM has an answer to this problem. It gives you the ability to define these types of transitions at the domain level. `Todo` has `lastModifiedDate` and `createDate`. In GORM, you can add two methods to the domain that are automatically called before inserting and before updating the database. Obviously, the `beforeInsert` method is called before insertion, and `beforeUpdate` is called before updating. Listing 6-17 shows the code you need to add to `Todo` in order to have your dates modified at insertion and creation.

Listing 6-17. Code for Adding the Automatic Events for Todo

```
def beforeInsert = {
   createDate = new Date()
    lastModifiedDate = new Date()
}
def beforeUpdate = {
   lastModifiedDate = new Date()
}
```

Now whenever a save or update is called, these two methods are called regardless from where the save or update is called from. In addition, a `beforeDelete` event is called before a deletion.

Do you detect a pattern here? Having create and modify dates is a fairly standard pattern. In order to have this same functionality on more than one class, you would have to add those seven lines of code plus the two lines to define the domains in each of your domain classes.

Luckily, as you may have guessed, GORM has a way around this. If you have `lastUpdated` and `dateCreated` named properties, you can configure GORM to automatically update them by adding the following line in the mapping:

```
static mapping = {
        ...
        autoTimestamp false
}
```

Note that the properties *have* to be named `lastUpdated` and `dateCreated`. In addition, `lastUpdated` only gets updated when the domain is actually updated and *not* on a creation like before.

Finally, there is one other way to adjust items, and that is on the actual loading of the item, or rather after the item has been loaded and all the properties have been set. Listing 6-18 contains a method that displays a message upon loading the domain object.

Listing 6-18. Method Called upon Loading the Domain

```
def onLoad = {
    print 'We have loaded the item'
}
```

Database Model

Before moving onto validation, let's see how all the updates to the domain model affect a MySQL database.

In Figure 6-3, you can see the output of the database structure after being created by GORM.

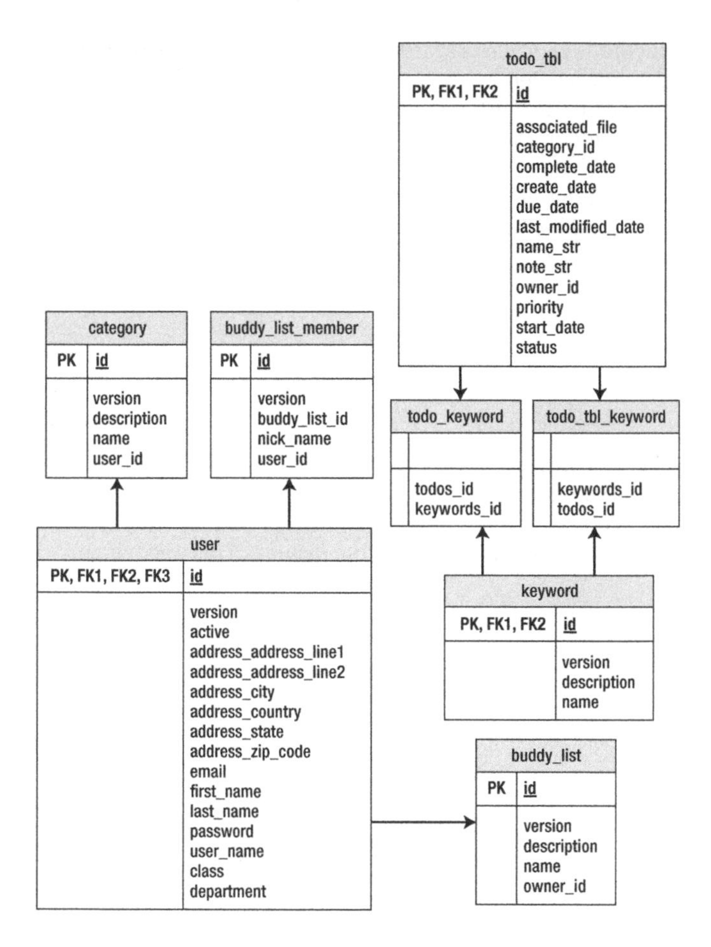

Figure 6-3. *The database model after being created by GORM*

■ **Note** We kept the modifications to the generator, and we included the lack of versioning and the name change, so Figure 6-3 includes some extra tables you might not have expected.

Validation

In the previous chapters, you saw that when you executed `save()` on the `Todo` instance, GORM would only persist the data if the validations (set in the constraints) passed for the domain. The `save()` would return a `true` or `false` depending on whether persisting was successful. Now the real question is, "How do you know what to validate?"

Constraints are somewhat of a dual-use item. Their main functionality is to validate items before they're persisted to the database, but they can also adjust some of the settings on the database itself for the column. For example, if you mark a column in your constraints as nullable or set a maximum length, then these changes will be reflected at the database level as well. Out of the box, GORM comes with quite a few validations, and it even provides the framework for creating a few custom validations of your own.

For the purpose of the sample application, you only need a small subset of those validations, so while we will list all of them here, you'll only use a few. In addition, just like any application, it would be impossible for all the built-in validations to cover every situation, so we'll also introduce the idea of custom validations. We will then close with a discussion about how to change the messages to something more meaningful.

Constraints

You've already seen constraints in Chapter 4. These were used to determine whether some properties had to be filled in on the domain object, and also to set the order of display when scaffolding the domain. Let's look at other features for which you can use constraints.

You have seen the `nullable` constraint, which not only verifies that the object is not `null`, but also sets the database property to "not `null`" (in Figure 6-2, you can see many properties are set to "not `null`"). Of course, this assumes you're using GORM to create or update your database.

Let's start with the familiar `Todo` object, since this is the object to which you'll apply the most validations. Start with the basic skeleton shown in Listing 6-19.

Listing 6-19. The Todo Object with the Validation Constraints

```
1. class Todo {
2.     ...
3.     static constraints = {
4.         owner(nullable:false)
5.         name(blank:false)
6.     }
7. }
```

In line 3, `static constraints = {` starts the constraint area. This line makes sense when you think about it. Constraints are static because they span multiple instances. The next two lines define two of the constraints for you. Line 4 tells you that the owner cannot be `nullable`; however, it could be a blank string. Line 5 not only doesn't allow for `nulls`, but it also doesn't allow the name to be blank.

Using Built-In Constraints

You can add many different constraints to your domain object, including everything from `null` checking to credit-card validation. In our application, we will use quite a few of these validations, although there's no way for us to use them all. Table 6-2, however, shows all the possible constraints provided by GORM.

Table 6-2. Constraints Built into GORM

Name	Description
blank	Validates that the string either is or is not blank
creditCard	Validates that the string either is or is not a valid credit card number
email	Validates that the string either is or is not a valid e-mail address
inList	Validates that the constraint is contained within the supplied list
matches	Validates that the object matches the supplied regular expression
max	Validates that the number is not larger than the supplied maximum value
min	Validates that the number is not smaller than the supplied minimum value
minSize	Validates that the object's string's length or collection's size is larger than the supplied amount
maxSize	Validates that the object's string's length or collection's size is smaller than the supplied amount
notEqual	Validates that the object is not equal to the supplied object
nullable	Validates that the object is not null
range	Validates that the object falls within the given range
scale	Constrains the supplied number to a particular decimal place
size	Validates that the object's string's length or collection's size is equal to the supplied amount
url	Validates that the supplied string is formatted as a valid URL

Of course, it is impossible for the Grails team to predict all the possible constraints needed by an application. Using pre-created constraints is the easy part. In the next section, we'll show you how to create your own customized constraints using closures.

Creating Custom Constraints

Let's take another look at that Todo object and what other constraints you need to define for it. Let's examine the startDate property and see what you need to constrain on it. For starters, you don't want to allow users to use start dates in the past. The purpose of this application is to create tasks that start now or in the future; in theory, this is something that is probably created at the beginning and never changed. Nothing in the built-in constraints shown in Table 6-2 does what you need, so you need to create your first custom constraint. You need to allow the constraint to be null, and if the constraint is filled in, you need to make sure the date doesn't occur in the past.

To define custom constraints in GORM, mark the custom constraint with a validator. Take a look at this in action in Listing 6-20.

Listing 6-20. Applying a Simple Custom Validator to Todo

```
static constraints = {
    ...
    startDate(nullable:true,
        validator: {
            if (it?.compareTo(new Date()) < 0 ) {
                return false
            }
```

```
            return true
        })
}
```

As you can see, this starts off like normal validations with `nullable:true`, but then it adds custom validation. All custom validators start with the word `validator`, followed by a closure. Inside the closure, you need to return `true` if the validation passes, and `false` if the validation doesn't pass. Of course, you cannot create a decent validation with a random closure that has no information. However, that is why you have access to the property, demarked with `it`, inside the `validator` closure. The `it` represents the item that is being validated. For our validation, we are going to check that the start date doesn't occur before the current date. As you can see, it's pretty easy to create a custom validation, but you can make it even more advanced.

For this next example of functionality, let's take a look at the `completeDate` field. It makes sense that `completeDate` has to occur after `startDate`. To create a custom validator to show this, you need to have access to the `startDate` object. No problem. Check out its implementation in Listing 6-21.

Listing 6-21. Applying aMore Complex Validator to Todo

```
static constraints = {
    ...
COMPLETEDATE(NULLABLE:TRUE,
        validator: {
            val, obj ->
                if (val != null) {
                    return val.after(obj.createDate)
                }
                return true
        })
}
```

As you can see, this looks similar to the validator you defined in Listing 6-20, with one small change: you also pass in the variables `val, obj ->`. `val` is the variable that is passed in; the previous example, it represented the value of `startDate`. In addition, you're now also passing in `obj`, which is the domain object you're using—in this case, the `Todo` object. This allows you to compare `completeDate` directly with that domain's `createDate`.

This gives you a fairly dynamic way of creating validations. In fact, you can even create queries inside the validator, allowing for some slick validations. Let's take a look at the `Keyword` domain, which is one of the constraints. To reduce redundancy, you want to put a constraint on the name, because you don't want to have any names that are also used as names for the `description`. You can easily make the name a unique field, but you also want to make sure that no description is the same as the name. If there is, you're probably creating a name twice or not properly defining the other one. Listing 6-22 shows how to find all the instances of `description` to make sure it doesn't have the same text as the `name` property.

Listing 6-22. A Custom Constraint That Performs aQuery

```
class Keyword {
    ...
    String name
    String description
    static constraints = {
        name(validator: {
            if (Keyword.findAllByDescription(it).size() > 0) {
                return false
            }
```

```
            return true
        })
    }
}
```

Calling the Validator

Validation is called behind the scenes when you do a save or when there is an update to the domain object. Of course, this prevents you from persisting objects that don't pass your own validations. However, there may be times when you want to call the validator manually, so you can do some additional checking on it or test that specific messages get returned. Listing 6-23 shows a simple check for a validation that is called twice. The first time, it fails; the second time, it passes.

Listing 6-23. Example of aValidation Called Twice

```
void testValidationsOnTodo() {
    def todo = new Todo(
        owner: user1, name: "Validation Test", note:"Detailed web app description",
        createDate: new Date(), dueDate: new Date(), lastModifiedDate:
        new Date(), priority: '1', status: '1' )
    assert true == todo.validate()

    // shouldn't validate
    todo.completeDate = new Date() - 1
    todo.name = null
    assert false == todo.validate()

    // readjust the date to be in the future
    todo.completeDate = new Date() + 3
   assert true == todo.validate()
}
```

In this example, you can see that you set `completedDate` to the past, which is not allowed with the constraints. When the first validation fails, you update the completed date to the future; now, as you can see, the validation passes. This example shows you how you can use validation in your test cases to make sure you have an item that works. This isn't as necessary for out-of-the-box validators, but for your custom validators, you'll want to use this to make sure you wrote the validation correctly.

Validation Messages

In Chapters 4 and 5, we showed the error messages that Grails provides when a validation fails on a page. In Chapter 5, we went over more extensively how to write the error outputs to the page without using scaffolding. However, we haven't yet explained how those message names are derived. Now that we've gone over constraints, we'll explain the validation messages.

As you may have guessed from looking at the messages in `messages.properties` and looking at the constraints, there is a roughly one-to-one ratio between constraints and messages, with an added error message for the custom constraints.

Let's take a look at the `Todo` example. We'll be focusing on three constraints: `name`, `priority`, and `completeDate`. Listing 6-24 shows what those three validations look like.

Listing 6-24. The name, priority, and completeDate Validations in Todo

```
name(blank:false)
priority(blank:false)
completeDate(nullable:true,
    validator: {
        val, obj ->
           if (val != null) {
               return val.after(obj.createDate)
           }
           return true
    }
)
```

Querying the Database

Starting in Chapter 4, we gave you a fully functioning web site with database persistence. In this chapter, we have expanded that relatively crude database, and now you essentially have a fully functioning schema complete with constraints and relations. Now that you have this wonderful database to use, it's time to start using it. We'll assume that if you're reading this book, you have at least cursory knowledge of creating SQL queries. However, if that's not the case, don't worry. Grails has made creating SQL queries extremely easy—in fact, it's almost too easy, if you ask us.

To begin, we'll go over five different ways to query the database. This might seem like an excessive way of querying the database, but in the end, you will find that you have the flexibility to create a query with as little or as much information as you need to provide.

We'll show you how to do simple CRUD operations. We demonstrated this in the previous two chapters, but we'll briefly rehash it so you can see how to build up your querying ability. We'll then explain how GORM really shows off its DSL capabilities by being able to create dynamic queries in the form of method names. You saw a bit of this in the earlier chapters when we did `findBy`, but now we'll show you all the options and parameters. We'll cover this for both straight single retrievals and for retrieving multiple objects.

Finally, we'll show you how to use Hibernate Query Language (HQL) queries instead of the more dynamic DSL queries. Sometimes using HQL is the only way to get the query you want.

GORM's CRUD Support

When interacting with a database, you need to know how to do basic CRUD operations. Most Java developers reading this are probably used to the standard DAO domain model, where after you create the domain, you create a DAO with various operations. These DAO models usually have the standard `void delete(Domain d)` and `get(String primaryKey)` methods. Before Hibernate, these methods would usually interact with the database directly with straight SQL calls. This methodology made sense when you had to write the SQL code directly, but with today's tools and a dynamic language like Groovy, these constraints are no longer necessary.

Hibernate helped eliminate the problem of having to hard-code SQL by allowing you to use more abstract terminology to persist to the database. But that solved only half the problem. Why do you even need DAO at that point? It's still a waste of programmers' time to create these DAO objects, and time is money.

Because we're using Groovy as the underlying language for Grails, we now have more options available to us. We'll start by looking at a test case that steps through the individual CRUD operations. Afterward, we'll discuss the ease of operations. Listing 6-25 shows a test case for updating the `User` object.

Listing 6-25. Performing CRUD Operations on the User

```
void testCRUDOperations() {
   // Let's create the user
    def userTemp = new User(userName: 'testUser', firstName:'John',
                               lastName:'Smith', password:'pass',
                               email:"smith@gmail.com")

    // Create - let's save it
    userTemp.save()
    // grab the user id
    def userId = userTemp.id

    // Update - since we are still within the session we caught it
    // we shouldn't need to do anything explicit
    userTemp.password = 'A new password'
    // let's see if it got updated
    userTemp = User.get(userId)
    assert "A new password" == userTemp.password
    assert "John" == userTemp.firstName

    // let's show the delete
    userTemp.delete()
    // let's make sure it got deleted
    assert null == User.get(userId)
}
```

As you can see, creating, updating, and deleting are as easy as pie. None of the domain objects have a `get`, `delete`, or `save` method, and there are no base classes. So how does this work? It's a simple method interception, as we discussed in Chapter 3. Grails has the ability to intercept methods and provide functionality for them. The same functionality of retrieving, deleting, and saving could be done in straight Java with aspects or dynamic proxies, but you wouldn't be able to get that far, because the previous tests wouldn't compile in straight Java. Using a dynamic language like Groovy gives you the best of both worlds. It keeps the object a lightweight object for passing between layers and storing into `HttpSession`, and it gives you the functionality of a bloated object with the get, save, and delete methods on it.

CRUD operations don't give you everything you'll need to do in an application, so you still need to create some dynamic queries. You need the options to select one or more than one record. You also may want to select records based on parameters or by interacting with multiple tables. In the next section, we'll go over creating these dynamic queries.

Creating Queries

To create the code for the Collab-Todo project, you have to create many dynamic queries throughout the book. You'll use these queries later on for a variety of things, from creating user-registration pages to creating the fancier Ajax items in Chapter 8. All of these actions require various types of dynamic support, and although the query portion is not the focus of those chapters, you'll need to understand how those queries are created and how to create some of your own queries.

Queries in GORM are different than queries in ActiveRecord or in EJB3. Because we're using Hibernate as the back end, they're obviously more like Hibernate queries. Actually, GORM has *more* options than Hibernate, because it makes use of Groovy's dynamic ability to make some DSLtype queries. The number of options you have are the same here. Each type serves its own purpose. If you want to become a Grails guru, it's important to understand the different types. GORM supports a number of powerful ways to query as described in the next few sections:

- Dynamic queries
- HQL queries
- Criteria queries
- Detached criteria
- Where queries

GORM's Dynamic Queries

As you just saw, creating dynamic CRUD queries is fairly easy. However, you're only able to do a simple retrieval based on the primary key (the ID). While this is necessary to most applications, you obviously need to do more than that. In the example application, you'll need to retrieve not only lists, but also lists of people and ever more specific queries.

In the upcoming sections, we'll go over multiple types of queries, ranging from fairly simple single finds to lists, criteria queries, and HQL queries. The criteria queries will make use of Groovy the most by allowing you to create a DSL of the query you want to create. This makes for some wonderfully easy queries to create. The downside is, unlike with the HQL queries, the criteria queries are limited to querying off only one class.

We'll start by showing you how to grow some single result-set queries, and then we'll go over how they work. We'll list the options for creating the queries, and finally, we'll show you how to create the query lists.

Counts

Probably the easiest query to create is to do a simple count. The code in Listing 6-26 counts the amount of `Todos`.

Listing 6-26. Counting the Amount of Todos

```
Todo.count()
```

Besides the standard count, you can also count the amount of `Todos` where the columns equal a particular value. Listing 6-27 counts the amount of `Todos` that have a priority of `"1"`.

Listing 6-27. Example of a countBy Query

```
Todo.countByPriority('1')
```

Single Result-Set Queries

Now we'll take a look at queries that return a single result set. You use these when you want to find one item. We'll go over these two types in this section:

- `findBy`
- `findWhere`

Although there are two different ways of performing a query, the end result and the usefulness are mostly equal. The main difference is how the query looks and how you pass the values into the query.

Let's take a look first at the `findBy` example, as shown in Listing 6-28. In this query, you find that `Todo` has a `priority` of `2` and a `status` of `3`.

Listing 6-28. Example of a findBy Query

```
Todo.findByPriorityAndStatus("2", "3")
```

As you can imagine, there is no method called `findByPriorityAndStatus` on `Todo`. This is one of our first examples of a dynamic query. In Figure 6-4, we broke up this query into its individual parts.

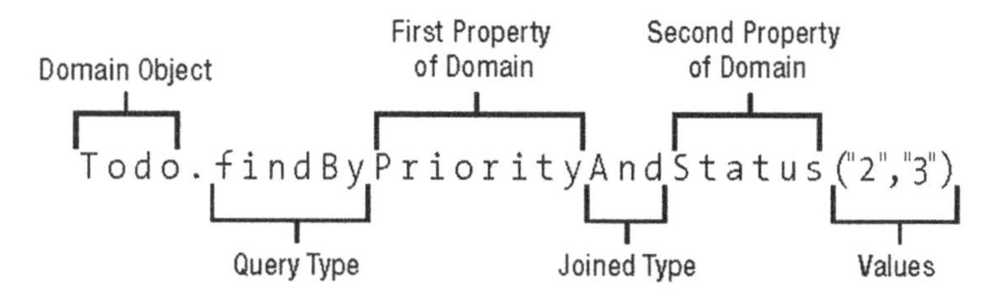

Figure 6-4. *The dynamic query broken up into its parts*

As you can see, the DSL method starts with a static `findBy` call. It then has a property name separated with an `And` and another property name. In fact, we could have added a few more `And`s if we wanted to; you're only limited by the amount of properties on the domain object. Additionally, you can separate the properties with either an `And` or an `Or`.

This approach is useful, especially if you want to mix `And`s and `Or`s. However, if you want to build something simpler that contains only `And`s, you can use the query shown in Listing 6-29.

Listing 6-29. Example of a findWhere Query

```
Todo.findWhere([ "priority": "1", status: "2"])
```

Although a bit simpler than the previous example, this example passes the properties and values into the class as a map. You pass the name of the domain's property as the key, and you pass the item you want it to equal as the value. This query is also more useful if you received a map of name values from another call.

Multiple Results Queries

The previous queries were only able to return single results; they would have thrown errors much like Hibernate does if you returned multiple results. In this section, we'll show you how to return multiple results. The way these are written looks much like the previous examples, except they return much more. In this section, we'll also add a few more select types:

- `findAllBy`
- `findAllWhere`
- `getAll`
- `listOrderBy`
- `list`

findAllBy

The `findAllBy` call is similar in functionality and use to the `findBy` method we used earlier. Listing 6-30 shows an example of two `findAllBy`s.

Listing 6-30. Two Examples of a findAllBy Query

```
Todo.findAllByName("Our First Web App")
Todo.findAllByPriorityOrStatus("2", "4")
```

In the first one, you're finding all records where the name equals one item; in the second, you're separating the retrieval with an `Or`, to denote if a record has a priority of "2" or a status of "4". As with `findBy`, this query is able to use `And` or `Or` operations to separate the domain properties.

findAllWhere

Again, `findAllWhere` is similar to the previously defined `findWhere`. Listing 6-31 shows an example of using `findAllWhere` to retrieve all `Todos` that have a `priority` of `1` and a `status` of `2`.

Listing 6-31. Example of a findAllWhere Query

```
Todo.findAllWhere([ "priority": "1", status: "2"])
```

getAll

`getAll` is much like the `get` method we covered in the "GORM's CRUD Support" section. However, `get` retrieves one item for an ID, while this method allows multiple items to be passed through. This is a basic convenience method when you already have the IDs. Listing 6-32 shows an example of retrieving three `Todos` with the IDs of `1`, `3`, and `5`.

Listing 6-32. Retrieving Three Todos

```
Todo.getAll(1,3,5)
Todo.getAll([1,3,5])
```

This code contains two examples, because you can pass in the objects either as a comma-separated list or as a map.

List

The next method is probably the most basic type of retrieval: retrieving all records. This returns all the items of the domain. Listing 6-33 retrieves all the items in `Todo`.

Listing 6-33. Example of a list Query

```
Todo.list()
```

listOrderBy

`listOrderBy` also retrieves the complete list of records from a domain, but it lets you arrange them by column. Listing 6-34 retrieves the entire list, ordering by the name column.

Listing 6-34. Example of a listOrderBy Query

```
Todo.listOrderByName()
```

Filtering Queries

We haven't gone over *all* the options for queries, because there are some overlapping configurations. In this section, we'll look at those overlapping configurations, which provide the ability to set the maximum results, the fetch modes, what to sort on, and the ordering. We'll only show the code for one type, but you can use the query types equally with any of these options:

- `list`
- `listOrderBy`
- `findAllBy`
- findBy

Some of this code is useful when you want to get a partial set of records back—for example, when doing pagination. Listing 6-35 gets results that should be 20 through 30, sorting on priority and in descending order.

Listing 6-35. Example of Filtering the Results

```
Todo.list(max: 10, offset: 20, sort: "priority", order "desc")
```

HQL Queries

The previous methods for query creation allowed you to use powerful DSLs to create simple user queries. However, using these queries is like eating sushi—an hour later, you're hungry for more. These GORM dynamic queries could not perform anything too complex, such as ranges, and more importantly, they can only query off themselves.

In many applications, you not only need to query other tables to get the data, but you often want bits and pieces of the data back—for example, a few columns from table A mixed with a few columns from table B. With HQL queries, you can perform this task easily.

Once again, if you're familiar with Hibernate, this will be second nature to you. However, if you're new to Hibernate, understanding HQL is simply realizing that you're creating a query based on what the domain says as opposed to what is actually in the database (like in an SQL query).

In the "GORM's Dynamic Queries" section, we went over two sets of queries: returning one result set and returning multiple result sets. With HQL queries, you have the same scenario, plus a more general query mechanism with `executeQuery`:

- `find`
- `findAll`
- `executeQuery`

find

The first query type we'll look at is `find`. Listing 6-36 shows a few examples of setting up a find query.

Listing 6-36. An HQL Query with find

```
1. Todo.find("From Todo as t order by t.priority asc")
2. Todo.find("From Todo as t
                        where t.name = ?
                        and t.priority = ?
                        order by t.priority asc", ["Test", "2"])
3. Todo.find("From Todo as t
                        where t.name = :name
                        and t.priority = :priority
                        order by t.priority asc", [priority :"2", name : "Test"])
```

```
4. def todo = new Todo()
    todo.name = "Test"
    todo = Todo.find(todo)
```

As you can see, the one thing they all have in common is an HQL query. In the first example, the `find` retrieves all the items in the database. However, being that this is only a `find`, you better hope you have only one item in the database. The next three queries are much more specific. In the second and third ones, you're searching for a query with the name `Test` and the priority of `2`. The difference between the two is how you label the variables. In second one, you do it by the order of variables. This works well in the example, because we know the order. However, if you had more of a dynamic query coming in from another source, the key/value map of the third one might be a better fit. The fourth example is what is called a *query by example*. Basically, you pass in a partially completed `Todo`, and GORM finds a match based off the items passed in.

findAll

`findAll` looks the same as the examples in Listing 6-36, except this time, you're able to return multiple entries. As you were able to filter your list and other queries previously, now you will be able to do the same here with `max`, `offset`, and so on. For example, if you took the example in Listing 6-35 and converted it to a `findAll` HQL query, you would get the following code:

```
Todo.findAll("From Todo t", max: 10, offset: 20, sort: "priority", order "desc")
```

If you'd like, you could even add a selection based on priority with this query:

```
Todo.findAll("From Todo t where t.priority = ?",

                        ["1"], max: 10, offset: 20, sort: "priority", order "desc")
```

executeQuery

`executeQuery` is a bit different than the other queries, because you don't necessarily need to retrieve an actual domain object. You can simply return columns off the domain. For example, if you want to get the names of every `Todo` with a priority of `"1"`, you would use the query shown in Listing 6-37.

Listing 6-37. Query to Find the Names of All the Todos with a Priority of "1"

```
Todo.executeQuery("select t.name from Todo t where t.priority = ? ", "1")
```

In addition, all the normal rules of passing parameters work for executing the query.

Hibernate's Criteria Queries

If you've ever worked with Hibernate, you're probably familiar with Hibernate's Criteria API. Perhaps you tried to do some of the concepts of projections and so on, but got confused. Sometimes the simplest criteria query seems overly complex. For those of you not familiar with the Criteria API, it's a Hibernate API designed to provide elegance to creating dynamic queries. You might be wondering why this is necessary. Well, let's think back to the HQL queries we previously created.

What if you want to create a dynamic query? Doing so would require multiple dynamic `where` clauses, which would require you to do multiple string concatenations and a bunch of if-then-else statements. Yuck! That just gets messy fast, and lends itself to easy runtime SQL errors—and that's never a good thing. Using the Criteria object allows you to abstract away creating the query and make it in a readable DSL way.

As we said, creating the Criteria queries in pure Hibernate is a bit of a pain; however, with the Groovy language, GORM has created some fairly smooth ways for creating these queries. In this section, we'll go over how to create advanced Criteria queries. First, we'll show a small example that demonstrates the difference between creating a query with Criteria and creating a query with HQL.

Our first example is a relatively simple problem that you could have with any web application—even ours. Take `Todo`—what if you want to search based on the note, the description, or another field? This requires you to create a dynamic query. You need to store the possible values in the map where the key is the name of the field and where the value is the value.

We'll build this in a few steps to make this as easy as possible. First, we'll create the base test methods for `TodoTest`. Next, we'll show you the implementation of this logic in HQL. Finally, we'll show you how to do this the proper way in Criteria.

You'll create a query that can take in this map and do multiple ands of it on the key/value pair. Listing 6-38 shows the parameters to pass through to the query runners.

Listing 6-38. The Entry Test Case

```
void testFindingTodosWithHQL() {
    def params = [ name: '%Second%', status: '4' ]
    def todos = executeHQLQuery( params )
    assert todos[0].name == "Our Second Web App"
}

void testFindingTodosWithCriteria() {
    def params = [ name: '%Second%', status: '4' ]
    def todos = executeCriteriaQuery( params )
    assert todos[0].name == "Our Second Web App"
}
```

These tests are relatively simple; they look on the `Todo` list for a name with the word `"Second"` in it and a status of 4. With our sample data, this should only return one record with the name `"Our Second Web App"`. This is the easy part. Now let's take a look at how to implement this for an HQL query. Listing 6-39 defines `executeHQLQuery`.

Listing 6-39. The Dynamic `HQL Query`

```
List executeHQLQuery(def params) {

    def hqlQuery = "Select t From Todo t "

    if (params.size() > 0) {
        def first = true
        params.each { key, value ->
        if (first) {
            hqlQuery += ' where '
        } else {
            hqlQuery += ' and '
        }
        first = false
        hqlQuery += " t.${key} like :${key} "
        }
        }
        return Todo.executeQuery(hqlQuery, params)
    }
```

We won't try to claim that this is the *only* way of creating the necessary query, but it is one of the ways. The solution contains multiple steps:

1. Create the `select`—in this case, `Select t From Todo t`.
2. Check whether there are any parameters. This is necessary because you don't want a `where` clause if there are no parameters.
3. Add `where` or `and` depending on whether it's the first or subsequent property you're selecting.
4. Add the comparison. The `key` is the name of the property, and the `value` is the value to compare against. You see the word `key` twice, because the second instance will be replaced by a prepared statement when `executeQuery` is called.
5. Execute the query, pass in the supplied parameters, and voilà.

If you look at that code and explanation, you'll see that it's not a pretty way of performing that query. Luckily, Hibernate has an easier solution: the Criteria query. With this, you can write dynamic queries without ever having to write any SQL or HQL code. And with Groovy, this gets even easier, because you get to use builders to create your Criteria query instead. Listing 6-40 defines the method you'll use for creating the Criteria query.

Listing 6-40. The Criteria Query

```
List executeCriteriaQuery(def params) {
        def todos = Todo.createCriteria().list {
            and {
                params.each {key, value ->
                    like(key, value)
              }
            }
        }
    }
```

Not only does this look better, but it's much easier to read as well. Here's the breakdown for this one:

1. Create a dynamic query on the `Todo` domain.
2. Use `and` to define a closure that then allows you to iterate through a list of expressions.
3. Set `like` with a name/value pair without any formatting.

As you can see, this is much easier than creating a dynamic HQL query. Once you're familiar with creating Criteria queries in your average Java code, you'll see that the ability to use the Groovy builder with closures is cleaner and more robust. This will become even more apparent when we increase the complexity of our Criteria examples throughout the book.

Detached Criteria

Detached Criteria, commonly used to create common reusable criteria queries, are not associated with any given database session/connection and are constructed using a `grails.gorm.DetachedCriteria` class that accepts a domain class as the only argument to its constructor:

```
import grails.gorm.*
...
def criteria = new DetachedCriteria(User)
```

You can execute criteria queries or where queries (discussed in the next section)on a detached criteria instance to build up the appropriate query. To build a normal criteria query, you can use the build method as illustrated in Listing 6-41.

Listing 6-41. Building the Criteria

```
def criteria = new DetachedCriteria(User).build {
  eq 'lastName', ''Smith'
}
```

You can also execute dynamic finders on `DetachedCriteria` just like on domain classes, as illustrated in Listing 6-42.

Listing 6-42. Executing Dynamic Finders on Detached Criteria

```
def criteria = new DetachedCriteria(User).build {
    eq 'lastName', 'Smith'
}
def bart = criteria.findByFirstName("John")
```

Where Queries

The where queries provide compile-time checked query DSL for common queries. The object returned by the where query is a Detached criteria instance, which makes it possible to define common queries at the class level, or execute batch operations such as batch updates and deletes.

The where method accepts a closure that defines the logical criteria, as illustrated in 6-43.

Listing 6-43. Using a where Query

```
def query = User.where {
   firstName == "John"
}
Person vishal = query.find()
```

Listing 6-44 illustrates using the where method to define queries at the class level.

Listing 6-44. Using the where Method to Define Queries at the Class Level

```
class User{
    static smiths = where {
         lastName == "Smith"
    }
    ...
}
...
User.smiths.each {
    println it.firstname
}
```

Listing 6-45 illustrates using the where method to execute batch operations.

Listing 6-45. Using the where Method to Execute Batch Operations

```
def query = Person.where {
    lastName == 'Simpson'
}
int total = query.deleteAll()
```

Services

If you're a Java developer who has spent the last few years doing "enterprise development" work, you'll have to get used to the idea of controllers. It might be hard to get used to putting so much business logic inside the controller. On top of that, sometimes this is not even the correct answer. Many times, it is necessary to send the code off to a service class where you can also control the transactioning of it, the scope, and so on.

Enter Grails services. These classes are stored in the `grails-app/services` directory. Like other Groovy objects in Grails, these classes are simple POJOs.

Of course, the next logical question is, "If they're Groovy POJO scripts, why use them instead of controllers? Is it segregation for segregation's sake?" As you can guess, the answer is no. Controllers differ by the fact that they are the only items accessible directly via the GSP UI. As such, they're where the bulk of your initial interactions should go. However, imagine something like e-mail, which needs to be reused over and over again. Why would you want it in a controller? The answer is, you wouldn't. (By the way, we mention an e-mail service as an example here, because that's exactly what we're going to build in Chapter 8.)

Besides the ability to segregate reusable data, services serve two other purposes as well: one is controlling transactioning, and the other is controlling the context for the service.

Creating a Service

Creating a service is a relatively simple task, and like other Grails items, there is a command-line call. To make a `todo` service, type the following command:

```
> grails create-service todo
```

This creates the service class, as illustrated in Listing 6-46.

Listing 6-46. The TodoService and TodoServiceTests Classes

```
class TodoService {

    def serviceMethod() {

    }
}
```

In the service, you can do whatever you'd want to do in a controller: you can call other classes, access the domain, pass in parameters, and so on.

Calling the Service

As we said earlier, you still have to go through the controller first when calling from a web page. To access the service, you use simple injection. In Listing 6-47, the controller accesses the service you just created.

Listing 6-47. TodoController Accesses todoService

```
class TodoController {

    def todoService

    def process() = {
        todoService.serviceMethod()
    }
}
```

If you've used Spring, Seam, HiveMind, or any other injection framework, this concept should be familiar to you.

Injecting into the Service

In addition to being able to inject the service into the controller, you can inject other services into the service as well. If want to use Spring, or if you have some legacy Spring code, you can also inject Spring beans into the service.

If you had the following bean defined in `spring\resources.xml`:

```
<bean id="customBean" class="com.CustomBeanImpl"/>
```

you could inject this bean into your bean using the ID as the name. Simply define it as `def customBean` inside your service. This works by using Spring's functionality to auto-wire by name.

Initializing the Service

If you recall, Spring and EJB don't always rely on constructors for initialization. The main reason for this is because often a constructor might rely on items that need to be injected (like Spring services), but these items may not be available during instantiation. If you have any items that need to be looked up at creation, use Spring's `InitializingBean`, which calls the `afterPropertiesSet()` method. Listing 6-48 shows `TodoService` with a postinitialization method.

Listing 6-48. TodoService with a PostInitialization Method

```
import org.springframework.beans.factory.InitializingBean

class TodoService implements InitializingBean
{
    boolean transactional = true
    void afterPropertiesSet()
    {
        println "Post Initialization"
    }

    def serviceMethod() {
        println "TodoService - serviceMethod"
    }
}
```

The bold areas are the new sections. As you can see, calling an initialize method is simple to do, and you have access to any other services that have been injected into that service.

Setting a Bean to Be Transactional

As you might have noticed, `transactional = true` exists everywhere. You can control the transaction boundaries of items inside the services. When set to `true`, Grails defaults the service to `PROPAGATION_REQUIRED`. Within the services, you can even inject the data sources and get even finer-grain control.

Service Context Available in the Service

The last subject we'll cover is service contexts. Contexts have been around for a while; for a long time, we've had application, request, session, and page contexts. However, in recent years with frameworks such as Seam and, more recently, Spring, contexts have expanded to include the conversation context and others.

You can think of the conversation context as more than a request and less than a session. The data has a start, a middle, and an end. For example, take a credit card application, which can take multiple pages to complete. It contains data that you'll want to have until the end.

We won't cover conversation contexts (also known as *flows*) in this book. However, here we'll show you how you can set the service for these contexts. By default, every context is a singleton, meaning that the whole application shares this one instance. This means that you don't want to have any data as a global property with its state specific to the user. To adjust the context of a service, add the following line to your service:

```
static scope = "singleton"
```

The `singleton` is the default, and if you don't define the scope, the service is automatically assumed to be a singleton. Table 6-3 provides a list of the available contexts.

Table 6-3. *Available Contexts for Services*

Name	Description
`prototype`	Every time the service is injected in a new class, a new service is instantiated.
`request`	Each time a request to the server is made, a service is instantiated.
`flash`	The service is instantiated for the current and next requests only.
`flow`	The service lives for the lifetime of a controller's web flow.
`conversation`	The service lives for the lifetime of a controller's web flow and subflows.
`session`	The service is instantiated and kept for the life of the user's `HttpSession`.
`singleton`	This default service is treated like a singleton and shared across the application scope.

Summary

In this chapter, we covered quite a bit of ground in a relative short amount of space. Database interaction is an important piece of the framework puzzle, and many books and sites are devoted to it alone.

We showed you how to create domain objects, and we explained the options used to create them. This is important to understand, so you know how our domains operate. Hopefully, you'll be able to create some of your own.

From there, we showed you how to query the domains; as you saw, there are quite a few options. Throughout the rest of this book, we will use bits and pieces of each, picking the best one that suits our needs at the time. Hopefully, you've gotten an idea of when to use each, but be forewarned that for many, there is no one right answer.

Lastly, we dove into services. We will use them in various forms as the book progresses. In future chapters, you'll see how services can be useful and how the different scopes can boost your application's performance, especially when coupled with web flows.

Now that the domain is all ready to go, we'll dive into more interesting code in the next few chapters. First, though, you need to secure the application so you don't have other people changing your `Todos`. That's what we'll tackle next in Chapter 7.

CHAPTER 7

Security in Grails

Now that you have a good foundation in Grails, it's time to move on in our programming adventure. After creating a basic application and completing the domain model, what's next? The answer: addressing security.

Security concerns can range from actually securing a server to securing the application itself. Since this is a book about the Grails application framework, we will discuss only the latter. So when you read about "securing the application" or "security," we are referring to *application-level security*.

So far, we have not addressed security at all. In Chapter 5, we used an extremely unsafe generic login, which allowed you to choose which user to log in as. This was certainly easy to implement, but now we can move to a more mature approach to web security.

So, what are the goals of security? One goal is to allow the ability to sign on as a specific user. We will want to know how to secure certain pages for those who have logged in. In addition, many web sites require different levels of access for different users. Designing your security model can get fairly convoluted, depending on your application's needs, and it can reach the point where the application's design is wrapped around the security. The security needs of this book's sample application, Collab-Todo, are middle ground—requiring access control but nothing so complex that we need to build an entire system from scratch.

The security apparatus we will use is not just to meet the needs of the application we have created so far, but also the needs of the application going forward. Let's quickly examine what those needs are:

- *Domain/model-level security for a user*: We need to make sure that when users retrieve their todos, they are retrieving theirs and no one else's. If users could view others' todos, our application would be very unpopular.
- *Administrator vs. regular user access*: In Chapter 10, we will create a few reports that are only for administrators. This means we need to be able to secure certain pages of the site for administrators.
- *Basic access authentication*: For the web services we'll add in Chapter 9, we need to secure the site so it can be accessed through basic URL authentication.

If we dove straight into a solution for just our sample application's security needs, not only would that be a bit dull, but it also wouldn't help if your application happens to have different requirements.

In some Java frameworks, like JBoss Seam, there is a built-in security framework. That is not the case for Grails. However, quite a few security plugins are available for Grails. In this chapter, we will go over three of the plugins, along with our very own custom security implementation for the application. But before we start looking at the different security solutions, let's take a step back and review what we actually mean by *security*.

What Is Security?

Before we dive into our security examples with Grails, we should reach a common understanding of what security means for a web application and the issues involved with adding security to a web application. Depending on your experience in web development, this may or may not be familiar.

Although there are many aspects to security, two techniques are very common: authentication and access control. These two basic areas will serve as the core aspects for each of the security plugins and the custom solution covered in this chapter.

Authentication

Even parttime web surfers are familiar with *authentication*, which is the process of logging into and out of a site. A client (typically the user on a web browser) sends over a username and a password. The client is then either authenticated and forwarded to a welcome screen or rejected and kept on the login page. Figure 7-1 illustrates basic authentication.

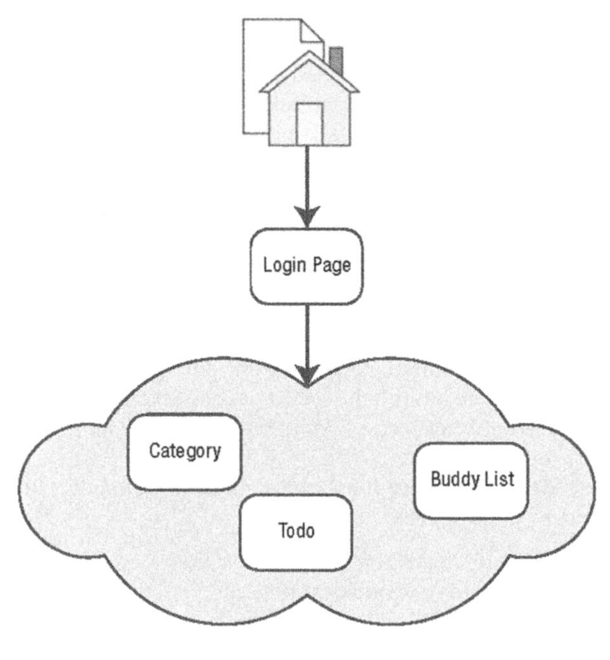

Figure 7-1. *Basic authentication*

The login username and password sent to the server typically correspond with entries in a database. Since this information is in a database, it is not that secure, so most web sites will not store the password in clear text. Generally, the password is hashed, and the hash of it is saved. The value of using a hash is that it is only a oneway manipulation of the data, as opposed to encryption, where data can be scrambled and then unscrambled given the right key. When a password is hashed, if someone gains access to the database and retrieves the password in an illegal way (like hacking the box), he will need to spend some trying to determine what the original string was.

HASHING TECHNIQUES

Throughout this chapter, we will be hashing passwords prior to storing them in the database. *Hashing* is a cryptographic technique to take a string and output a fixed-length string that is unintelligible. Here are two examples of hashing a word with Message Digest algorithm 5 (MD5), a commonly used hash function:

```
password                - 5f4dcc3b5aa765d61d8327deb882cf99
josephsPassword        - 32c6f5140cbd510d57e87bc5aeea1f60
```

As you can see, although the lengths of the strings to be hashed differ, the hash length is the same—a 32-character hex string.

A variety of techniques to produce hashes are available. The more secure the hash, the longer it will take to create and the more space it will consume in the database.

For hashing in Java, and specifically Grails, a common technique is to use `DigestUtils` in the package `org.apache.commons.codec.digest.DigestUtils`. This class contains a variety of methods to produce different types of hashes. Let's take a quick look at the three methods we will be using in this chapter:

- `DigestUtils.md5(java.lang.String data)`: This method produces a 16-element `byte[]` using MD5 as its digest mechanism.
- `DigestUtils..md5Hex(java.lang.String data)`: This method also uses MD5, but creates a 32-character hex string.
- `DigestUtils.shaHex(java.lang.String data)`: This method creates a 32-character hex string as well, but uses SHA-1 as the digest mechanism.

See the `DigestUtils` API for other hashing options.[1]

When creating authentication for a corporate web site, you don't want to overburden the user with the need to remember a lot of login credentials, nor do you want to overburden yourself with the task of managing them. If you are creating an internal site for a big business, or even an external site where multiple business entities can interact, you probably do not want a person to need to create a new username and password for each site. For one thing, it's annoying. For another, if you need to remove someone's login credentials (for example, because she left her job and should no longer be able to log in to an internal site), it would be difficult to contact every single business unit with which she has an account and get them to delete her. That is why many companies use a centralized authentication server, something like a Lightweight Directory Access Protocol (LDAP) server.

As we go through each of the solutions in this chapter, you will notice that there are slightly different ways to authenticate a user.

Access Control

So now that we have discussed the ability to log in, what's next? We also need some sort of permissions mechanism. The following are common forms of access control:

> *Session validation*: This is probably the simplest form of authentication. It just involves checking if there is a valid session. Generally, this is used in conjunction with user authentication. For the Collab-Todo site, we will take this approach to make sure that users have been authenticated and their session is active.

[1] `http://commons.apache.org/codec/apidocs/org/apache/commons/codec/digest/DigestUtils.html`.

User: One way to secure pages and data is on the user level itself. Many web sites that require authentication use data at the user level to retrieve items that are specific to a particular user. With this level, you store user data to the session, and then whenever you need to do a query against a back-end system, you retrieve only the data for that user. This is how our application will work.

Roles: You can assign users to roles to provide coarsegrained permissions to pages or even just areas of a page. An internal site may have roles like manager, developer, trainee, and so on. For example, a site that handles work orders could allow a worker to work on a variety of tickets, but the page that assigns or approves the tickets is accessible only to the manager. In addition, the ticket itself may have a Delete button available only to the manager. A more common approach, and the one we will take for our application, is to have two roles: an admin and a regular user. The admin role can access more functionality than is available to the regular user role. The nice thing about roles is that you can assign multiple people to a single role, and even provide multiple roles to a single user. Unfortunately, roles do not, in general, provide for fine-grained control.

Permissions: For finegrained control, we turn to permissions. With permissions, you can give only certain users access to certain portions of a site. Returning to the example of work order tickets, what if you wanted to allow some users to create and delete tickets; others to just view them; and others to create, edit, and delete them? This could be accomplished with roles, but you would need a lot of them, so it would get messy fast. Both assigning and managing all those roles would be a burden. Using permissions is easier.

Rules: Some sites use a rule-based access control. Systems like JBoss Seam use a rules engine (like JBoss Drools) to determine authentication privileges while also using permissions and roles. This provides for an extremely flexible authentication mechanism. However, it also requires more configuration and general knowledge of how to use the rules engine.

These are basic security concepts. As you may have noticed, each successive one provides more flexibility, but with the added flexibility comes more overhead. So the trick for you as the developer is to pick the items you need that give you a balance between flexibility and ease of implementation. Keep this in mind as we discuss each security solution in this chapter.

BOOTSTRAPPING

One of the directories that Grails creates for you when you create a Grails application is `grails-app/ conf`. This directory contains configuration files, including a bootstrap file, `Bootstrap.groovy`. We have not made use of this file yet; however, that will change in this chapter. If you are familiar with the Java Persistence API (JPA), the `Bootstrap.groovy` is much like the `import.sql` file, only smarter and more powerful.

The traditional Java EE bootstrapping mechanism is to preload the database. This could be to populate a preferences type table or to load some sample data. However, Grails not only allows for the population of the database, but also to the servlet context if desired. You can use actual Groovy code for the bootstrap file, as opposed to just SQL code, as in JPA.

When we add security in this chapter, we will want to do some prepopulation of the database. One reason is that we are going to store permissions in the database. Additionally, we want to have a few users prepopulated for the examples.

Bootstrapping itself is relatively easy. Here is an example of the bare minimum code in the `Bootstrap.groovy` file:

```
class BootStrap {
    def init = { servletContext ->
    }
}
```

The `init` method is the method the application will call, passing in the `servletContext`. This will allow us to have access to the servlet context in case we need to add data to it. Within this context, we can do normal database insertions to add sample data. For example, to insert a user, you would add the following line:

```
new User(userName: 'joseph', firstName: 'Joseph', lastName: 'Nusairat',
     email: 'jnusairat@integrallis.com', password: pass).save()
```

You just instantiate a `new User` and then save it. This method of adding data will be the same throughout this chapter and the rest of the book.

While using the bootstrap file can be a useful tool to warm the database, if you are using this in a full development, test, or production environment, you should consider one additional item. If you are using it to prepare static tables like roles or permission names, these are, across the board, global constraints. However, if you are going to prepare sample data, like users and todos, you do not want this data in your production database. Luckily, within Grails, there is an easy way to configure your bootstrap file to only write to different environments. You can detect the environment for which you packaged the application and specify that variable in the bootstrap file. For example, using the following code, you can create common methods or custom methods for the development and production environments:

```
import grails.util.GrailsUtil
. . .

switch(GrailsUtil.environment) {
    case "development":
        configureForDevelopment()
        break
    case "production":
        configureForProduction()
        break
}
```

In this chapter, we will not present all of the `Bootstrap.groovy` file, but will show bits and pieces of what we are adding to it.

An Overview of Grails Security Solutions

Two popular shows on TV right now are *Project Runway* and *Hell's Kitchen*. These shows have experts in their fields (either designers or chefs) who are given the task of creating something unique and awesome, and then their efforts are judged. It's decided which is best, or at least, which one each judge likes the best. Security, and especially security in Grails, is something like that. You have many experts in the field creating different security frameworks, each with pluses and minuses, and you must judge which one is better.

Grails is truly a unique Java framework. While some frameworks suffer from the underlying code being unstable, Grails does not have this problem since it uses two well-established frameworks at its core (JBoss Hibernate and Spring). However, it suffers from being new, which brings about a lack of 100% mature plugins for it. Although the developers of these plugins are working hard to keep up with changes in Grails, all of the plugins are relatively new, as indicated by their `.1` or `.2` statuses. Therefore, when you deal with these plugins, you may encounter some not-so-polished features.

Much like our favorite TV shows, when it comes to security plugins, there is rarely a clear winner, and odds are, there never will be. Each plugin serves a particular niche market. Which one you choose depends on your specific requirements.

The Grails security plugins we will examine in this chapter are CAS and Spring Security. Additionally, we will demonstrate how to implement your own custom security, which can work well for either simple sites or very complex sites where control is strict.

We will start with the custom security implementation, and then move on to the different plugins (note that the order in which we discuss the solutions is purely arbitrary and does not infer that any is superior). In the end, we will use the Spring Security plugin as our solution, because it meets the needs outlined at the beginning of this chapter.

Because our approach in this chapter is to show you multiple paths but only go with one, we decided to do something a bit different with the code examples in this chapter. In the previous chapter, we added quite a bit to our domain model. Most of this is unnecessary from a pure security point of view. We feel it's not necessary to add that complexity here.

One of the first items you will notice when we talk about the plugins is that many have their own `User` classes. This can pose a problem, because you will want to tie your `User` object on your domain to the plugin's user class. You will want to tackle this problem during authentication, and there are essentially two ways to solve this problem:

- If the domain model is created after plugin creation, the set of user domain objects the plugin creates can either be moved into the `grails-app/domain` directory or referenced directly in your application. The only reason to move them is if you want to make changes to the domain.
- You can have the plugin's domain object and your domain object linked by username after authentication. Since this is a unique field, after authentication is verified, you can look up your user in the database and save your user to the session. This provides a nice balance of keeping your application uncoupled while at the same time totally relying on the plugin for security. This is the approach we'll take in this chapter.

Custom Security Implementation

We start with the most basic approach to securing a web site, which is our custom security implementation. But using a simple security apparatus does not means your web site is simple. The two are not really related. It is just about picking the right security for your application.

■ **Note** The term *custom implementation* may be a bit confusing. This approach is not truly "custom." Many applications use this same approach. In fact, it's a very common implementation. We call it custom because it doesn't use a security plugin (other than the CAPTCHA one).

One of the main needs of any user-based application is to authenticate the users. With our application, the majority of the pages are driven by which user is accessing the page. The todos that appear are only for the logged-in user, users add buddy lists for themselves, and so on. We also need to make sure the user is authenticated before accessing any page except the login page. This is a fairly simple authentication pattern, and we will be using a `User` object in the session to check the access to the pages. (We will use the `User` object in the session in the other plugins, but the difference is we are not using it for page-level authentication purposes.)

In this section, we will adjust the user-creation procedure. Note that for our custom security implementation, we do not need any new domain classes. We will use the domain classes we created in Chapter 5. Our main focus is on manipulating the `User` class. Now we will add a password confirmation and a CAPTCHA challenge.

CAPTCHA

While you may not be familiar with the term *CAPTCHA*, you probably have encountered such a challenge. For example, you may have gone to a web site and seen an image like this:

This image is part of a CAPTCHA (for Completely Automated Public Turing Test to Tell Computers and Humans Apart). You're asked to type in the text you see in the image. The purpose is to help prevent automated computer programs from gaining access to your site, and for the most part, CAPTCHAs work. They are not unbreakable, but depending on the complexity of the CAPTCHA, decoding the image requires a fairly complex neural network. CAPTCHAs are used on a variety of sites. For example, `ticketmaster.com` has a fairly complex set (and we admit to missing a few on that site).

Even simple sites are subject to spammers. When we launched our company's web site at `http://www.integrallis.com`, within a few days, we were getting hit by spam via our Contact Us link. Now that we have added the CAPTCHA, the only e-mail we get is from real people.

In order to create the custom security solution, we will cover three aspects of its design and implementation:

- Registering a user
- Logging users in and out
- Securing the controllers

Registering a User

In order to register a user, we need to add two items: a registration page (`register.gsp`) and an action to register the user in the `UserController`. As noted, we will use a CAPTCHA challenge on the registration page, so we need to install the plugin for that.

Installing the Captcha Plugin

The CAPTCHA is added only to the registration page because it is the only page on the site that could be easily affected by spammers. The other parts of the application require authentication before users even get to the page.

For the registration page with the CAPTCHA, we will use the Simple Captcha plugin[2] for the creation of the CAPTCHA. To install the plugin from command-line or GGTS' command line, use the following command:

```
> grails install-plugin simple-captcha
```

Or you can use Grails Plugin Manager instead, as shown in Figure 7-2.

[2]`http://grails.org/Simple+Captcha+Plugin`.

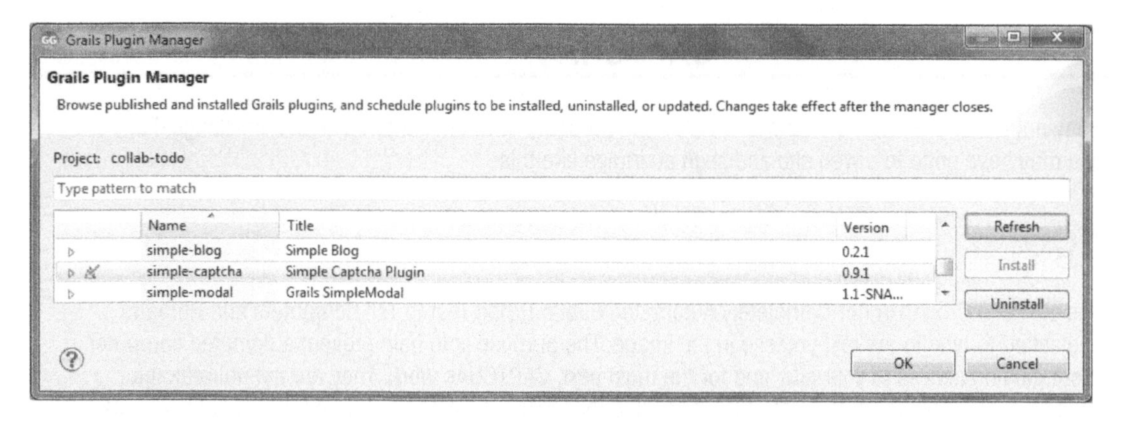

Figure 7-2. *Installing thesimple-captchaplugin using Grails Plugin Manager*

JCAPTCHA

There actually is another, more advanced CAPTCHA plugin out there called JCaptcha.[3] It allows for more customization on the output of the look of the CAPTCHA. It also lets you use a `.wav` file CAPTCHA (for web users with vision difficulties).

JCaptcha does require a bit more configuration, and we did not include it here for that reason. But we highly recommend it for a production site, as there have been lawsuits against sites that are not usable by the blind.

Now that the Grails Captcha plugin and the domain objects from the previous chapter are installed, it's time to get this working. Let's start with the registration page section.

Implementing the Registration Page

Our registration page will look like the page where you add a user, except it will have a field to confirm the password and the CAPTCHA image. So, we start by copying the file `views/user/add.gsp` to `register.gsp`. This allows us to preserve the `add.gsp` page.

Listing 7-1 shows the code for `register.gsp`, with the new sections for the password confirmation and the CAPTCHA link in bold.

Listing 7-1. The Form Section of register.gsp

```
<g:form action="handleRegistration" method="post">
<div class="dialog">
<table>
<tbody>
<tr class='prop'>
<td valign='top'class='nameClear'>
<label for="login">Login:</label>
</td>
```

[3] `http://grails.org/JCaptcha+Plugin`.

```
<td valign='top'
              class='valueClear ${hasErrors(bean:user,field:'userName','errors')}'>
<input type="text" name="userName" />
</td>
</tr>
<tr class='prop'>
<td valign='top' class='nameClear'>
<label for="password">Password:</label>
</td>
<td valign='top'
              class='valueClear ${hasErrors(bean:user,field:'password','errors')}'>
<input type="password" name="password" />
</td>
</tr>
<tr class='prop'>
<td valign='top' class='nameClear'>
<label for="confirm">Confirm Password:</label>
</td>
<td valign='top'
              class='valueClear
                     ${hasErrors(bean:user,field:'password','errors')}'>
<input type="password" name="confirm" />
</td>
</tr>
<tr class='prop'>
<td valign='top' class='nameClear'>
<label for="firstName">First Name:</label>
</td>
<td valign='top'
               class='valueClear
                      ${hasErrors(bean:user,field:'firstName','errors')}'>
<input type="text" name="firstName" />
</td>
</tr>
<tr class='prop'>
<td valign='top' class='nameClear'>
<label for="lastName">Last Name:</label>
</td>
<td valign='top'
    class='valueClear ${hasErrors(bean:user,field:'lastName','errors')}'>
<input type="text" name="lastName" />
</td>
</tr>
<tr class='prop'>
<td valign='top' class='nameClear'>
<label for="email">Email:</label>
</td>
<td valign='top'
    class='valueClear ${hasErrors(bean:user,field:'email','errors')}'>
<input type="text" name="email" />
</td>
</tr>
```

```
<tr class='prop'>
<td valign='top' class='nameClear'>
<label for="code">Enter Code:</label>
</td>
<td valign='top' class='valueClear'>
<input type="text" name="captcha"><br/>
<img src="${createLink(controller:'captcha', action:'index')}" />
</td>
</tr>
</tbody>
</table>
</div>

<div class="buttons">
<span class="button">
<input class="save" type="submit" value="Register"></input>
</span>
</div>
</g:form>
```

The line with the CAPTCHA reference is the plugin's CAPTCHA controller. The controller will create a word, save the word in clear text to a session variable, and then output the image in a distorted manner. Figure 7-3 shows the registration page.

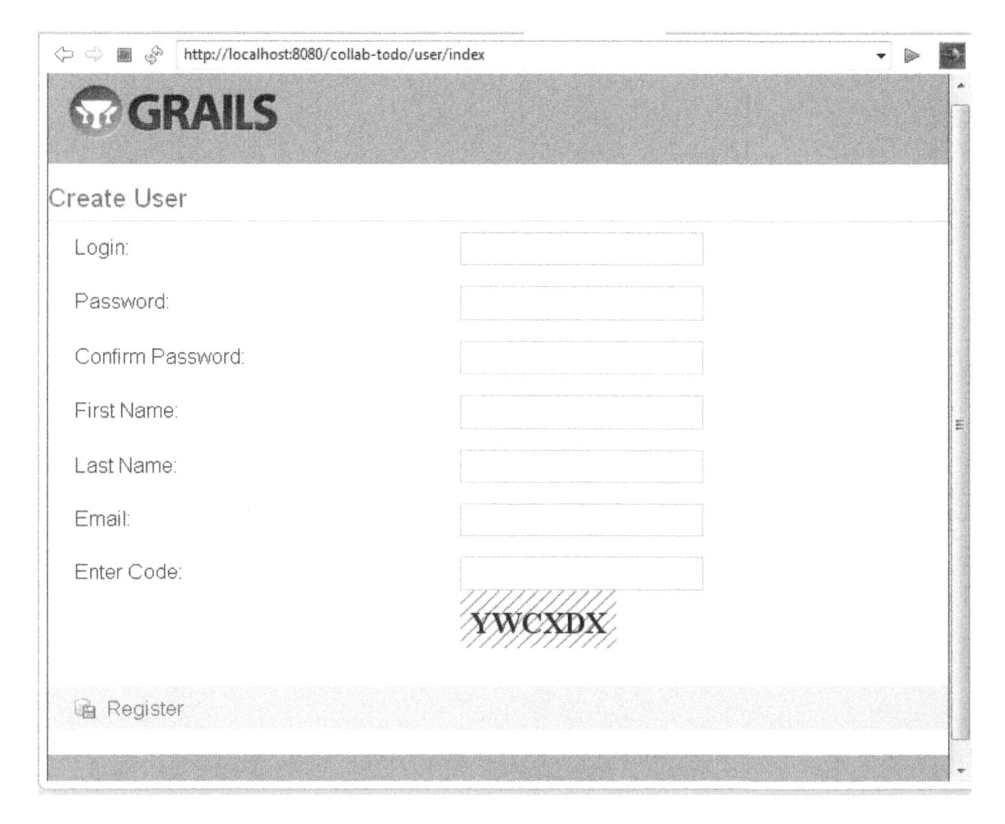

***Figure 7-3.** The register.gsp page with the password confirmation and CAPTCHA image*

Adding the Registration Action to the Controller

Putting the CAPTCHA on the GSP is only half the battle in creating our CAPTCHA challenge. The other half is handling it on the server side. Unfortunately, there is nothing that automatically intercepts the CAPTCHA when used to verify the image. We need to code this by hand.

In our UserController registration action, we will add a check to make sure the CAPTCHA the user entered matches the CAPTCHA given. You can see our registration action in Listing 7-2. This checks that the CAPTCHA matches, and then if it passes validation, allows the user to register.

Listing 7-2. The Action to Register a User in the UserController

```
def handleRegistration(){
                def user = new User()
                log.info("HANDLE REGISTRATION")
                // using the log.info here will only print out the object, not a listing of it
                println params
                // create the property object
                user.properties = params
                // Process the captcha request
                boolean captchaValid = simpleCaptchaService.validateCaptcha(params.captcha)
                if (captchaValid) {
                  if(params.password != params.confirm) {
                        flash.message = "The two passwords you entered dont match!"
                        render(view:'register', model:[user:user])
                  }
                  else if (user.password?.length() <= 3) {
                        flash.message = "The password length is under 3 characters."
                        render(view:'register', model:[user:user])
                  } else {
                        log.info "before save"
                        // lets hash the password
                        user.password = DU.md5Hex(user.password)

                        if(user.save()) {
                                // also add this user to the authority system
                                //def userAuth = Authority.findByAuthority("ROLE_USER")
                                //userAuth.addToPeople(user)
                                // not sure if the save is necessary.
                                //userAuth.save()

                                // send a confirmation email
                                //sendAcknowledgment (user)
                                log.info "saved redirecting to user controller"

                                // they will be prompted to login when they
                                // go to an internal place anyway.
                                redirect(controller:'todo')
                        }
```

```
                    else {
                            log.info "didn't save"
                            println "didn't save"
                            flash.user = user
                            render(view:'register', model:[user:user])
                    }
              }
            }
            else {
                    log.info "Captcha Not Filled In"
                    flash.message = "Access code did not match."
                    render(view: 'register', model:[user:user])
            }
    }
```

You may notice that the CAPTCHA created is in the session scope. Unfortunately, at the time of this writing, this was necessary to allow the image to spawn multiple requests (with some of the new service-level scopes written after the plugin's creation, this requirement may change in the future). We have overcome this issue slightly by saving the data from the session to a local variable, and then removing the CAPTCHA information from that session.

In addition, you will notice that, as a convenience factor, we set the `session.user` to the user that was just created. We did this because once users are logged in, we want other pages to know that. This information can be used to display the username or simply to get the ID for querying.

Also notice that we've hashed the password. As mentioned earlier in the chapter, hashing is a critical step, because we do not want to keep a password in the database in clear text form.

■ **Note** Remember that many people use the same password for multiple sites. If you stored a clear text password and your site was compromised, you could potentially expose users' passwords to all sorts of sites and therefore valuable data. The one downside (and it's arguable if it's a downside) is that if you have a password-reminder routine, it cannot remind people of their password; instead, it will simply need to reset the password to a random string.

Logging In and Out

Now that the user is registered, the next step is to log the user in and out. This could be difficult depending on your back-end system. Logging in could involve going through an LDAP server or whatever other systems you use. However, for our example, logging in is relatively simple, as we are just authenticating against a local database.

We will preserve the general feel of the login page we had before, except now instead of choosing from a drop-down list, the user must actually enter a proper username and password. The modified login page is shown in Figure 7-4.

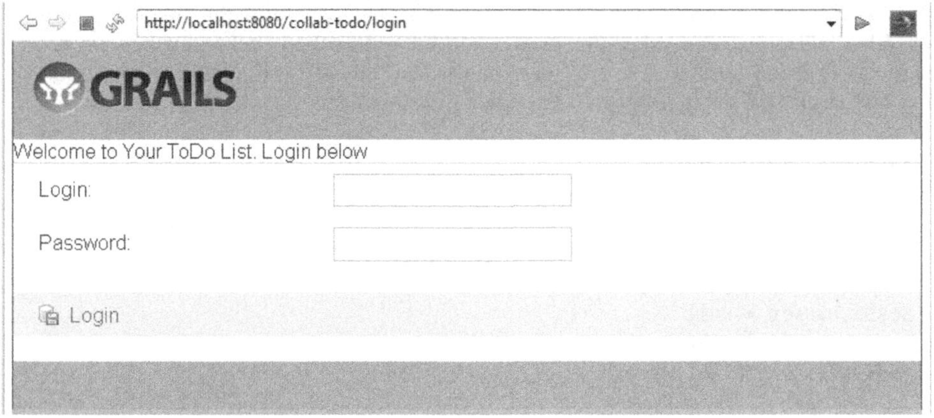

Figure 7-4. The login page with username and password validation

As you see in Listing 7-3, we check the user and the password in the database for a match, hashing the password passed in by the front end with an MD5 hash. If a user is not found, we send a message to the page and redirect back to the login page. If a match is found, we set the user in the session and redirect to the todo page.

Listing 7-3. The handleLogin Action of the LoginController

```
def handleLogin(){
println "Handle Login"
        def hashPassd = DU.md5Hex(params.password)
println params.userName
println params.password

        // find the user name
        def user = User.findByUserNameAndPassword(params.userName, hashPassd)

        if (!user) {
            flash.message = "User not found for userName: ${params.userName}"
            redirect(action:'index')
            return
        } else {
            session.user = user
            redirect(controller:'todo')
        }
    }
```

■ **Note** You will notice that we send one generic message back. Some sites will search for the user first, and then do a check against the password. This is done so that a more specific message is sent back to the user. While this can be helpful for the user, it is also another point of exposure—it can tell a would-be hacker which part of his attempt was successful.

Logging out is a fairly universal process in web design, and the way we do it here will more than likely look the same as you've seen in other web applications. The only differences can lie in preprocessing before logging out, such as sending notifications, writing to an events table, and so on. However, we do not need any of that for our system. We will just invalidate the session and redirect to the index page. The code for the logout action is shown in Listing 7-4.

Listing 7-4. The Logout Action of the LogoutController

```
def logout() {
log.info 'logout'
        if(session.user) {
                        session.user = null
                        session.invalidate()
                        redirect(controller:'login')
                }
        }
```

Securing the Controllers

So far, we have covered the ability to log in and out of the site and to register a user. These are the first two steps in securing the site. Now what's left? We need to secure the actual controller pages so that a nonauthenticated user cannot access the `TodoController` and other controllers. The registration and logging in and out were relatively simple to code. Controller security is a slightly more difficult piece of our authentication model.

We will control access to the pages using tried-and-true servlet technology: filters. Filters are great for simple, all-encompassing procedural captures. And since all but three pages (the index, login, and registration pages are the exceptions) require a session, filters are the cheapest and most effective way to implement access control.

Filters are relatively easy to create in Grails. Unlike servlet filters, they do not require any `web.xml` configuration. Here, we will walk through the steps to create the filter.

■ **Note** We will use filters in the other security solutions covered in this chapter. The configuration here applies to those other solutions as well.

Let's start with the filter's name and location. Filters must be placed in the `grails-app/conf` directory, and the name of the Groovy class must end with the word `Filters`. Since our filters are for security, we will name the file `SecurityFilters`:

```
class SecurityFilters {
}
```

The next part is defining the filters. We will be defining an action called `filters`. This is the method that the Grails framework will use to look for any and all filters we have created:

```
class SecurityFilters {
    def filters = {
    }
}
```

With the framework set up for the filters, now we define the filters. We can have one or more filters defined inside the same class. If you have programmed regular servlet filters before, you will realize that this is a huge advantage;

with regular servlet filters, you must define a different class for each filter. You can create a new set of filters in a class called grails-app/conf/SecurityFilters.groovy by running:

```
> grails create-filters security
```

As a result of running this command, the SecurityFilters class shown in Listing 7-5 is generated.

Listing 7-5. Creating the Security Filter

```
class SecurityFilters {

    def filters = {
        all(controller:'*', action:'*') {
            before = {

            }
            after = { Map model ->

            }
            afterView = { Exception e ->

            }
        }
    }
}
```

You can create two types of filters:

- The more traditional type, where you define the URI to be intercepted, like this: uriCheck(uri: /user/*). The method defining this check is intercepted anytime anyone calls anything with the /user URI.
- Capture based on the controller and action. This way, you can capture all controllers and actions or just selective ones. This is the approach we will take here.

For our application, we can either capture all controllers or be selective and individually capture certain controllers. We opted for the capture-all approach and will ignore the login and registration page in the code. Otherwise, if we added more controllers later, we would need to keep adding the login check code to each filter, which could get messy fast, depending on how much functionality we add to the site. Listing 7-6 shows the final definition of the filter.

Listing 7-6. The Filter for Securing the Application

```
    def filters = {
        collabTodoFilter(controller:'*', action:'*') {
            before = {
                if(!session.user
                  && !controllerName.equals('login')
                  && !controllerName.equals('captcha')
                  && (!controllerName.equals('user')
                  && !actionName.equals("register"))
                  ) {
```

```
                    // There is no log access in the filter
                    //log.info('Redirect to login page')
                    redirect(controller:'login')
                    return false
                }
            }
        }
    }
```

Here, we are checking the session as well as the controller and action names. The `controllerName` tells us which controller was just accessed. The `actionName` tells us the action that was accessed. Grails injects several properties and makes them accessible in the filters, including the following:

- `request`
- `response`
- `session`
- `servletContext`
- `applicationContext`
- `params`

Our custom security solution is a fairly lightweight security wrapper. For many applications, all you need to worry about is whether users are logged in, and this solution handles that.

However, some applications have more complex requirements. For example, a banking application might have an administration portion of the site. The admin could log in to the same application as the regular user, so that he could mimic being a particular user if necessary (such as to assist a customer if she were having a problem with the online application). At the same time, you *wouldn't* want the admin to be able to do some things, such as actually submitting a payment. Creating such a solution requires more than just a simple authenticated validation. It requires assigning roles and permissions, and then giving each task access based on the roles and permissions. The plugins covered in the remainder of this chapter provide mechanisms for this type of security.

CAS

Our third option is unique from our other choices in that it is the only one that cannot work as a stand-alone solution. The CAS Grails plugin is a fairly simple wrapper for the Java CAS client[4] for use with a CAS server.

CAS is the Central Authentication Server developed at Yale. It is designed to allow for a single authentication system. This is useful when you have numerous organizations or systems that want to authenticate against the same system. For example, an insurance company could be selling home insurance, auto insurance, investment accounts, and term life insurance. Each of these items could be run from different business units. Each of these business units will be developing its own web site, so their users have access to their individual accounts. One of the biggest challenges of companies that have this type of setup is to avoid having the sites look like they are totally separate. They should allow a single sign-on. Users would get annoyed if they had to keep registering and using different usernames and passwords for the various systems.

Another issue with corporate multiple-application development is that the applications may not all be written using the same language. CAS is provideragnostic and can be consumed by a variety of languages. This means you could have a .NET application, Java application, and Rails application, with all using the same authentication.

[4]`http://www.ja-sig.org/products/cas/client/javaclient/index.html`

Since our application is not part of a multiple-application environment, the level of sophistication provided by CAS is unnecessary. In this section, we will go over some basic implementations and usage of the plugin itself. While you will be able to deploy and run the sample code, it will not actually authenticate against anything (we don't have a CAS server).

■ **Note** This section is provided to demonstrate the use of the plugin, and should not be considered a CAS client/server tutorial. A basic understanding of the CAS client/server architecture may be needed in order to fully understand the plugin. To learn more, check out the main CAS web site.[5]

CAS Installation

The installation for the CAS plugin is straightforward and does not create any additional artifacts in the `grails-app` directory; all that is created is in the `plugins` directory. You can download the plugin at `http://grails.org/CAS+Client+Plugin` or install it with the following command:

```
> grails install-plugin cas-client
```

CAS Configuration

Since this application is using an outside authentication system, configuring it is rather simple. You just need to define the URLs of the CAS servers. These definitions will go in `grails-app/conf/Config.groovy`, as shown in Listing 7-7.

Listing 7-7. The Config.groovy File with the CAS Configurations

```
// cas client configuration, required by CasClientPlugin
cas {
    urlPattern = '/someurl/*'
//    urlPattern = ['/oneurl/*', '/another', '/anotheranother/*']
    disabled = false
}

// log4j configuration
log4j {
    // . . . removed for brevity . . .
}
environments {
    development {
        cas.loginUrl = 'https://localhost:8080/casSecurity/login'
        cas.validateUrl = 'https://localhost:8080/casSecurity/serviceValidate'
        cas.serverName = 'localhost:8080'
        cas.serviceUrl = 'http://dev.casclient.demo.com/access'
         log4j {
```

---

[5]`http://www.ja-sig.org/products/cas/`.

```
            logger {
                grails.'app.controller'="trace,stdout,logfile"
                grails.app="error,stdout"
             }
        }
    }
    // . . . production and test removed . . .
}
```

Here, we added two sections to the Config.groovy file. The first one is a required item for the CAS plugin, which defines a URL pattern. The second is in the environments section, and it is important when you want to access the CAS server itself. It defines all the URLs to be used for filtering. These attributes once again go into web.xml, but they are automatically added during compilation of the Grails application. Table 7-1 shows the additional configuration options as well as the corresponding web.xmlinit-param values.

Table 7-1. *CAS URL Definition Entries*

Config.groovy Entry	Required	Web.xml Reference Value
cas.urlPattern	Yes	
cas.loginUrl	Yes	edu.yale.its.tp.cas.client.filter.loginUrl
cas.validateUrl	Yes	edu.yale.its.tp.cas.client.filter.validateUrl
cas.serverName	Yes	edu.yale.its.tp.cas.client.filter.serverName
cas.serviceUrl	Yes	edu.yale.its.tp.cas.client.filter.serviceUrl
cas.proxyCallbackUrl	No	edu.yale.its.tp.cas.client.filter.proxyCallbackUrl
cas.authorizedProxy	No	edu.yale.its.tp.cas.client.filter.authorizedProxy
cas.renew	No	edu.yale.its.tp.cas.client.filter.renew
cas.wrapRequest	No	edu.yale.its.tp.cas.client.filter.wrapRequest
cas.disabled	No	

■ **Caution** cas.serverName and cas.serviceUrl are mutually exclusive. You need to fill in one or the other, but not both.

In addition, Listing 7-7 defines one other field—the cas.disabled flag. It works as you may have guessed. If you set it to true, the plugin is disabled; if it is set to false, the plugin is enabled.

CAS Usage

The usage of the CAS security is entirely up to you. The main goal is to pull the name of the loggedin user for the controller. You can then secure the controllers either through filters or by extending the base controller classes. Listing 7-8 illustrates how to pull the user from the session.

Listing 7-8. Retrieving the Username from the Session

```
def username = session?.getAttribute(CASFilter.CAS_FILTER_USER)
```

You could then use this in a base class's interceptor to perform a validation, or you could use it in a custom filter to perform the check.

The CAS security plugin is quite easy to use and allows for simple authentication against a middle system. As we pointed out, this can be very useful in a big corporate system where you care about authentication.

Spring Security

Last but not least, we will discuss how to implement security in Grails with a tried-and-true favorite from the Spring Portfolio: Spring Security. The Spring Security framework is a subproject of the Spring Framework and was designed to give developers a single place to go for security when using Spring.

The flexibility of Spring Security is one of the main reasons for its growing popularity when it comes to securing Spring applications. (Remember that Grails uses Spring as its Inversion of Control, or IoC, pattern, and, as such, Grails is in many ways a glorified Spring application.) The Spring Security plugin simplifies the integration of Spring Security (formerly Acegi Security) into Grails applications. The plugin provides defaults with many configuration options for customization. The Spring Security plugin maintains its configuration in the standard `Config.groovy` file. Default values are in the plugin's grails-`app/conf/DefaultSecurityConfig.groovy` file, and you add application-specific values to the `grails-app/conf/Config.groovy` file. The two configurations will be merged, with application values overriding the defaults.

Installation of the spring security-core plugin is a relatively painless process. Either use Grails Plugin Manager (shown in Figure 7-5) or issue the following command:

```
> grails install-plugin spring-security-core
```

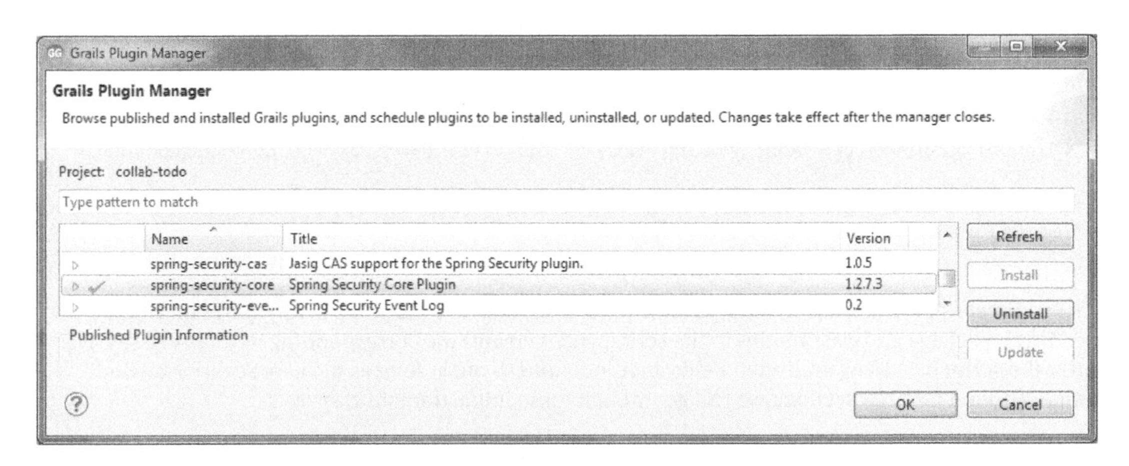

Figure 7-5. *Installing the spring-security-core plugin using Grails Plugin Manager*

Security Domain Classes

By default, the plugin uses regular Grails domain classes to access its required data. To use the standard user lookup you'll need, at a minimum, a "person" and an "authority" domain class. In addition, if you want to store URL<->Role mappings in the database, you need a "requestmap" domain class. If you use the recommended approach for mapping the many-to-many relationship between "person" and "authority," you also need a domain class to map the join table. We can use the `s2-quickstart` script to create the initial domain classes as explained next. The general format of the script is:

```
> grails s2-quickstart DOMAIN_CLASS_PACKAGE USER_CLASS_NAME ROLE_CLASS_NAME [REQUESTMAP_CLASS_NAME]
```

For example, in the command shown in GGTS in Figure 7-6, Chapter 7 is the package name, SecurityUser is the user class, and the Role is the role class. The request map class is optional in the command and we will discuss it later in this section.

Figure 7-6. *Running the s2-quickstart script*

The output is:

```
| Loading Grails 2.1.0
| Configuring classpath.
| Environment set to development.....
| Packaging Grails application.....
| Compiling 1 source files.....

Creating User class SecurityUser and Role class Role in package chapter7.
| generated D:\devl\workspace\chapter7\grails-app\domain\chapter7\SecurityUser.groovy.
| generated D:\devl\workspace\chapter7\grails-app\domain\chapter7\Role.groovy.
| generated D:\devl\workspace\chapter7\grails-app\domain\chapter7\SecurityUserRole.groovy.....
| ************************************************************
* Created domain classes, controllers, and GSPs. Your *
* grails-app/conf/Config.groovy has been updated with ** the class names of the configured domain
classes;    *
* please verify that the values are correct.          *
************************************************************
```

The s2-quickstart script creates a user and role class (and optionally a requestmap class) in the specified package. We specify the package and class names in the script, and it creates the corresponding domain classes. We can also customize the script by adding unlimited fields, methods, and so on, as long as the core security-related functionality remains. In the next few sections we will go through these initial domain classes.

Person Class

Spring Security uses an Authentication object to determine whether the current user has the right to perform a secured action, such as accessing a URL, manipulating a secured domain object, accessing a secured method, and so on. This object is created during login. Typically overlap occurs between the need for authentication data and the need to represent a user in the application in ways that are unrelated to security. By default, the plugin uses a Grails "person" domain class to manage this data. The class name is Person, and username, enabled, and password are the default names of the required properties. You can easily plug in your own implementation, and rename the class, package, and fields. In addition, you should define an authorities property to retrieve roles; this can be a public field or a getAuthorities() method, and it can be defined through a traditional GORM many-to-many or a custom mapping. Listing 7-9 shows the User class generated by the s2-quickstart script.

Listing 7-9. The Person Class Generated by the s2-quickstart Script

```
package chapter7

class SecurityUser {

        transient springSecurityService

        String username
        String password
        boolean enabled
        boolean accountExpired
        boolean accountLocked
        boolean passwordExpired

        static constraints = {
                username blank: false, unique: true
                password blank: false
        }

        static mapping = {
                password column: 'password'
        }

        Set<Role> getAuthorities() {
                SecurityUserRole.findAllBySecurityUser(this).collect { it.role } as Set
        }

        def beforeInsert() {
                encodePassword()
        }

        def beforeUpdate() {
                if (isDirty('password')) {
                        encodePassword()
                }
        }

        protected void encodePassword() {
                password = springSecurityService.encodePassword(password)
        }
}
```

The `getAuthorities()` method is analogous to defining static `hasMany = [authorities: Authority]` in a traditional many-to-many mapping. This way `GormUserDetailsService` can call `user.authorities` during login to retrieve the roles without the overhead of a bidirectional many-to-many mapping.

Authority Class

The Spring Security plugin also requires an “authority” class to represent a user’s role(s) in the application. In general, this class restricts URLs to users who have been assigned the required access rights. A user can have multiple roles to indicate various access rights in the application, and should have at least one. Like the “person” class, the “authority” class has a default name, `Authority`, and a default name for its one required property, `authority`. If you want to use another existing domain class, it simply has to have a property for the name. As with the name of the class, the names of the properties can be whatever you want—they’re specified in `grails-app/conf/Config.groovy`.

Listing 7-10 shows the `Authority` class generated by the `s2-quickstart` script.

Listing 7-10. The Authority Class generated by the s2-quickstart Script

```
package chapter7

class Role {

        String authority

        static mapping = {
                cache true
        }

        static constraints = {
                authority blank: false, unique: true
        }
}
```

PersonAuthority Class

The typical approach to mapping the relationship between “person” and “authority” is a many-to-many. Users have multiple roles, and roles are shared by multiple users. This approach can be problematic in Grails, because a popular role, for example, `ROLE_USER`, will be granted to many users in your application. GORM uses collections to manage adding and removing related instances and maps many-to-many relationships bidirectionally. Granting a role to a user requires loading all existing users who have that role because the collection is a Set. So even though no uniqueness concerns may exist, Hibernate loads them all to enforce uniqueness. The recommended approach in the plugin is to map a domain class to the join table that manages the many-to-many, and using that to grant and revoke roles to users.

Like the other domain classes, this class is generated for you, so you don’t need to deal with the details of mapping it.

Besides these domain classes, the `s2-quickstart` script also creates the login and logout functionality. In order to test the secured log in functionality created by `s2-quickstart` script, we will add the test data to `conf/Bootstrap.groovy`, as illustrated in Listing 7-11.

Listing 7-11. Test Data in Bootstrap.groovy

```
import chapter7.*

class BootStrap {

        def init = { servletContext ->
```

```
                def userRole = new Role(authority: 'ROLE_USER').save()
                String password = 'password'
                def user = new SecurityUser(username: 'testUser', password: password, enabled:
true).save()
                SecurityUserRole.create user, userRole, true
        }

        def destroy = {
        }
}
```

Now you can run the application using run-app and click on the `LoginController` link, which renders the screen shown in Figure 7-7. You can test the login functionality using the `username:testUser` we created in `Bootstrap.groovy`.

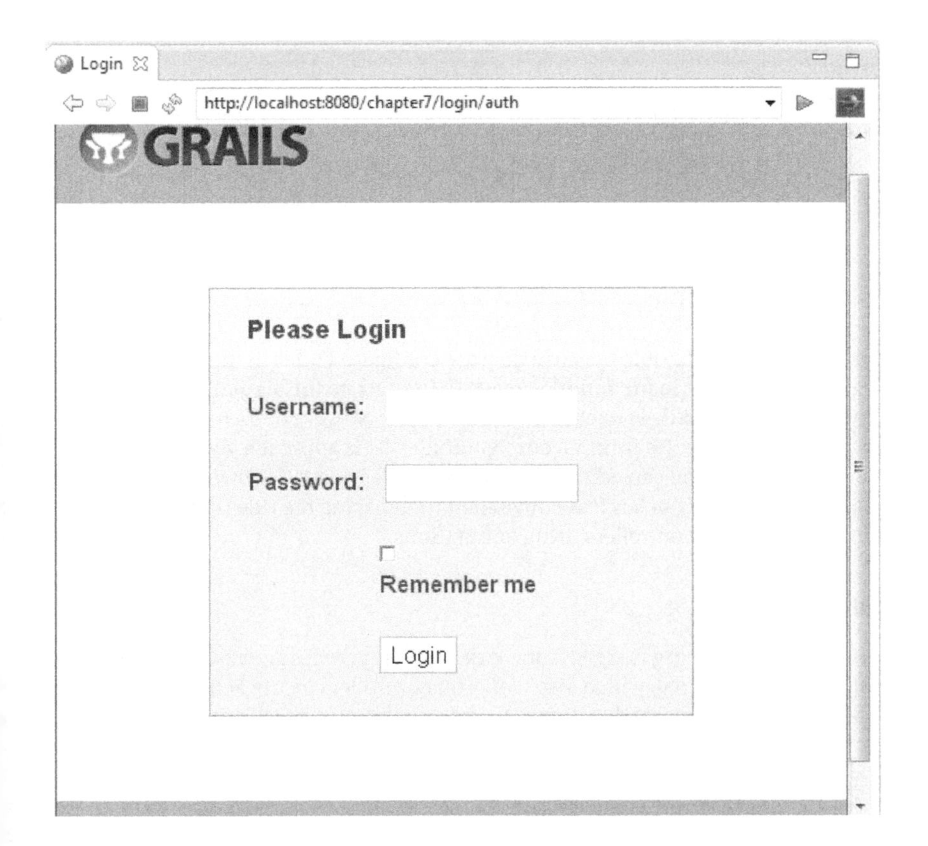

Figure 7-7. *Login functionality*

Requestmap Class

Optionally, use this class to store request mapping entries in the database instead of defining them with annotations or in `Config.groovy`. This option makes the class configurable at runtime; you can add, remove, and edit rules without restarting your application.

Securing URLs

Securing URLs entails mapping URL patterns to the roles required to access those URLs. You can choose one of the following approaches to configuring request mappings for secure application URLs.

- @Secured annotations (default approach)
- A simple Map in Config.groovy
- Requestmap domain class instances stored in the database

URLs and Authorities

In each approach of securing URLs, you configure a mapping for a URL pattern to the role(s) that are required to access those URLs; for instance, /admin/user/** requires ROLE_ADMIN. In addition, you can combine the role(s) with tokens such as IS_AUTHENTICATED_ANONYMOUSLY, IS_AUTHENTICATED_REMEMBERED, and IS_AUTHENTICATED_FULLY.

Table 7-2. *Preconfigured Requestmap Attributes*

Attribute	Description
IS_AUTHENTICATED_FULLY	Requires the user to be fully authenticated with an explicit login
IS_AUTHENTICATED_REMEMBERED	Requires the user to be authenticated through a remember-me cookie or an explicit login
IS_AUTHENTICATED_ANONYMOUSLY	Signifies that anyone can access this URL

Annotations and the Config.groovy Map are less flexible because they are configured once in the code and you can update them only by restarting the application (in prod mode anyway). In practice this limitation is minor, because security mappings for most applications are unlikely to change at runtime.

On the other hand, storing requestmap entries enables runtime configurability. This approach gives you a core set of rules populated at application startup that you can edit, add to, and delete as needed. However, it separates the security rules from the application code, which is less convenient than having the rules defined in grails-app/conf/Config.groovy or in the applicable controllers using annotations.

Defining Secured Annotations

You can use an @Secured annotation (either the standard org.springframework.security.access.annotation.Secured or the plugin's grails.plugins.springsecurity.Secured, which also works on controller closure actions) in your controllers to configure which roles are required for which actions. To use annotations, specify securityConfigType="Annotation", or leave it unspecified because it's the default:

```
grails.plugins.springsecurity.securityConfigType = "Annotation"
```

You can define the annotation at the class level, meaning that the specified roles are required for all actions, or at the action level, or both. If the class and an action are annotated, the action annotation values are used since they're more specific.

Simple Map in Config.groovy

To use the Config.groovy Map to secure URLs, first specify securityConfigType="InterceptUrlMap":

```
grails.plugins.springsecurity.securityConfigType = "InterceptUrlMap"
```

Define a Map in Config.groovy:

```
grails.plugins.springsecurity.interceptUrlMap = [
   '/secure/**':     ['ROLE_ADMIN'],
   '/finance/**':    ['ROLE_FINANCE', 'IS_AUTHENTICATED_FULLY'],
   '/js/**':         ['IS_AUTHENTICATED_ANONYMOUSLY'],
   '/css/**':        ['IS_AUTHENTICATED_ANONYMOUSLY'],
   '/images/**':     ['IS_AUTHENTICATED_ANONYMOUSLY'],
   '/*':             ['IS_AUTHENTICATED_ANONYMOUSLY'],
   '/login/**':      ['IS_AUTHENTICATED_ANONYMOUSLY'],
   '/logout/**':     ['IS_AUTHENTICATED_ANONYMOUSLY']
]
```

When using this approach, make sure that you order the rules correctly. The first applicable rule is used, so for example if you have a controller that has one set of rules but an action that has stricter access rules (such as in the following code), this would fail.

```
'/secure/**':                ['ROLE_ADMIN', 'ROLE_SUPERUSER'],
'/secure/reallysecure/**': ['ROLE_SUPERUSER']
```

It would fail because it wouldn't restrict access to /secure/reallysecure/list to a user with ROLE_SUPERUSER since the first URL pattern matches, so the second would be ignored. The correct mapping is:

```
'/secure/reallysecure/**': ['ROLE_SUPERUSER']
'/secure/**':                ['ROLE_ADMIN', 'ROLE_SUPERUSER'],
```

Requestmap Instances Stored in the Database

With this approach, you use the Requestmap domain class to store mapping entries in the database. Requestmap has a url property that contains the secured URL pattern and a configAttribute property containing a comma-delimited list of required roles and/or tokens such as IS_AUTHENTICATED_FULLY, IS_AUTHENTICATED_REMEMBERED, and IS_AUTHENTICATED_ANONYMOUSLY.

To use Requestmap entries, specify securityConfigType="Requestmap":

```
grails.plugins.springsecurity.securityConfigType = "Requestmap"
```

You create Requestmap entries as you create entries in any Grails domain class:

```
new Requestmap(url: '/js/**', configAttribute:'IS_AUTHENTICATED_ANONYMOUSLY').save()
new Requestmap(url: '/css/**', configAttribute:'IS_AUTHENTICATED_ANONYMOUSLY').save()
new Requestmap(url: '/images/**', configAttribute:
'IS_AUTHENTICATED_ANONYMOUSLY').save()
new Requestmap(url: '/login/**', configAttribute:
'IS_AUTHENTICATED_ANONYMOUSLY').save()
new Requestmap(url: '/logout/**', configAttribute:
```

```
'IS_AUTHENTICATED_ANONYMOUSLY').save()
new Requestmap(url: '/*', configAttribute: 'IS_AUTHENTICATED_ANONYMOUSLY').save()
new Requestmap(url: '/profile/**', configAttribute: 'ROLE_USER').save()
new Requestmap(url: '/admin/**', configAttribute: 'ROLE_ADMIN').save()
new Requestmap(url: '/admin/role/**', configAttribute: 'ROLE_SUPERVISOR').save()
new Requestmap(url: '/admin/user/**', configAttribute: 'ROLE_ADMIN,ROLE_SUPERVISOR').save()
new Requestmap(url: '/j_spring_security_switch_user',
            configAttribute: 'ROLE_SWITCH_USER,IS_AUTHENTICATED_FULLY').save()
```

The configAttribute value can have a single value or multiple comma-delimited values. In this example, only users with ROLE_ADMIN or ROLE_SUPERVISOR can access /admin/user/** URLs, and only users with ROLE_SWITCH_USER can access the switch-user URL (/j_spring_security_switch_user) and in addition, must be authenticated fully; for example, not using a remember-me cookie. Note that when specifying multiple roles, the user must have at least one of them, but when combining IS_AUTHENTICATED_FULLY, IS_AUTHENTICATED_REMEMBERED, or IS_AUTHENTICATED_ANONYMOUSLY with one or more roles means the user must have one of the roles and satisfy the IS_AUTHENTICATED rule.

SecurityTagLib

The plugin includes GSP tag libraries to support conditional display based on whether the user is authenticated, and/or has the required role to perform a particular action. These tags are in the sec namespace and are implemented in grails.plugins.springsecurity.SecurityTagLib.

Table 7-3. *Spring Security Core Plugin Tag Libraries*

Tag	Description
sec:ifLoggedIn	Displays the inner body content if the user is authenticated.
sec:ifNotLoggedIn	Displays the inner body content if the user is not authenticated.
sec:ifAllGranted	Displays the inner body content only if all of the listed roles are granted.
sec:ifAnyGranted	Displays the inner body content if at least one of the listed roles are granted.
sec:ifNotGranted	Displays the inner body content if none of the listed roles are granted.
sec:username	Displays the value of the authentication username field if logged in.
sec:ifSwitched	Displays the inner body content only if the current user switched from another user.
sec:ifNotSwitched	Displays the inner body content only if the current user has not switched from another user.
sec:loggedInUserInfo	Displays the value of the specified authentication field if logged in.
sec:access	Renders the body if the specified expression evaluates to true or specified URL is allowed.
sec:noAccess	Renders the body if the specified expression evaluates to false or URL isn't allowed.
sec:switchedUserOriginalUsername	Renders the original user's username if the current user switched from another user.

Summary

Security is important to any application. While most of the Grails security plugins are relatively new, they all are based on frameworks that have been built over time. Security has a broad spectrum in which a variety of options are available. A framework like Spring Security can make it easy to add access control. The coverage of other plugins should help you select which plugin is best for your own application.

Now that we have security in place, we can embrace more user functionality in the next chapter, which covers Ajax and other fun Web 2.0 items.

CHAPTER 8

Web 2.0—Ajax and Friends

So far in this book, we have relied on a few basic items to create our site, and, as of right now, it is fully functioning. Users have the ability to log in, create todos, and so on. And while these make for a good application, good applications will not generate revenue. The Web is filled with many bad applications, a lot of good ones, and very few excellent ones. In this and the following two chapters, we will try to add some excellence to our web application by applying some Web 2.0 techniques.

What do we mean by *excellence*? Some developers try to cram every Ajax component and every Web 2.0 concept under the sun into their applications. Many times, this approach fails. You end up complicating the page and making it difficult to use. In this chapter's examples, we will try to toe the line between enhancing the page and making it unmanageable. Each component we add will supply functionality that the users should be able to enjoy.

We will start slowly, with basic plugins that add some Web 2.0 functionality. From there, we will add a mail service, which we will use in this chapter and in Chapter 10 (which covers reporting). After that, we will dive into some good old-fashioned Ajax and demonstrate the flexibility of Ajax in Grails. We will finish up with an RSS feed, which can be useful if you want to be able to displayyour todoson an RSS reader like iGoogle.

Advanced Presentation Components

In this section we will focus on three areas to enrich the presentation:

- Allow for the use of rich text in the todo notes.
- Make the todos searchable.
- Allow for uploading a file associated with a todo.

To add these features, we will make use of an ever-growing list of plugins for Grails.

Adding RichText Capabilities

Currently, todo note entry is limited. You cannot style text (such as italics or boldface) or format it (say, into a bulleted list). Adding a rich text editor can provide near Microsoft Word–type functionality to a web site. Not only can you allow rich text, but you can also let the users upload images, Flash movies, and even files to your web application. The CK editor plugin[1] is a good example of this sort of editor. You can install `ckeditor` using this command:

```
>grails install-plugin ckeditor
```

Or you can use Grails Plugin Manager, as shown in Figure 8-1.

[1] `http://grails.org/plugin/ckeditor`

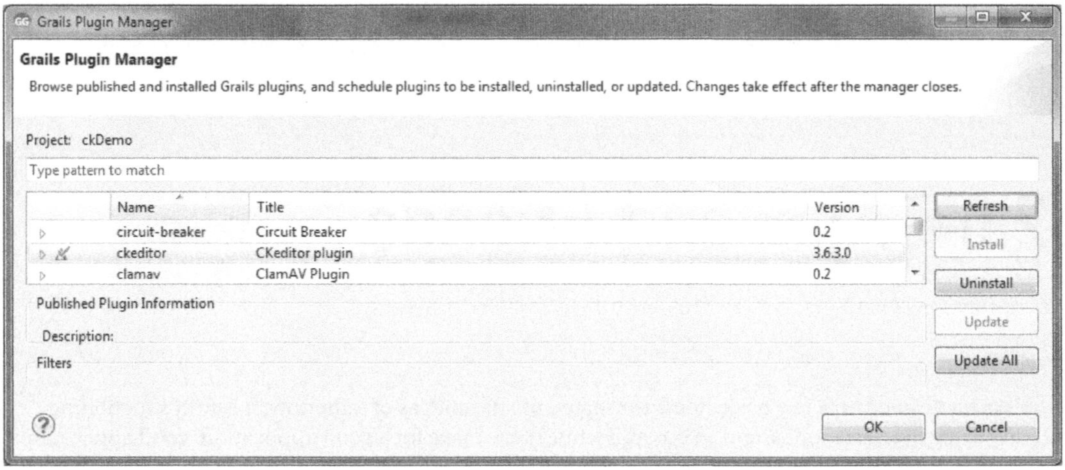

Figure 8-1. Installing CK editor plugin using Grails Plugin Manager

To start using the plugin, add the `ckeditor` tag in the `head` and page sections as illustrated in Listing 8-1 and Listing 8-2:

Listing 8-1. Adding ckeditor Tag to head

```
<head>
. . .
<ckeditor:resources/>
. . .
</head>
```

Listing 8-2. Adding ckeditor Tag to page

```
<ckeditor:editor name="myeditor" height="400px" width="80%">
${initialValue}
</ckeditor:editor>
```

Figure 8-2 shows an example of the CK editor embedded into an application. Although this is, as Borat would say, "very nice," it is overkill for our needs. Not only that, it might break some of the smooth lines of our page.

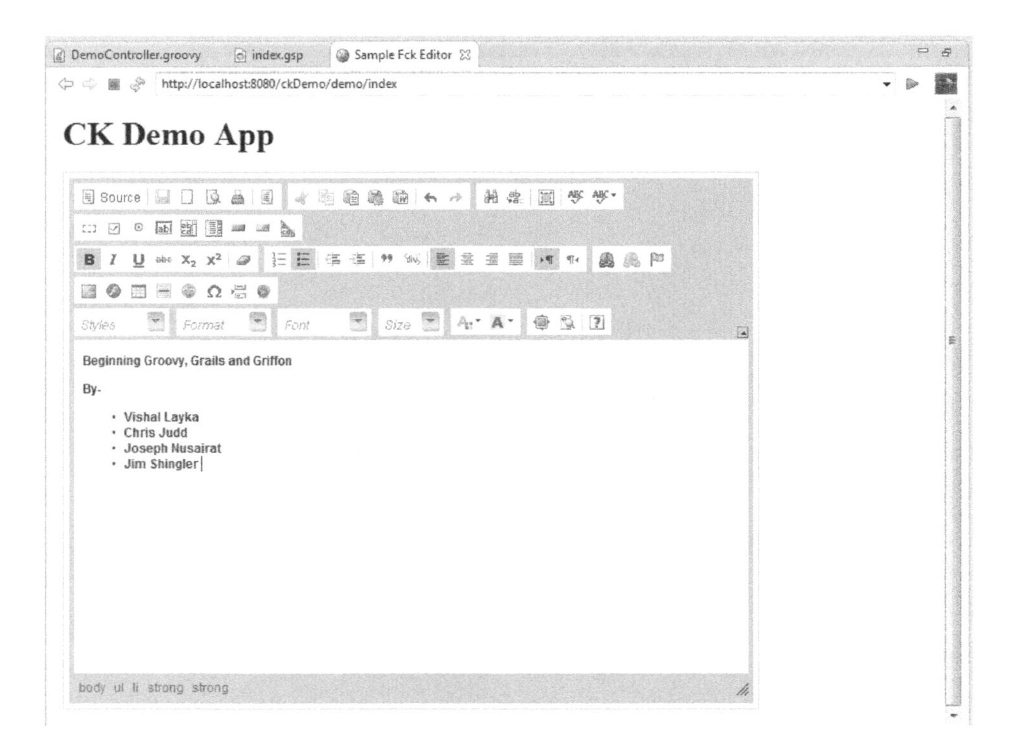

Figure 8-2. *The CK editor plugin in action*

Adding Search Capabilities

Currently, the only way to search for a particular task is to literally open up every task and see what is in there. While this may work if you have a small number of tasks, it quickly becomes cumbersome as the application grows—especially if you're looking for akeyword that is buried in the notes.

As in previous chapters, we are not only going to make use of a plugin, but a plugin that is based on triedand-true Java technologies. The Searchable plugin is based on the OpenSymphony Compass Search Engine framework, which in turn uses Apache Luceneunder the covers.

The Searchable plugin is supplied with Grails. Install it by issuing the following command:

```
> grails install-plugin searchable
```

Or you can use Grails Plugin Manager, as shown in Figure 8-3.

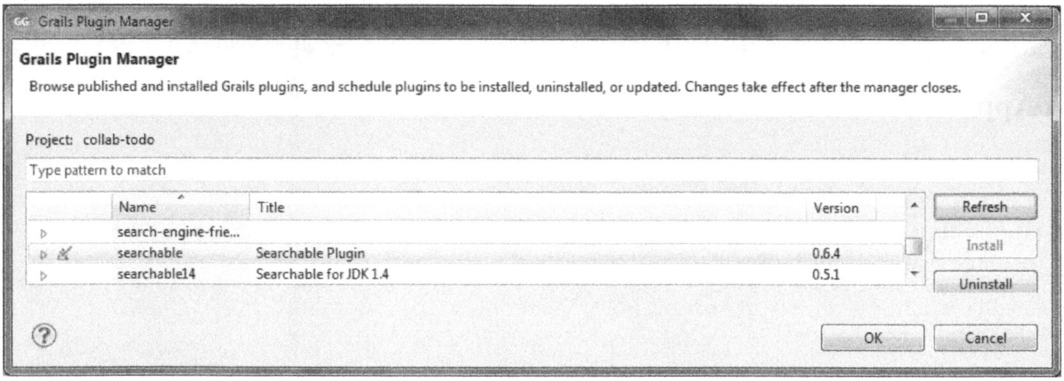

Figure 8-3. *Installing searchable plugin using Grails Plugin manager*

The Searchable plugin is a snap to set up and use. The plugin allows you to decide which domain objects should be searchable. We want to make the todos searchable, so we add the line `static searchable = true` to our `Todo` domain object, as shown in Listing 8-3.

Listing 8-3. Marking Our Todo as Searchable in domain/Todo.groovy

```
class Todo {
    static searchable = true
    // . . . continued . . .
}
```

And that is all we need to do. So what does that give us? If you go to `http://localhost:8080/collab-todo/searchable`, you see the default searchable page (see Figure 8-4).

Figure 8-4. *Default searchable*

To see the searchable plugin in action, let's search through the list of tasks shown in Figure 8-5.

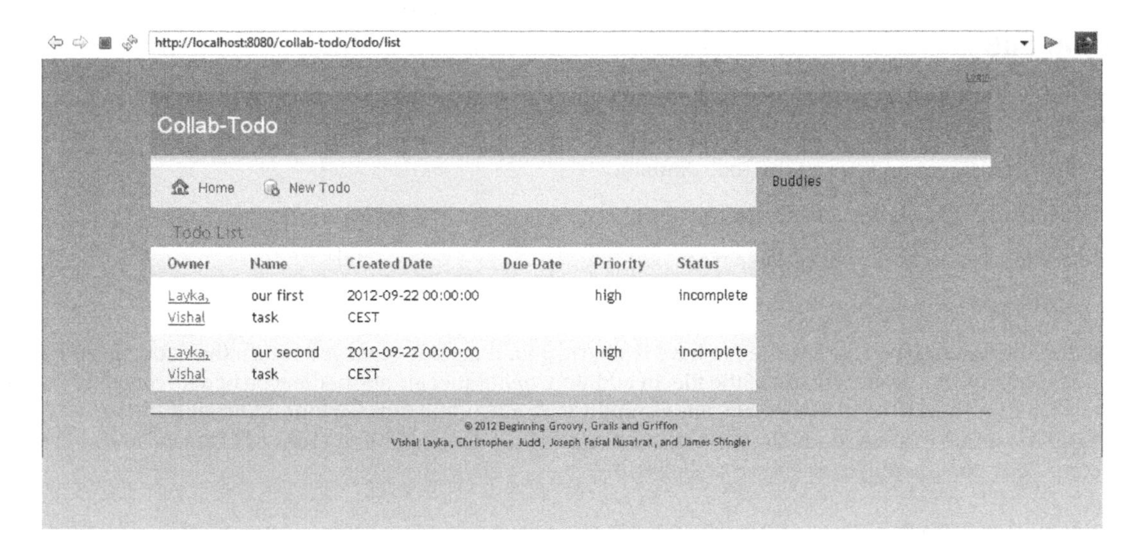

Figure 8-5. *List of tasks*

You can type in a word to search for and get the results. Figure 8-6 shows the results of searching for *task*.

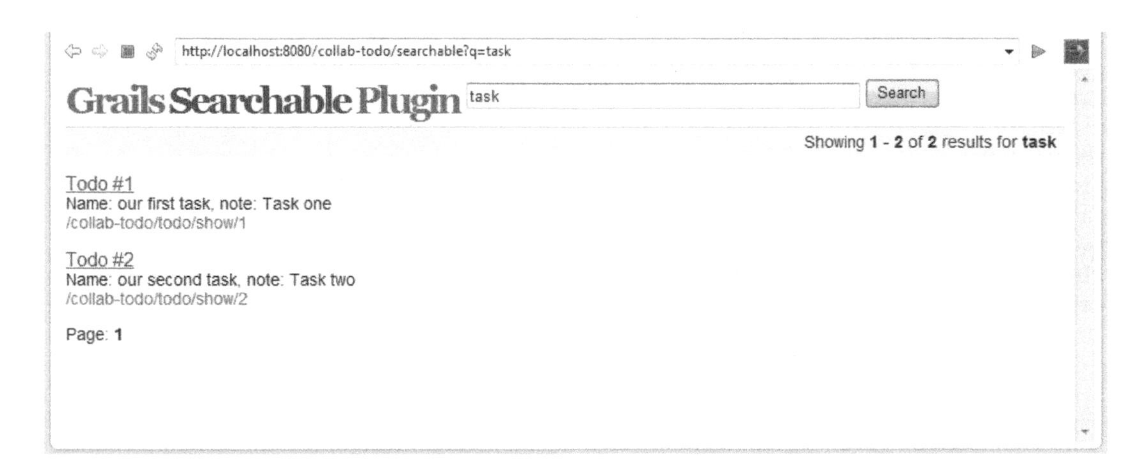

Figure 8-6. *The results of searching for the word "task"*

Allowing File Uploads

Some web applications allow users to upload files. For our application, we'll add the ability to upload a file for each of the todos, and then retrieve (download) that file later. The uploaded files can be stored either on the application server or the database itself. For our example, we wantto store the file in the database, mainly since that's easy and because we're working with only one file, so space is not an issue.

Uploading the File

Grails will use Spring's file upload capability to help upload the file. Uploading a file is a fairly simple process, requiring the following steps:

1. Review necessary properties on the `Todo` domain.
2. Add a link to upload it in our list page.
3. Add configurations to the Spring `resources.xml` file.
4. Create the necessary code in our controller to store and retrieve the file.

In order to store the data, all you are required to have is a `byte[]` for data. But when you return the data, the end user probably wants to have the original name of the file. In addition, being specific about the type of data returned will help the browser know how to process the data. For example, if it's a PDF, the browser automatically knows to open it as a PDF. To handle this, we added the variable `associatedFile byte[]` and `Strings` of `filename` and `contentType` to our `Todo` domain object, as shown in Listing 8-4.

Listing 8-4. Updating the Todo Domain Object (in domain/Todo.groovy)

```
class Todo {
    User owner
    Category category
    String name
    String note
    Date createDate
    Date startDate
    Date dueDate
    Date completeDate
    Date lastModifiedDate
    String priorityf
    String status
    byte[] associatedFile
    String fileName
    String contentType
    . . .
}
```

Once you restart the server, it automatically creates the entry in the database as a BLOB, or TINYBLOB if you are using MySQL.

The next part is to add a section to our page to upload the file. As shown in Listing 8-5, we add a file upload tag after the due date.

Listing 8-5. The File Upload Tag for the Todo (in views/todo/list.gsp)

```
<tr class='prop'>
<td valign='top' class='name'><label for='dueDate'>File:</label></td>
<td valign='top'
    class='value ${hasErrors(bean:todo,field:'asociatedFile','errors')}'>
<input type="file" name="associatedFile" />
</td>
</tr>
```

Performing file uploads also requires a change in the form tag itself. You must change the form to a multipart request. To do this, add the attribute shown in Listing 8-6 to the form tag.

Listing 8-6. The Multipart Tag for the Form (in views/todo/list.gsp)

```
enctype="multipart/form-data"
```

Figure 8-7 shows an example of the result of our additions: a todo is created, with a file selected to upload.

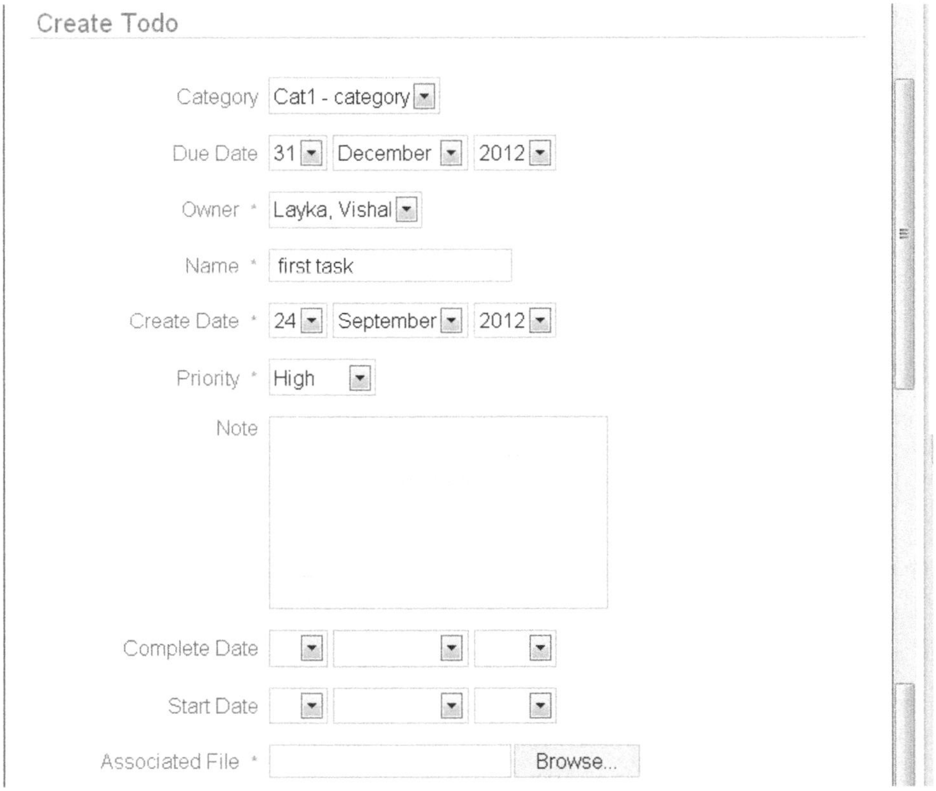

Figure 8-7. *Choosing a file to upload with a new todo*

As we said earlier, we make use of Spring for our file upload capability, and you cansee when we update the controller, next, that there are calls to Spring objects. However, in order to use the Spring objects, we need to add a bean in Spring's `resources.xml` file. This is where we define Spring resources to be used in Grails. Add the following linesto `conf/spring/resources.xml`.

```
<bean class="org.springframework.web.multipart.commons.CommonsMultipartResolver">
<property name="maxUploadSize"><value>1000000</value></property>
</bean>
```

The final step is to actually save the file. This is not complicated, but it does require making use of some Spring objects. We will cast the request coming in as a `MultipartHttpServletRequest` and retrieve the items off the file as necessary. Listing 8-7 shows the new method to handle the file upload.

Listing 8-7. The uploadFileData Method on the TodoController (in controllers/TodoController.groovy)

```
import org.springframework.web.multipart.MultipartHttpServletRequest;
import org.springframework.web.multipart.commons.CommonsMultipartFile;
. . .
def uploadFileData = { todo ->
    if (request instanceof MultipartHttpServletRequest) {
        MultipartHttpServletRequest multiRequest
            = (MultipartHttpServletRequest)request;
        CommonsMultipartFile file =
            (CommonsMultipartFile)multiRequest.getFile("associatedFile");
        // Save the object items.
        todo.fileName = file.originalFilename
        todo.contentType = file.contentType
        todo.associatedFile = file.bytes
    }
}
```

Simply call this method before you persist on your save method in order to set the appropriate properties on the Todo.

Downloading the File

Now that it is stored, we want to be able to retrieve the file on the fly. The file that is returned from the database is in a byte[], hence you can use any common method of response rendering to render the returned item. When you return a file, you put the byte[] into the output stream of the response, setting some header data. A basic example of a file return is shown in Listing 8-8.

Listing 8-8. A Download File Method for TodoController (in controller/TodoController.groovy)

```
def downloadFile = {
    def todo = Todo.get( params.id )
    response.setHeader("Content-disposition",
"attachment; filename=${todo.fileName}")
    response.contentType = todo.contentType
    response.outputStream << todo.associatedFile
}
```

This method can be called by a link on our todo page, just by passing in the ID of the todo. As you can see in the method, the header and contentType returns are why we needed to save those two items in the first place.

Adding Mail Services

Another common feature of web sites is the ability to send e-mail from them. We will add this capability to our application. For now, we will use the mail service to send an e-mail when a user registers. In Chapter 10, we will use it again to send reports.

If you are familiar with the Spring e-mail service, you will be right at home with the Grails system, since it uses Spring Mail underneath.

We will create an e-mail service, and then adjust our user registration process to call it and send an e-mail. This requires the following steps:

1. Create the service to send an e-mail.
2. Create the authenticator to use for logging in to an SMTP server.
3. Update the Spring `resources.xml` file.

Creating the E-Mail Service

Because Grails uses Spring's e-mail support, we will use the `org.springframework.mail. MailSender` class to actually send the e-mail. In order to make this easier for all of us, we will wrap the call to the class in a service. The service will provide an easy, generic set of parameters to send the e-mail. That way, the callers do not need to worry about creating MIME messages. Listing 8-9 shows the `EMailAuthenticatedService`.

Listing 8-9. The EMailAuthenticatedService, Responsible for Sending E-Mail

```
 1. import org.apache.log4j.Logger;
 2.
 3. import org.springframework.core.io.InputStreamResource
 4. import org.springframework.core.io.ByteArrayResource
 5.
 6. import org.springframework.mail.MailException
 7. import org.springframework.mail.MailSender
 8. import org.springframework.mail.javamail.MimeMessageHelper
 9.
10. import javax.mail.internet.MimeMessage
11. import javax.mail.internet.InternetAddress;
12.
13. class EMailAuthenticatedService {
14.     boolean transactional = false
15.     MailSender mailSender
16.
17.     def sendEmail = { mail, eMailProperties, attachements ->
18.         MimeMessage mimeMessage = mailSender.createMimeMessage()
19.
20.         MimeMessageHelper helper
                = new MimeMessageHelper(mimeMessage, true, "ISO-8859-1")
21.         helper.from = eMailProperties.from
22.         helper.to = getInternetAddresses(mail.to)
23.         helper.subject = mail.subject
24.         helper.setText(mail.text, true);
25.         if(mail.bcc) helper.bcc = getInternetAddresses(mail.bcc)
26.         if(mail.cc) helper.cc = getInternetAddresses(mail.cc)
27.
28.         attachements.each { key, value ->
29.             helper.addAttachment(key, new ByteArrayResource(value))
30.         }
31.
32.         mailSender.send(mimeMessage)
33.     }
34.
```

```
35.     private InternetAddress[] getInternetAddresses(List emails) {
36.         InternetAddress[] mailAddresses = new InternetAddress[emails.size()]
37.         emails.eachWithIndex {mail, i ->
38.             mailAddresses[i] = new InternetAddress(mail)

39.         }
40.         return mailAddresses
41.     }
42. }
```

On line 15, we have a reference to MailSender. Since this is not set explicitly, you can assume it will be injected by Grails. You will see later how we reference MailSender in Spring's resources.xml file.

The only public method starts on line 17. This is the method that any clients using the service will use. The parameters passed to it are simple. We will send a mail object, which will be passed to the method as a Map.

Creating the Mail Sender

The EMailAuthenticatedSender has a MailSender as an injectable component. This is relatively easy to create but does require a few steps. We need to add a few entries into resources.xml and one new service. We will work this sort of in reverse by building up the top entries, and then going through their dependents.

We begin by defining the mailSender in resources.xml, as shown in Listing 8-10.

Listing 8-10. mailSender Defined in resources.xml

```
<bean id="mailSender" class="org.springframework.mail.javamail.JavaMailSenderImpl">
<property name="host" value="smtp.apress.com" />
<property name="session" ref="mailSession" />
</bean>
```

As you can see, the mailSender itself defines two variables: a host and a session. The host is a String bean identifying the host through which we send the e-mail. For a production server, it could easily be localhost or anther host on the network. In our example, we use a fictional Apress SMTP server.

The session is a bit more complex and requires us to define another injectable object. So, we need to add another bean, mailSession, in our resources.xml file, as shown in Listing 8-11.

Listing 8-11. mailSession Defined in resources.xml

```
<bean id="mailSession" class="javax.mail.Session" factory-method="getInstance">
<constructor-arg>
<props>
<prop key="mail.smtp.auth">true</prop>
<!-- If SSL needed...
<prop key="mail.smtp.socketFactory.port">465</prop>
<prop key="mail.smtp.socketFactory.class">
        javax.net.ssl.SSLSocketFactory
</prop>
<prop key="mail.smtp.socketFactory.fallback">
        false
</prop>
      -->
</props>
```

```
</constructor-arg>
<constructor-arg ref="smtpAuthenticator" />
</bean>
```

Here, we defined the session to work with a nonSSL source, but as you can see by the commented-out code, switching to an SSL source is quite easy as well.

As you may have guessed, we have yet another item to inject, the `smtpAuthenticator`. We need to create an object and define the bean for it. First, let's define the bean in `resources.xml`, as shown in Listing 8-12.

Listing 8-12. smtpAuthenticator Defined in resources.xml

```
<bean id="smtpAuthenticator" class="SmtpAuthenticator">
<constructor-arg value="xxx@xxx.net" />
<constructor-arg value="xxxxxx" />
</bean>
```

We defined a constructor that takes in a username and a password (blanked out because, well, we don't need everyone checking our e-mail).

Now we need to create a bean for this. We'll create this class in the `services` folder, and simply extend `javax.mail.Authenticator`. Listing 8-13 shows our authentication bean.

Listing 8-13. The Custom SmtpAuthenticator Bean

```
import javax.mail.Authenticator

class SmtpAuthenticator extends Authenticator {

  private String username;
  private String password;

public SmtpAuthenticator(String username, String password) {
    super();
    this.username = username;
    this.password = password;
  }

  public javax.mail.PasswordAuthentication getPasswordAuthentication() {
    return new javax.mail.PasswordAuthentication(username, password);
  }
}
```

Updating the Registration Page

Now that our bean and all of its subcomponents are defined, it's time to put it to use. We will modify the registration page to send an e-mail message. Listing 8-14 shows the method that we will use.

Listing 8-14. Registration Page to Send E-mail (in controller/UserController.groovy)

```
private sendAcknowledgment = { user ->
    // Let's first design the email that we want to send
    def emailTpl = this.class.classloader.getResource(
"web-app/WEB-INF/templates/regisrationEmail.gtpl")
```

```
def binding = ["user": user]
def engine = new SimpleTemplateEngine()
def template = engine.createTemplate(emailTpl).make(binding)
def body = template.toString()

// Set up the email to send.
def email = [
    to: [user.email],
    subject: "Your Collab-Todo Report",
    text: body
]

try {
    // Check if we "need" attachments
    eMailAuthenticatedService.sendEmail(email, [])
            } catch (MailException ex) {
    log.error("Failed to send emails", ex)
    return false
}
     true
}
```

This e-mail call is actually relatively simple. We will pass in a map defining the To and Subject lines and text. The email message body is generated by using a Groovy template engine on the file `registrationEmail.gptl`.

Note that you can reuse this code in other places to send e-mail messages.

Tag Libraries

Tag libraries provide sets of custom actions that you perform inside pages. Generally, the actions are repetitive or would be too long to write scriptlets within the page.

You have seen many of the Grails built-in tag libraries in use in our examples so far. We have used these tags to output data, render lists, and so on, and we will continue to use them throughout the book. See the "Grails Tags" section in Chapter 5 for an overview of the Grails tags.

Here, we cover how to create your own custom tag library. If you created tag libraries in the past with Java frameworks, you know that it is actually quite a pain. Your tag library class must extend a base class. You then need to define the tag and its attributes in your tag library definition. Optionally, you can then reference that tag library in the `web.xml`. Finally, you reference the specific tag you are using in the page itself. Wow—that'squite a bit of work just to create something that may be only a formatter. Fortunately, creating a tag library with Grails is simpler than that.

You may have noticed that on our application's todo page, the option to add a todo is always shown. But users may go to that page and just want to see the list. It would be good to be able to hide the add section and open it when necessary. We can create a tag library to handle this. It will mark an area with `div` tags and allow the user to click a JavaScript link to open that section. Creating this will require two sets of code segments: one to display the JavaScript and the other to actually call that JavaScript for any `div` section. Normally, with JSP, this requires two classes and a host of XML. Thanks to Grails, we can handle this with one class and no XML.

Creating the Tag Library

Tag libraries reside in the `grails-app/taglib` folder, so that is where we will create our new tag library. Listing 8-15 shows the outline of our tag library with all the global objects we will use.

Listing 8-15. The ShowHideTagLib Outline

```
class ShowHideTagLib {
}
```

As you can see, this doesn't contain much; that's because this is all we need for the basic outline.

We are actually creating two separate tag libraries. While this is normally done with different classes, with Grails, we merely have separate methods. Listing 8-16 shows the methods we are adding to ShowHideTagLib.

Listing 8-16. The Contents of ShowHideTagLib

```
    def showHide = { attrs, body ->

        def divId = attrs['update']
        out <<"""<a href="javascript:showhide('$divId');">${body()}</a>"""
    }
    def preLoadShowHide = { attrs, body ->
        out <<"""<script language="javascript">
<!--
            function showhide(layer_ref) {
                // Let's get the state.
                var state = document.getElementById(layer_ref).style.display;
                if (state == 'block') {
                    state = 'none';
                } else {
                    state = 'block';
                }
                if (document.all) { //IS IE 4 or 5 (or 6 beta)
                    eval("document.all." + layer_ref + ".style.display = state");
                }
                if (document.layers) { //IS NETSCAPE 4 or below
                    document.layers[layer_ref].display = state;
                }

                if (document.getElementById &&!document.all) {
                    hza = document.getElementById(layer_ref);
                    hza.style.display = state;
                }
            }
            //-->
</script>
"""
    }
```

Here, we have two tag library calls. Each of them shows how great it is to use Groovy when creating tag libraries.

Since creating tag libraries requires the output of the code to be HTML markups, this generally involves a lotof string building. Not only that, but when you have output with quotation marks, you need to escape them with backslashes (\) throughout the code. Yuck! However, with Groovy, we can use triple quotes. The triple quote style allows us to not only fully embed strings with markups, but also to return characters and referenced values.

The first method, showHide, passes in two objects: attrs and body. The body is simply the section of the page between the opening and closing bracket of your tag library. The attrs is a map of attributes you want to pass into the method. With regular JSP tag libraries, you need define them individually as getters and setters on the page, and in the tag library XML. With Grails and Groovy, that is not necessary. As you can see, we mapped a value called `update`, which is the `div` tag section we want activated.

The second method, `preLoadShowHide`, doesn't contain any dynamic code per se. We are simply outputting the JavaScript in there.

Referencing the Tag Library

Referencing the tag library is simple as well. By default, the tag library is referenced in the g namespace—the same one in which all the built-in Grails tags are referenced. Then the method name is used as the tag's reference name. Listing 8-17 shows the calls to the tags in `todo/list.gsp`.

Listing 8-17. Excerpts from todo/list.gsp Showing the Calls to the Custom Tags

```
<g:preLoadShowHide/>
<g:javascript library="scriptaculous" />
<div class="body">
<h2>Todo List<g:showHide update="addToDo">
<img border=0 src="${createLinkTo(dir:'images',file:'add_obj.gif')}"
        alt="[ADD]"/>
</g:showHide>
```

But what if you don't want to use the g namespace? Perhaps you are bundling the application as a tag library and are worried about name conflicts, or you simply want to remember it's not part of the core Grails functionality. In order to change the namespace used, add a static namespace reference in your tag library. For example, to use the namespace `todo` for our code, you would add the following line to `ShowHideTagLib`:

```
static namespace = 'todo'
```

Ajax in Grails

We certainly could not have a Web 2.0 chapter without including a discussion of Ajax. *Ajax* stands for Asynchronous JavaScript and XML, which oddly enough, is not a 100% accurate definition. Although Ajax is usually asynchronous, usually written in JavaScript, and often deals with transmission of XML, none of these items is a *must* for it. You can send Ajax messages synchronously, you do not have to use JavaScript to send them, and your response can be an XML file but can also be a regular string.

■ **Note** The term *Ajax* was originally coined by Jesse James Garrett. But the technology was first developed by Microsoft in an attempt to deal with remote scripting.

One of the biggest "secrets" about Ajax is that, for the most part, it's not that complex, at least conceptually. There is nothing you can do with Ajax that you could not do in a normal application; however, using Ajax can help your application not only perform better, but also give a richer user experience.

The core of Ajax is just sending data to the server and parsing the data on the return without forcing the display to refresh. The complexity lies in making use of the data, and this is where you start to see frameworks emerge. The fact is that these frameworks are not 100% Ajax—if they were, they wouldn't be very big. Instead, these frameworks wrap Ajax with JavaScript UI enhancements. Some of the calls won't even involve Ajax. However, here we will refer to these frameworks as *Ajax frameworks*.

Using Ajax Frameworks in Grails

Popular Ajax frameworks include Prototype, Dojo:`http://dojotoolkit.org/`, script.aculo.us, and Yahoo! User Interface (YUI) Library:`http://developer.yahoo.com/yui/`. Even Google has come onboard with its own rather complex Ajax framework, Google Web Toolkit (GWT).

Most of the popular web frameworks have implemented Ajax. The majority of these did not create their own Ajax framework, but merely wrapped code from previous Ajax frameworks. Ruby on Rails uses script.aculo.us, Tapestry's Tacos uses Dojo, and so on. So what does Grails use? The answer is all of the above.

In an effort to provide maximum flexibility, Grails currently accepts all of the frameworks out there. So what does this mean? Is this good or bad? It's a bit of both. While it allows us more flexibility in choosing a framework, in the end, we need to write more code than other frameworks usually demand, especially when it comes to the JavaScript UI portions of the Ajax items. If you are familiar with other Java or Rails Ajax uses, this will become apparent to you in the upcoming examples.

By default, Grails ships with the jQuery library, but through the Plugin system provides support for other frameworks such as Prototype, DojoYahoo UI, and the Google Web Toolkit.

Each of these frameworks has its own custom UI components. If you are familiar with Rails or Tapestry's Tacos, you know that they generally provide complete support for the underlying framework. In other words, there is usually a tag library wrapper for the whole framework. This makes it easy to not only support the Ajax components, but also the JavaScript components. Unfortunately, this is not the case in Grails.

Grails includes several Ajax tags, which call a controller action and update a page element with the results. Grails supports a variety of popular JavaScript libraries with regard to its Ajax tags. To use these tags, we need to tell Grails which library we are using. We do this with the `<g:javascript>` tag and its library attribute. This tag is placed in the <head> section of a page.

In Grails we extensively use GSP templates to render the response to Ajax calls. A GSP template is a GSP file that begins with an underscore (`_example.gsp`). GSP templatesprovide an easy way to share common code across multiple pages. You can include a GSP template in a GSPpage with the `<g:render>` tag, like this:

```
<g:render template="sampleTemplate" />
```

This line would render a template called `_sampleTemplate.gsp` in the same directory as the page from which it is called.

Grails supports just the standard Ajax components, as listed in Table 8-1. However, this does give us a good subset of components to use.

Table 8-1. *Ajax Components in Grails*

Tag	Description
`remoteField`	Creates a text field that sends its value to a remote link when it changes
`remoteFunction`	Creates a remote JavaScript function that can be assigned to a DOM event
`remoteLink`	Creates a link that calls a remote function
`formRemote`	Creates a form that executes an Ajax call on submission
`javascript`	Loads a JavaScript function
`submitToRemote`	Creates a button that submits the form as an Ajax call

Using remoteField

This tag creates an input field that fires an Ajax request when its value changes (typically when the user presses Return inside the field). We will use the controller in Listing 8-18 to illustrate the usage of the `remoteField` tag, as shown in Listing 8-19.

Listing 8-18. Example Controller for the Usage of remoteField Tag

```
class CategoryController {
def changeDescription() {
        def cat = Category.get(params.id)
        cat.description = params.value
        cat.save()
    }
}
```

Listing 8-19. Using remoteField Tag

```
<g:remoteField action="changeDescription" update="descDiv"
               name="description" value="${category?.description}" />
<div id="descDiv">
This div is updated
</div>
```

By default the parameter name sent is called `value` as shown in Listing 8-19; you can change this by specifying a `paramName` attribute.

Using remoteFunction

This tag creates a remote Javascript function call that fires an Ajax request to call the remote method. We will use the controller in Listing 8-20 to demonstrate the usage of the `remoteFunction` tag.

Listing 8-20. Example UserController for the Usage of Ajax Tags

```
class UserController {
def list() {
        [users: User.list(params)]
    }
def show() {
        [user: User.get(params.id)]
    }
def byFirstName() {
        [user: User.findByName(params.firstName)]
    }
        def byLastName() {
        [users: User.findByName(params.lastName, params)]
    }
}
```

Listing 8-21. Using remoteFunction Tag

```
$('mydiv').onclick = <g:remoteFunction action="show" id="1" />
```

Using remoteLink

This tag creates an HTML link to a controller action that generates an Ajax request when it is clicked. Listing 8-22 illustrates the usage of the `submitToRemote` tag for the controller in Listing 8-20.

Listing 8-22. Using remoteLink Tag

```
<g:remoteLink action="show" id="1">Test 1</g:remoteLink>
<g:remoteLink action="show" id="1" update="[success:'success',failure:'error']"
    on404="alert('not found');">Test 2</g:remoteLink>
```

Using formRemote

This tag creates a form that fires an Ajax request when it is submitted, serializing the form elements and falling back to a normal form submit if JavaScript is not supported. Listing 8-23 illustrates the usage of the `submitToRemote` tag for the controller in Listing 8-20.

Listing 8-23. Using formRemote Tag

```
<g:formRemote name="myForm" on404="alert('not found!')" update="updateDiv"
              url="[controller: user, action:'show']">
User Id: <input name="id" type="text" />
</g:formRemote>
<div id="updateDiv">this div is updated with the result of the show call</div>
```

Using javascript

This tag Includes JavaScript libraries and scripts as well as providing a kind of shorthand for inline JavaScript, as illustrated in Listing 8-24.

Listing 8-24. Using javascript Tag

```
1. <g:javascript src="script.js" />
2. <g:javascript library="scriptaculous" />
3. <g:javascript>alert('hello')</g:javascript>
```

Listing 8-24 illustrates three different uses of the `javascript` tag. The tag on line 1 actually imports `script.js`, and the tag on Line 2 imports all the necessary js for the scriptaculous library. The tag on line 3 does not include a `library` or `src` attribute but instead provides a body; the result is an inline script.

Using submitToRemote

This tag creates a submit button that fires an Ajax request when it is pressed and submits the containing form as a remote Ajax call, serializing the fields into parameters. Listing 8-25 illustrates the usage of the `submitToRemote` tag for the controller in Listing 8-20.

Listing 8-25. Using submitToRemote Tag

```
<g:form action="show">
    Login: <input name="login" type="text" />
<g:submitToRemote update="updateDiv" />
</g:form>
<div id="updateDiv ">this div will be updated with the form submit response</div>
```

Handling Ajax Events

Specific JavaScript can be called if certain events occur. All the events start with the "on" prefix and let you give feedback to the user where appropriate, or take other action.

Listing 8-26. Handling Ajax Events

```
<g:remoteLink action="show"
        id="1"
        update="success"
        onLoading="showProgress()"
        onComplete="hideProgress()">
Show task 1
</g:remoteLink>
```

The code in Listing 8-26 executes the showProgress() function, which may show a progress bar or whatever is appropriate.

Table 8-2 shows the different events.

Table 8-2. *Ajax Events*

Field Name	Description
onSuccess	The JavaScript function to call if successful
onFailure	The JavaScript function to call if the call failed
on_ERROR_CODE	The JavaScript function to call to handle specified error codes
onUninitialized	The JavaScript function to call if the Ajax engine failed to initialize
onLoading	The JavaScript function to call when the remote function is loading the response
onLoaded	The JavaScript function to call when the remote function hascompleted loading the response
onComplete	The JavaScript function to call when the remote function is complete, including any updates

Dynamic Rendering of Data

Our first example demonstrates using one of the most basic and popular types of Ajax components. This is where you type data into the page, submit it, remotely call the server, process the data, and re-render only a portion of the page. For our example, we will modify the todo add page to do a partial page re-rendering. Now when adding a new todo, instead of doing an entire page refresh, the page will dynamically render the todo list section of the page.

In order to perform this, we need to take a few steps, the first of which is not necessarily Ajax-specific:

1. Move the list section of the page into its own page (called a *template* or *partial page*).
2. Change our current add call to do an Ajax remote call instead of submitting the whole page.
3. Change the TodoController's return to render the new page we created instead of the whole page.

■ **Note** One of the big issues you will run into when performing the dynamic rendering of data is *partial page updates*. Partial page updating refers to re-rendering a part of the page. Some frameworks, like Tapestry's Tacos, allow you to perform this in line. However, the majority of web frameworks, including Grails and Ruby on Rails, force you to call to another page. In reality, this is not a big deal. It does add to the number of GSPs you need to write, but on the plus side, it keeps the GSPs clean.

Rendering a Template

Rendering a page from another page is fairly simple to do. First, we need a page to call from, which obviously must be a GSP page. We will use the `<g:render />` tag library to define the area of the page that will call out to another GSP page. Grails refers to these partial pages as *templates*.

Our first step is to take our list of todos in `todo/list.gsp` and pull that section out to its own page. We will replace the list with what is in Listing 8-27. Also, instead of taking the entire code, we will take everything but the `for` loop. This is because we can tell the renderer to render a collection.

Listing 8-27. A Template of todo/list.gsp with the Modified Todo List Display

```
<div id="todoList">
<g:render template="detail" var="todo" collection="${todoList}" />
</div>
```

Here, we simply tell Grails to take our collection labeled `todoList` and iterate through the list, rendering the `detail` page each time for every item in the collection. The item in the collection is then referenced in the page by the variable `var`.

Creating a Template

The name of the page we are creating will not actually be `detail.gsp`. Instead, Grails chooses the page to render by taking the rendered template attribute and adding underscores at the beginning to indicate the page is a template. The page must also be located in the same directory as the calling controller. Thus, for this example, we will create `_detail.gsp` in the todo directory, as shown in Listing 8-28.

Listing 8-28. The _detail.gsp Page

```
<div id="todoDetail${todo.id}" class="todo">

<div class="todoTitle">${todo.name?.encodeAsHTML()}
<g:link action="edit" id="${todo.id}">
<img border=0
          src="${createLinkTo(dir:'images',file:'write_obj.gif')}" alt="[EDIT]"/>
</g:link>
<g:remoteLink
           action="removeTask"
           id="${todo.id}"
           update="todoDetail$todo.id"
           onComplete="highlight('todoDetail$todo.id');">
<img border=0 src="${createLinkTo(dir:'images',file:'delete_obj.gif')}"
           alt="[EDIT]"/>
</g:remoteLink>
```

```
<g:showHide update="todoDetailFull${todo.id}">
<img border=0
              src="${createLinkTo(dir:'images',file:'add_obj.gif')}"
               alt="[Show All]"/></g:showHide>
</div>

<div id="todoDetailFull${todo.id}" class="todo" style="display:none">
    Status: ${todo.status?.encodeAsHTML()} <br />
    Priority: ${todo.priority?.encodeAsHTML()} <br />
    Created date: ${todo.createDate?.encodeAsHTML()} <br />
    Last Modified date: ${todo.lastModifiedDate?.encodeAsHTML()} <br />

<g:if test="${todo.completeDate == null}">
        Complete Task: <input type="checkbox"
                             onclick="${remoteFunction(
                                          action:'completeTask',
                                          id:todo.id,
                                          update:'todoDetail' + todo.id,
                                          onComplete:'highlight(\'todoDetail' + todo.id+'\')'
)};"/><br />
</g:if>
<g:else>
        Completed Date: ${todo.completeDate?.encodeAsHTML()} <br />
</g:else>
<!-- show notes -- mark in the code that we should use a todo -->
<g:radeoxRender>${todo?.note}</g:radeoxRender>
<!-- update:[success:'great', failure:'ohno'], -->
<!--

<g:remoteLink action="showNotes" id="${todo.id}"
         update="todoDetailNote${todo.id}">
        Notes
</g:remoteLink><br/>
<div id="todoDetailNote${todo.id}">
</div>
    -->
</div>
</div>
```

Our first step is complete. In reality, there is nothing in the page that is Ajax-enabled yet. Right now, the page works exactly as it did before, and in theory, you could have used these techniques to help segregate the code.

Making the Page Dynamic

Now we will do the partial page form rendering, which is a two-step process:

1. Change the form to take an Ajax form tag.
2. Have the save call on the controller render the tag instead of the whole page.

For the first part, change the form encapsulation in `list.gsp` to the code shown in Listing 8-29.

Listing 8-29. Adding an Ajax Form Tag (in views/todo/list.gsp)

```
<g:formRemote name="todoForm"
              url="[controller:'todo',action:'save']"
              update="todoList"
              onComplete="showhide('addToDo')"
              enctype="multipart/form-data">
    . . .
</g:formRemote>
```

This calls the save action on our TodoController, and then on completion, hides the add section. In addition, the update attribute will tell us which <div> section we are updating. In Listing 8-27 notice that we surrounded our rendered items with the <div> tag todoList. This is the section that the Ajax JavaScript will re-render upon return.

The changes to the save action are equally as easy. Instead of the standard return, where we redirect to the list page, we have a line to get the collection and call out to render the GSP we marked, as shown in Listing 8-30.

Listing 8-30. Rendering Just the Tag (in views/todo/list.gsp)

```
render(TEMPLATE:'DETAIL',  VAR: 'TODO', COLLECTION:LISTBYOWNER())
```

As you can see, besides having to move some data, this was all relatively simple. And that is all that is needed. If you go back to the page now, it will do an update without needing to return the whole page.

RSS Feeds

RSS feeds have become an increasingly popular feature to incorporate on a web site. Contributing to RSS feed popularity is the increasing number of RSS readers out there, including the new iGoogle[2] and the RSS Web Clip in Gmail. So we will go over creating a basic RSS reader. This will be an extremely basic example; in a real-world application, you would want to add more items for security checking.

Creating an RSS feed basically requires creating an XML output in a fairly strict format. The reader then takes that XML and parses it for content.

We could do this by hand, but the format based on the feeds can be somewhat complex, and you would also need to write quite a bit of repetitive code. Luckily, there is aplugin that will help us cheat a bit and create the feeds. The Feeds plugin[3] shown in Figure 8-8 supports creating feeds in the popular RSS and Atom formats (with multiple versions of each supported). Start by installing the plugin:

```
> grails install-plugin feeds
```

---

[2] http://www.google.com/ig.

[3] http://grails.codehaus.org/Feeds+Plugin.

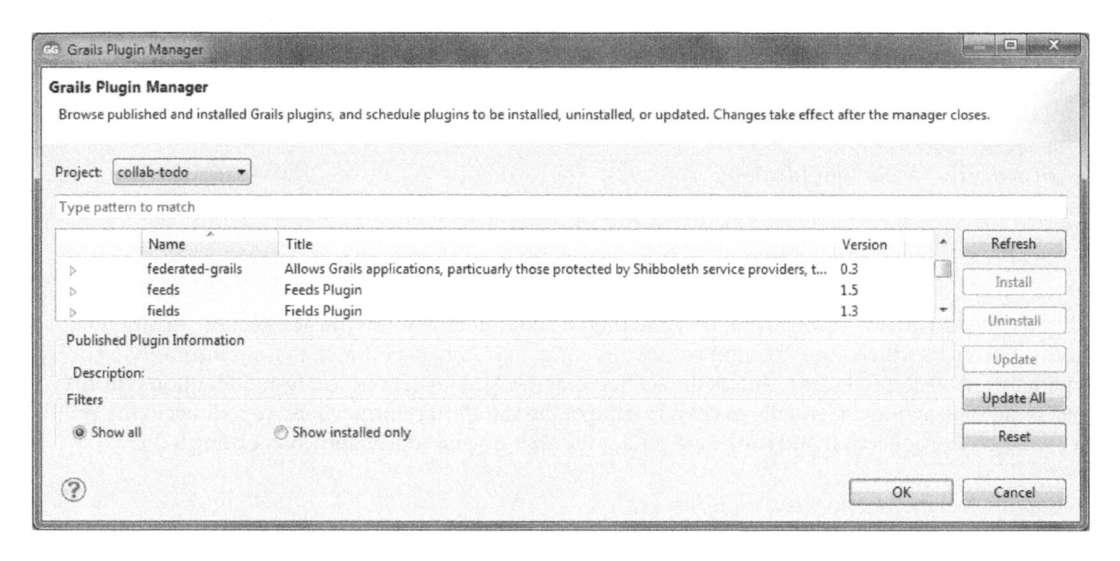

Figure 8-8. *Installing feeds plugin using Grails Plugin Manager*

The next step is to create a controller with one method in it. This method will be rendering the XML in a way that the renderer can understand. For this example, we will use the Atom format to format the output. Listing 8-31 shows our `RSSControllerwith` a `feed` method.

Listing 8-31. Our RSSController with the feed Method (in controller/RssController.groovy)

```
import feedsplugin.FeedBuilder
class RssController {

    def feed = {
        render(feedType:"atom") { // optional - , feedVersion:"2.0") {
            title = "Todo List"
link = "http://localhost:8080/collab-todo/rss"

            Todo.list(sort: "name", order: "asc").each {
                def todo = it
                entry(it.name) {
                    title = "${todo.name}"
                    link = "http://localhost:8080/collab-todo/todo/view/${todo.id}"
                    author = "${todo.owner.lastName}, ${todo.owner.firstName}"
                }
            }
        }
    }
}
```

Here we use a standard renderer, and in it we define a few items. We define the title and the link. Then we iterate through a list of items queried from the database sorted in ascending order. For each item, we need to define an entry. The entry has three items on it: itstitle, its URL link, and its contents. Table 8-3 lists a few of the common fields you would expect to have in a feed.

Table 8-3. *Some Common Fields for a Feed*

Field Name	Description
`publishedDate`	The date the entry of the field is published
`categories`	The list of categories related to the entry
`author`	The name of the author of the entry
`link`	The link to a full description of the entry
`title`	The title of the entry

In our example, we used `title`, `link`, and `author`. We sorted based on creation date (actually, we could have sorted based on anything). Note that if you supply `publishedDate`, your feeder may automatically sort on that date instead. An example of the output for this example is shown in Figure 8-9.

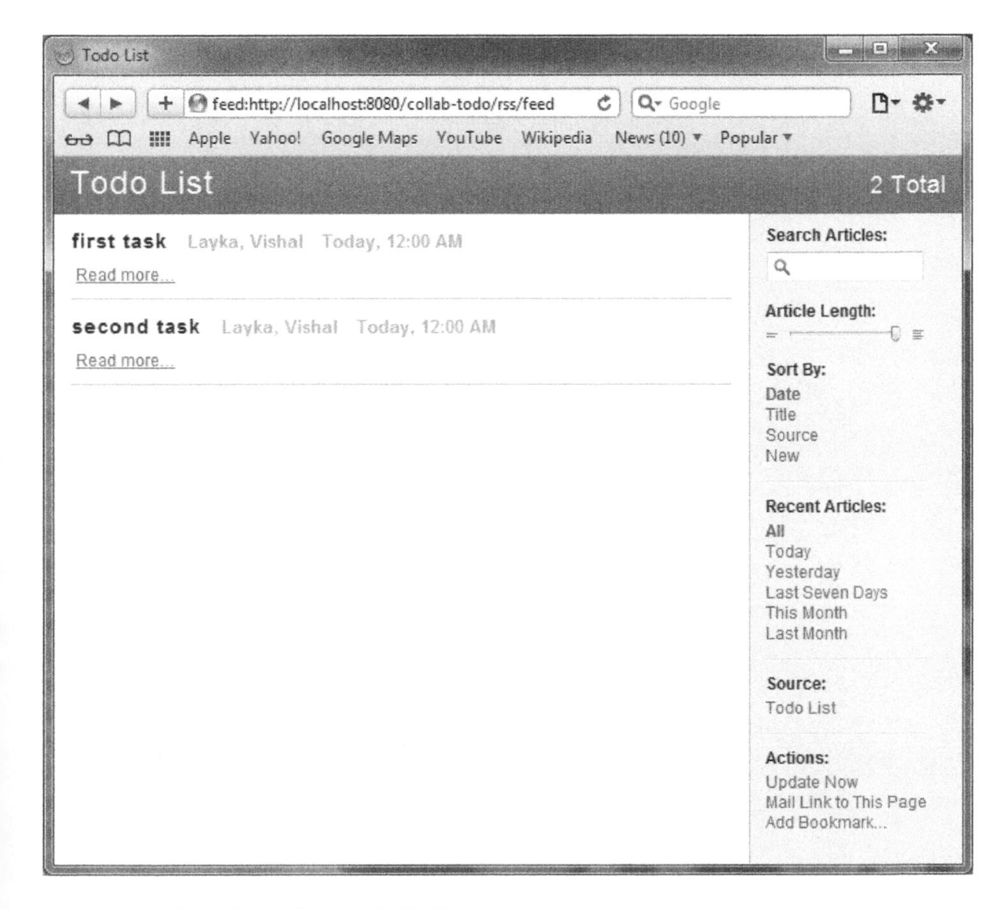

Figure 8-9. *Our RSS reader in a Safari browser*

Summary

This chapter was the start of transforming our working todo application into a more robust application. We added features that not only make it more useful, but also make it more visually appealing. These characteristics are extremely important for a web site.

The purpose of this chapter was to expose you to a variety of more advanced webstyling techniques for our application, taking advantage of the Ajax framework. There are more Ajax techniques and plugins available on the Grails site. We suggest taking a peek to see if any meet your needs. And if they don't, you always have the option of creating your own plugin and joining the Grails community that way.

In the next few chapters, we will expand the todo application and add even more functionality, including reporting and batch jobs.

CHAPTER 9

Web Services

Up until this point, you have seen how you can use Grails to develop user-oriented web applications. This chapter focuses on how to use web services to expose your application functionality to other applications. You can also use the techniques discussed in this chapter to drive Web 2.0 Ajax enabled web applications, like those discussed in Chapter 8.

Originally, web services grew in popularity as a means for system integration. But with the recent popularity of sites such as Google Maps and Amazon.com, and social networking sites like Facebook, there is an expectation that public APIs should be offered so users can create new and innovative client applications. When these clients combine multiple services from multiple providers, they are referred to as *mashups*.(See `http://en.wikipedia.org/wiki/Mashup_(web_application_hybrid)` for more information.) They can include command-line applications, desktop applications, web applications, or some type of widget.

In this chapter, you will learn how to expose your application functionality as a Representational State Transfer (REST) web service by extending the Collab- Todo application to provide access to domain objects. This RESTful web service will be able to return either XML or JavaScript Object Notation (JSON), depending on the needs of the client application. This web service will also be designed to take advantage of convention over configuration for exposing CRUD functionality for any Grails domain model, similar to the way Grails scaffolding uses conventions to generate web interfaces. Finally, you will discover how to write simple client applications capable of taking advantage of the web service.

RESTful Web Services

REST is not a standard or specification. Rather, it is an architectural style or set of principles for exposing stateless CRUD-type services, commonly via HTTP. Web services are all about providing a web API onto your web. That is, setting the web services for the application makes the application a source of data that other web applications can use. These web services can be implemented in either REST or SOAP. In the case of SOAP, the data exchange happens in a specialized XML with a SOAP-specific header and body, which adds to the complexity of building web services. Rest supports regular old XML (POX) as well as JSON for data exchange.

Unlike SOAP, the web services based on REST are resource-oriented. For example, if we implement a web service in the Collab-Todo application that returns an XML representation of the user, the URI to this web service, `http://localhost:8080/collab-todo/todo/user`, is resource oriented, as the *user* in the URI is a resource(noun). If the URI was like `http://localhost:8080/collab-todo/todo/showuser` , it was not resource-oriented, as the `showuser` is a method (verb) and such a URI is service-oriented. In addition to resource-oriented URI, in the RESTful web service, the access is achieved via standard methods such as HTTP's `GET`, `POST`, `PUT`, and `DELETE`. To understand this, we will first implement a web service that is not RESTful. The quickest way to get POX or JSON output from your Grails application is to import the `grails.converters.*` package and add a closure, as shown in Listing 9-1 and Listing 9-2, with output shown in Figure 9-1 and Figure 9-2, respectively.

Listing 9-1. Implementing a Non-RESTful Web Service for POX Output

```
import grails.converters.*

class UserController{
  def showUser = {
    render User.list() as XML
  }

  ...
}
```

```
  <?xml version="1.0" encoding="UTF-8" ?>
- <list>
  - <user id="1">
      <firstName>Vishal</firstName>
      <lastName>Layka</lastName>
      <userName>vishal</userName>
    </user>
  - <user id="2">
      <firstName>Chris</firstName>
      <lastName>Judd</lastName>
      <userName>chris</userName>
    </user>
  - <user id="3">
      <firstName>Joseph</firstName>
      <lastName>Nusairat</lastName>
      <userName>joseph</userName>
    </user>
  - <user id="4">
      <firstName>Jim</firstName>
      <lastName>Shingler</lastName>
      <userName>jim</userName>
    </user>
  </list>
```


Figure 9-1. *A POX output*

Listing 9-2. Implementing a Non-RESTful Web Service for JSON Output

```
import grails.converters.*

class UserController{
  def showUser = {
    render User.list() as JSON
  }

  ...
}
```

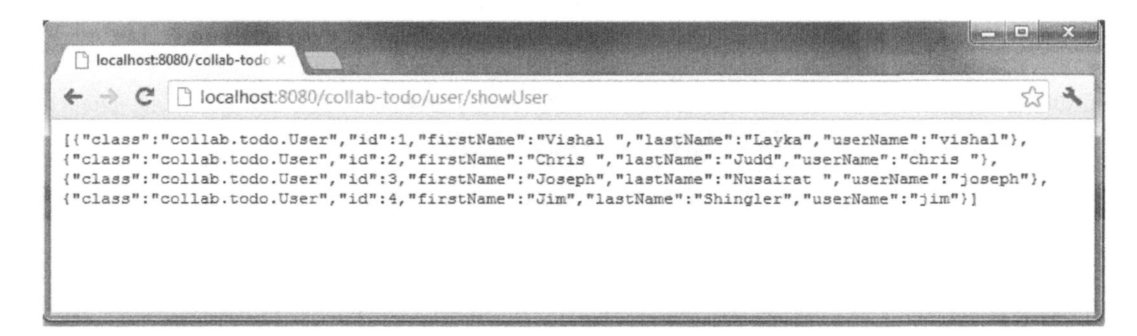

Figure 9-2. *JSON output*

A RESTful web service in the Collab-Todo application, which we will discuss in later sections, might look like this:

```
http://localhost:8080/collab-todo/todo/1
```

In this example, a representation of the `Todo` object with an `id` of `1` could get returned as XML, as shown in Listing 9-3.

Listing 9-3. POX Representation of a Todo Object Returned from a RESTful Web Service

```
<todo id="1">
<completedDate>2012-08-11 11:08:00.0</completedDate>
<createDate>2012-08-11 00:15:00.0</createDate>
<dueDate>2012-08-11 11:08:00.0</dueDate>
<name>Expose Web Service</name>
<note>Expose Todo domain as a RESTful Web Service.</note>
<owner id="1"/>
<priority>1</priority>
<status>1</status>
</todo>
```

Another alternative might be to return a representation as JSON, like the example shown in Listing 9-4.

Listing 9-4. JSON Representation of a Todo Object Returned from a RESTful Web Service

```
{
"id": 1,
"completedDate": new Date(1197389280000),
"status": "1",
```

```
"priority": "1",
"name": "Expose Web Service",
"owner": 1,
"class": "Todo",
"createDate": new Date(1197350100000),
"dueDate": new Date(1197389280000),
"note": "Expose Todo domain as a RESTful Web Service."
}
```

In both Listings 9-3 and 9-4, you see that the Todo representation includes all the properties of the object, including the IDs of referenced domain models like owner. The one difference is the lack of the action, or verb. RESTful accessed via HTTP uses the standard HTTP methods of GET, POST, PUT, or DELETE to specify the action. Table 9-1 provides a mapping of CRUD actions to SQL statements, HTTP methods, and Grails URL conventions.

Table 9-1. *Relationship Between SQL Statements, HTTP Methods, and Grails Conventions*

Action	SQL Statements	HTTP Method	Grails Convention
Create	INSERT	PUT	create
Read	SELECT	GET	show
Update	UPDATE	POST	update
Delete	DELETE	DELETE	delete
Collection	SELECT		list

The relationships described in Table 9-1 are self-explanatory and follow the REST principles, except for the last action of the collection. Because REST is purely focused on CRUD, it doesn't really address things like searching or returning lists. So the collection is borrowed from the Grails concept of the list action and can easily be implemented by doing a REST read without an ID, similar to the following:

```
http://localhost/collab-todo/todo
```

The result of this URL would include a representation of all Todo objects as XML, as shown in Listing 9-5.

Listing 9-5. POX Representation of a Collection of Todo Objects Returned from a RESTful Web Service

```
<list>
<todo id="1">
<completedDate>2012-08-11 11:08:00.0</completedDate>
<createDate>2012-08-11 00:15:00.0</createDate>
<dueDate>2012-08-11 11:08:00.0</dueDate>
<name>Expose Web Service</name>
<note>Expose Todo domain as a RESTful Web Service.</note>
<owner id="1"/>
<priority>1</priority>
<status>1</status>
</todo>
<todo id="2">
<completedDate>2012-08-11 11:49:00.0</completedDate>
<createDate>2012-08-11 00:15:00.0</createDate>
<dueDate>2012-08-11 11:49:00.0</dueDate>
```

```
<name>Expose Collection of Todo objects</name>
<note>Add a mechanism to return more than just a single todo.</note>
<owner id="1"/>
<priority>1</priority>
<status>1</status>
</todo>
</list>
```

Notice that in Listing 9-5, two Todo objects are returned within a `<list>` element representing the collection.

RESTful in Grails

Grails provides several features that make implementing a RESTful web service in Grails easy. First, it provides the ability to map URLs. In the case of RESTful web services, you want to map URLs and HTTP methods to specific controller actions. Second, Grails provides some utility methods to encode any Grails domain object as XML or JSON.

In this section, you will discover how you can use the URL mappings, encoding, and the Grails conventions to create a RestController, which returns XML or JSON representations for any Grails domain class, similar to how scaffolding is able to generate any web interface.

URL Mappings

As you learned in the previous section, URLs are a major aspect of the RESTful web service architectural style. So it should come as no surprise that URL mappings are involved. But before we explain how to map RESTful web services, let's look at the default URL mappings.

Default URL Mappings

You can find the URL mappings' configuration file, UrlMappings.groovy, with the other configuration files in grails-app/conf/. It uses a simple domain-specific language to map URLs. Listing 9-6 shows the default contents of the file.

Listing 9-6. Default UrlMappings.groovy

```
1.  class UrlMappings {
2.     static mappings = {
3.         "/$controller/$action?/$id?"{
4.             constraints {
5.                 // apply constraints here
6.             }
7.         }
8.             "500"(view:'/error')
9.     }
10. }
```

In case you thought the Grails URL convention was magic, well, it isn't. Line 3 of Listing 9-6 reveals how the convention is mapped to a URL. The first path element, $controller, as explained in Chapters 4 and 5, identifies which controller handles the request. $action optionally (as noted by the ? operator, similar to the safe dereferencing operator in Groovy) identifies the action on the controller to perform the request. Finally, $id optionally specifies the unique identifier of a domain object associated with the controller to be acted upon.

Listing 9-6 shows how this configuration file maps the default URLs. It is completely customizable if you don't like the default or if you want to create additional mappings for things such as RESTful web services. Mappings are explained in the next section.

RESTful Mappings

The basic concept behind RESTful URL mappings involves mapping a URL and an HTTP method to a controller and an action.

Listing 9-7. RESTful URL Mapping

```
static mappings = {
   "/user/$id?"(resource:"user")
}
```

This maps the URI /user onto a UserController. Each HTTP method such as `GET`, `PUT`, `POST`, and `DELETE` map to unique actions within the controller. You can alter how HTTP methods are handled by using URL Mappings to map to HTTP methods, as shown in Listing 9-8.

Listing 9-8. URL Mappings to Map to HTTP Methods

```
"/user/$id"(controller: "user") {
                         action = [GET: "show", PUT: "update", DELETE: "delete", POST: "save"]
}
```

As we discussed earlier, Grails provides automatic XML or JSON marshalling. However, unlike the resource argument used in Listing 9-7, Grails will not provide automatic XML or JSON marshalling in the case of Listing 9-8, unless you specify the `parseRequest` argument as shown in Listing 9-9.

Listing 9-9. URL Mappings to Map to HTTP Methods with Auto Marshalling

```
"/product/$id"(controller: "product", parseRequest: true) {
                  action = [GET: "show", PUT: "update", DELETE: "delete", POST: "save"]
}
```

This technique also simplifies making the generic `RestController` in the next section, because using a common base URL can always be mapped to the `RestController`. So the URL to invoke a RESTful web service that returns an XML representation like that found in Listing 9-3 would look like this:

```
http://localhost:8080/collab-todo/rest/todo/1
```

The URL for returning a JSON representation like that found in Listing 9-4 would look like this:

```
http://localhost:8080/collab-todo/json/todo/1
```

You can implement this mapping by adding an additional URL mapping to `UrlMappings.groovy`. Listing 9-10 shows what the mapping looks like.

Listing 9-10. Using rest Format Type

```
1. "/$rest/$controller/$id?"{
2.     controller = "rest"
```

```
3.      action = [GET:"show", PUT:"create", POST:"update", DELETE:"delete"]
4.      constraints {
5.          rest(inList:["rest","json"])
6.      }
7. }
```

Line 1 of Listing 9-10 shows the format of the URL. It includes a required `$rest`, which is the resulting format type, followed by the required `$controller` and an optional `$id`. Because `$rest` should only allow the two format types we are expecting, line 5 uses an `inList` constraint much like the constraints discussed in the GORM discussions of Chapter 6. Anything other than a "`rest`" or a "`json`" will cause an HTTP 404 (Not Found) error. Line 2 specifies that the `RestController` will handle any URL with this mapping. Finally, line 3 maps the HTTP methods to Grails conventional actions on the `RestController`.

Content Negotiation

Content negotiation is a mechanism defined in the HTTP specification that makes it possible to deal with different incoming requests to serve different versions of a resource representation at the same URI. Grails has built-in support for content negotiation using either the HTTP Accept header, an explicit format request parameter, or the extension of a mapped URI.

With the content negotiation, a controller can automatically detect and handle the content type requested by the client. Before you can start dealing with content negotiation, you need to tell Grails what content types you wish to support. By default, Grails comes configured with a number of different content types within `grails-app/conf/Config.groovy` using the `grails.mime.types` setting, as shown in Listing 9-11.

Listing 9-11. Default Content Types

```
grails.mime.types = [ xml: ['text/xml', 'application/xml'],
                                          text: 'text-plain',
                                          js: 'text/javascript',
                                          rss: 'application/rss+xml',
                                         atom: 'application/atom+xml',
                                         css: 'text/css',
                                         csv: 'text/csv',
                                         all: '*/*',
                                         json: 'text/json',
                                         html: ['text/html','application/xhtml+xml']
                                        ]
```

The above bit of configuration allows Grails to detect to format of a request containing either the `'text/xml'` or `'application/xml'` media types as simply `'xml'`.

Content Negotiation using the Accept Header

Every browser that conforms to the HTTP standards is required to send an Accept header. The Accept header contains information about the various MIME types the client is able to accept. Every incoming HTTP request has a special Accept header that defines what media types (or mime types) a client can "accept." Listing 9-12 illustrates an example of a Firefox Accept header.

Listing 9-12. Example of Accept Header

```
text/xml, application/xml, application/xhtml+xml, text/html;q=0.9,
text/plain;q=0.8, image/png, */*;q=0.5
```

Grails parses this incoming format and adds a property to the response object that outlines the preferred response format.

To deal with different kinds of requests from Controllers, you can use the `withFormat` method, which acts as kind of a switch statement, as shown in Listing 9-13.

Listing 9-13. Using withFormat Method

```
import grails.converters.XML
class UserController {
            def list()  {
                    def users = User.list()
                           withFormat {
                                  html userList: users
                                  xml { render users as XML }
                    }
            }
    }
```

If the preferred format is html, Grails executes the `html()` call only. If the format is xml, the closure is invoked and an XML response is rendered. When using `withFormat`, make sure it is the last call in your controller action, as the return value of the `withFormat` method is used by the action to dictate what happens next. The request format is dictated by the CONTENT_TYPE header and is typically used to detect if the incoming request can be parsed into XML or JSON, while the response format uses the file extension, format parameter, or Accept header to attempt to deliver an appropriate response to the client. The `withFormat` available on controllers deals specifically with the response format. To add logic that deals with the request format, use a separate `withFormat` method on the request, as illustrated in Listing 9-14.

Listing 9-14. Using withFormat with Request

```
request.withFormat {
                 xml {
                        // read XML
                }
                json {
                 // read JSON
                }
        }
```

Content Negotiation with the Format Request Parameter

Another mechanism of content negotiation is to use the format request parameter, which is used to override the format used in the request headers by specifying a format request parameter:

```
/user/list?format=xml
```

You can also define this parameter in the URL Mappings definition:

```
"/user/list"(controller:"user", action:"list") {
            format = "xml"
}
```

Content Negotiation with URI Extensions

Grails also supports content negotiation using URI extensions. For example, suppose you have the following URI:

```
/user/list.xml
```

In this case, Grails will remove the extension and map it to `/user/list` instead, while simultaneously setting the content format to xml based on this extension. This behavior is enabled by default; to turn it off, set the `grails.mime.file.extensions` property in grails-app/`conf/Config.groovy` to `false`:

```
grails.mime.file.extensions = false
```

RestController

Because Grails already has conventions around CRUD as well as dynamic typing provided by Groovy, implementing a generic RESTful controller that can return XML or JSON representations of any domain model is relatively simple. We'll begin coverage of the `RestController` by explaining the common implementation used by all actions. We'll then explain each action and its associated client, which calls the RESTful service.

Common Functionality

The common functionality of the `RestController` is implemented as an interceptor, as discussed in Chapter 5, along with two helper methods. Listing 9-15 contains a complete listing of the common functionality.

Listing 9-15. RestController

```
import static org.apache.commons.lang.StringUtils.*
import org.codehaus.groovy.runtime.InvokerHelper
import org.codehaus.groovy.grails.commons.GrailsDomainClass
import Error

/**
 * Scaffolding like controller for exposing RESTful web services
 * for any domain object in both XML and JSON formats.
 */
class RestController {
  private GrailsDomainClass domainClass
  private String domainClassName

  // RESTful actions excluded
```

```
  def beforeInterceptor = {
    domainClassName = capitalize(params.domain)
    domainClass = grailsApplication.getArtefact("Domain", domainClassName)
  }

  private invoke(method, parameters) {
    InvokerHelper.invokeStaticMethod(domainClass.getClazz(), method, parameters)
  }

  private format(obj) {
    def restType = (params.rest == "rest")?"XML":"JSON"
    render obj."encodeAs$restType"()
  }
}
```

The `beforeInterceptor` found in Listing 9-15 is invoked before any of the action methods are called. It's responsible for converting the `$controller` portion of the URL into a domain class name and a reference to a `GrailsDomainClass`, which are stored into private variables of the controller. You can use the `domainClassName` later for logging and error messages. The name is derived from using an interesting Groovy import technique. Since the controller in the URL is lowercased, you must uppercase it before doing the lookup. To do this, use the static Apache Commons Lang `StringUtilscapitalize()` method. Rather than specifying the utility class when the static method is called, an import in Groovy can also reference a class, making the syntax appear as if the static helper method is actually a local method. A reference to the actual domain class is necessary so the `RestController` can call dynamic GORM methods. Getting access to that domain class by name involves looking it up. However, because Grails domain classes are not in the standard classloader, you cannot use `Class.forName()`. Instead, controllers have an injected `grailsApplication` with a `getArtefact()` method, which you can use to look up a Grails artifact based on type. In this case, the type is domain. You can also use this technique to look up controllers, tag libraries, and so on.

■ **Note** The `RestController` class is framework-oriented, so it uses some more internal things such as `grailsApplication.getArtefact()` and `InvokerHelper` to behave generically. If you get into writing Grails plugins, you will use these type of techniques more often than in normal application development.

In Listing 9-15, the helper methods are the `invoke()` method and `format()` method. The `invoke()` method uses the `InvokerHelper` helper class to simplify making calls to the static methods on the domain class. The methods on the domain class that are invoked by the `RestController` are all GORM-related. The format method uses the `$rest` portion of the URL to determine which Grails `encodeAsXXX()` methods it will call on the domain class. Grails includes `encodeAsXML()` and `encodeAsJSON()` methods on all domain objects.

There is one other class involved in the common functionality, and that is the `Error` domain class found in Listing 9-16.

Listing 9-16. Error Domain Class

```
class Error {

  String message
}
```

Yes, the Groovy `Error` class in Listing 9-16 is a domain class found in the `grails-app/domain` directory. Making it a domain class causes Grails to attach the encoding methods, therefore enabling XML or JSON to be returned if an error occurs during the invocation of a RESTful web service.

RESTful show

The `show` action has double duty. It displays both a single domain model and a collection of domain models. Listing 9-17 exhibits the `show` action implementation.

Listing 9-17. show Action

```
def show = {
  def result
  if(params.id) {
    result = invoke("get", params.id)
  } else {
    if(!params.max) params.max = 10
    result = invoke("list", params)
  }

  format(result)
}
```

In Listing 9-17, you should notice that the action uses `params` to determine if an ID was passed in the URL. If it was, the GORM `get()` method is called for that single domain model. If it wasn't, the action calls the GORM `list()` method to return all of the domain objects. Also, notice that just like scaffolding, the action only returns a maximum of 10 domain objects by default. Using URL parameters, you can override that, just like you can with scaffolding. So adding `?max=20` to the end of the URL would return a maximum of 20 domain classes, but it does break the spirit of REST.

Listing 9-18 contains example code of a client application that calls the `show` action and returns a single domain model.

Listing 9-18. RESTful GET Client (GetRestClient.groovy)

```
import groovy.util.XmlSlurper

def slurper = new XmlSlurper()

def url = "http://localhost:8080/collab-todo/rest/todo/1"
def conn = new URL(url).openConnection()
conn.requestMethod = "GET"
conn.doOutput = true

if (conn.responseCode == conn.HTTP_OK) {
  def response

  conn.inputStream.withStream {
    response = slurper.parse(it)
  }
```

```
  def id = response.@id
  println "$id - $response.name"
}
conn.disconnect()
```

There are a couple of things to notice in Listing 9-18. First, the example uses the standard Java URL and URLConnection classes defined in the java.net package. This is true of all client applications through the rest of the chapter. You could also use other HTTP client frameworks, such as Apache HttpClient.[1] Second, notice that the request method of GET was used. Finally, the Groovy XmlSlurper class was used to parse the returned XML. This allows you to use the XPath notation to access things such as the name element and the id attribute of the result.

RESTful delete

Because DELETE is so similar to GET, both the action code and the client code are similar to that shown in the previous show action section. Listing 9-19 shows the delete action implementation.

Listing 9-19. delete Action

```
def delete = {

  def result = invoke("get", params.id);

  if(result) {
    result.delete()
  } else {
    result = new Error(message: "${domainClassName} not found with id ${params.id}")
  }

  format(result)
}
```

In Listing 9-19, the GORM get() method is called on the domain class. If it is found, it is deleted. If it isn't, it will return an error message. Listing 9-20 shows the client code that calls the delete RESTful web service.

Listing 9-20. RESTful DELETE Client (DeleteRestClient.groovy)

```
def url = "http://localhost:8080/collab-todo/rest/todo/1"
def conn = new URL(url).openConnection()
conn.requestMethod = "DELETE"
conn.doOutput = true

if (conn.responseCode == conn.HTTP_OK) {
  input = conn.inputStream
  input.eachLine {
    println it
  }
}
conn.disconnect()
```

---

[1]http://jakarta.apache.org/httpcomponents/httpclient-3.x/

The only differences between Listing 9-20 and Listing 9-18 are that the request method used in Listing 9-20 is DELETE, and instead of using the XmlSlurper, the contents of the result are just printed to the console, which is either an XML or JSON result of the deleted domain.

RESTful update

A POST is used to update the existing domain models in the RESTful paradigm. Listing 9-21 shows the implementation of the method that updates the domain models.

Listing 9-21. update Action

```
def update = {
  def result
  def domain = invoke("get", params.id)
  if(domain) {
    domain.properties = params
    if(!domain.hasErrors() && domain.save()) {
      result = domain
    } else {
      result = new Error(message: "${domainClassName} could not be saved")
    }
  } else {
    result = new Error(message: "${domainClassName} not found with id ${params.id}")
  }
  format(result)
}
```

Like previous examples, Listing 9-21 invokes the GORM get() method to return the domain model to update. If a domain model is returned, all the parameters passed from the client are copied to the domain. Assuming there are no errors, the domain model is saved. Listing 9-22 shows a client that calls the POST.

Listing 9-22. RESTful POST Client (PostRestClient.groovy)

```
def url = "http://localhost:8080/collab-todo/rest/todo"
def conn = new URL(url).openConnection()
conn.requestMethod = "POST"

conn.doOutput = true
conn.doInput = true

def data = "id=1&note=" + new Date()

conn.outputStream.withWriter { out ->
  out.write(data)
  out.flush()
}
```

```
if (conn.responseCode == conn.HTTP_OK) {
  input = conn.inputStream
  input.eachline {
    println it
  }
}
conn.disconnect()
```

Notice that Listing 9-22 uses a POST method this time. Also, pay attention to the fact that the data is passed to the service as name/value pairs separated by &s. At a minimum, you must use the id parameter so the service knows on which domain model to operate. You can also append other names to reflect changes to the domain. Because this is a POST, the container automatically parses the name/value pairs and puts them into params. The result will either be an XML or a JSON representation of the updated domain.

RESTful create

Finally, the most complicated of the RESTful services: the create service. Listing 9-23 shows the implementation.

Listing 9-23. create Action

```
def create = {
  def result
  def domain = InvokerHelper.invokeConstructorOf(domainClass.getClazz(), null)

  def input = ""
  request.inputStream.eachLine {
    input += it
  }



  // convert input to name/value pairs
  if(input  && input != '') {
    input.tokenize('&').each {
      def nvp = it.tokenize('=');
      params.put(nvp[0],nvp[1]);
    }
  }
  domain.properties = params

  if(!domain.hasErrors() && domain.save()) {
    result = domain
  } else {
    result = new Error(message: "${domainClassName} could not be created")
  }

  format(result)
}
```

Listing 9-23 begins by using InvokerHelper to call a constructor on the domain class. Unlike POST, PUT's input stream of name/value pairs is not automatically added to the params. You must do this programmatically. In this case, two tokenizers are used to parse the input stream. After that, the rest of the implementation follows the update example found in Listing 9-21. Listing 9-24 demonstrates a client application that does a PUT.

Listing 9-24. RESTful PUT Client (PutRestClient.groovy)

```
def url = "http://localhost:8080/collab-todo/rest/todo"
def conn = new URL(url).openConnection()
conn.requestMethod = "PUT"

conn.doOutput = true
conn.doInput = true

def data = "name=fred&note=cool&owner.id=1&priority=1&status=1&"+
"createDate=struct&createDate_hour=00&createDate_month=12&" +
"createDate_minute=15&createDate_year=2012&createDate_day=11"

conn.outputStream.withWriter { out ->
  out.write(data)
  out.flush()
}
if (conn.responseCode == conn.HTTP_OK) {
  input = conn.inputStream
  input.eachLine {
    println it
  }
}
conn.disconnect()
```

Listing 9-24 is nearly identical to Listing 9-22, except that the PUT request method and a more complicated set of data are passed to the service. In this example, the data includes the created date being passed. Notice that each element of the date/time must be passed as a separate parameter. In addition, the createDate parameter itself must have a value of struct. The result is either an XML or JSON representation of the created domain object.

Summary

In this chapter, you learned about the architectural style of RESTful web services, as well has how to expose domain models as RESTful web services. As you build your applications, look for opportunities to expose functionality to your customers in this way. You may be amazed at the innovations you never even imagined. In Chapter 13, you will see one such innovation of a Groovy desktop application.

CHAPTER 10

Reporting

In most projects, reporting is often overlooked until the last minute. Everyone is focused on getting information into the system and making the views look and feel right. Then someone starts using the application and says, "Wouldn't it be nice if users could print out a copy of the information to take with them?" "Oops, we didn't think about that." (Insert chirping crickets here.)

It makes sense that users would want to take their todo information with them. But you're in a hurry and want to get this application rolled out quickly. What do you do?

In this chapter, you will learn how to create a reporting facility using the Collab-Todo domain and a popular open source reporting engine, JasperReports.[1] Creating a reporting facility will give you a slightly different view of Grails. You will use dynamic invocation to retrieve data for the report and pass the data to JasperReports. Along the way, you will see how easy it is to use third-party libraries in a Grails application.

The Report

The goal of this chapter is to allow users to run a report that contains their lists of todo items.

Start by adding some technical constraints to help frame the solution:

- You want to be able to create multiple reports.
- Reports should be available in multiple formats, including PDF, HTML, TXT, RTF, XLS, CSV, and XML.
- You believe in the DRY principle and want to maintain a separation of concerns and encapsulation.
- You'll leverage the Grails domain model and dynamic methods to retrieve the report data.

Taking these technical constraints into consideration, you can construct the solution illustrated in Figure 10-1.

[1] http://www.jasperforge.org

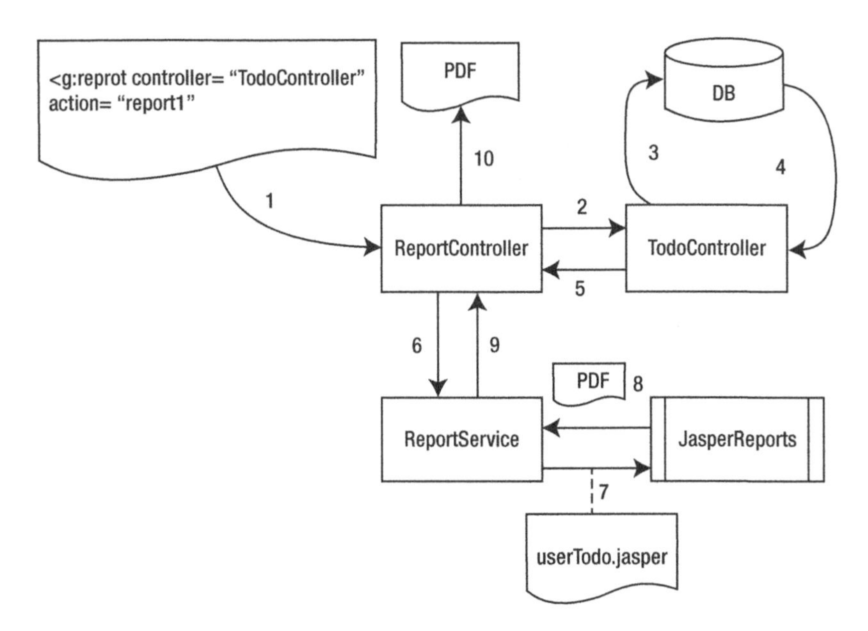

Figure 10-1. *Reporting facility overview*

The first component in the top-left of Figure 10-1 represents an HTML page. The HTML page needs to provide a way for users to indicate that they want to generate a report. You accomplish this by creating a report tag. You could just hard-code all the logic required to invoke the next step in the process, but since there are multiple reports, that would be a lot of copying, pasting, and tweaking. It wouldn't be very user friendly to the HTML developer either. By creating a tag, you're able to encapsulate all of the invocation knowledge.

Just like most links in Grails, a tag invokes an action on a controller. If you consider the technical constraints, the controller should have very little knowledge about the actual report to be created. It should control (pun intended) the execution of the reporting process. In this case, it calls the `TodoController` to gather the data for the report.

The `TodoController` uses dynamic finder methods on the `Todo` class to retrieve the report data from the database, and returns the result to the `ReportController`. Now that the `ReportController` has data for the report, it calls the `ReportService` to create the report.

The `ReportService` prepares the data, locates the appropriate report template, and invokes the report engine, JasperReports. The report engine merges the data and the template to create the report. It returns the report to the `ReportService`, which in turn returns the report to the `ReportController`. The `ReportController` then wraps the report in the appropriate headers and returns it to the browser to be displayed.

This is just an overview. The rest of the chapter will explore each step in more detail and will hopefully answer most, if not all, of your questions.

DYNAMIC FINDERS OR EMBEDDED SQL?

A question that needs to be addressed straightaway is, "Why does the `ReportController` pass the report data to the report instead of the report looking up the data using a simple SQL statement embedded in the report template?" The answer is pretty simple. That would be a perfectly legitimate approach in many situations (see the "An Alternate Approach" section at the end of the chapter), but using the dynamic finder and the domain model provides a couple of advantages.

First, when the domain model becomes more complicated, writing the SQL to navigate all of the tables and relationships is error-prone and difficult. You already defined all of this information in the domain model using GORM, so why not just reuse it?

Second, your goal is to learn Grails, and using embedded SQL would cause you to miss out on using dynamic finders and dynamically calling the appropriate action on the `TodoController` to gather the data.

Now that you have an idea of how to approach creating the reporting facility, you need to add JasperReports to the application and create the report template. The next couple of sections will take you through that process. With that accomplished, you will construct the individual components and tie everything together. By the end of this chapter, you will have a pretty nice reporting facility that will allow you to easily create reports in multiple output formats.

Reporting Tools

In this section, you will receive a high-level overview of JasperReports (the runtime reporting engine) and iReports (the report designer). You will install iReports and add the appropriate JasperReports libraries to the application.

Overview

JasperReports is a popular open source Java reporting engine from JasperSoft.[2] You can use JasperReports to define robust, professional reports that include graphics and charts. You set up and define JasperReports reports using XML. The reporting engine uses the report definition and a data source to produce a report in a variety of output formats, including PDF, XML, HTML, CSV, XLS, RTF, and TXT.

JasperReports uses third-party libraries to render reports. The engine itself is not an executable application. It is intended to be embedded into a client or server-side application. The application is responsible for passing the XML report definition, data source, parameters, and configuration information to a report exporter. The exporter returns a `ByteArrayOutputStream` containing the report content to the application. In the case of a typical server application, the application sets the appropriate content type on an HTML response and streams the results to the browser.

■ **Tip** JasperReports relies on Abstract Window Toolkit (AWT) to render the report. If you intend to run Collab-Todo in a Linux/Unix environment without graphics support, you will need to specify the headless environment by setting `-Djava.awt.headless=true`. You can do this by setting the `JAVA_OPT` environmental variable (e.g., `JAVA_OPT='-Djava.awt.headless=true'`).

---

[2] `http://www.jaspersoft.com`

The XML report definition, known as a *report template* in Jasper terms, defines the content and layout of the report. You can define the report by hand using an XML editor, but this is time-consuming and error-prone. Luckily, JasperSoft created iReports, a graphic report designer for JasperReports that defines and compiles JasperReports. It is much easier to build reports using iReports than it is to build the XML report definition by hand.

■ **Note** A full exploration of JasperReports and iReports is beyond the scope of this book. In addition to the JasperSoft web site, the Apress books *The Definitive Guide to JasperReports*[3] and *The Definitive Guide to iReports*[4] are good sources of information.

Installing JasperReports and iReports

Installing JasperReports and iReports is easy. You can download iReports from the iReports home page[5] or from SourceForge.[6] Download and execute the Windows installer version.

■ **Note** If you're using an operating system other than Windows, you need to download the `.zip` or `.tar` file and install it manually by unzipping or unpacking it into an appropriate location.

The Windows installer installs iReports in the directory of your choice; remember where it's installed. iReports includes JasperReports and all of the required third-party libraries. Copy the following files from the `iReports/lib` directory to the `collab-todo/lib` directory:

- `poi-x.x.x-FINAL-x.jar`
- `commons-beanutils-x.x.jar`
- `commons-collections-x.x.jar`
- `commons-dbcp-x.x.x.jar`
- `commons-digester-x.x.jar`
- `commons-logging-x.x.x.jar`
- `commons-logging-api-x.x.x.jar`
- `commons-pool-x.x.jar`
- `itext-x.x.x.jar`
- `jasperreports-x.x.x.jar`

Grails uses these JAR files to invoke JasperReports.

---

[3]TeodorDanciu and Lucian Chirita, *The Definitive Guide to JasperReports* (Berkeley, CA: Apress, 2007).

[4]GiulioToffoli, *The Definitive Guide to iReports* (Berkeley, CA: Apress, 2007).

[5]`http://jasperforge.org/sf/projects/ireport`

[6]`http://sourceforge.net/projects/ireport`

Creating the Todo Report

Now that iReports is installed, you're ready to build the todo report, as shown in Figure 10-1. You will take the following steps to create the report:

1. Define a JavaBeans data source for Collab-Todo.
2. Create the first iteration of the report using the iReport Wizard.
3. Enhance the report.
4. Compile the report.

Defining the Data Source

If you recall from the overview, the `ReportController` gathers the report data from another controller and ultimately passes the data to the reporting engine. This means that instead of using a JDBC database connection, the report uses a JavaBeans data source. Let's define the data source:

1. From iReports, select the Data ➤ Connections/Data Sources menu option. A list of currently defined and example data sources is shown.
2. Click the New button to define a new data source. The "Connections properties" dialog box opens.
3. Select the "JavaBeans set data source" option from the list of available data sources, and click the Next button. The "JavaBeans set data source" options are shown.
4. Set the name to Collab-Todo and blank out the factory class and static method fields. Figure 10-2 shows the contents of this page.

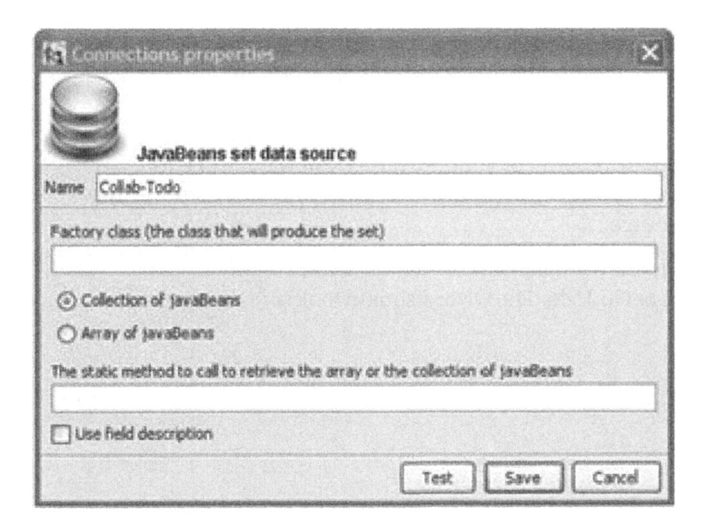

Figure 10-2. *The "JavaBeans set data source" page*

5. Click the Save button. You should see your new data source in the list of available data sources.

6. Close this window.

You're now ready to define the report using the wizard.

Using iReports

Now that you've defined a data source, you're ready to start building the report. If you're already familiar with iReports, you can skim through this section and move on to the "The Report Tag" section.

MAKING IREPORTS AWARE OF THE COLLAB-TODO CLASSES

iReports uses the Collab-Todo domain class to create the report, so you need to make iReports aware of the domain classes. Ideally, you would just add the location of the CollabTodo classes to the iReports classpath. At the time of writing, however, a bug in iReports prevents this from working as expected. You have to decide whether to manually describe the JavaBean fields within iReports, or create a JAR file of the classes and put it in the iReports `lib` directory.

For our purposes, it's easier and less errorprone to create a JAR file of the Collab-Todo classes. By default, the Collab-Todo classes should be located in `workspace\collab-todo\target`. You can use your favorite JAR/ZIP tool to create a JAR of the classes and place it in the iReports `lib` directory. This will make iReports aware of the Collab-Todo domain classes.

If you're familiar with iReports, you can go ahead and create the report however you see fit. However, we're assuming that you're new to iReports, so follow these steps to use the iReports Wizard.

1. Select the File ➤ Report Wizard menu option.

2. Specify the data that you want in the report. For your purposes, you want to set the Connections/Data Sources field to Collab-Todo, if it isn't already. This tells iReports that you're using a JavaBeans data source.

3. Specify which domain class contains the data. You're creating a todo report, so the "JavaBean class" field should be set to `Todo`. The wizard should look something like Figure 10-3.

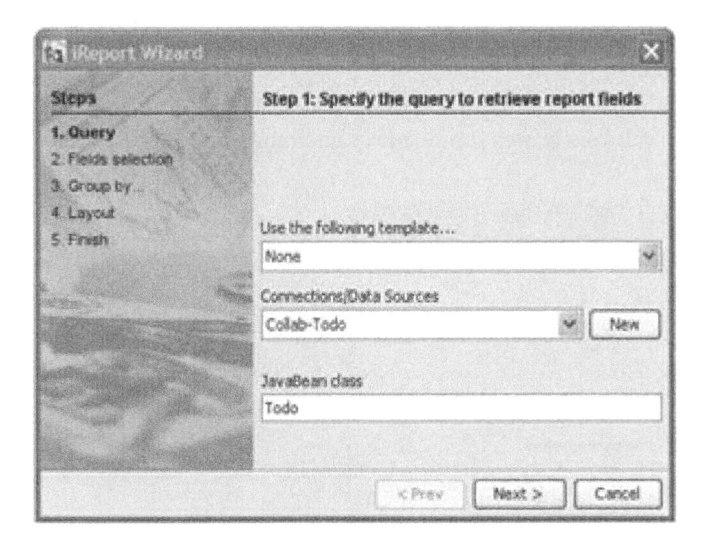

Figure 10-3. *Specifying the data source*

4. Assuming that you followed the instructions in the "Making iReports Aware of the Collab-Todo Classes" sidebar, when you click the Next button, you select the fields that should be included in the report. The wizard should look something like Figure 10-4.

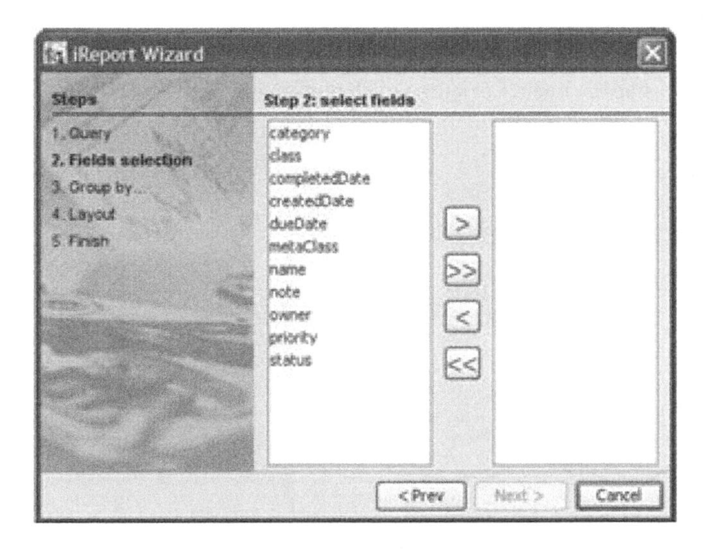

Figure 10-4. *Selecting fields*

Add all of the fields except for the class and metaClass, and click the Next button. The metaClass is internal Grails metadata and isn't appropriate for a report. The next screen lists the fields and their datatypes. Click the Next button to continue.

5. You should now be on step 3, "Group by." You don't have any work to do here, so click the Next button to move to step 4, Layout.

6. The wizard lets you pick from predefined layouts. As a starting point, check "Columnar layout" and highlight `classicC.xml`. Your screen should look something like Figure 10-5.

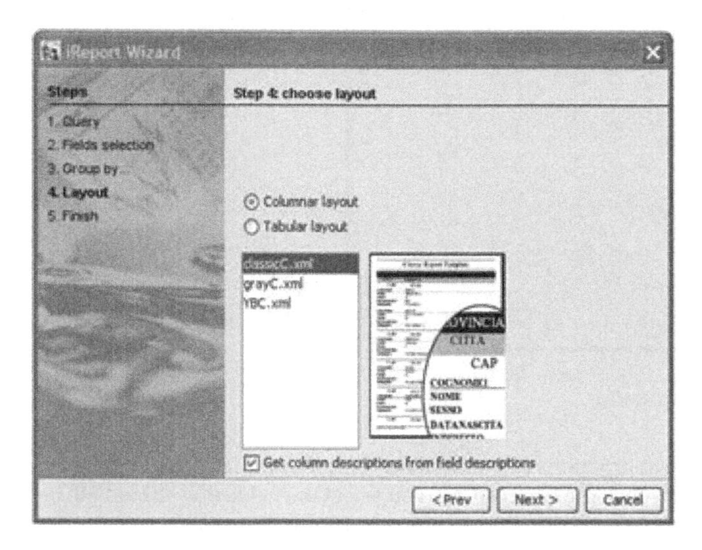

Figure 10-5. *Selecting the layout*

7. Click the Next button to move to step 5, Finish. Click the Finish button to generate the report template. You should have a report template that looks like Figure 10-6.

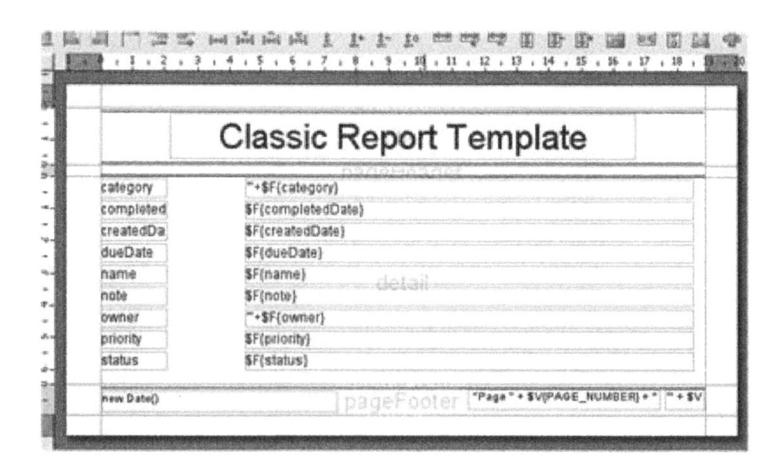

Figure 10-6. *The todo report template*

Congratulations; you have your first report. It isn't pretty, but it is functional. At this point, you could compile the report and run it. If that's what you want to do, skip forward to "Compiling the Report." Otherwise, let's make the report a little more usable first.

As you can see, iReports used the attribute names to create the labels. As a first step in making the report more usable, type in your own text for the labels. You may have to resize the field by dragging the right side of the label.

Enhancing the Report

As you can see, iReports used the Todo property names to create the labels. You should rearrange the labels and fields to an order that makes more sense. You may want to copy the example shown in Figure 10-7.

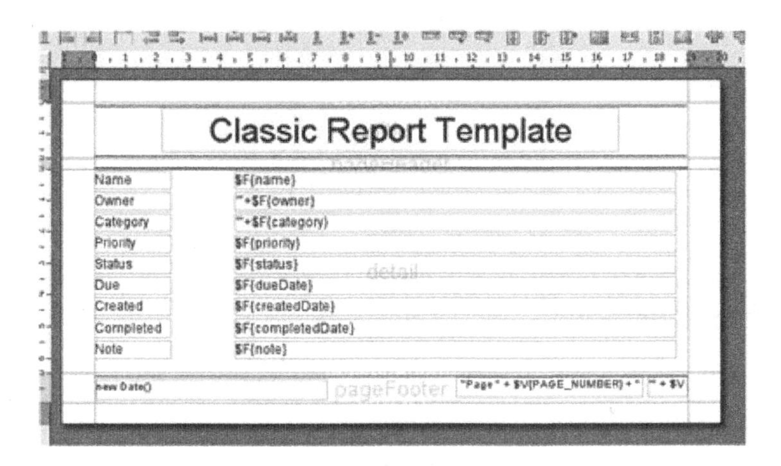

Figure 10-7. *Rearranged labels and fields*

The report is starting to look better, but you could do more. Follow these steps to enhance the report:

1. Take a good look at the Note field. It's a little small, so expand it by dragging the bottom edge of the field down.
2. The title could use a little work, so add the username, which is passed to the report as a parameter. To define the username, right-click the parameter entry in the Document Structure window and select Add ➤ Parameter. iReports displays a pop-up window that lets you input the parameter name. Set the Parameter Name field to userName, as shown in Figure 10-8.

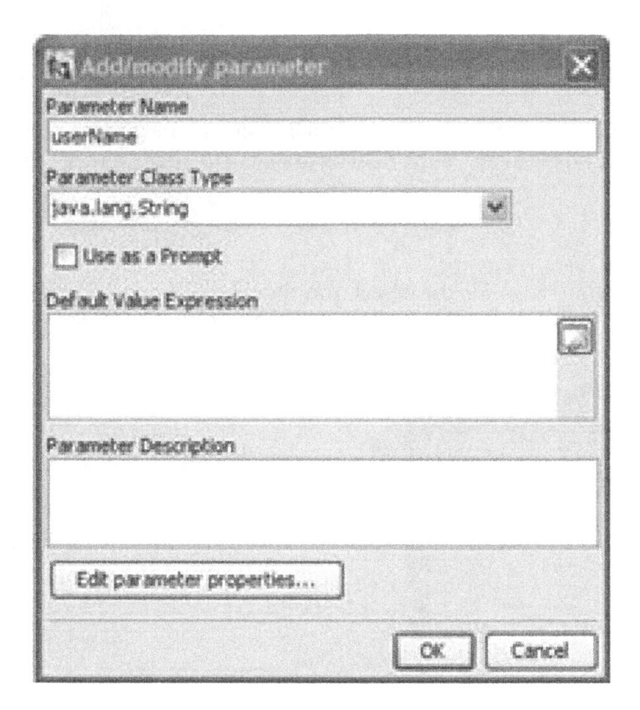

Figure 10-8. *Setting up the parameter*

3. Now that you defined the parameter, you can use it in the report header. Insert the userName parameter into the header by dragging it from the list of parameters in the Document Structure window to the report header. Also, change the current text to read "Todo for:". Figure 10-9 shows an example of the new header.

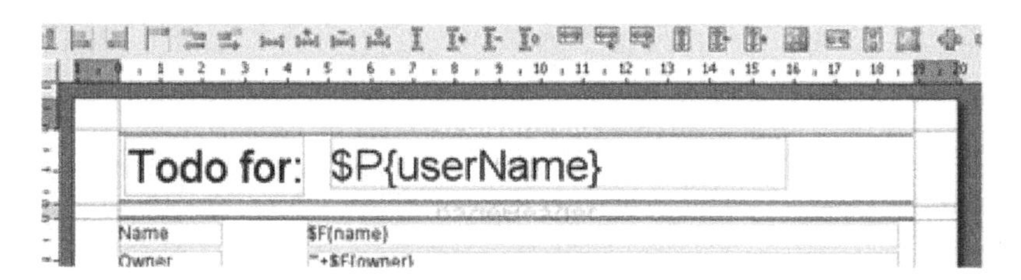

Figure 10-9. *The new header*

4. Save the report as `userTodo.jrxml` in the Collab-Todo application directory.

You're now ready to compile the report and start integrating it into the application.

Compiling the Report

Now that you've set up the report, it's time to make it available to the application. You need to compile it and copy the compiled file to the appropriate application directory.

Select Build ➤ Compile in iReports. You will see the results of the compilation at the bottom of iReports in the output console. Hopefully, the build is successful the first time, but if it isn't, work through the error messages and try again. Once you have a successful build, copy the `userTodo.jasper` file from the iReports home directory to the `collab-todo/web-app/reports` directory.

The Report Tag

You have used several tags, but now it's time to create your own. If you have developed tags before, you will be pleasantly surprised by how easy it is in Grails. You will create a report tag library to hold the report tag and then implement the tag as a closure.

Tag Library Overview

It is a best practice to group tags by topic into a tag library. In this case, all report tags are grouped in the `grails-app/taglib/ReportTagLib.groovy`. Notice the Grails conventions again: tag libraries end with `TagLib.groovy` and are located in the `grails-app/taglib` directory. The following command illustrates creating the tag library:

```
> grails create-tag-lib Report
```

The results of the command can be seen here:

```
| Created file grails-app/taglib/collab/todo/ReportTagLib.groovy
| Created file test/unit/collab/todo/ReportTagLibTests.groovy
```

As you have come to expect, Grails created the tag library and a unit test. The next step is to create the tag.

Creating the Tag

As you saw in Chapter 8, a tag is a closure that has two arguments: a map of tag attributes and the body of the tag. Listing 10-1 illustrates the tag library class.

Listing 10-1. Tag Library Class

```
class ReportTagLib {

    def report = { attrs, body ->

    ...

    }
}
```

Now you have to figure out what to put between the curly braces. You know you have to let the users choose in which format they want to receive the report, and you know that you have to invoke the `ReportController` to generate the report. With this in mind, you can start designing the tag inputs. Let's take a look at it from a usage point of view. Listing 10-2 illustrates how that tag might look inside a view.

Listing 10-2. Report Tag

```
<g:report id="todoReport" controller="TodoController"
          action="userTodo" report="userTodo"
          format="PDF,HTML,CSV,XLS,RTF,TXT,XML">
<input type="hidden" name="userName" value="${todoList[0]?.owner}" />
</g:report>
```

Based upon the requirements, this should make some sense. The `report` tag has an `id` attribute to uniquely identify it. The `controller` and `action` attributes work together to specify which action to run to get the report data. The `report` attribute specifies which report to generate, and the `format` attribute supplies a list of report formats for users to select. The hidden input determines which user's information to gather. With this information, you can turn your attention back to the tag implementation. The tag body gives you a hint about the implementation. The tag generates a `<form>` element that invokes the `ReportController`'s `index` action. The `format` attribute is used to display icons representing each of the report formats. Listing 10-3 contains the implementation of the `report` tag.

Listing 10-3. Report Tag Implementation

```
1.  def report = { attrs, body ->
2.
3.    validateAttributes(attrs)
4.    def appPath = grailsAttributes.getApplicationUri(request)
5.
6.    out <<"""
7.        <form id=\"${attrs['id']}\" name=\"${attrs['report']}\"
8.          action=\"${appPath}/report\">
9.        <input type=\"hidden\" name=\"format\"/>
10.        <input type=\"hidden\" name=\"file\" value=\"${attrs['report']}\"/>
11.        <input type=\"hidden\" name=\"_controller\"
12.          value=\"${attrs['controller']}\"/>
13.        <input type=\"hidden\" name=\"_action\" value=\"${attrs['action']}\"/>
14.   """
15.   TreeSet formats = attrs['format'].split(",")
16.   formats.each{
17.     out <<"""
18.         <a href=\"#${attrs['report']}Report\"
19.                    onClick=\"document.getElementById('${attrs['id']}').
20.                     format.value = '${it}';
21.                     document.getElementById('${attrs['id']}').submit()\">
22.         <img width=\"16px\" height=\"16px\" border=\"0\"
23.                    src=\"${appPath}/images/icons/${it}.gif\" />
24.         </a>
25.     """
26.   }
27.   out << body()
28.   out <<"</form>"
29. }
30.
31. private void validateAttributes(attrs) {
32.   //Verify the 'id' attribute
33.   if(attrs.id == null)
34.     throw new Exception("The 'id' attribute in 'report' tag mustn't be 'null'")
35.
```

```
36.   //Verify the 'format' attribute
37.   def availableFormats = ["CSV","HTML","RTF","XLS","PDF","TXT","XML"]
38.   attrs.format.toUpperCase().split(",").each{
39.     if(!availableFormats.contains(it)){
40.       throw new Exception("""Value ${it} is a invalid format attribute.
41.             Only ${availableFormats} are permitted""")
42.     }
43.   }
44.
```

Let's take a look at the tag implementation line by line. In line 1, the tag takes two arguments: an attribute map and the body. Because you specified the report formats on the tag, the tag in line 3 has to validate that you specified supported report formats. Line 4 creates a local variable for the application path. Lines 6-14 create the form and hidden input fields to allow tag attributes to be passed to the `ReportController`. But wait, where was `out` defined? The `out` variable is a handle to the output stream that is injected by Grails.

Lines 15-25 iterate over the tag `format` attribute to create icons for each of the report formats. Looking closely, note that when the user selects the report format, the hidden input field `format` is set and the form is submitted. Line 27 outputs the tag body, and line 28 completes the form definition. Lines 31-44 are the body of the `validateAttributes` method called on line 3. This method iterates through the tag `format` attribute to validate that you specified valid report formats.

The ReportController and the ReportService

The `ReportController` follows these three steps to create the report:

1. Gather data for the report by invoking a controller/action.
2. Locate a compiled report.
3. Ask the `ReportService` to generate the report, and wrap the output with the appropriate content type.

Start by running the following code to create the `ReportController`:

```
> grails create-controller Report
```

Now you need to implement the three previously listed steps. Listing 10-4 illustrates gathering the report data

Listing 10-4. Gathering the Report Data

```
   def index() {
      // Gather data for the report.
      // 1) Find the controller
      ApplicationContext ctx = (ApplicationContext) session.
         getServletContext().
         getAttribute(GrailsApplicationAttributes.APPLICATION_CONTEXT);
DEF CONTROLLER = CTX.GETBEAN("${PARAMS._CONTROLLER}");

      // 2) Invoke the action
      def inputCollection = controller."${params._action}"(params)
      params.inputCollection = inputCollection
...
}
```

The first step in gathering data for the report is to dynamically invoke the action supplied by the report tag. The tag specifies the controller and the action to be invoked to gather the data. The controller and the action to invoke are passed in the params map. The problem is that the values are just strings. You use the Spring application context to get an instance of the controller. Then you invoke the action on the controller, passing the params map to it.

Next, you need to locate the report. The compiled reports are located in the web-app/reports directory. Listing 10-5 illustrates using the servletContext to locate and load the report.

Listing 10-5. Locating and Loading the Report

```
// Find the compiled report
def reportFileName = reportService.reportFileName("${params.file}")
def reportFile = servletContext.getResource(reportFileName)

if(reportFile == null){
    throw new FileNotFoundException("""\"${reportFileName}\" file must be in
        reports repository.""")
}
```

Finally, you need to generate the report and wrap the output with the proper content type. The ReportController calls the ReportService to generate the report. You could collapse the service into the controller, but the controller's purpose is to control, not do the actual work. The controller should delegate the actual work to some other component. Delegating the actual report generation to the report service maintains a separation of concerns and encapsulates knowledge of the JasperReports libraries into a single location, the ReportService. Listing 10-6 illustrates delegating to the ReportService and wrapping the output in the appropriate context type.

Listing 10-6. Calling the ReportService

```
// Call the ReportService to invoke the reporting engine
   switch(params.format){
      case "PDF":
         createPdfFile(reportService.generateReport(reportFile,
            reportService.PDF_FORMAT,params ).toByteArray(),params.file)
         break
      case "HTML":
         render(text:reportService.generateReport(reportFile,
            reportService.HTML_FORMAT,params),contentType:"text/html")
         break
      case "CSV":
         render(text:reportService.generateReport(reportFile,
            reportService.CSV_FORMAT,params),contentType:"text")
         break
      case "XLS":
         createXlsFile(reportService.generateReport(reportFile,
            reportService.XLS_FORMAT,params).toByteArray(),params.file)
         break
      case "RTF":
         createRtfFile(reportService.generateReport(reportFile,
            reportService.RTF_FORMAT,params).toByteArray(),params.file)
         break
```

```
        case "XML":
            render(text:reportService.generateReport(reportFile,
                reportService.XML_FORMAT,params),contentType:"text")
            break
        case "TXT":
            render(text:reportService.generateReport(reportFile,
                reportService.TEXT_FORMAT,params),contentType:"text")
            break
        default:
            throw new Exception("Invalid format")
            break
    }
}

/**
* Output a PDF response
*/
def createPdfFile = { contentBinary, fileName ->
    response.setHeader("Content-disposition", "attachment; filename=" +
         fileName + ".pdf");
    response.contentType = "application/pdf"
    response.outputStream << contentBinary
}

/**
* Output an Excel response
*/
def createXlsFile = { contentBinary, fileName ->
    response.setHeader("Content-disposition", "attachment; filename=" +
       fileName + ".xls");
    response.contentType = "application/vnd.ms-excel"
    response.outputStream << contentBinary
}

/**
* Output an RTF response
*/
def createRtfFile = { contentBinary, fileName ->
    response.setHeader("Content-disposition", "attachment; filename=" +
         fileName + ".rtf");
    response.contentType = "application/rtf"
    response.outputStream << contentBinary
}
```

Now that you have the controller, you need to set up the `ReportService`. You can create the `ReportService` by running this command:

```
> grails create-service Report
```

The main functionality in the ReportService is encapsulation of the logic to generate the report using the JasperReports API. Listing 10-7 contains the ReportService.

Listing 10-7. ReportService

```
1.  import java.io.ByteArrayOutputStream
2.  import java.io.InputStream
3.  import java.sql.Connection
4.  import java.sql.Timestamp
5.  import java.util.HashMap
6.
7.  import net.sf.jasperreports.engine.JRException
8.  import net.sf.jasperreports.engine.JRExporter
9.  import net.sf.jasperreports.engine.JasperPrint
10. import net.sf.jasperreports.engine.JasperFillManager
11. import net.sf.jasperreports.engine.JRExporterParameter
12. import net.sf.jasperreports.engine.export.JRCsvExporter
13. import net.sf.jasperreports.engine.export.JRHtmlExporter
14. import net.sf.jasperreports.engine.export.JRHtmlExporterParameter
15. import net.sf.jasperreports.engine.export.JRPdfExporter
16. import net.sf.jasperreports.engine.export.JRXlsExporter
17. import net.sf.jasperreports.engine.export.JRXmlExporter
18. import net.sf.jasperreports.engine.export.JRRtfExporter
19. import net.sf.jasperreports.engine.export.JRTextExporter
20. import net.sf.jasperreports.engine.export.JRTextExporterParameter
21. import net.sf.jasperreports.engine.data.JRBeanCollectionDataSource
22.
23. class ReportService {
24.
25.   boolean transactional = true
26.
27.   int PDF_FORMAT = 1;
28.   int HTML_FORMAT = 2;
29.   int TEXT_FORMAT = 3;
30.   int CSV_FORMAT = 4;
31.   int XLS_FORMAT = 5;
32.   int RTF_FORMAT = 6;
33.   int XML_FORMAT = 7;
34.
35.
36.
37.   /**
38.   * Generate the Report
39.   */
40.   def generateReport = {jasperFile, format, parameters ->
41.
42.     // Setup the Data Source
43.     JRBeanCollectionDataSource ds = new JRBeanCollectionDataSource(
44.           parameters.inputCollection);
45.
46.     InputStream input = jasperFile.openStream()
47.     JRExporter exporter
```

```
48.     ByteArrayOutputStream byteArray = new ByteArrayOutputStream()
49.     JasperPrint jasperPrint = JasperFillManager.fillReport(input, parameters,ds)
50.     switch (format) {
51.       case PDF_FORMAT:
52.         exporter = new JRPdfExporter()
53.         break
54.       case HTML_FORMAT:
55.         exporter = new JRHtmlExporter()
56.         exporter.setParameter(JRHtmlExporterParameter.
57.             IS_USING_IMAGES_TO_ALIGN, FALSE)
58.         break
59.       case CSV_FORMAT:
60.         exporter = new JRCsvExporter()
61.         break
62.       case TEXT_FORMAT:
63.         exporter = new JRTextExporter()
64.         exporter.setParameter(JRTextExporterParameter.CHARACTER_WIDTH,
65.             new Integer(10));
66.         exporter.setParameter(JRTextExporterParameter.CHARACTER_HEIGHT,
67.             new Integer(10
68.         break
69.       case XLS_FORMAT:
70.         exporter = new JRXlsExporter()
71.         break
72.       case RTF_FORMAT:
73.         exporter = new JRRtfExporter()
74.         break
75.       case XML_FORMAT:
76.         exporter = new JRXmlExporter()
77.         break
78.       default:
79.         throw new Exception("Unknown report format
80.     }
81.     exporter.setParameter(JRExporterParameter.OUTPUT_STREAM, byteArray)
82.     exporter.setParameter(JRExporterParameter.JASPER_PRINT, jasperPrint)
83.     exporter.exportReport()
84.     return byteArray
85.   }
86.
87.     def reportFileName = { reportName ->
88.        return "/reports/"+reportName+".jasper"
89.     }
90. }
```

Let's walk through this. Line 40 is the beginning of the generateReport closure. As you can see, generateReport takes three input parameters: the report template, the report format, and parameters. Lines 42-44 define and populate a JavaBeans collection data source. Looking closely, note that the data source is populated from an input collection contained with the parameters. This is the collection that the ReportController created.

Lines 46-48 do some additional setup. Line 49 passes the report template, parameters, and JavaBeans data source to the reporting engine. Lines 50-80 set up the appropriate rendering component based upon the report format type requested, while lines 81-82 set some additional parameters on the renderer. Line 83 is where the real magic happens: it causes the report to be generated. The results are returned to the caller on line 84.

In Listing 10-5, you may recall seeing something like the following:

```
reportService.reportFileName($params.file)
```

Lines 87-89 contain the implementation of this method, which, as you can tell, is pretty basic. You simply prepend the directory and append the file extension to create the report file name. You could easily have done this in the ReportController, but you really don't want the ReportController to know that you're using JasperReports. By doing it this way, you maintain a separation of concerns and encapsulation.

You're now ready to tie it all together and see the result of your work.

Tying It All Together

You're about to see the result of your work. You installed iReports and copied the appropriate libraries to the application. You created the report and the report tag library. You created the ReportService and the ReportController. The only thing left to do is to write the code that gathers the report data and hook the report tag into the application.

Gathering the Report Data

Recall from "The Report Tag" section that the tag allows you to specify the controller and the action to call to gather the report data. In this case, you'll specify the TodoController and the userTodo action, so you'll need to create a userTodo action on the TodoController. Listing 10-8 contains the content of the action.

Listing 10-8. Gathering the Report Data

```
def userTodo = {
    def user = User.get(session.user.id)
    return Todo.findAllByOwner(user)
}
```

The code in Listing 10-8 finds all of the todos for the current user and returns the results. Now, you have to hook the report tag into the application.

Adding the Report Tag to the Application

The last step is to add the report tag to the Todo List view and then edit the Todo List view (grails-app/views/todo/list.gsp). At the bottom of the file, after the paginate logic, add the report tag. Follow Listing 10-9 as an example.

Listing 10-9. Adding the Report Tag

```
    ...
<div class="paginateButtons">
<g:paginate total="${Todo.count()}" />
</div>
<g:report id="todoReport" controller="TodoController"
action="userTodo" report="userTodo"
format="PDF,HTML,CSV,XLS,RTF,TXT,XML">
<input type="hidden" name="userName" value="${todoList[0]?.owner}" />
```

```
</g:report>
</div>
</body>
</html>
```

Now let's take a look at the results. Start the application, log in, and select the PDF icon. Figure 10-10 shows the report.

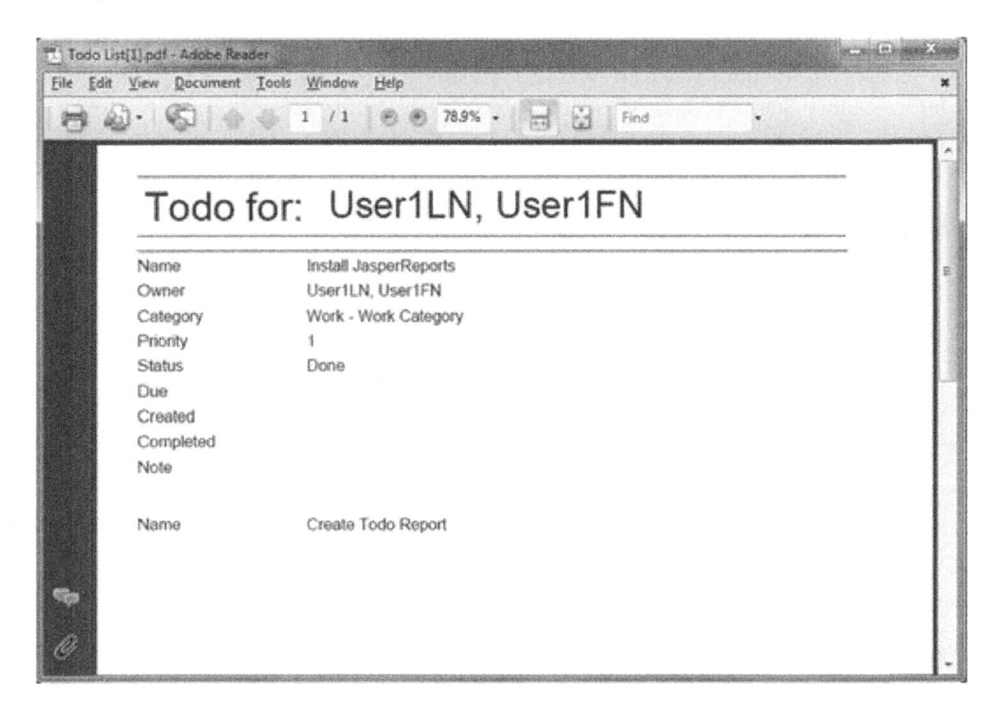

Figure 10-10. *The report*

Congratulations, you successfully built a reporting facility. Now that you have one, it would be a shame to not reuse it.

The Report List

You did a lot of good work; you constructed all of the core components of a reporting facility and enhanced a view with the `report` tag to give users access to reports. You also saw how to use the following command to pass report parameters to the data collection action:

```
<input type="hidden" name="userName" value="${todoList[0]?.owner}" />
```

In this case, the parameter was a hidden field, but it could have just as easily been a visible input field.

It would be reasonable for users expect to be able to specify a due-date range and only see todo items that are within the range. What would it take to fulfill such a request? Well, you would need to construct a Reports List view and hook it into the application. This view would need to list all of the available reports. If a report doesn't require any additional parameters, you could execute it directly from the Reports List view. If a report requires additional parameters, it will launch another page that allows users to specify the input parameters for the report.

The best thing is, you can reuse all of the components you just created. Pretty cool. Given that this is all a rehash of everything you have learned, we will leave this as an exercise for you to develop on your own.

An Alternate Approach

Earlier in the chapter, we discussed using the domain model to give data to the reports or using embedded SQL. We decided to use the domain model approach for several good reasons, but the alternative is worth considering.

Marcos Fábio Pereira created a Jasper plugin for Grails. As a matter of fact, Marcos' work provided some of the inspiration for this chapter. So here is a big shoutout to Marcos: thank you Marcos; your good work is appreciated.

The Jasper plugin takes the embedded SQL approach. Depending upon your circumstances, this may be a good solution for you. You can take a look at the Jasper plugin by running Grails Plugin Manager as shown in Figure 10-11.

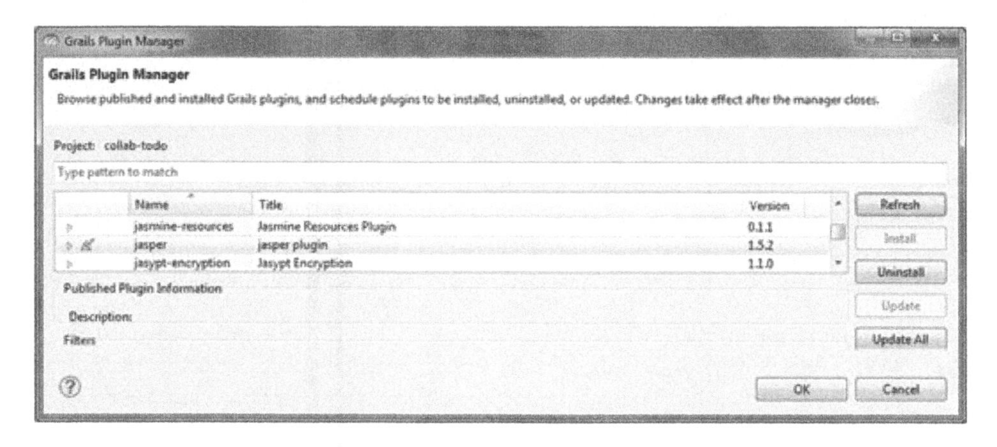

Figure 10-11. *Installing the Jasper plugin*

This installs the Jasper plugin as shown in the output:

```
| Loading Grails 2.1.0
| Configuring classpath.
| Environment set to development.....
| Resolving plugin jasper. Please wait…
| Installing zip jasper-1.5.2.zip.....
| Installed plugin jasper-1.5.2
| Resolving plugin JAR dependencies.....
| Plugin installed.
```

Similar to the approach we discussed in the previous section, to create a report from Jasper, we need to create a `.jrxml` and compile it to the `.jasper` report file. In addition, we use `jasperReport` tags as illustrated in Listing 10-10.

Listing 10-10. Using the jasperReport Tag

```
<g:jasperReport controller="todo" action="todoReport" jasper="userTodo" format="PDF"  />
<g:jasperReport controller="todo" action="todoReport" jasper="userTodo" format="XLS"  />
```

The `controller` and `action` attributes of the `jasperReport` tag work together to specify which action to run to get the report data. The `jasper` attribute specifies which report to generate, and the `format` attribute supplies a format/list of report formats for users to select. Listing 10-11 illustrates the action `todoReport` fragment.

Listing 10-11. Action Attribute of the jasperReport Tag

```
def createReport() {
        def todos = Todo.list()
        chain(controller:'jasper',action:'index',model:[data:todos],params:params)
}
```

Figure 10-12 shows the result of using Listing 10-10 and Listing 10-11.

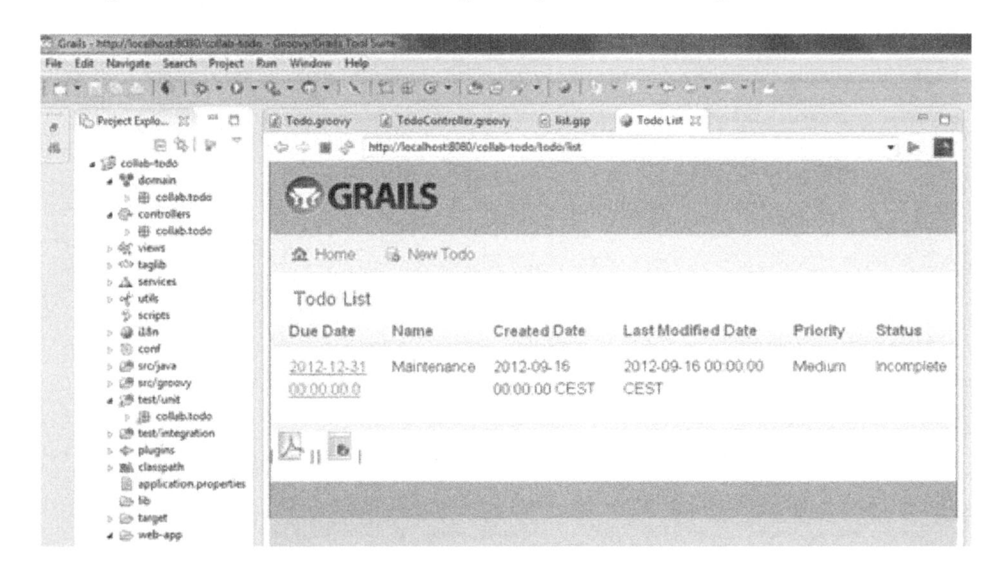

Figure 10-12. *pdf and xls icons for reports*

As we added the `jasperReport` tag in the `list.gsp`, the Todo list screen shows the pdf and xls icons for PDF and XLS reports.

Summary

You accomplished a lot in this chapter. Instead of building a static solution for one report, you built a dynamic reporting facility that supports multiple reports and multiple formats, and accepts input to drive the selection of report data.

In the process of building the reporting facility, you installed and configured the JasperReports reporting engine and the iReports report designer. You used iReports to define and compile the report template.

You then moved on to creating a report tag library. You created the `ReportController` for the `report` tag to call. The `ReportController` took care of facilitating the data collection and invoking the `ReportService` to generate the report. In the `ReportService`, you wrapped the `Todo` domain objects in a JavaBeans data source, and you passed the data source, parameters, and report template to the JasperReports reporting engine for processing. The reporting engine returned a binary version of the report, which the `ReportController` then returned to the user.

This chapter allowed you to learn some new things, and it reinforced some things you learned earlier. It showed you how to build a reporting facility that supports multiple reports and formats. The next chapter leverages the `ReportService` in a nightly batch job to generate and e-mail user todo reports.

CHAPTER 11

Batch Processing

Grails is more than just a web framework—it is an application framework. And almost all applications contain functionality that must be executed on a periodic basis (every 15 minutes, once an hour, twice a day, daily, weekly, month, quarterly, or yearly). This is known as *batch processing*. The Grails team anticipated the need for batch processing and decided to leverage a popular open source third-party enterprise job scheduling library: Quartz[1]. Since the Spring Framework is a core component of Grails, and the Spring Framework already includes a Quartz integration, this was a natural choice. A Quartz Grails plugin makes it easy to use the Quartz library.

Quartz is similar to the Unixcron facility in that it provides the ability to execute a job in the future. However, Quartz is different from the Unixcron facility because it runs within the application server and has full access to all of the application components.

This chapter explores batch-processing functionality. We will start by installing the Quartz plugin and creating a simple job. Then we will move on to creating a sample batchreporting facility.

Installing the Quartz Plugin

As we mentioned, Grails leverages Quartz for job-scheduling functionality. The Quartz plugin integrates Quartz into Grails and makes Quartz easy to use.

To begin, from within the project directory, execute the following command:

```
> grails install-plugin quartz
```

Or you can use the plugin manager of GGTS. This will yield the output as illustrated in Figure 11-1.

---

[1]http://www.quartz-scheduler.org/

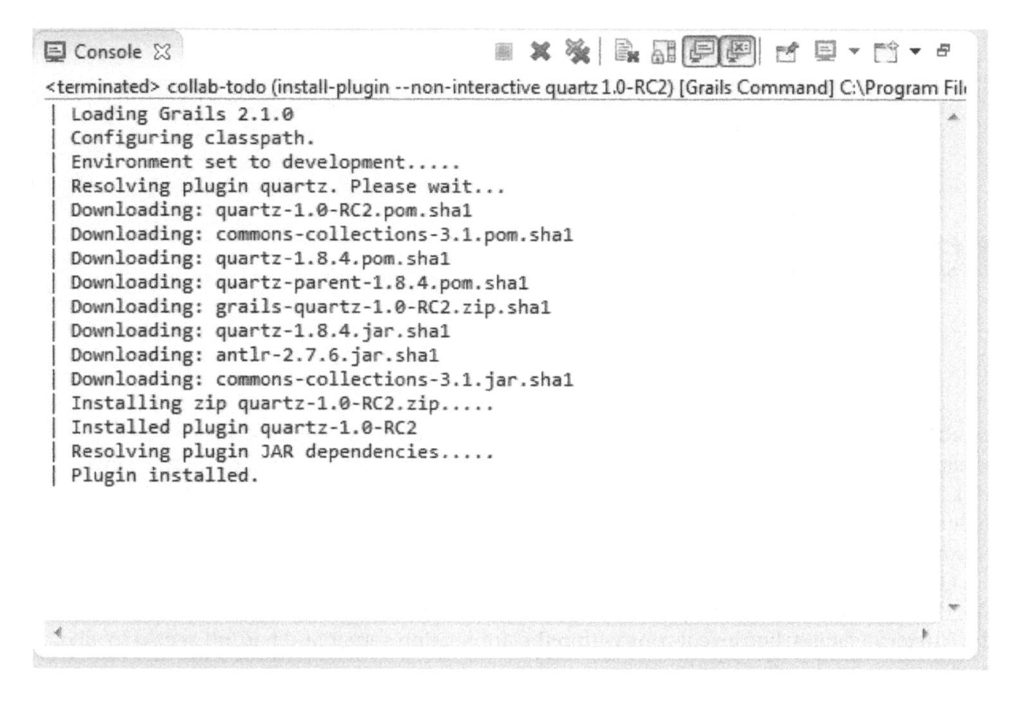

Figure 11-1. *Installing Quartz*

Installing the plugin created the `jobs` directory under `grails-app`.

Creating a Job

A *job* is a program that contains the code you wish to run. In Grails, the job defines what to do and when to do it.

As a simple demonstration of Quartz in action, let's create a job that prints a message and the current time. The first step is to create the job, as follows:

```
> grails create-job first
```

The command generates the `FirstJob` class, in the `grails/job` directory:

```
package collab.todo
class FirstJob {
static triggers = {
simple repeatInterval: 5000l // execute job once in 5 seconds
    }

def execute() {
        // execute job
    }
}
```

■ **Note** Look closely at the `timeout` value, and you'll see an `l` after the `5000`. The `l` makes the variable a `Long`. Also notice that `create-job` follows conventions just like other `create-*` commands, and appends the suffix `Job` to the end of the job name.

The `create-job` command creates a skeleton job that is preconfigured to run once, five seconds after the application server starts. So, five seconds after the server starts, the code in the `execute()` method is executed. Add the following code to the `execute()` method:

```
println "Hello from FirstJob: "+ new Date()
```

Listing 11-1 shows the completed `FirstJob` class.

Listing 11-1. Completed FirstJob

```
package collab.todo
class FirstJob {
static triggers = {
simple repeatInterval: 5000l // execute job once in 5 seconds
    }

def execute() {
println "Hello from FirstJob: "+ new Date()     }
}
```

Start the application by issuing the following command:

```
> grails run-app
```

While you could interpret the comment for the `timeout` property in Listing 11-1 to mean that the `FirstJob` is executed only once, you can see from the output in Figure 11-2 that it is executed every five seconds.

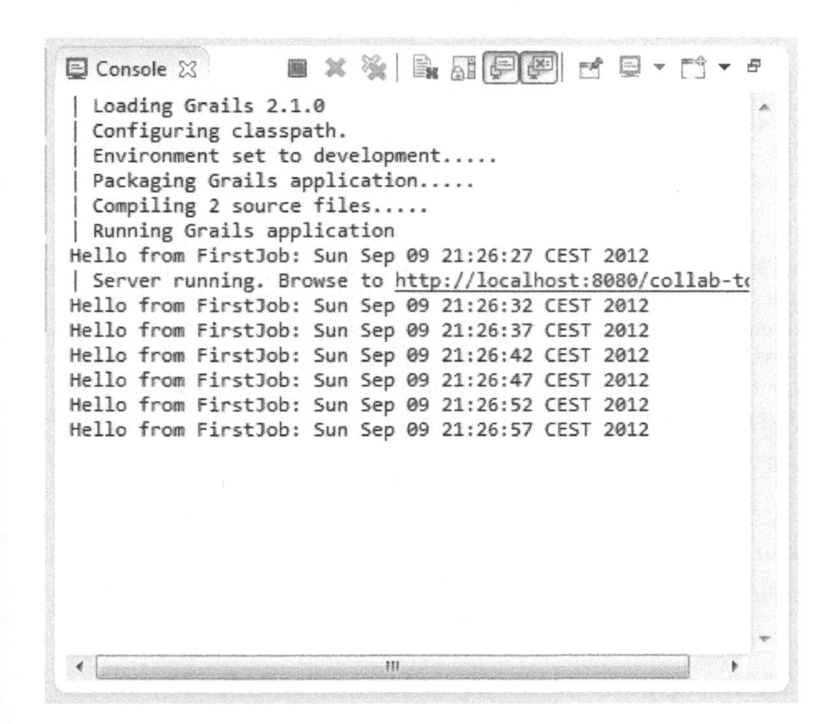

Figure 11-2. *Output every five seconds*

Now that you've seen how to create a simple job, let's move on to something a bit more useful: a batch-reporting facility.

Building a Batch-Reporting Facility

As an example, we will build a batch-reporting facility that generates todo reports and e-mails them to the user nightly. We will leverage a couple of services created in earlier chapters: `EMailAuthenticatedService` from Chapter 8 and `ReportService` from Chapter 10. Figure 11-3 shows an overview of the nightly reporting process.

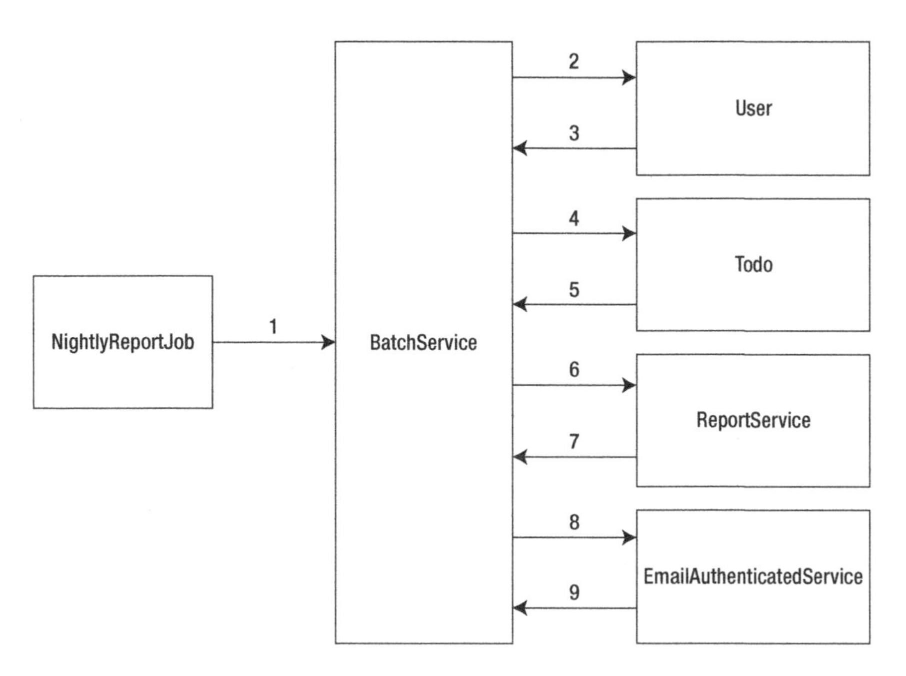

Figure 11-3. *Nightly reporting process*

The process starts with the `NightlyReportJob`. When the `NightlyReportJob` is invoked by Quartz, it immediately invokes the `BatchService`. The `BatchService` is the main control routine. It facilitates the interaction with other solution components. First, the `BatchService`retrieves all `User` objects that have an e-mail address. For each user, the `BatchService` retrieves the `Todo` objects. The `BatchService` then uses the `ReportService` to generate a PDF report. Finally, the `BatchService` uses the `EmailAuthenticatedService` to send the user an e-mail attachment of the report.

Building the batch-reporting facility requires the following steps:

1. Create and configure the execution of the `NightlyReportJob`.
2. Retrieve the user's todos.
3. Invoke the report service (created in Chapter 10).
4. Invoke the e-mail service (created in Chapter 8).

Creating a Nightly Reporting Job

Issue the following command to create the NightlyReportJob:

```
> grails create-job NightlyReport
```

In addition to the timeout property, which you saw earlier in the FirstJob job, you can use several additional properties to control job execution.

Setting the Name and Group

You can use the name and group properties to help you identify jobs when interacting with the Quartz scheduler:

```
class NightlyReportJob {
    def name = "NightlyReport" // Job name
    def group = "CollabTodo"   // Job group
```

Controlling Execution Frequency

There are two techniques for controlling the job execution frequency:

- Use the startDelay and timeout properties: these two properties allow you to control the execution frequency of the job. The startDelay property delays starting the job for a number of milliseconds after the application starts. This can be useful when you need to let the system start up before the job starts. Grails defaults the startDelay property to 0. The timeout property is the number of milliseconds between executions of the job. Grails defaults the timeout property to 60,000 milliseconds, or 1 minute.
- Use the cronExpression property: for all of the Unix geeks out there, this works just as you would expect. It is a string that describes the execution frequency using a crontab format. If you're not familiar with this approach, don't worry—we'll explain the format in more detail here.

Both techniques have their place in controlling execution frequency. Determining which technique to use depends on the job requirements. If the job can be handled by a timer, setting the startDelay and timeout properties should be sufficient, as in this example:

```
def startDelay = 20000      // Wait 20 seconds to start the job
def timeout = 60000         // Execute job once every 60 seconds
```

If the job is very time sensitive, using the cronExpression property is probably more appropriate. But note that during development and initial testing of the job, you will probably want to use the startDelay/timeout technique, and then switch to the cronExpression approach later.

■ **Caution** Depending on the execution frequency and duration of the job, it's possible to have multiple instances of a job executing concurrently. This could happen if a job is long running and still running when the cronExpression property causes it be invoked again. Having jobs running concurrently may or may not be desirable. By default, the Quartz plugin permits the job to run concurrently. Most of the time, you probably won't want to allow a job to run concurrently. You can change this behavior by setting the concurrent property on the job to false.

A cron expression tells the job scheduler when to run the job. The cronExpression property value is composed of six fields, separated by whitespace, representing seconds, minutes, hours, day, month, day of week, and an optional seventh field for the year. A cron expression expresses the fields left to right:

```
Seconds Minutes Hours DayOfMonth Month DayOfWeek Year
```

For example, we define a `cronExpression` property to have the job run 1:00 a.m. every day as follows:

```
def cronExpression = "0 0 1 * * *"   // Run every day at 1:00 a.m.
```

Table 11-1 describes the cron expression fields, and Table 11-2 summarizes some of the more commonly used special characters. (See the Quartz documentation for a more complete explanation of the special characters: `http://www.quartz-scheduler.org/documentation/quartz-1.x/tutorials/crontrigger.`)

Table 11-1. *Cron Expression Fields*

Field	Values	Special Characters
Seconds	0-59	, - * /
Minutes	0-59	, - * /
Hours	0-23	, - * /
DayOfMonth	1-31	, - * ? / L W
Month	1-12 or JAN-DEC	, - * /
DayOfWeek	1-7 or SUN-SAT	, - * ? / L#
Year (optional)	Empty or 1970-2099	, - * /

Table 11-2. *Cron Expression Special Characters*

Character	Function	Example
*	All values-matches all allowed values within a field.	* in the Hours field matches every hour of the day, 0-23.
?	No specific value-used to specify something in one of the two fields in which it is allowed, but not the other.	To execute a job on the tenth day of the month, no matter what day of the week that is, put 10 in the DayOfMonth field and ? in the DayOfWeek field.
-	Used to specify a range of values.	2-6 in the DayOfWeek field causes the job to be invoked on Monday, Tuesday, Wednesday, Thursday, and Friday.
,	Used to create a list of values.	MON, WED, FRI in the DayOfWeek field causes the job to be invoked on Monday, Wednesday, and Friday.
/	Used to specify increments. The character before the slash indicates when to start. The character after the slash represents the increment.	0/15 in the Minutes field causes the job to be invoked on the quarter hour—0, 15, 30, and 45 minutes.

Cron expressions are very powerful. With a little imagination, you can specify a multitude of times. Table 11-3 shows some sample cron expressions.

Table 11-3. Cron Expression Examples

Expression	Meaning
`0 0 1 * * ?`	Invoke at 1:00 a.m. every day
`0 15 2 ? * *`	Invoke at 2:15 a.m. every day
`0 15 2 * * ?`	Invoke at 2:15 a.m. every day
`0 15 2 * * ? *`	Invoke at 2:15 a.m. every day
`0 15 2 * * ? 2008`	Invoke at 2:15 a.m. every day during the year 2008
`0 * 13 * * ?`	Invoke every minute starting at 1 p.m. and ending at 1:59 p.m., every day
`0 0/5 14 * * ?`	Invoke every 5 minutes starting at 2 p.m. and ending at 2:55 p.m., every day
`0 0/5 14,18 * * ?`	Invoke every 5 minutes starting at 2 p.m. and ending at 2:55 p.m., and invoke every 5 minutes starting at 6 p.m. and ending at 6:55 p.m., every day
`0 0-5 14 * * ?`	Invoke every minute starting at 2 p.m. and ending at 2:05 p.m., every day
`0 10,45 14 ? 3 WED`	Invoke at 2:10 p.m. and at 2:45 p.m. every Wednesday in the month of March
`0 15 2 ? * MON-FRI`	Invoke at 2:15 a.m. every Monday, Tuesday, Wednesday, Thursday, and Friday
`0 15 2 15 * ?`	Invoke at 2:15 a.m. on the fifteenth day of every month
`0 0 12 1/5 * ?`	Invoke at 12 p.m. (noon) every 5 days every month, starting on the first day of the month
`0 11 11 25 12 ?`	Invoke every December 25 at 11:11 a.m.

Listing 11-2 shows the definition for the `NightlyReportJob`. Notice that it includes both techniques for controlling execution frequency, with the `startDelay`/`timeout` definitions commented out.

Listing 11-2. NightlyReportJob Name, Group, and Execution Frequency Configuration

```
class NightlyReportJob {
  def cronExpression = "0 0 1 * * *" // Run every day at 1:00 a.m.
  def name = "Nightly"               // Job name
  def group = "CollabTodo"           // Job group

//  def startDelay = 20000           // Wait 20 seconds to start the job
//  def timeout = 60000              // Execute job once every 60 seconds
```

You can see why the Grails team chose to integrate Quartz instead of creating something new. It is very powerful. Armed with this knowledge, you are ready to move on and implement the core logic of the nightly report job.

Retrieving the User's Todos

The next step is to leverage Spring's auto-wired dependency injection to inject the `BatchService` into the job, as follows:

```
> grails create-service Batch
```

Listing 11-3 illustrates injection and execution of the `BatchService`.

Listing 11-3. NightlyReportJob with Batch Service

```
class NightlyReportJob {
  def cronExpression = "0 0 1 * * *" // Run every day at 1:00 a.m.
  def name = "Nightly"               // Job name
  def group = "CollabTodo"           // Job group

//  def startDelay = 20000           // Wait 20 seconds to start the job
//  def timeout = 60000              // Execute job once every 60 seconds

  def batchService
  def execute() {
      log.info "Starting Nightly Job: "+new Date()
      batchService.nightlyReports.call()
      log.info "Finished Nightly Job: "+new Date()
  }
}
```

The code is straightforward. It defines when the job is to run and delegate to the BatchService.

The next step is to create the nightly closure on the batch service. It will contain the code to retrieve the user's todos. Listing 11-4 illustrates adding the nightly closure and retrieving the user's todos.

Listing 11-4. Batch Service Nightly Closure

```
class BatchService

  . . .

  /*
  *  Runs nightly reports
  */
  def nightlyReports = {
      log.info "Running Nightly Reports Batch Job: "+new Date()
      // 1. Gather user w/ email addresses.
      def users = User.withCriteria {
              isNotNull('email')
      }

      users?.each { user ->
          // 2. Invoke report service for each user.
          //    Can't reuse ReportController because it makes too
          //    many assumptions, such as access to session.class.
          //
          //    Reuse Report Service and pass appropriate params.
          // Gather the data to be reported.
          def inputCollection = Todo.findAllByOwner(user)

          // To be completed in the next section

      }

      log.info "Completed Nightly Reports Batch Job:  "+new Date()
  }
```

The BatchService.nightlyReports gets all users with an e-mail address, and then for each user, gets their todos and prepares to invoke the report service.

Invoking the Report Service

In Chapter 10, you used JasperReports to build a report facility. You can reuse components of the report facility to create a todo report PDF to attach to the e-mail.

Your first thought might be to use the ReportController. Well, that doesn't work. The report controller is dependent on the HTTP session and renders the PDF to the output stream. You need to go one level deeper and use the ReportService directly.

We have already retrieved the user's todos. Now all we need to do is pass the todos, report template, and a username parameter to the report service. The highlighted section of Listing 11-5 illustrates the required steps.

Listing 11-5. Invokingthe Report Service

```
class BatchService {
ReportServicereportService  // Inject ReportService

  def nightlyReports = {

. . .

      users?.each { user ->
          // 2. Invoke Report Service for each user.
          //    Reuse Report Service and pass appropriate params.
          // Gather the data to be reported.
          def inputCollection = Todo.findAllByOwner(user)
          Map params = new HashMap()
          params.inputCollection = inputCollection
          params.userName = user.firstName+""+user.lastName

          // Load the report file.
          def reportFile = this.class.getClassLoader().getResource(
           "web-app/reports/userTodo.jasper")
          ByteArrayOutputStream byteArray = reportService.generateReport(reportFile,
          reportService.PDF_FORMAT,params )
          Map attachments = new HashMap()
          attachments.put("TodoReport.pdf", byteArray.toByteArray())

          // 3. Email results to the user.
          sendNotificationEmail(user, attachments)

      }
  }
```

The new code works as follows:

1. Injects the ReportService into the BatchService.
2. Creates a HashMap of parameters that will be passed to the ReportService. The parameters include the list of todos for the current user.
3. Loads the JasperReports template from the classpath.
4. Invokes reportService.generateReport to pass the report template, report format (PDF), and parameters.

Now that you have a PDF report, the next step is to e-mail it to the user.

Invoking the E-Mail Service

In Chapter 8, you implemented an SMTP e-mail service, called EMailAuthenticatedService. You can use your e-mail service to send the todo report to the user. Listing 11-6 contains the code required to create and send the e-mail.

Listing 11-6. Sending the E-mail

```
1.  class BatchService implements ApplicationContextAware {
2.    boolean transactional = false
3.
4.  public void setApplicationContext(ApplicationContext applicationContext) {
5.    this.applicationContext = applicationContext
6.  }
7.  def ApplicationContext applicationContext
8.  def EMailAuthenticatedService EMailAuthenticatedService  // injected
9.
10. ReportService reportService
11.
12. def nightlyReports = {
13.
14. ...
15.
16.       // Load the report file
17.       def reportFile = this.class.getClassLoader().getResource(
18.           "web-app/reports/userTodo.jasper")
19.       ByteArrayOutputStream byteArray =
20.           reportService.generateReport(reportFile,
21.           reportService.PDF_FORMAT,params )
22.
23.       Map attachments = new HashMap()
24.       attachments.put("TodoReport.pdf", byteArray.toByteArray())
25.
26.       // 3. Email results to the user.
27.       sendNotificationEmail(user, attachments)
28.       }
29.       log.info "Completed Nightly Batch Job:  "+new Date()
30.  }
31.
```

```
32. def private sendNotificationEmail = {User user, Map attachments ->
33.   def emailTpl = this.class.getClassLoader().getResource(
34.       "web-app/WEB-INF/nightlyReportsEmail.gtpl")
35.   def binding = ["user": user]
36.   def engine = new SimpleTemplateEngine()
37.   def template = engine.createTemplate(emailTpl).make(binding)
38.   def body = template.toString()
39.   def email = [
40.           to: [user.email],
41.     subject: "Your CollabTodo Report",
42.     text:   body
43.   ]
44.   try {
45.     EMailProperties eMailProperties =
46.           applicationContext.getBean("eMailProperties")
47.     eMailAuthenticatedService.sendEmail(email, eMailProperties, attachments)
48.   } catch (MailException ex) {
49.     log.error("Failed to send emails", ex)
50.   }
51.  }
52. }
```

The highlighted lines contain the changes made to the batch service. Lines 1 and 4-7 make the batch service (Spring) application context-aware; in other words, the Spring application context is injected into the service. You will use the application context later to look up some information. Line 8 takes advantage of Spring auto-wiring to inject the `EmailAuthenticatedService`. Lines 23 and 24 add the PDF report to a map of attachments for e-mail. Line 27 invokes a local `sendNotificationEmail` closure.

Lines 32-51 contain the code to send the todo report e-mail to the user. Line 33 loads an e-mail template. Lines 36-38 use the Groovy `SimpleTemplateEngine`[2] to generate the e-mail body. Lines 39-43 define a map of e-mail parameters that are passed to the e-mail service. Line 45 uses the Spring application context to look up e-mail properties, including the "from" address. Line 47 invokes the e-mail service, sending the e-mail map, e-mail properties, and the attachments.

Summary

This chapter demonstrated Grails' ability to reuse open source, third-party Java libraries. You installed the Quartz plugin, created a simple job, and saw how to control the frequency of execution using the `timeout` property.

Next, you started to build the batchreporting facility. You created a `NightlyReportJob` and configured it to run at 1:00 a.m. using the `cronExpression` property. You learned that cron expressions are robust and provide fine-grained control over when the `NightlyReportJob` is invoked.

The `NightlyReportJob` delegated to a batch service that was injected using Spring auto-wiring and invoked `nightlyReports`. `nightlyReports` iterated through a list of users, gathered their todos, invoked the report service built in Chapter 10 to generate a PDF attachment, and e-mailed the attachment to the user using the `EmailAuthenticatedService` built in Chapter 8.

---

[2]http://groovy.codehaus.org/Groovy+Templates

CHAPTER 12

Deploying and Upgrading Grails Applications

The previous chapters were related to developing Grails applications. One of the strengths of Grails is that it comes bundled with everything you need to begin developing and testing your application. Grails embeds a web container (Tomcat) and a relational database (H2). All you have to do is execute the Grails `run-app` target, and you have your entire runtime environment. However, at some point in time, you will want to expose your application to your users. The embedded runtime environment is for development and testing only, and it is not intended to scale or support the load necessary in a production environment.

This chapter focuses on deploying Grails applications to Java EE application servers and more robust database servers. It also covers some other miscellaneous, operational aspects, such as upgrading a Grails application when a new version of the Grails framework is released and automating tasks using Gant.

Deploying Grails Applications

Deploying a Grails application involves three steps:

1. Configure the application. This typically involves environmentspecific configurations.
2. Package the application. For Grails applications, this means bundling all the code and related artifacts into a Web Application Archive (WAR) file.
3. Deploy the application to an application server or web container.

Using Environments

Many organizations have multiple environments or gates that an application must pass through before reaching production and users. At a minimum, each application should have to pass through development, test, and production environments. The development environment is the developer's machine. In the test environment, which mimics production, somebody other than the developer completes quality assurance by validating that the application meets requirements and generally works. The production environment is where real users use the application. In each of these environments, you're likely to have environment-specific configurations and, rarer, behavioral differences. For example, in development, you may want to point to a local H2 in-memory database, but in the test and production environments, you may need to point at a remote server database such as MySQL.[1]

[1]`http://dev.mysql.com/`

As you might expect, Grails follows these best practices and is aware of these three environments. You can use these environments when calling the `grails` command line as the second parameter or in configuration files such as `DataSource.groovy`, `BootStrap.groovy`, and `Config.groovy`, which you'll see in the next section. Table 12-1 shows the mapping per environment.

Table 12-1. *Environment Mappings*

Environment	Command Line	Configuration File Reference
Development	`dev`	`development`
Test	`test`	`test`
Production	`prod`	`production`

Depending on the size of the organization and the criticalness of the application or the system, you may have additional environments such as integration testing (IT), user acceptance testing (UAT), and performance testing (PT). You can use custom environments as well. The only requirement is that the `grails.env` system property must be passed to the Grails command line. For example, the following specifies the performance environment:

```
> grails -Dgrails.env=PT run-app
```

Grails supports the concept of per-environment configuration. The `Config.groovy`, `DataSource.groovy`, and `BootStrap.groovy` files in the `grails-app/conf` directory can use per-environment configuration, as illustrated in the default `dataSource` definition provided by Grails and shown in Listing 12-1.

Listing 12-1. Using Per-Environment Configuration

```
dataSource {
    pooled = false
    driverClassName = "org.h2.Driver"
    username = "sa"
    password = ""
}
environments {
    development {
        dataSource {
            dbCreate = "create-drop"
            url = "jdbc:h2:mem:devDb"
        }
    }
    test {
        dataSource {
            dbCreate = "update"
            url = "jdbc:h2:mem:testDb"
        }
    }
    production {
        dataSource {
            dbCreate = "update"
            url = "jdbc:h2:prodDb"
        }
    }
}
```

In Listing 12-1, notice how the common configuration is provided at the top level and then an `environments` block specifies per-environment settings for the `dbCreate` and `url` properties of the `dataSource`. We will revisit this code in the `dataSource` section of this chapter.

Within a Gant script or a bootstrap class, explained later in this chapter, you can detect the environment using the Environment class, as illustrated in the Listing 12-2.

Listing 12-2. Detecting the Environment

```
import grails.util.Environment
......
switch (Environment.current) {
    case Environment.DEVELOPMENT:
        configureForDevelopment()
        break
    case Environment.PRODUCTION:
        configureForProduction()
        break
}
```

Understanding Grails Configurations

With Grails' default settings, you can actually develop an application without doing any configuration whatsoever, but it's important to learn where and how to override the conventions when you need to.

For general configuration, Grails provides two files:

- `grails-app/conf/BuildConfig.groovy`
- `grails-app/conf/Config.groovy`

The `BuildConfig.groovy` file is for settings that are used when running Grails commands and the `Config.groovy` file is for settings that are used when your application is running. This means that `Config.groovy` is packaged with your application, but `BuildConfig.groovy` is not. Grails contains four primary configuration categories. The first is URL mapping, which we explained in earlier chapters, so we won't revisit it here. The second is behavior when the application starts up and shuts down. The third and fourth are data source and logging configurations. You can find all these configurations in the `grails-app/config` directory.

Startup and Shutdown Behavior

Sometimes when an application starts up and/or shuts down, you need to do things such as acquire and release resources, respectively, or cache data. Grails makes this possible in the `grails-app/config/BootStrap.groovy` file.

Listing 12-3 is an example of a `BootStrap.groovy` file. It includes comments where startup and shutdown code should go.

Listing 12-3. Using BootStrap.groovy to Perform Startup and Shutdown Activities

```
classBootStrap {
       definit = { servletContext ->
       // perform startup activities here
       }
       def destroy = {
       // perform shutdown activities here
       }
}
```

In Listing 12-3, the `init` action is invoked when the application starts up or is redeployed. The `javax.servlet.ServletContext`[2] is passed in, providing access to the application attributes, initialization parameters configured in web.xml, the context path, and more. The destroy action is invoked when the application is shut down, but it is not guaranteed to be called. For example, it is not likely the destroy method will be called when the application server is shut down, but it is likely to be called when the application is redeployed or undeployed.

Data Source Configurations

By default, Grails is configured out of the box to use an embedded, in-memory H2 database. This is not likely to be the database used in the test and production environments and possibly not even in most development environments. This is because, as you've seen, each time the application restarts, the database gets re-created in memory and is therefore empty. It's more likely that an application will use a server database such as MySQL, Oracle,[3] DB2,[4] Microsoft SQL Server,[5] or maybe even Apache Derby.[6]

You can set database and Hibernate configurations in the `grails-app/config/DataSource.groovy` file. Listing 12-4 shows an example of a `DataSource.groovy` file that was customized to include a production database configuration for a local MySQL database.

Listing 12-4. DataSource.groovy Containing a MySQL Production Configuration

```
1.  dataSource {
2.      pooled = true
3.      driverClassName = "org.h2.Driver"
4.      username = "sa"
5.      password = ""
6.  }
7.  hibernate {
8.      cache.use_second_level_cache=true
9.      cache.use_query_cache=false
10.      cache.region.factory_class = 'net.sf.ehcache.hibernate.EhCacheRegionFactory'
11. }
12. // environment specific settings
13. environments {
14.     development {
15.         dataSource {
16.             dbCreate = "create-drop" // one of 'create', 'create-drop','update', 'validate', "
17.             url = "jdbc:h2:mem:devDb;MVCC=TRUE;LOCK_TIMEOUT=10000"
18.         }
19.     }
20.     test {
21.         dataSource {
22.             dbCreate = "update"
23.             url = "jdbc:h2:mem:testDb;MVCC=TRUE;LOCK_TIMEOUT=10000"
24.         }
25.     }
26.     production {
```

---

[2]http://www.oracle.com/technetwork/java/javaee/servlet/index.html

[3]http://www.oracle.com

[4]http://www.ibm.com/db2/

[5]http://www.microsoft.com/sql/

[6]http://db.apache.org/derby/

```
27.         dataSource {
28. pooled = true
29. driverClassName = "com.mysql.jdbc.Driver"
30. username = "root"
31. password = "<password>"
32. dbCreate = "update"
33. url = "jdbc:mysql://localhost:3306/collab_todo"
34.                              dialect = org.hibernate.dialect.MySQL5InnoDBDialect
35.                              properties {

                                        maxActive = -1
                             minEvictableIdleTimeMillis=1800000
                             timeBetweenEvictionRunsMillis=1800000
                             numTestsPerEvictionRun=3
                             testOnBorrow=true
                             testWhileIdle=true
                             testOnReturn=true
                             validationQuery="SELECT 1"
                                        ...
     }
36.         }
37.     }
38. }
```

The configuration file in Listing 12-2 is separated into three main parts: `dataSource` (lines 1–6), `hibernate` (lines 7–11), and environment-specific settings (lines 12–38). The `dataSource` section provides default database settings that environmentspecific settings may override or append to. Other than the `pooled` property, these default settings all relate to standard JDBC configuration information, such as the JDBC driver class name, the username, and the password for the database.

The `hibernate` section relates to Hibernate-specific settings. By default, it configures Hibernate caching settings. See the Hibernate documentation[7] for more configuration options.

The environment-specific settings can provide specific data source or Hibernate configurations for a particular named environment. Notice in lines 28–33 that the `productiondataSource` is configured to use a MySQL database by setting the `driverClassName` and `url` to be MySQL-specific. It also overrides the `pooled` property by setting it to `true`, since most production environments have more concurrent needs than a developer's workstation.

Finally, note that the `dbCreate` property is configured only for `update`. This means that at deployment time, Hibernate will update any of the tables it is able to, but it will leave the existing data intact. On the other hand, the default development configuration will create the table at startup and destroy the tables and data when the application is shut down. In line 35, properties set extra properties on the `dataSource` bean.

The `dbCreate` property of the `dataSource` definition in line 32 is important, as it dictates what Grails should do at runtime with regard to automatically generating the database tables from GORM classes. The options are described in the `dataSource` section:

- create
- create-drop
- update
- validate
- no value

---

[7]`http://www.hibernate.org/docs`

In development mode, dbCreate is by default set to create-drop, but at some point in development (and certainly once you go to production), you'll need to stop dropping and re-creating the database every time you start up your server.

Logging Configurations

Logging is an important part of gathering feedback about the state of an application. As you learned earlier, Grails provides logging support using the Apache Commons Logging component[8] and Apache log4j.[9] You can create the log4j configurations, as well as a couple other configurations, in grails-app/config/Config.groovy. Listing 12-5 shows the default version of Config.groovy.

Listing 12-5. Config.groovy File Containing Logging Configurations

```
1.  // log4j configuration
2.  log4j {
3.    appender.stdout = "org.apache.log4j.ConsoleAppender"
4.    appender.'stdout.layout'=""org.apache.log4j.PatternLayout"
5.    appender.'stdout.layout.ConversionPattern'='[%r] %c{2} %m%n'
6.    rootLogger="error,stdout"
7.    logger {
8.      grails="info,stdout"
9.      org {
10.       codehaus.groovy.grails.web.servlet="off,stdout"  //  controllers
11.       codehaus.groovy.grails.web.pages="off,stdout" //  GSP
12.       codehaus.groovy.grails.web.sitemesh="off,stdout" //  layouts
13.       codehaus.groovy.grails."web.mapping.filter"="off,stdout" // URL mapping
14.       codehaus.groovy.grails."web.mapping"="off,stdout" // URL mapping
15.       codehaus.groovy.grails.commons="off,stdout" // core / classloading
16.       codehaus.groovy.grails.plugins="off,stdout" // plugins
17.       codehaus.groovy.grails.orm.hibernate="info,stdout" // hibernate integration
18.       springframework="off,stdout"
19.       hibernate="off,stdout"
20.     }
21.   }
22.   additivity.'default' = false
23.   additivity {
24.     grails=false
25.     org {
26.       codehaus.groovy.grails=false
27.       springframework=false
28.       hibernate=false
29.     }
30.   }
31. }
32.
33. // The following properties have been added by the Upgrade process...
34. grails.views.default.codec="none" // none, html, base64
35. grails.views.gsp.encoding="UTF-8"
```

---

[8]http://commons.apache.org/logging/

[9]http://logging.apache.org/log4j/2.x/

Listing 12-3 does the following:

- Lines 2–31 configure log4j, while the remaining lines set some default configurations for views. When the application logs a message, something has to be done with the message.
- Lines 3–5 configure a `ConsoleAppender`, which takes the message and writes it to standard out, with the format defined by the pattern in line 5.
- Line 6 instructs log4j to send only messages with severities of `error` or greater to the appender unless explicitly overwritten.
- Lines 7–20 show examples of overriding some logging. For example, on line 8, the `grails` logger says to include anything with a log level of `info` or above, while line 10 turns off `org.codehaus.groovy.grails.web.servlet` completely.

■ Note There are a lot of options for log4j. Check out "Short Introduction to log4j."[10]

Grails provides some special loggers for the different types of artifacts that it already understands by conventions. Table 12-2 documents the special loggers you will find helpful for seeing your log messages.

Table 12-2. *Special Grails Artifact Loggers*

Logger	Description
`grails.app.controller`	Configures logging for all your controllers
`grails.app.domain`	Configures logging for all your domains
`grails.app.service`	Configures logging for all your services
`grails.app.tagLib`	Configures logging for all your tag libraries

The most likely log configuration you will want to make is adding environment-specific logging for your artifacts; you can use the loggers described in Table 12-2. For example, in your development environment, you may want to log messages at a debug level (as shown in Listing 12-6), but in your production environment, you may want to log fewer messages for performance reasons and to ensure that the log file doesn't consume all your disk space.

Listing 12-6. Example of Adding Logging Specific to Your Development Environment

```
environments {
  development {
    log4j {
      logger {
        grails {
          app.controller="debug"
        }
      }
    }
  }
}
```

[10]`http://logging.apache.org/log4j/2.x/manual/`

Listing 12-6 shows an example of logging all controllers at a debug level. You can simply add this configuration to the end of the `Config.groovy` file and then restart the application for the new development-specific logging configuration to take effect.

Packaging the Application for Deployment

The `run-app` command is thus best suited for development only. For deployment onto a production system, use a packaged WAR file. Deploy your application by setting up Grails on your production environment and simply type:

```
grails> run-war
```

This command packages up Grails as a WAR file and then runs Tomcat using the packaged WAR.

The `run-war` command shown above is convenient, but you might want more control over your deployment environment, or you might want to deploy onto another container, such as BEA WebLogic, instead of Tomcat. What you need in these cases is a WAR file. To create a WAR archive, use Grails' `war` command:

```
grails> war
```

After you complete the application functionality for an iteration or a release, you or your build master need to package your application so it can be deployed on a machine other than your computer. At the most basic level, all you have to do is run the Grails `war` target to create a deployable WAR file. In reality, though, you should follow a more disciplined process to make it easier to identify the version of your application as it goes through environments. We recommended you follow this procedure for milestone releases:

1. Update the code from your version control repository to make sure it's in sync with the head/trunk.
2. Run unit and smoke tests to verify that the release is ready.
3. Increment the `app.version` property in `application.properties` either manually or by using the grails set-version target to identify a milestone release number, such as X.X.X.
4. Clean the project using the `grails clean` target to make sure there are no leftover artifacts.
5. Package the application into a WAR file using the `Grails war` target and an environment designation—for example, `grails prod war`. This creates a WAR file in the root of the project with a name containing the project name and version number.
6. Increment the `app.version` property and append a `-SNAPSHOT` in `application.properties` either manually or by using the `grailsset-version` target to indicate this version is a work in progress and not a milestone release.
7. Commit the `application.properties` file back into your version control repository.

Now you have a WAR file ready for deployment. We'll discuss how to deploy it in the next section.

Deploying to an Application Server

A Grails application packaged as a WAR file can be deployed to Java EE application servers such as JBoss, GlassFish, Apache Geronimo, BEA WebLogic, or IBM WebSphere, or to a web container such as Apache Tomcat or Jetty. Deployment between containers varies greatly, so consult your application server or web container documentation for details. However, standard mechanisms include special deployment directories where the WAR can be copied, a web-based administrator console, a command-line client, and/or Apache Ant tasks. Grails does not provide anything for simplifying deployments, so now we'll discuss how you can write your own script to automate the process.

■ **Note** The Grails FAQ (`http://www.grails.org/FAQ`) has specific configurations and tips for deploying Grails applications to some common application servers.

HTTPS

Many applications require that the information passed from the browser to the server be encrypted to ensure the data is not intercepted along the way. This is usually done using a secure HTTP connection, otherwise known as HTTP over Secure Socket Layer (SSL), or HTTPS. Configuring HTTPS is an application server–specific configuration, so you should check your application server documentation to learn how to configure it. However, it can be critical to test your application within an HTTPS context, so Grails provides the ability to start your Grails application using HTTPS instead of HTTP. Instead of executing grails run-app, you use `run-app -https`. This starts your server so it is available under port 8080 as well as port 8443 using an HTTPS protocol—for example, `https://localhost:8443/collab-todo/`. Running the server in this mode causes a temporary certificate to be generated, as shown in the following figure. You'll be prompted with an unknown certifying authority error, which makes this method unsuitable for production use but fine for testing.

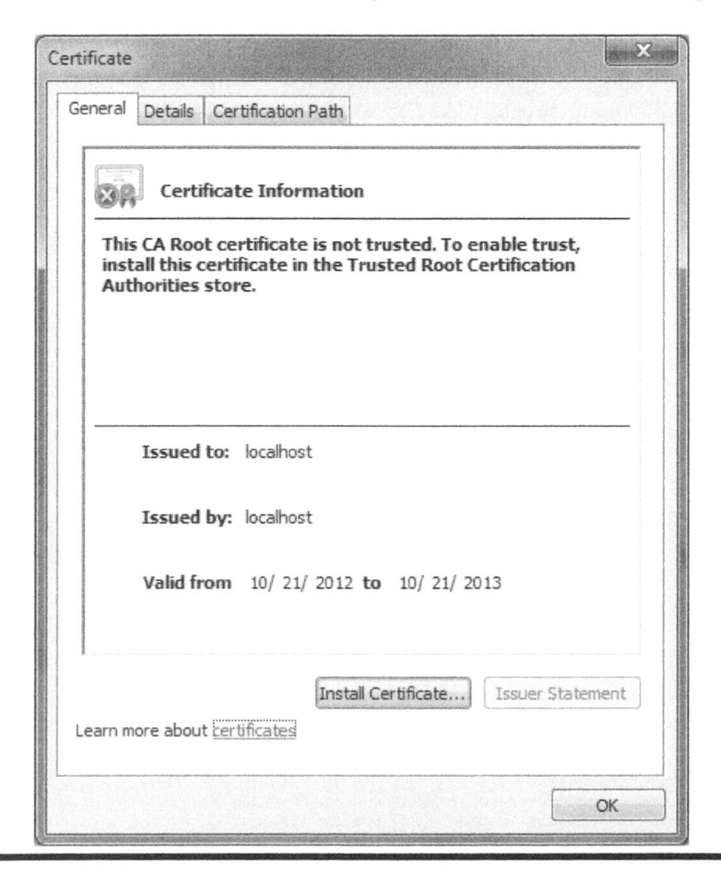

Development is full of cycles and repetitive tasks, such as compiling, packaging, and deploying. Performing such tasks manually can be boring and error prone. It is considered a best practice to automate such tasks. Many books have been written to this effect, and many frameworks were developed to solve the problem. In fact, one of the primary conventions for Grails is the Grails command line, which is used to automate common tasks in Grails development. The Grails command line utilizes Gant,[11] a build system that uses the Groovy language to script Apache Ant tasks rather than Ant's XML format. Ant, and therefore Gant, are primarily made up of name collections of tasks referred to as targets, which you can execute to complete a unit of work.

As you have seen throughout this book, the Grails command line provides a lot of functionality. However, it may not automate every task you perform during your development. For example, there is no task for deploying, and yet it is common to deploy your application to infrastructure that matches the application server and database you use in a production environment. So from time to time, you may want to simplify your development efforts by creating your own Gant scripts or modifying existing ones.

Grails makes it easy to incorporate your scripts into your development process. After all, every Grails command-line task is itself a Gant script already. The Grails command line uses the following directories to locate scripts for execution and incorporate them into the help system:

- `USER_HOME/.grails/scripts`
- `PROJECT_HOME/scripts`
- `PROJECT_HOME/plugins/*/scripts`
- `GRAILS_HOME/scripts`

After writing your Gant script, you can place it in one of these directories, and it will automatically be available from the Grails command line and in the Grails help list.

Grails does not include a deployment script, because there are too many application servers and configuration options to keep up. Listing 12-7 shows an example of a simple script you can use to deploy a WAR file to an application server that supports automatic deployments via a deployment directory like JBoss has.

Listing 12-7. Basic Deployment Script Deploy.groovy

```
1.  /**
2.  * Gant script that copies a WAR file to an application
3.  * server deployment directory.
4.  */
5.
6.
7.
8.
9.  includeTargets <<grailsScript("War")
10.
11. target ('default':'"Copies a WAR archive to a Java EE app server's deploy
12. directory.
13.
14. Example:
15. grails deploy
16. grails prod deploy
17. "") {
18.   deploy()
19. }
20.
```

[11]http://gant.codehaus.org

```
21. target (deploy: "The implementation target") {
22.   depends( war )
23.
24.   def deployDir = ant.antProject.properties.'deploy.dir'
25.
26.   ant.copy(todir:"${deployDir}", overwrite:true) {
27.     fileset(dir:"${basedir}", includes:"*.war")
28.   }
29.
30.  event("StatusFinal", ["Done copying WAR to ${deployDir}"])
31. }
```

In the Deploy.groovy script shown in Listing 12-7, line 9 imports another Gant script—specifically, the War.groovy script. The deploy script is dependent on the War.groovy script to build the WAR file, so it has something to deploy.

Lines 11-19 represent the first of two targets in this script. The first target is the default target, which means if no other target is specified, this will be the one executed. Since Grails calls the default target, it will definitely be the one executed. Notice that the default name is in single quotes; this is because the word default is a reserved word in Groovy. Quotes are not normally needed for target names. Following the name is the target description, which the Grails help system uses. The only behavior the default target has is to call the deploy target.

The deploy target, shown on lines 21-31, does all the real work. It begins by calling the war target from the War.groovy script. After the WAR file is created, it looks up the deploy.dir property. It then copies the WAR file to the location of this property. You can put the destination of the WAR file in the application.properties file, since the Grails command line automatically loads it. Lines 26-28 use the Ant copy task to copy all WAR files to the deployment directory. Finally, a message is printed to the system out to indicate to the user that the script is complete and in which directory the WAR file was copied.

Running the following target performs the deployment by copying the WAR file to your application server:

```
> grails deploy
```

Upgrading Grails Applications

Early in the development of the Grails framework, it must have become obvious that the framework would go through many iterations and that some mechanism was needed to ensure that applications could migrate easily to new releases of the Grails framework. As with many of the Grails conventions, this is accomplished through a Grails target, upgrade. This section gives a brief summary of what you might encounter when upgrading to Grails 2. The detailed description can be found in Grails documentation.[12]

Grails 2.0 contains updated dependencies including Servlet 3.0, Tomcat 7, Spring 3.1, Hibernate 3.6, and Groovy 1.8. This means that certain plugins and applications that depend on earlier versions of these APIs may no longer work. For example, the Servlet 3.0 HttpServletRequest interface includes new methods, so if a plugin implements this interface for Servlet 2.5 but not for Servlet 3.0, then said plugin will break. The same can be said of any Spring interface. Grails 2 does not work on JDK 1.4, so if you wish to continue using Grails, use Grails 1.0.x until you are able to upgrade your JDK.

---

[12]http://grails.org/doc/latest/guide/upgradingFromPreviousVersionsOfGrails.html

Configuration Changes

The following settings have been moved from `grails-app/conf/Config.groovygrails` to `app/conf/BuildConfig.groovy`:

- `grails.config.base.webXml`
- `grails.project.war.file` (renamed from `grails.war.destFile`)
- `grails.war.dependencies`
- `grails.war.copyToWebApp`
- `grails.war.resources`

Command Line Changes

The `run-app-https` and `run-war-https` commands no longer exist and have been replaced by an argument to `run-app`:

```
> grails run-app -https
```

H2

HSQLDB was replaced with H2 as default in-memory database, but it is still bundled with Grails. Upgrade options include replacing HSQLDB references in `DataSource.groovy` with H2 references or adding HSQLDB as a runtime dependency for the application.

If you want to run an application with different versions of Grails, add HSQLDB as a runtime dependency, which you can do in `BuildConfig.groovy`, as illustrated in Listing 12-8.

Listing 12-8. Adding HSQLDB as a Runtime Dependency

```
grails.project.dependency.resolution = {
    inherits("global") {
    }
    repositories {
        grailsPlugins()
        grailsHome()
        grailsCentral()
    }   dependencies {
        // Add HSQLDB as a runtime dependency
        runtime 'hsqldb:hsqldb:1.8.0.10'
    }
}
```

jQuery

jQuery Replaces Prototype. The Prototype JavaScript library was removed from Grails core and now new Grails applications have the jQuery plugin configured by default. This will only impact you if you are using Prototype with the adaptive Ajax tags in your application (for example, `<g:remoteLink/>`) because those tags will break as soon as you upgrade. To resolve this issue, simply install the Prototype plugin in your application. If you want you can also remove the prototype files from your `web-app/js/prototype` directory.

Controller Public Methods

As of Grails 2.0, public methods of controllers are now treated as actions in addition to actions defined as traditional closures. If you were relying on the use of methods for privacy controls or as helper methods, then this could result in unexpected behavior. To resolve this issue, mark all methods of your application that you do not want to expose as actions as private methods.

Unit Test Framework

Grails 2 introduces a new unit testing framework that is simpler and behaves more consistently than the old one. The old framework based on the `GrailsUnitTestCase` class hierarchy is still available for backward compatibility, but it does not work with the new annotations. Migrating unit tests to the new approach is non-trivial, but recommended. Here are a set of mappings from the old style to the new:

1. Remove `extends *UnitTestCase` and add a `@TestFor` annotation to the class if you're testing a core artifact (controller, tag lib, domain class, and so on) or `@TestMixin(GrailsUnitTestMixin)` for non-core artifacts and non-artifact classes.
2. Add `@Mock` annotation for domain classes that must be mocked and use new `MyDomain().save()` in place of `mockDomain()`.
3. Replace references to `mockRequest`, `mockResponse`, and `mockParams` with `request`, `response`, and `params`.
4. Remove references to `renderArgs` and use the view and model properties for view rendering, or `response.text` for all others.
5. Replace references to `redirectArgs` with `response.redirectedUrl`. The latter takes into account the URL mappings as it is a string URL rather than a map of `redirect()` arguments.
6. The `mockCommandObject()` method is no longer needed, as Grails automatically detects whether an action requires a command object or not.

Summary

This chapter covered a lot of the operational aspects of developing Grails applications. Many of the topics related to things that happen after the code is written or described ways to facilitate the development process. The topics included packaging and deploying the application, as well as configuring environmental data sources and logging. It also covered how to automate your daily development processes and upgrade your applications to work with new versions of Grails. This chapter also ends the server-side discussion of Grails.

CHAPTER 13

Introduction to Griffon

The griffon is a mythological creature with the body of a lion and the head and wings of an eagle. As the lion was traditionally considered the king of the beasts and the eagle was the king of the birds, the griffon was thought to be an especially powerful and majestic creature. Similar to this majestic mix, Griffon, a Model-View-Controller (MVC)-based desktop application framework, uses Grails, the web application framework, as its foundation to enable the developer to switch between web and desktop development. The knowledge acquired in one transmutes to the other, thus bringing you the best of both worlds. Both frameworks share a lot of traits, Griffon's MVC design and plugin facility is based on those provided by Grails, and the command-line tools and scripts found in one framework can also be found in the other.

Inspired by Grails, Griffon follows the "convention over configuration" paradigm, paired with an intuitive MVC architecture and a command line interface. Griffon also follows the spirit of the Swing Application Framework, which defines a simple yet powerful application life cycle and event publishing mechanism. Grails developers should feel right at home when trying out Griffon. Many of Grails' conventions and commands are shared with Griffon.

The Griffon framework is extensible via plugins, and there are many to choose from. For example, you'll find plugins for third-party Swing components like SwingX, Jide, and Macwidgets; persistence-related plugins like DataSource, GSQL, and Hibernate, among others; and 3D graphics and animation support is possible via JOGL and LWJGL. Griffon also supports additional UI toolkits like JavaFX and SWT.

This chapter, by no means comprehensive, introduces you to the basics of Griffon. For a detailed treatment on Griffon, we recommend:

- *Griffon in Action* (Manning Publications, 2012), co-authored by James Shingler, also the co-author of this book
- The Griffon documentation (`http://griffon.codehaus.org/guide/latest/`)

Installing Griffon

The first step to getting up and running with Griffon is to install the distribution. To do so, follow these steps:

1. Download a binary distribution of Griffon and extract the resulting zip file to a location of your choice from here:`http://griffon.codehaus.org/Download`. This chapter uses Griffon 1.1.0.
2. Set the GRIFFON_HOME environment variable to the location where you extracted the zip file. On Unix/Linux based systems, this is typically a matter of adding something like `export GRIFFON_HOME=/path/to/griffon` to your profile. On Windows, you typically set an environment variable under My Computer ➤ Advanced ➤ Environment Variables.
3. Now you need to add the bin directory to your `PATH` variable. On a Unix/Linux base system, you can do this by adding `export PATH="$PATH:$GRIFFON_HOME/bin"`. On Windows, modify the Path environment variable under My Computer ➤ Advanced ➤ Environment Variables.

If Griffon is working correctly, you should now be able to type `griffon` in the terminal window and see output similar to the below:

```
Welcome to Griffon 1.1.0 - http://griffon-framework.org/
Licensed under Apache Standard License 2.0
Griffon home is set to: /usr/local/griffon-1.1.0
No script name specified. Use 'griffon help' for more info
```

If you type `griffon help` at your command prompt as specified below, a list of available Griffon commands is displayed, confirming that `GRIFFON_HOME` was set as expected and that the griffon command is available on your path.

```
> griffon help
```

The output should be similar to this:

```
Welcome to Griffon 1.1.0 - http://griffon.codehaus.org/
Licensed under Apache Standard License 2.0
Griffon home is set to: /opt/griffon
```

■ **Note** Griffon may produce output in addition to this, especially when you run it for the first time, when Griffon makes sure it can locate all the required dependencies, which should be available in the folder where Griffon was installed.

Now you're ready to start building your first application. You'll start with a default Griffon application and then enhance it using plugins.

Creating Your First Application

To create a Griffon application, use the following `griffon` command, which is similar to Grails, as Grails developers will notice.

```
> griffon create-app user
```

The `create-app` command creates the appropriate directory structure, the application, and even skeleton code that you can use to launch the application. To launch the application, navigate to the application directory and call the `run-app` command:

```
> griffon run-app
```

This command should compile all sources and package the application. After a few seconds, you'll see a result similar to Figure 13-1.

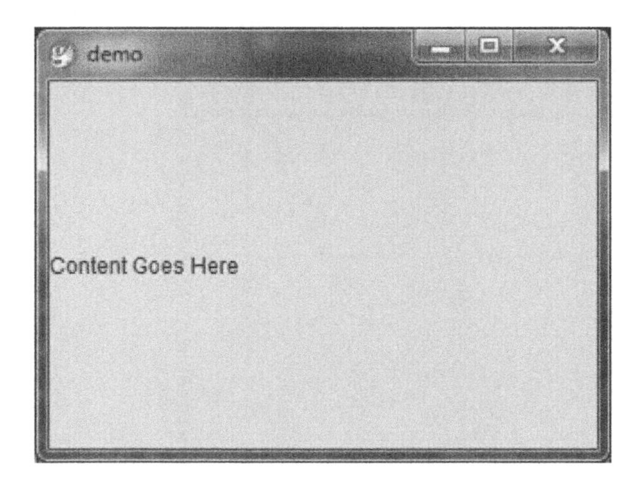

Figure 13-1. *The default view*

This does not look much of an application so far, but it is a full Griffon application with the complete directory structure created as explained in the next section. The `griffon run-app` command runs the application in the stand-alone mode, but it is not the only way to run your application. Every Griffon application can be deployed in three modes: stand-alone, Web Start, and applet.

Java Web Start is a framework developed by Sun Microsystems (now Oracle) that allows users to start application software for the Java Platform directly from the Internet using a web browser. Using JavaWS, desktop applications can be delivered across network. To launch the current application in Web Start mode in Griffon, use the following command:

```
> griffon run-webstart
```

Finally, you can run the application in applet mode with the following command:

```
> griffon run-applet
```

In both the cases, Web Start mode and applet mode, the result is similar, as depicted in Figure 13-1.

As we mentioned earlier, the `create-app` command creates the appropriate directory structure, the application, and even skeleton code. We will go through the directory structure next.

Directory Structure

One of the strengths of the Grails framework is its convention over configuration paradigm. Along the same lines, Griffon's conventions are dictated by the common application structure shared by all applications; this structure was created when you invoked the Griffon `create-app` command.

Let's see what else is created by that command. The core of the application resides in the griffon-app directory, as illustrated in Figure 13-2. There you can find the code for all models, views, and controllers, which together are the mainstay of the application. You'll also find other useful artifacts there.

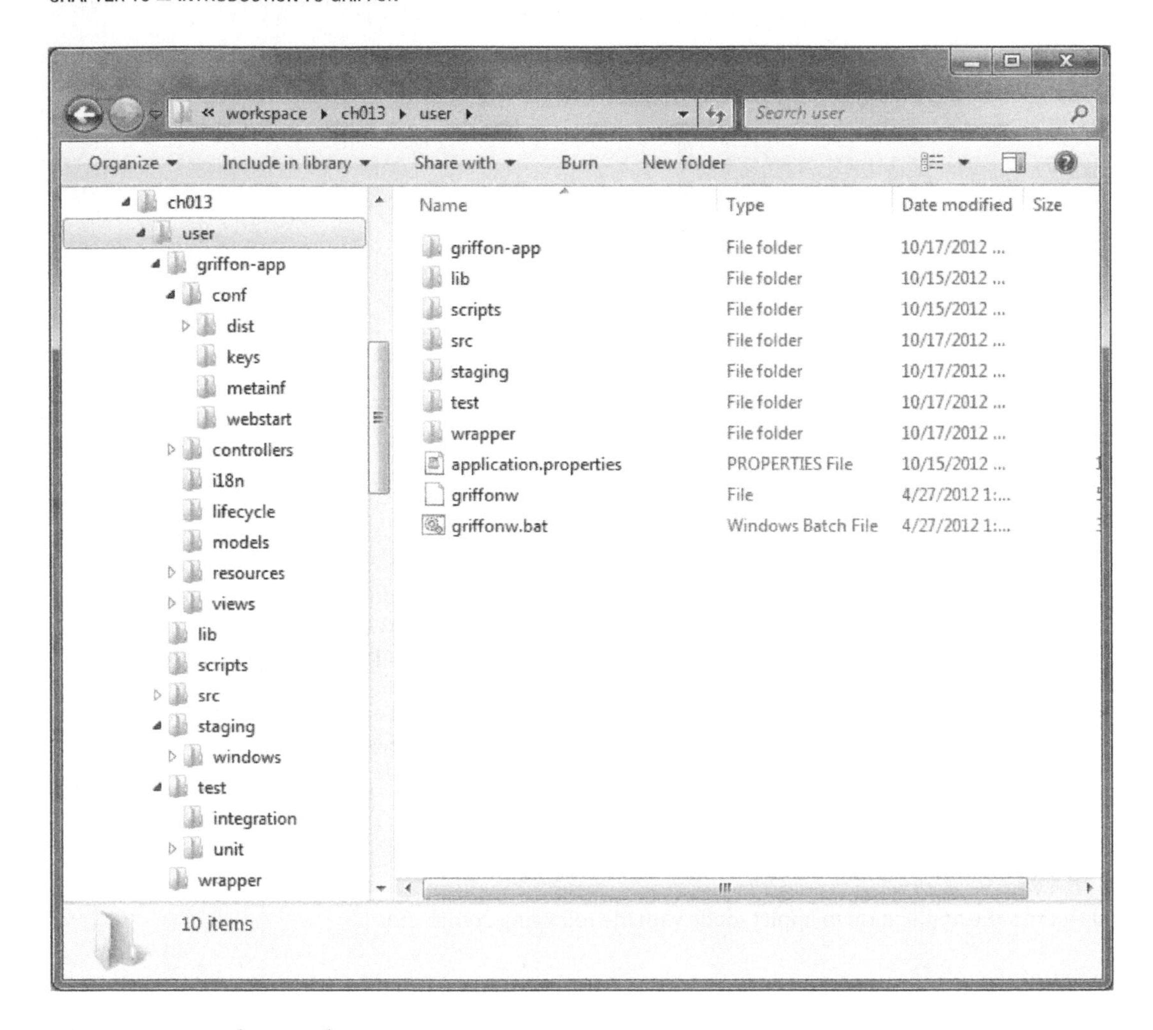

Figure 13-2. *Application directory structure*

Table 13-1 shows a breakdown of the contents of each directory. As you develop more and more Griffon applications, you'll come to appreciate that the applications all follow a common structure and layout. It makes moving between applications much easier. You don't have to spend time to search your way through the application to see where the views, models, and controllers might be located. You just *know* where they are located.

Table 13-1. *Important Directories in the Griffon Convention*

Directory	Description
`griffon-app`	Core Griffon artifacts
`griffon-app/conf`	Configuration sources
`griffon-app/conf/keys`	JAR signing keys
`griffon-app/conf/dist`	Package specific files
`griffon-app/conf/dist/shared`	Common files to all packaging targets

(continued)

Table 13-1. (*continued*)

Directory	Description
griffon-app/conf/metainf	Files that should go in META-INF inside the application/addon JAR
griffon-app/conf/webstart	Webstart templates
griffon-app/controllers	Controllers
griffon-app/models	Models
griffon-app/services	Services
griffon-app/resources	Images, properties files, and so on
griffon-app/views	GSP
lib	Third-party JAR files, such as database drivers
scripts	Build-time scripts
src	Supporting sources
src/main	Other Groovy/Java sources
test	Unit and integration tests
test/integration	Integration tests
test/unit	Unit tests
test/cli	Directory for command line tests

Let's now navigate through the MVC Triad created by Griffon in the models, views, and controllers directory named after the application. Griffon follows the MVC pattern (Model-View-Controller). The smallest unit of structure in a Griffon application is an MVC group. An MVC group is a set of three components, one for each member of the MVC pattern: model, view, and controller. Each member follows a naming convention that's easy to follow. Griffon created an initial MVC group for the application when you issued the `create-app` command. We begin with looking at the view: the part of the application the user can touch and feel (in the literal sense). This file is located at griffon-`app/view/user/UserView.groovy`, as illustrated in Listing 13-1.

Listing 13-1. The Default View

```
package user
application(title: 'user',
  preferredSize: [320, 240],
  pack: true,
  //location: [50,50],
  locationByPlatform:true,
  iconImage: imageIcon('/griffon-icon-48x48.png').image,
  iconImages: [imageIcon('/griffon-icon-48x48.png').image,
imageIcon('/griffon-icon-32x32.png').image,
             imageIcon('/griffon-icon-16x16.png').image]) {
// add content here
    label('Content Goes Here') // delete me
}
```

The view script in the Listing 13-1 is a fairly straightforward `SwingBuilder` script. Griffon will execute this Groovy script in the context of its UberBuilder, a compositing `FactoryBuilderSupport` class, which allows seamless merging of existing Builders. From this code, you can see that the `create-app` command defines an application titled User with a default size of 320 by 240, some icons, and a Content Goes Here label. The application node resolves to a `javax.swing.JFrame` instance when run in stand-alone mode and a `javax.swing.JApplet` instance when run in applet mode. After the code sets some basic properties, such as the title and the location, in the application node, the label component resolves to `javax.swing.JLabel`.

Listing 13-2 illustrates the model class `UserModel` created by Griffon in the `models` directory.

Listing 13-2. Default UserModel Generated by Griffon

```
package user

import groovy.beans.Bindable

class UserModel {
   // @Bindable String propName
}
```

As you can see in Listing 13-2, the model in Griffon is Groovy-powered to map the fields to the properties following the JavaBeans convention. The Groovy compiler will generate the appropriate bytecode for a pair of methods (the getter and setter) and a private field. Also, notice the `@Bindable` attribute, which sets up Griffon data binding. The `@Bindable` annotation is on the individual fields. We can also move the `@Bindable` up to the class level, to make all the fields observable properties. We'll look at binding in the next section. (If you are wondering about "observable" properties are, rest assured that we will cover them later in this chapter.) Now, let's go through the default controller, as shown in Listing 13-3.

Listing 13-3. Default UserController Generated by Griffon

```
package user

class UserController {
    // these will be injected by Griffon
    def model
    def view

    // void mvcGroupInit(Map args) {
    //    // this method is called after model and view are injected
    // }

    // void mvcGroupDestroy() {
    //    // this method is called when the group is destroyed
    // }

    /*
        Remember that actions will be called outside of the UI thread by default. You can change
this setting of course.Please read chapter 9 of the Griffon Guide to know more.
    def action = { evt = null ->
    }
    */
}
```

As you can see, Listing 13-3 includes a lot of comments in the cod. The commented code and the comments are created by Griffon when it creates the controller for the default application. The fields model and view in the controller will be *injected* by the Griffon framework. This allows us to access the view widgets and the model data if needed. At this point, the astute reader might notice that Griffon is an MVC framework blended with avant-garde concepts like injection and convention over configuration. The two methods in Listing 13-3 serve as initialization and destruction hooks respectively for any MVC member. We will discuss these methods in the controller section later in this chapter. As mentioned earlier, Griffon creates an initial MVC group for the application when you issue the `create-app` command. Listing 13-4 illustrates the MVC group configuration created in `Application.groovy` located in `griffon-app/conf` in the application's structure.

Listing 13-4. Application.groovy in the default application

```
application {
    title = 'User'
    startupGroups = ['user']

    // Should Griffon exit when no Griffon created frames are showing?
    autoShutdown = true

    // If you want some non-standard application class, apply it here
    //frameClass = 'javax.swing.JFrame'
}
mvcGroups {
    // MVC Group for "user"
    'user' {
        model      = 'user.UserModel'
        view       = 'user.UserView'
        controller = 'user.UserController'
    }

}
```

In Listing 13-4, the `user` MVC group was created when the application was created and serves as the master group of the whole application. The property named `application.startup-Groups` serves as a list of the MVC groups that should be automatically started up when the application framework starts up. By default, the MVC group created as a part of the initial application is added to the list of startup groups. You can add any number of groups that you declare later. To create a new MVC group, invoke the following command from the command prompt from inside the user project.

```
> griffon create-mvc userDetails
```

The execution of `create-mvc` command generates four files, each in the appropriate functional directory: a model, a view, a controller, and a test file. Each of the files also has a name derived from the MVC group name.

```
C:\workspace\ch013\user>griffon create-mvc userDetails
Welcome to Griffon 1.1.0 - http://griffon-framework.org/
Licensed under Apache Standard License 2.0
Griffon home is set to: D:\griffon-1.1.0
```

```
Base Directory: C:\workspace\ch013\user
Running script D:\griffon-1.1.0\scripts\CreateMvc.groovy
Resolving dependencies...
Dependencies resolved in 404ms.
Environment set to development
Resolving framework plugin dependencies ...
Framework plugin dependencies resolved in 376 ms.
Resolving plugin dependencies ...
Plugin dependencies resolved in 344 ms.
Created Model for UserDetails
Created View for UserDetails
Created Controller for UserDetails
Created Tests for UserDetails
```

Apart from generating MVC member files, the create-mvc command also changes the configuration files to tell the framework that you have a new MVC group as illustrated in Listing 13-5.

Listing 13-5. Application.groovy after running create-mvc command

```
application {
    title = 'User'
    startupGroups = ['user']

    // Should Griffon exit when no Griffon created frames are showing?
    autoShutdown = true

    // If you want some non-standard application class, apply it here
    //frameClass = 'javax.swing.JFrame'
}
    mvcGroups {
    // MVC Group for "userDetails"
    'userDetails' {
        model      = 'user.UserDetailsModel'
        view       = 'user.UserDetailsView'
        controller = 'user.UserDetailsController'
    }

    // MVC Group for "user"
    'user' {
        model      = 'user.UserModel'
        view       = 'user.UserView'
        controller = 'user.UserController'
    }

}
```

As you can see in Listing 13-5, Griffon added a new MVC group for the userDetails, but it did not add the userDetails MVC group to list of startup groups. You may choose to add the new MVC group to the startup group to instantiate it automatically or you can instantiate it manually using methods available to every MVC member and the application instance: buildMVCGroup(), createMVCGroup(), and withMVCGroup(). We will discuss these methods in the controller section later in this chapter.

Now we will enhance the default application by modifying the view, model, and controller to create the application, which allows us to create new users. The form used to create the user will look as shown in Figure 13-3.

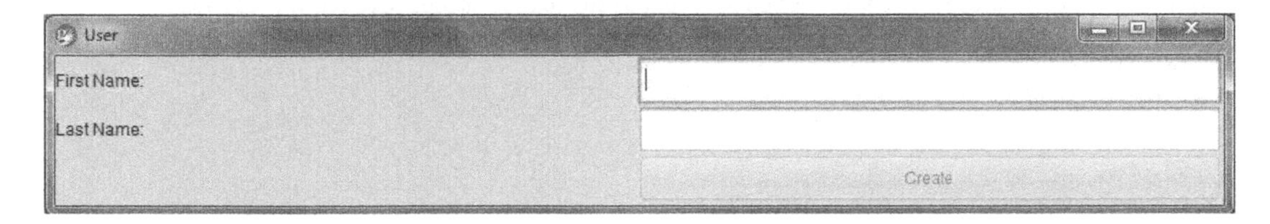

Figure 13-3. *View of enhanced application*

Looking at Figure 13-3, it's easy to see that the model will have the following properties: `firstName` and `lastName`. Also, we will enable the create button if the user provides both a first name and last name. Listing 13-6 illustrates the model that churns this out.

Listing 13-6. Enhancing the UserModel

```
package user

import groovy.beans.Bindable
import griffon.transform.PropertyListener
import static griffon.util.GriffonNameUtils.isBlank

@Bindable
@PropertyListener(clos)
class UserModel {

        String firstName
        String lastName
        boolean create
        private clos = { event->
                create = !isBlank(firstName) &&
                !isBlank(lastName)
        }
}
```

The model in Listing 13-4 is quite simple. Other than the `@Bindable` annotation, which looks familiar since Griffon created it for us in the default model, there is another annotation: `@PropertyListener`. The `@PropertyListener` annotation registers a `PropertyChangeListener` that handles change events. The `@PropertyListener` is set up at the class level to listen to all property-change events associated with the class. The `@Bindable` annotation adds `PropertyChangeSupport` to all fields of the class. This means that when any of the field values change, a property change event is fired. When an event is fired, the closure is invoked with the event. The closure `clos` takes an event as input. The closure uses the `isBlank` helper to determine the value of the boolean `create`. `isBlank` is a utility method provided by the Griffon runtime to check if the field is blank.

Now let's enhance the view. Referring to Figure 13-3, we need two labels, two text fields, and one button. Listing 13-7 illustrates the code for the view.

Listing 13-7. Enhancing the View

```
package user
actions { action(id: 'createAction', name: 'Create', enabled: bind{ model.create }, closure:
controller.create) }
application(title: 'User',
  preferredSize: [320, 240],
  pack: true,
  //location: [50,50],
  locationByPlatform:true,
  iconImage: imageIcon('/griffon-icon-48x48.png').image,
  iconImages: [imageIcon('/griffon-icon-48x48.png').image,
               imageIcon('/griffon-icon-32x32.png').image,
               imageIcon('/griffon-icon-16x16.png').image]) {

gridLayout(cols: 2, rows: 3)
label 'First Name:'
textField columns: 20,
text: bind(target: model, 'firstName', mutual: true)
label 'Last Name:'
textField columns:20,
text: bind(target: model, 'lastName', mutual: true)
label ''
button  createAction, constraints: 'span 2, right'

}
```

As illustrated in Listing 13-7, the view components are associated with the model property using the binding. The textField bindings contain an extra parameter, `mutual`. Setting `mutual` to `true` creates a bi-directional binding. When the view is changed, the model is updated, and when the model is changed, the view is updated. You also see that when the user clicks a button, the associated `createAction` is invoked on the controller. Let's look at the controller next. Listing 13-8 illustrates the code for the `UserController`.

Listing 13-8. Enhancing the Controller

```
package user

class UserController {
    def model
    def view

    def create = {
        println "First Name: ${model.firstName}"
        println "Last Name: ${model.lastName}"
    }
}
```

The controller in Listing 13-8 is trivial: when the Create button is clicked, the action in controller prints the model values.

Now you can the run the application using the following command:

```
> griffon run-app user
```

The Figure 13-4 depicts the running application. The create button is not enabled until the user fills the `lastName`. We will show you how to enhance the look and feel of the application in the next section but before that we will cover the topic that is important in terms of the facilities that must be provided by an application framework: the application life cycle.

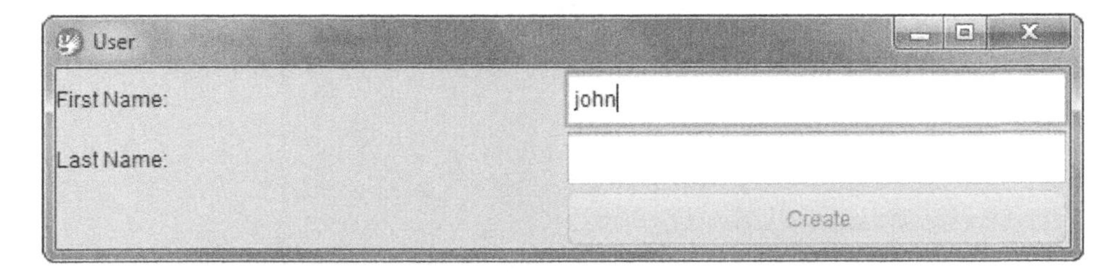

Figure 13-4. *The enhanced application*

Griffon Application Life Cycle

Griffon is an open source, rich client platform framework. In a rich client application, the client not only provides the UI (user interface), but is also responsible for data processing. Rich client applications are generally built on a framework, are extensible with the help of plugins, and can be seamlessly updated with globally distributed applications. The desktop applications share common features, such as menus, toolbars, and so on. For such features, a rich client platform provides a framework with which the features can quickly be rolled and assembled. The rich client platform also provides the configuration and extension infrastructure with which features such as menus can be declaratively loaded by the framework, thus allowing developers to focus on the core business of the application. To this end, one of the key concerns of the desktop applications is the lifecycle management of its components.

The desktop application should be responsible for bootstrapping itself, allocating resources to the components being loaded, and instantiated and relinquishing the allocated resources when they are not needed. Griffon addresses all these concerns with its well-defined life cycle management. Every Griffon application goes through the same life cycle phases no matter in which mode they are running, with the exception of applet mode, where there is an additional phase.. Every phase has an associated life cycle script that will be invoked at the appropriate time and these scripts are located in the `griffon-app/lifecycle` in the application's structure. The phases are as follows:

- Initialization
- Startup
- Ready
- Shutdown
- Stop

Initialization

The initialization phase is the first to be called by the application's life cycle. The application instance was just created and its configuration was read but you can't access any MVC members yet. This phase is typically used to tweak the application for the current platform, including its look and feel. Listing 13-9 illustrates the code in the script for this phase (`Initialize.groovy`).

Listing 13-9. Initialize.groovy

```
import groovy.swing.SwingBuilder
import static griffon.util.GriffonApplicationUtils.isMacOSX

SwingBuilder.lookAndFeel((isMacOSX ? 'system' : 'nimbus'), 'gtk', ['metal', [boldFonts: false]])
```

The code in this script configures the look and feel using a list of names that resolve to a particular `lookAndFeel` setting.

Startup

The Startup phase is responsible for instantiating all MVC groups that have been defined in the application's configuration (`Application.groovy`) and that also were marked as startup groups in the same configuration file.

Ready

The Ready phase is called right after Startup with the condition that no pending events are available in the UI queue. The application's main frame is displayed at the end of this phase. The application is fully initialized at this point; no further life cycle scripts will be called until the application is ready to shut down in the next life cycle phase.

Shutdown

The Shutdown phase begins when the application is about to close. Any artifact can invoke the shutdown sequence by calling `shutdown()` on the app instance. This is the last life cycle script called by Griffon. The shutdown phase represents the last chance for freeing used resources, saving configuration settings, and closing any connections your application might have opened.

Stop

The Stop phase is only available when running in applet mode. It is called when the applet container invokes `destroy()` on the applet instance.

These are all the phases in the Griffon application lifecycle. It's simple, but it's a powerful feature in Griffon's arsenal against painful desktop application development. Instead of figuring out when and how each of these tasks should be invoked, you let Griffon call the phase-handler scripts when needed. These scripts are guaranteed to be invoked inside the UI thread (the Event Dispatch Thread in Swing). The script names match each phase name; you'll find them inside `griffon-app/lifecycle`. In the next section, we'll dig into views.

■ **Note** The Swing toolkit has a rule: all long computations must be performed outside of the Event Dispatch Thread (or EDT for short). This rule also states that all interaction with UI components must be done inside the EDT, including building a component and reading/writing component properties. More information on concurrency in swing can be obtained from `http://docs.oracle.com/javase/tutorial/uiswing/concurrency/index.html`.

Views

Groovy can do anything Java can do. If you think about the goal of developing the user interface from a Java perspective, you have two options: Swing or Standard Widget Toolkit (SWT). Either choice would work. You could just start coding Groovy and use Swing or SWT the same way you would in a normal Java program. However, if you've ever coded Swing or SWT, you probably aren't too excited right now.

Groovy uses builders[1] to make the job easier. It has both the Swing family of builders (`SwingBuilder`,[2] `SwingXBuilder`, and `JideBuilder`[3]) and the SWT builder (`SwtBuilder`[4]). Using Groovy and a builder will make it much easier to create a client application. In general, Java developers are more likely to be familiar with Swing than SWT. Therefore, we'll show you how to use Swing as the presentation technology and `SwingXBuilder` to make it easier. `SwingXBuilder` extends `SwingBuilder` and provides access to all of the power of `SwingBuilder`, plus the Swing components from the folks at SwingLabs.[5]

Builder Overview

A Swing user interface can be thought of as a composite or a tree of graphical components. If you have programmed with Swing, you're undoubtedly familiar with the neverending pattern of adding a component to its parent. It can be a complex, verbose mess. Groovy tackles the mess using builders.

If you have spent any time with Groovy, you have probably seen or used `MarkupBuilder` to construct an HTML or XML document. Builders can be used equally as well to build a Swing UI.

The easiest way to gain appreciation for `SwingXBuilder` is to see an example. Listing 13-10 shows how to use `SwingXBuilder` to create a simple user interface.

Listing 13-10. Creating a Simple UI Using SwingXBuilder

```
import groovy.swing.SwingXBuilder
import static javax.swing.WindowConstants.EXIT_ON_CLOSE
import javax.swing.*

class SimpleUI {

    static void main(args) {
        def simpleUI = new SimpleUI()
        simpleUI.run()
    }
        def swing
    def count = 0


    def run = {
          swing = new SwingXBuilder()
          swing.lookAndFeel('system')
```

[1]Refer to Chapter 3 for a review of builders.
[2]`http://groovy.codehaus.org/Swing+Builder`
[3]`http://groovy.codehaus.org/JideBuilder`
[4]`http://groovy.codehaus.org/GroovySWT`
[5]`http://www.swinglabs.org`

```
        // create the actions
        swing.action(id: 'exitAction',
          name: 'Exit',
          closure: this.&exit,
          mnemonic: 'x',
          accelerator: 'F4',
          shortDescription: 'Exit SimpleUI'
        )
        swing.action(id: 'aboutAction',
          name: 'About',
          closure: this.&showAbout,
          mnemonic: 'A',

          accelerator: 'F1',
          shortDescription: 'Find out about SimpleUI'
        )
        swing.action(id: 'clickAction',
          name: 'Click',
          closure: this.&click,
          shortDescription: 'Increment the Click Count'
        )

        // Define the Frame
        swing.frame(id:'simpleUIFrame', title: 'SimpleUI',
              location: [100,100],
              defaultCloseOperation: EXIT_ON_CLOSE
          ) {
        // Define the Menubar
        menuBar {
            menu(text: 'File', mnemonic: 'F') {
                menuItem(exitAction)
            }
            glue()
            menu(text: 'Help', mnemonic: 'H') {
                menuItem(aboutAction)
            }
        }

        // Define some stuff
        button(id:'clickButton', text:"Click Me", action: clickAction)
        // INSERT MORE STUFF HERE
          }

        swing.simpleUIFrame.pack()
        swing.simpleUIFrame.show()
  }

  void click(event) {
    count++
    swing.clickButton.text = "Clicked ${count} time(s)."
  }
```

```
    void showAbout(event) {
       JOptionPane.showMessageDialog(swing.simpleUIFrame,
'"This is the SimpleUI Application''')
     }
     void exit(event) {
       System.exit(0)
     }
}
```

Executing the SimpleUI application creates the user interface shown in Figure 13-5.

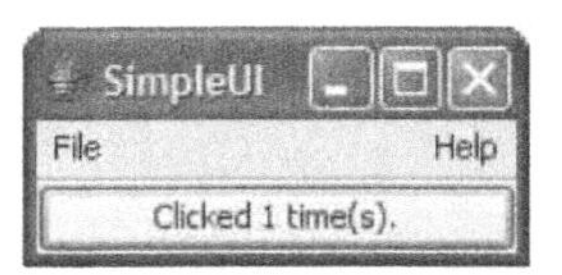

Figure 13-5. *The SimpleUI application*

The SimpleUI application creates a Swing user interface that features a menu bar that contains a File menu, a Help menu, and a button in the content area. The text on the button changes every time the user clicks it. When the program starts, it invokes the run closure to build the UI. The run closure sets up the builder, and then uses the builder to create three actions that will be used within the UI. Then the closure uses the builder to create the frame. The frame contains a menu bar, which contains the File and Help menus. Each of the menus contains menu items that reference the previously created actions. The frame also contains a button labeled Click Me, and a reference to the clickAction action.

If you take a closer look at the actions, you will notice that a parameter named closure was passed to the builder when creating the actions. In the case of clickAction, the closure to be executed is click. The click closure increments a counter and sets the button's text.

Griffon View

Views are usually written as Groovy scripts that create the UI by composing elements using builder nodes. Griffon supports all nodes provided by SwingBuilder by default.

Additional nodes can be configured in griffon-app/conf/Builder.groovy; the Griffon runtime will make sure to correctly setup the builder.

Listing 13-11 shows Builder.groovy located in the griffon-app/conf in the application's structure.

Listing 13-11. Builder.groovy

```
root {
  'groovy.swing.SwingBuilder' {
    controller = ['Threading']
    view = '*'
  }
}
```

In Listing 13-11 the root node is the top-level node used to mark the default namespace used by the builder. If you need to expose additional nodes to a controller, add a new builder to Builder.groovy and place all the libraries and dependencies of the new builder in your application's lib directory. Listing 13-12 illustrates adding MacWidgetsBuilder (http://griffon.codehaus.org/MacWidgetsBuilder) to Builder.groovy.

Listing 13-12. Adding MacWidgetsBuilder to Builder.groovy

```
root {
  'groovy.swing.SwingBuilder' {
    controller = ['Threading']
    view = '*'
  }
  'griffon.builder.macwidgets.MacWidgetsBuilder'{
    view = '*'
  }
}
```

You can also append the following line to the default `Builder.groovy` file as an alternative to the `MacWidgetsBuilder` block in Listing13-10.

```
root.'griffon.builder.macwidgets.MacWidgetsBuilder'.view = '*'
```

Adding builders to your builder configuration can be automated via plugins. All the builders shown at `http://griffon.codehaus.org/Builders` have companion plugins that adds the builder automatically so that you do not have to add it manually. Besides, there are many plugins (see `http://artifacts.griffon-framework.org/plugins/`) that can contribute additional nodes that you can use on views.

You can also get the list of all available plugins by invoking the `list-plugins` command target at your command prompt.

```
> griffon list-plugins
```

Invoking this command displays a table of all available plugins as shown in Figure 13-6

```
C:\workspace\ch013\user>griffon list-plugins
Welcome to Griffon 1.1.0 - http://griffon-framework.org/
Licensed under Apache Standard License 2.0
Griffon home is set to: D:\griffon-1.1.0

Base Directory: C:\workspace\ch013\user
Running script D:\griffon-1.1.0\scripts\ListPlugins_.groovy
Resolving dependencies...
Dependencies resolved in 381ms.
Environment set to development
Plugins available in the griffon-local repository are listed below:
-------------------------------------------------------------------------

Name                          Releases              Title

glazedlists                   1                     GlazedLists: hassle-free List
s, Tables and Trees
jide-builder                  1                     JideBuilder Plugin
lookandfeel                   1                     Swing Look & Feel selector
lookandfeel-jgoodies-looks    1                     Pluggable Look & Feel based o
n JGoodies Looks
macwidgets-builder            1                     MacWidgetsBuilder Plugin
miglayout                     2                     MigLayout integration
swing                         1                     Enables Swing support
```

Figure 13-6. *List of available plugins*

To get plugin specific information you can use plug-info command target with plugin's name as the parameter.

```
> griffon plug-info jide-builder
```

Invoking this command displays the plugin details with documentation information along with the author's name and email address, as shown in Figure 13-7.

```
C:\workspace>griffon plug-info jide-builder
Welcome to Griffon 1.1.0 - http://griffon-framework.org/
Licensed under Apache Standard License 2.0
Griffon home is set to: D:\griffon-1.1.0

Base Directory: C:\workspace
Running script D:\griffon-1.1.0\scripts\PluginInfo_.groovy
Resolving dependencies...
Dependencies resolved in 387ms.
Environment set to development

--------------------------------------------------------------------------------

Information about plugin listed at griffon-local
--------------------------------------------------------------------------------

Name          : jide-builder
Title         : JideBuilder Plugin
License       : Apache Software License 2.0
Source        : https://github.com/griffon/griffon-jide-builder-plugin
Documentation: No documentation link provided
--------------------------------------------------------------------------------

Toolkits      : swing
Platforms     : works in all platforms
Framework     : no
--------------------------------------------------------------------------------

Authors:
        Andres Almiray (aalmiray@yahoo.com)
--------------------------------------------------------------------------------

Releases:
Version             Griffon Version         Date

0.7                 0.9.5 > *               Sun Oct 14 23:47:35 CEST 2012
```

Figure 13-7. plugin details

Now we will enhance the look and feel of the view using plugins - JideBuilder and MigLayout. We will use the JideBuilder nodes for setting up the top banner and MigLayout to organize the components as illustrated in Listing 13-13.

Listing 13-13. View using JideBuilder and MigLayout

```
package user
import java.awt.Color
actions {
    action(id: 'loginAction',
    name: 'Login',
    enabled: bind{ model.enabled },
    closure: controller.login)
}
application(title: 'User', pack:true,
  locationByPlatform:true,
  iconImage: imageIcon('/griffon-icon-48x48.png').image,
```

```
  iconImages: [imageIcon('/griffon-icon-48x48.png').image,
  imageIcon('/griffon-icon-32x32.png').image,
  imageIcon('/griffon-icon-16x16.png').image]) {
      migLayout(layoutConstraints: 'fill')
      bannerPanel(constraints: 'span 2, growx, wrap',
      title: 'Login',
      subtitle: 'Please enter your credentials',
      titleIcon: imageIcon('/griffon-icon-48x48.png'),
      border: lineBorder(color: Color.BLACK, thickness: 1),
      subTitleColor: Color.WHITE,
      background: new Color(0,0,0,1),
      startColor: Color.WHITE,
      endColor: Color.BLACK,
      vertical: true)
    label 'Username:', constraints: 'left'
    textField columns: 20, text: bind('username', target: model), constraints: 'wrap'
    label 'Password:', constraints: 'left'
    passwordField columns: 20, text: bind('password', target: model), constraints: 'wrap'
    button loginAction, constraints: 'span 2, right'
}
```

You'll need to install twoplugins if you intend to run this application: `jide-builder` and `miglayout`, using the following commands:> griffon install-plugin miglayout

```
> griffon install-plugin jide-builder
```

The code in Listing 13-13 generates the screen shown in Figure 13-8. The code in Listing 13-14 and Listing 13-15 illustrates the model and the controller used for this application.

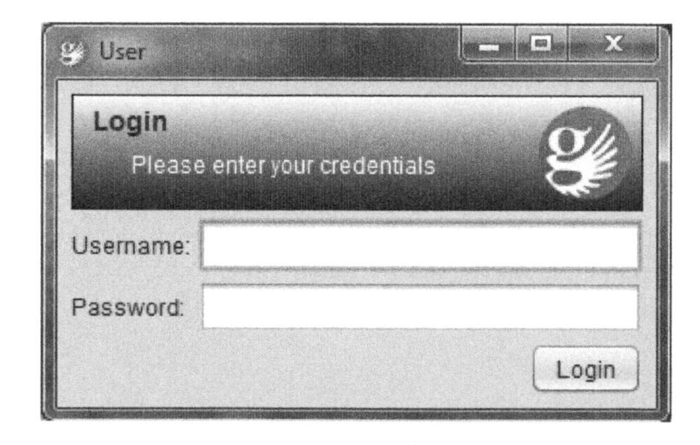

Figure 13-8. *View Using JideBuilder and MigLayout*

Listing 13-14. UserModel for Login Application

```
package user
import groovy.beans.Bindable
import griffon.transform.PropertyListener
@PropertyListener(enabler)
```

```
class UserModel {
    @Bindable String username
    @Bindable String password
    @Bindable boolean enabled
    private enabler = { evt ->
      if(evt.propertyName == 'enabled') return
      enabled = username && password
    }
}
```

Listing 13-15. Controller for Login Application

```
package user

import javax.swing.JOptionPane
class UserController {
    def login = {
        JOptionPane.showMessageDialog(app.windowManager.windows[0],
            """
              username = $model.username
              password = $model.password
            """.stripIndent(14).toString())
    }
}
```

Special Nodes

There are many Swing components and it would be a daunting task to find and make a `SwingBuilder` node for each one for them. Instead of tracking down each Swing component for their node names, drop the first J from the class name and uncapitalize the next character; for instance, `JButton => button`, `JLabel => label`. This rule applies to all Swing classes available in the JDK. In addition, `SwingBuilder` includes a few extra nodes that aren't related to a particular Swing class, but prove to be useful when you need to insert a custom Swing component. In this section, we'll look at six special nodes:

- Application
- Container
- Widget
- Bean
- Noparent
- Root

Application

This node is provided by Swing plugin and defines a top level container depending on the current running mode. Of all the properties suggested by the default template, you'll notice `iconImage` and `iconImages`. The first property is a standard property of JFrame. It usually defines the icon to display at the top of the frame (on platforms that support such a setting). The second property (`iconImages`) is a JDK 6addition to `java.awt.Window`. This property instructs the window to select the most appropriate icon according to platform preferences. Griffon ignores this setting if it's running in JDK 5. This property overrides the setting specified for `iconImage` if it's supported in the current JDK and platform.

Container

This node is provided by SwingBuilder and is a pass-through node that accepts any UI component as a value. This node allows for nesting of child content. It's quite useful when you need to embed a custom component for which a node is not available. Listing 13-16 illustrates its usage.

Listing 13-16. Using Container Node

```
container(new CustomPanel()) {
    label 'custom label'
}
```

Widget

This node is provided by SwingBuilder and is a pass-through node that accepts any UI component as a value. As opposed to container, this node does not allow nesting of child content. It's quite useful when you need to embed a custom component for which a node is not available. Listing 13-17 illustrates its usage.

Listing 13-17. Using Widget Node

```
widget(new CustomDisplay(), title: 'custom title') {
```

Bean

This node is provided by SwingBuilder and is a catch-all node. It allows you to set properties on any object using the builder syntax. Listing 13-18 illustrates its usage for setting up bindings on a model.

Listing 13-18. Using Bean Node

```
textField columns: 20, id: username
bean(model, value: bind{ username.text })
```

Noparent

This node is provided by SwingBuilder. Child nodes are always attached to their parents, but there are times when you don't want that to happen. In these cases, wrap those nodes with noparent, as illustrated in Listing 13-19.

Listing 13-19. Using Noparent Node

```
panel {
    gridLayout(cols: 2, rows: 2)
    button('Click 1', id: b1')
    button('Click 2', id: b2')
    button('Click 3', id: b2')
    button('Click 4', id: b4')    // the following line will cause the buttons
    // to be reordered
    // bean(button1, text: 'Click 11')
    noparent {
        // this is safe, buttons do not change places
        bean(button1, text: 'Click 11')
    }
}
```

Root

This node is provided by Griffon and it identifies the top level node of a secondary View script. View scripts are expected to return the top level node, but there may be times when further customizations prevent this from happening; for example, when wiring up a custom listener. When that happens, the result has to be made explicit; otherwise the script will return the wrong value. Using the `root()` node avoids forgetting this fact while also providing an alias for the node. Listing 13-20 illustrates its usage.

Listing 13-20. Using Root Node

```
root(
    tree(id: 'mytree')
)mytree.addTreeSelectionModel(new DefaultTreeSelectionModel() {
   ...
})
```

Models and Bindings

Swing uses the model-view-controller architecture (MVC) as the fundamental design behind each of its components. Essentially, MVC divides GUI components into three elements—the model, the view, and the controller. Each of these elements plays a crucial role in how the component behaves. The model encloses the state data for each component.

There are different models for different types of components. For example, the model of a menu may contain a list of the menu items from which the user can select. Note that this information remains the same no matter how the component is drawn on the screen; model data always exists independent of the component's visual representation. The view refers to how you see the component on the screen.

The controller is the portion of the user interface that dictates how the component interacts with events. Events come in many forms; for example, a mouse click or a keyboard event. The controller decides how each component will react to the event.

With MVC, each of the three elements requires the services of another element to keep itself continually updated. Likewise, the view determines if the component is the recipient of user events, such as mouse clicks. The view passes these events on to the controller, which decides how to handle them best. Based on the controller's decisions, the values in the model may need to be altered.

Griffon automates the creation of the model, view, and controller classes both at build time and at runtime. It configures them via injection to follow the original convention of paths of references, observed updates, and user interactions. It also has conventional file locations for the created groups and other conventions relating to the life cycle of the MVC group.

The MVC pattern is found in Griffon both at the architectural level and the presentation layer. In Griffon, any MVC member can be registered as a listener on a model class, by means of `PropertyChangeListeners` and `PropertyChangeEvents`. The responsibility of Models is to hold data that can be used by both Controller and View to communicate with each other. The Griffon Models are observable; all the properties in a Griffon model are observable. This means that whenever the value of any of the properties changes, an event is fired. To make a property observable, all you need to do is annotate the property with the `@Bindable` annotation. The `@Bindable` annotation, facilitated by Groovy's AST transformation, instructs the Groovy compiler to inject the byte code that makes the annotated property observable and ensure that a `PropertyChangeEvent` is fired for each observable property whenever the value of this observable property is changed. This considerably simplifies setting up bindings so that changes in the UI can automatically be sent to model properties and vice versa

When creating Swing UIs, you're often interested in monitoring the changes of value of certain UI elements. For this purpose, the usual approach is to use JavaBeans `PropertyChangeListeners` to be notified when the value of a class field changes. You then end up writing this very common boilerplate code in your Java beans, as illustrated in Listing 13-21.

Listing 13-21. Javabean Without @Bindable Annotation

```
import java.beans.PropertyChangeSupport;
import java.beans.PropertyChangeListener;

public class MyBean {
    private String prop;

    PropertyChangeSupport pcs = new PropertyChangeSupport(this);

    public void addPropertyChangeListener(PropertyChangeListener l) {
        pcs.add(l);
    }

    public void removePropertyChangeListener(PropertyChangeListener l) {
        pcs.remove(l);
    }

    public String getProp() {
        return prop;
    }

    public void setProp(String prop) {
        pcs.firePropertyChanged("prop", this.prop, this.prop = prop);
    }
}
```

Using @Bindable annotation in Groovy, the code in Listing 13-21 can be greatly simplified, as illustrated in Listing 13-22.

Listing 13-22. Bean with @Bindable Annotation

```
class MyBean {
    @Bindable String prop
}
```

Another annotation, @PropertyListener, helps you register PropertyChangeListeners without so much effort. The @PropertyListener accepts the in-place definition of a closure or reference of a closure property defined in the same class or a List of any of both.

The Code in Listing 13-23 is greatly simplified using @PropertyListener annotation, as illustrated in Listing 13-24.

Listing 13-23. Bean Without @PropertyListener Annotation

```
import groovy.beans.Bindable
import java.beans.PropertyChangeListener
class UserModel {
    def controller
    @Bindable String firstName
    @Bindable String lastName
def snoopAll = { evt -> ... }
```

```
UserModel() {
        addPropertyChangeListener(snoopAll as PropertyChangeListener)
        addPropertyChangeListener('lastName', {
            controller.someAction(it)
        } as PropertyChangeListener)
    }
}
```

Listing 13-24. Bean with @PropertyListener Annotation

```
import griffon.transform.PropertyListener
import groovy.beans.Bindable
@PropertyListener(snoopAll)
class MyModel {
    def controller
    @Bindable String name
    @Bindable @PropertyListener({controller.someAction(it)})
                String lastname    def snoopAll = { evt -> ... }
}
```

Binding in Griffon is achieved by leveraging JavaBeans' `PropertyChangeEvent` and their related classes. Thus binding will work with any class that fires this type of event, regardless of its usage (or non-usage(of `@Bindable`. The `SwingBuilder` class in Groovy contains bind node that allows you to cleanly bind the state of two objects. A simple `TestBean` with two properties, `property1` and `property2`, is shown below:

```
class TestBean {
  @Bindable String property1
  String property2
}
```

You can bind the field `property2` to be the same value as `property1` using the following:

```
bind(source: testBean, sourceProperty: 'property1',
     target: testBean, targetProperty: 'property2')
```

As a result of this binding, the value of the `property2` is same as the value of the `property1` and if the value of the `property1` is changed, the change is reflected in the `property2`.

There are the three options for writing a binding using the bind node:

- Long. The most complete of all three, you must explicitly specify both ends of the binding. The following snippet sets a unidirectional binding from `bean1.prop1` to `bean2.prop2`.

  ```
  bind(source: bean1, sourceProperty: 'prop1', target: bean2, targetProperty: 'prop2')
  ```

- Contextual. This type of binding can assume either the sources or the targets depending on the context. When used in this way, either `sourceProperty:` or `targetProperty:` can be omitted and considered implicit; the bind node's value becomes the property name.

  ```
  bean(bean1, prop1: bind('prop2', target: bean2))
  ```

- Short. This type of binding is only useful for setting implicit targets. It expects a closure as the definition of the binding value.

```
bean(bean2, prop2: bind{ bean1.prop1 })
```

Controllers

Controllers are the entry point for your application's logic. The controller has properties and methods injected by Griffon, hooks for post- initialization and handler actions. Some of the properties, methods, actions are created by Griffon when we created the default application, as shown in Listing 13-3. Along with these properties, we will introduce several other properties and methods in this section.

Injected Properties

The injected properties you need to understand are as follows:

- **App**—The app property points to the current running application, through which you can access the application's configuration. Using this property, an application can expose its configuration, controllers, views, models, and builders in the form of `app.config`, `app.controllers`, `app.views`, `app.models`, and `app.builders`.
- **Builder**—The builder property points to the builder used to create the view related to this controller. The view and the builder may share the same variables, but they're two distinct objects: the view is a script that tells you what you just built, and the builder is a `CompositeBuilder` instance that allows the controller to build new UI components if needed.
- **Model**—The model property, when defined, lets the controller access the model that's related to its group. A controller usually updates the view via the model, assuming the proper bindings are put into place. But there's no strict requirement for a controller to always have a model. If you think your controller doesn't require a model, you can safely delete this property from the code; there won't be an error, because Griffon will check for the property declaration before setting the value.
- **View**—The view property references the third member of the MVC triad: the view. Like the model, this property is optional. In some cases the controller may interact with the view solely by updating the model, in which case it's safe to delete this property from the code.

Injected Methods

The following sections provide examples of the injected methods you'll be using.

createMVCgroup

This method lets you create new instances of a MVC group. It always returns three elements: Model, View, and Controller, in that order.

Listing 13-25. Usage of createMVCgroup

```
class SampleController {
    def action = { evt = null ->
        def (m, v, c) = createMVCGroup('Other')
    }
}
```

This method is a restricted version of the more general `buildMVCGroup()`, explained next.

buildMVCgroup

This method lets you create new instances of an MVC group. Listing 13-26 illustrates its usage.

Listing 13-26. Usage of buildMVCgroup

```
class SampleController {
    def action = { evt = null ->
        MVCGroup group = buildMVCGroup('Other')
    }
}
```

This method is used when building a group that may contain additional MVC members, as `createMVCGroup()` returns strict MVC members only (Model, View, Controller).

destroyMVCgroup

The `destroyMVCGroup()` method removes the group reference from the application. Listing 13-27 shows its usage.

Listing 13-27. Usage of destroyMVCgroup

```
class SampleController {
    def action = { evt = null ->
        destroyMVCGroup('Other')
    }
}
```

This method performs the following steps in the following specified order:

1. Calls `mvcGroupDestroy()` on each MVC member that is not a Script.
2. Calls `dispose()` on the associated builder.
3. Removes all references of the MVC members from the applications cache.
4. Fires a `DestroyMVCGroup` event.

Once a group is destroyed, you cannot use it again.

withMVCgroup

This method lets you create new instances of a MVC group that is short-lived; for example, one that creates a dialog box. The `withMVCGroup()` method is a mix of `createMVCGroup()` and `destroyMVCGroup()` that makes sure the created group is destroyed immediately after it's no longer of use. Listing 13-28 illustrates its usage.

Listing 13-28. Usage ofwithMVCgroup

```
class SampleController {
    def action = { evt = null ->
        withMVCGroup('Other') { m, v, c ->
            // configure the group
        }
    }
}
```

Create a new MVC group instance, and then discard it once it is no longer of use.

newInstance

This method creates a new instance of a particular class and type. It is a convenience method that fires an event after the instance is created; the application will not perform additional management for an instance created in this way. Listing 13-29 illustrates its usage.

Listing 13-29. Usage of newInstance()

```
class SampleController {
    def action = { evt = null ->
        def myService = newInstance(MyServiceClass, 'service')
    }
}
```

Initialization and Destruction Hook

Other than listening to application events, creating and destroying MVC groups or holding references to service, controllers in Griffon can also react to MVC Initialization/Destruction through `mvcGroupInit` and `mvcGroupDestroy` methods which we will explain next.

mvcGroupInit

This method serves as an initialization hook for any MVC member that is neither a script nor a `CompositeBuilder` instance. It will be called right after an instance is created.

The signature of the method is this:

```
void mvcGroupInit(Map<String, Object> args)
```

The `args` parameter holds any additional data that has passed to either `createMVCGroup()` or `buildMVCGroup()`. Listing 13-30 shows its usage.

Listing 13-30. Usage of mcvGroupInit

```
class SampleController {
    def someProperty
    def mvcGroupInit(Map args) {
        someProperty = args.random
    }
}
```

mvcGroupDestroy

This method serves as a destruction hook for any MVC member that is neither a script nor a CompositeBuilder instance. It will be called when the instance is about to be removed from the application's cache during the destroy sequence of an MVC group. Listing 13-31 shows the usage of mvcGroupDestroy().

Listing 13-31. Usage of mvcGroupDestroy

```
class SampleController {
    def mvcGroupDestroy() {
        // perform cleanup
    }
}
```

Actions

Controller actions are usually defined using a closure property form, as illustrated in Listing 13-32.

Listing 13-32. Actions in Controller

```
class MyController {
    def someAction = { evt = null ->
        // do some stuff
    }
}
```

An action is nothing more than a closure property or a method that follows a conventional set of arguments, which is the event generated by the UI.

Summary

You started this chapter by setting up your development environment and using the Griffon create-app command to create your first Griffon application. You took a brief tour of how Griffon's convention-over-configuration paradigm makes the application structure predictable and easy to follow. You saw that data binding between views and controllers comes naturally with Griffon. The view components display the current status of the model, whereas the related controllers change them.

Finally, you saw how the power and expressiveness of Groovy help you write concise, expressive, powerful code. Our goal was to give you a sample of what is possible with Griffon. You are only limited by your imagination.

Index

A

B

F

G

H

I

J, K

L

M

N

O

P

Q

R

S

X, Y, Z

CPSIA information can be obtained at www.ICGtesting.com
Printed in the USA
LVOW020110090313

323485LV00008B/275/P